to the Collection
of the
Museum of Fine Arts,
Boston

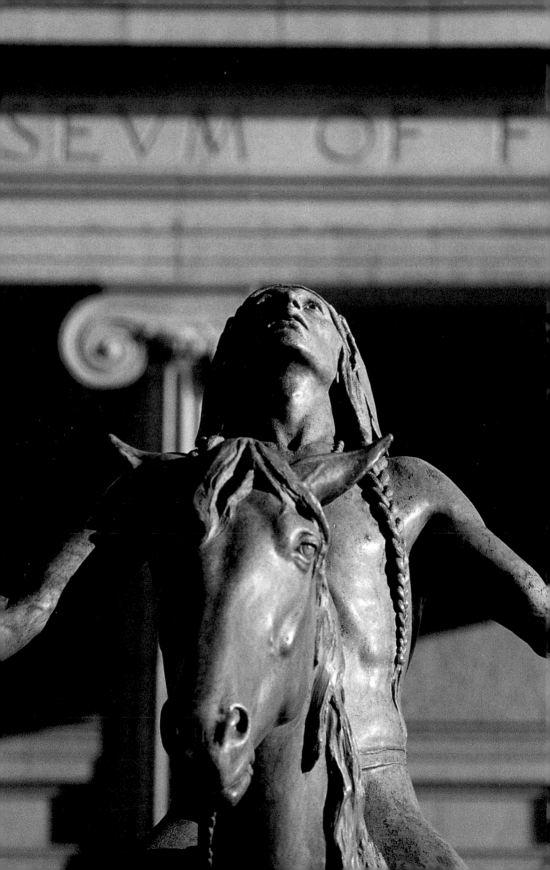

MFA A Guide to the Collection
of the Museum of Fine Arts,
Boston

Entries by
Gilian Shallcross Wohlauer
Introduction by
Malcolm Rogers

Museum of Fine Arts, Boston

This catalogue was funded in part by the National Endowment for the Arts.

NATIONAL
ENDOWMENT
FOR THE ARTS

Author: Gilian Shallcross Wohlauer
Designer: Janet O'Donoghue
Researcher: Benjamin Weiss
Production assistant: Dacey Sartor
Proofreader: Denise Bergman
Managing editor: Cynthia Purvis

Printed and bound by CS Graphics PTE LTD, Singapore

Cover: The Museum's Huntington Avenue entrance © Lou Jones 1999
Frontispiece: Cyrus Dallin's 1909 bronze sculpture *Appeal to the Great Spirit*
© Lou Jones 1999

CONTENTS

A BRIEF HISTORY OF THE MUSEUM

by Malcolm Rogers, Ann and Graham Gund Director

The Museum of Fine Arts, Boston, welcomes more than a million visitors each year. From scholars to schoolchildren, they come from our urban neighborhoods and from countries around the globe. Our collections of Egyptian, Asian, French Impressionist, and colonial New England arts, in particular, are world famous. Some visitors come to see beloved or celebrated works, familiar from frequent visits or from the pages of books; others, like Alice in Wonderland, tumble down the rabbit hole to find an unexpected visual adventure, an introduction to new places, cultures, personalities, and ideas. But for everyone, a visit to the Museum is a voyage of discovery.

The Museum of Fine Arts opened its doors to the public on July 4, 1876. One of a number of institutions that had been encouraged to build on land in the recently filled Back Bay, the Museum soon found itself in distinguished architectural company, with two of the finest buildings in America, H.H. Richardson's masterpiece, Trinity Church (1872–77), and McKim, Mead, and White's Boston Public Library (1888–95) to its north-east and north-west respectively. Recognizing the potential of the proximity of the three institutions, in 1883 the city removed a street to create Copley Square as the focal point of the Back Bay. Named for the great Boston painter John Singleton Copley, the square is now recognized as one of the most distinguished public spaces in America.

Even on its opening, the Museum already owned a number of distinguished works of art, acquired primarily by gift and bequest from public-spirited Bostonians. (It would be decades before the new

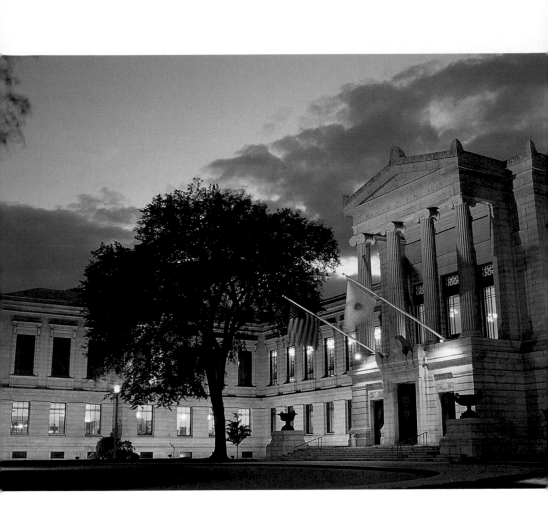

Museum would have funds available for the purchase of works of art.) Ranging across geography and time, many of these early acquisitions retain their prominence in the collections today. Among them are Washington Allston's *Elijah in the Desert*, the first oil painting to enter the collection, Thomas Crawford's marble *Hebe and Ganymede*, two monumental paintings by François Boucher, seven Egyptian mummies, and the Eighteenth-Dynasty sculpture of the lion-headed goddess Sekhmet. Other outstanding works were lent by private collectors, notably J.M.W. Turner's *The Slave Ship*.

As the quality and size of the collections grew, the responsibility for enhancing and shaping the col-

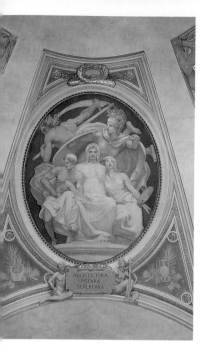

Murals and bas reliefs by John Singer Sargent adorn the Ruth and Carl J. Shapiro Rotunda and Colonnade. This scene, *Architecture, Painting, and Sculpture Protected by Athena from the Ravages of Time,* conveys the Museum's role as the guardian of culture.

lection was transferred from the trustees to a professional curatorial staff. The first curatorial department, the Print Department, was established in 1887. It was followed in the same year by departments of Classical art, Japanese art in 1890, Egyptian art in 1902, and, in 1908, Western art.

In 1897 the Museum acquired the print collection of Henry F. Sewall of New York. Comprising some 23,000 impressions, the collection systematically represented the history of Western printmaking from its beginnings through the eighteenth century. The purchase was made possible by the bequest of $100,000 from Peter Parker, the founder of Boston's Parker House Hotel and the eponym of the Parker House dinner roll.

The Classical collection owes its shape to Edward Perry Warren, scion of a wealthy Boston paper manufacturing family. Warren lived in Sussex in the British countryside, and virtually cornered the market in classical antiquities at the turn of the century. Boston's prudishness had frustrated Warren, who was to commission the celebrated statue *The Kiss* from the French sculptor Rodin, and he now took a certain pleasure in submitting to the Museum Greek vases whose decoration was frankly erotic. The Museum responded by editing compromising areas with strategically placed daubs of paint (removed in recent years). Warren directed works of major significance to the Museum between 1895 and 1905, to be purchased and donated by local supporters, notably Catharine Page Perkins, Henry Lillie Pierce, and Francis Bartlett.

The Museum's collection of Japanese art—unsurpassed anywhere outside of Japan itself—is largely the work of three nineteenth-century Bostonians: Edward Sylvester Morse, Ernest Fenollosa, and William Sturgis

Bigelow. Each came to collecting in a different way. Morse, a zoologist, traveled to Japan in 1877 to study marine brachiopods, and became fascinated with Japanese ceramics, which he collected systematically by region, city, and kiln, garnering a collection of some 6,000. Fenollosa went to Japan to teach philosophy and political economy at Tokyo University in 1879 on Morse's recommendation, and quickly amassed a collection of some 2,000 Japanese paintings. Bigelow first encountered Japanese art in Paris, while studying under Louis Pasteur. He subsequently heard Morse lecture in Boston, traveled with him to Japan in 1882, and began to build a collection that eventually comprised some 15,000 paintings, sculpture, and decorative arts, as well as tens of thousands of prints, drawings, and illustrated books. As early as 1882 the three men were discussing among themselves their hope that the Museum of Fine Arts would become the eventual repository of their collections. Their dreams

Intended to encourage contemplative viewing, the Japanese Buddhist Temple Room was designed in 1909 to evoke the dignified simplicity of the temples where these sculptures were once revered. The collection of Japanese Buddhist art is the finest outside of Japan.

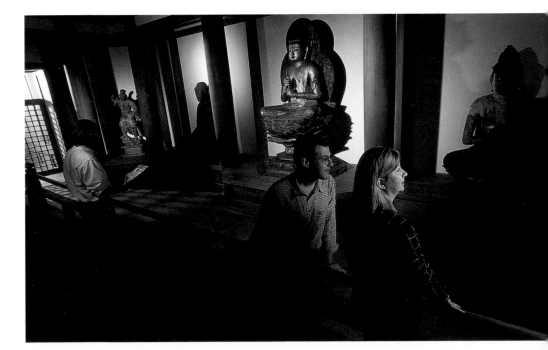

were realized in 1890 when the Museum opened a wing to house their collections, which were subsequently acquired by purchase and gift.

The Museum's collection of Egyptian art is the result of systematic archaeological excavations by the joint Harvard University–Museum of Fine Arts Expedition between 1905 and 1942 (see page 30). In this the key figure was George Reisner, who in 1903, while working for a University of California Expedition funded by Phoebe Apperson Hearst, mother of William Randolph Hearst, was granted a concession to excavate the Third Pyramid and funerary temple of Mycerinus at Giza, and the northern third of the west cemetery. When Mrs. Hearst curtailed her support, Harvard and the MFA seized the opportunity to join forces to continue funding Reisner's work. His finds at sites throughout Egypt and the Sudan were shared between the Museum and the Egyptian government, but it was to Harvard University that Reisner

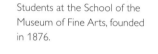

Students at the School of the Museum of Fine Arts, founded in 1876.

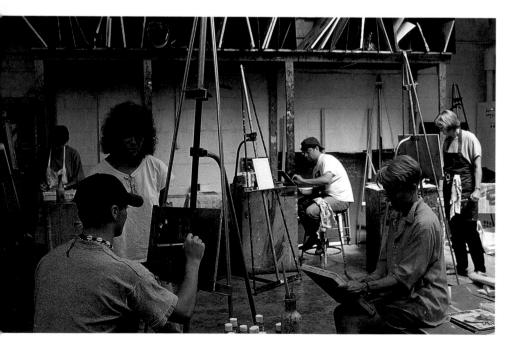

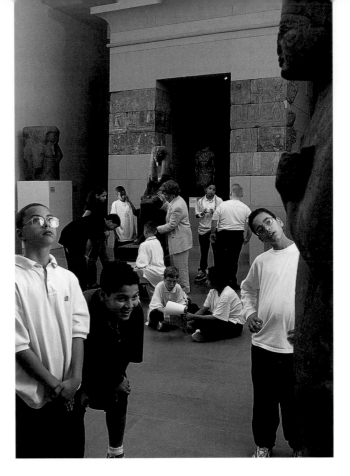

The ancient Egyptian galleries are the favorites of the 70,000 school-children who visit the Museum every year.

bequeathed his library of 1,300 volumes of detective stories, a telling end to long years spent in the Egyptian desert in the service of the Museum.

By the late 1880s, the growing collection, along with concerns over danger of fire and loss of light caused by the buildings that had grown up around the Copley Square building prompted the Trustees to search for a larger site close to the downtown area, but safe from encroachment by neighboring buildings. In 1899, coincidentally the year of the Museum's first operating surplus, the Trustees purchased twelve acres on Huntington Avenue for $703,000 on which to build a new Museum.

The Trustees—who had looked to European models when designing the building in Copley

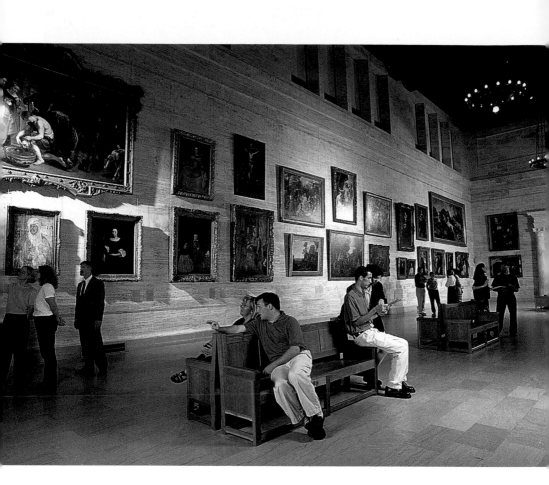

At the heart of the Museum, the Koch gallery displays masterpieces of 16th- and 17th-century European painting, including works by Rubens, El Greco, Velázquez, and Titian.

Square—were now keenly aware of their opportunity to conceive and construct a building that would not only be ideal for their own collections, but also establish a model for future museum structures. They explored contemporary theories of museum design (apparently carefully selected to support the building committee's known preferences), visited more than 100 European museums during 1904, and built an experimental gallery—an entirely flexible mock-up on the Huntington site—in order to test a range of methods of gallery illumination for both paintings and sculpture.

The design of the building was entrusted to the Boston architect Guy Lowell (1870–1927), whose

1907 master plan evokes his formal training in the Beaux-Arts tradition. His plan is a remarkable realization of the committee's guiding principles, and provided a flexible framework for future growth. This proved fortunate, for very soon after the central portico and Huntington facade opened on November 2, 1909, Mrs. Robert Dawson Evans donated one million dollars for the construction of the present Fenway facade and connecting galleries in memory of her late husband. Subsequent additions in the 1920s to the east, and in 1968 and 1981 to the west, were eventually to fulfill Lowell's initial concept, enclosing east and west garden courtyards with today's complete circuit of galleries.

The Museum's Japanese collections continued to grow in the new Museum. John T. and William S. Spaulding were entranced by a Japanese print by Hiroshige given to them at the end of a visit to Japan in 1909, and in 1913, they commissioned Frank Lloyd Wright to travel to Japan in search of prints to build their collection which came to number some 6,000 impressions, notable for their superb state of preservation. The Spauldings gave the collection in 1921, with the unusual stipulation that it never be publicly exhibited, though it is, of course, available for study. John T. Spaulding went on to collect a splendid group of Impressionist paintings, including still lifes by Manet and Cézanne, six Renoirs, and two van Goghs, which he bequeathed to the Museum in 1948.

While many of the Museum's collections derived their overall shape and character from the vision of just one or a handful of collectors, the European paintings collection is much more a blend of tastes and points of view. Individual donors have had a significant influence on specific aspects of the collection—Quincy Adam Shaw's sixty-five paintings and pastels by Jean François

Millet, for example, or the Edwards, Paine, Tompkins, and Spaulding collections of French Impressionism and Post-Impressionism. Of the Museum's thirty-eight paintings and pastels by Claude Monet—second in number to only the National Museums of France—only two were purchases; the remaining works, some acquired directly from the artist in Giverny, were the gift of no less than twenty, primarily local, collectors.

In contrast, just two collectors, the remarkable husband and wife team of Maxim and Martha Karolik (see page 322), were to transform our holdings of the arts of the Americas. The donation of their collections—eighteenth-century American art, in 1939; American paintings, 1815–1865, in 1945; and American watercolors and drawings, 1800–1875, in 1962—gives the Museum's remarkable holdings of American art their breadth and depth. The Karolik collections were formed in sequence, in consultation with the Museum's curators, and from the start were ear-marked for the Museum. In a letter of 1945 announcing the gift of the paintings collection, they

Art students, here at work in the Indian sculpture gallery, are inspired by direct experiences of works of art from cultures and civilizations around the world.

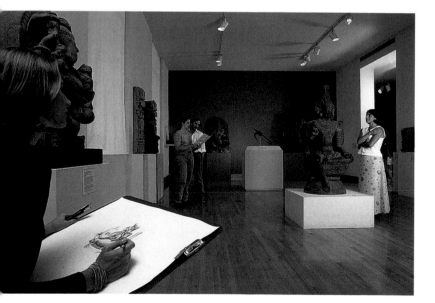

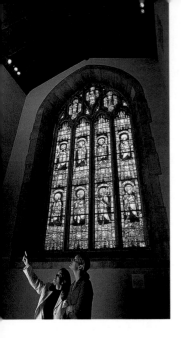

Natural light streams through the early 15th-century Apostles Window. The window was installed in the Museum in 1927 and again in 1944, after having been taken down for safety during World War II.

noted, "We discarded the motto of the fashionable connoisseur: 'Tell me who the painter is and I will tell you whether the painting is good.' Our motto was: 'Tell me whether the painting is good and I will not care who the painter is.'" Maxim Karolik summed up his feelings in a letter of 1962 announcing the gift of the collection of drawings: "I want the Museum's authorities and the people of this nation to know that the twenty-seven years, from 1935 to 1962, of this collaboration are the brightest chapter in my life."

What the Karoliks were to American art, Forsyth Wickes, a successful New York attorney, was to French art of the eighteenth century. Although his collection was installed at his home in Newport, he had never visited Boston. Perry Rathbone, then director of the Museum, recalls fondly a conversation in which Wickes asked if the Museum had any columns. Rathbone assured him that, indeed, the Fenway facade of the Museum featured twenty-two Ionic columns. Wickes must have been reassured, for he bequeathed his collection of some 800 works of art to the Museum in 1965. The Museum, in turn, undertook its first expansion—adding to the decorative arts wing—in forty years to house the collection.

Forsyth Wickes was not the only non-Bostonian to enrich the collections of the MFA. Elizabeth Day McCormick of Chicago gave the Museum her splendid collection of textiles and costumes, with its unique strength in English embroidery of the Elizabethan and Stuart periods, in 1943. Theodora Wilbour, who, like Wickes, never visited the Museum, began in 1933 a series of anonymous gifts of English silver in memory of her mother, and of coins and medallions in memory of her sister. These gifts continued until her death in 1947, upon which she bequeathed some $700,000 to establish two endowed funds that continue to bear her name and to permit significant acquisitions in her beloved English silver and Classical coins.

An important moment in the history of photography was the acquisition in 1924 of a gift of twenty-seven photographs by Alfred Stieglitz. Ananda Coomaraswamy, then Keeper of the Indian and Muhammedan Art at the Museum, a friend of Stieglitz, and an amateur photographer himself, solicited the gift and convinced the Trustees, not without some difficulty, that photography belonged among the Museum's collections. Stieglitz personally selected the photographs, which were augmented following his death by forty-two prints selected to complement them by his wife, Georgia O'Keeffe. These were the first photographs accepted as works of art by a major American museum. It must be noted that no other photographs were acquired by the Museum until the 1960s.

Some dominant personalities in the history of the Museum's collections spanned more than a single department or collection. For instance, Denman Waldo Ross, who is primarily associated with the Asiatic and textile collections, has the perhaps unique distinction of having been a significant donor to every department in the Museum. His wide-ranging gifts include the seventh-century Chinese *Thirteen Emperors Scroll*, inlays for the eyes of a mummy case, three paintings by Claude Monet, and two spectacular pastels over monotype by Edgar Degas, acquired as contemporary art and given during the artist's lifetime. Ross taught theory of design at Harvard and was a trustee of the MFA for four decades. His donations to the Museum, amounting to some 11,000 objects, range across geography, culture, and time period,

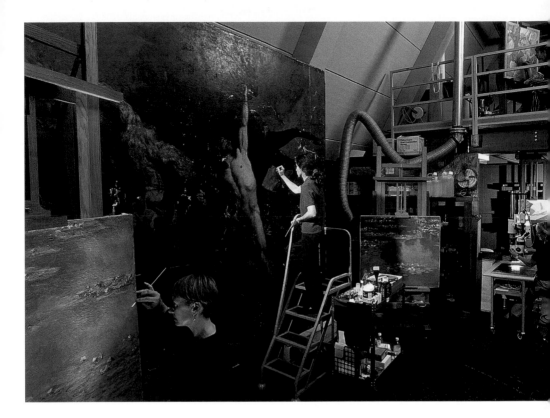

exemplifying his sole collecting criterion: visual quality. He expressed his goals clearly in a 1913 essay: "In collecting we proceeded regardless of archaeological or historical considerations. We were not archaeologists. We were not historians. We were simply lovers of order and the beautiful as they come to pass in the works of man supplementing the works of Nature. . . Our aim was to select and collect the best."

This sentiment continues to inspire benefactors in the late twentieth century, yet every great collector has his or her own vision and motivation. William H. Lane's collection of American modernist painting reflects his passions for jazz, Elvis, and Arthur Dove, as well as his requirement that every acquisition fit in the back of his Ford station wagon! William E. and Bertha L. Teel's collection of African and Oceanic sculpture was amassed in part because it was a field in which their resources permitted them to collect. Landon T. Clay's passionate commitment to ancient American cultures and his unwavering recognition of quality permeate his donations of Olmec, Maya, and Andean art.

The Museum of Fine Arts as it appears today is a rich whole comprising many parts, a collection of collections. This brief introduction has focused on pioneering and formative donations, but there are countless other gifts, both of individual works of art and of entire collections, that have also enriched our holdings. The fascinating individuals who made these gifts are associated with every area of the Museum. You will meet them and share their breadth of vision, knowledge, and taste, as well as their oversights and personal quirks, in the stories of the works of art they loved, which are told in the pages that follow.

Tucked away in a corner of the Museum, the George Putnam Ship Model Gallery is a perennial favorite with visitors. The collection includes models of American and European warships and merchant vessels from the 17th and 18th centuries.

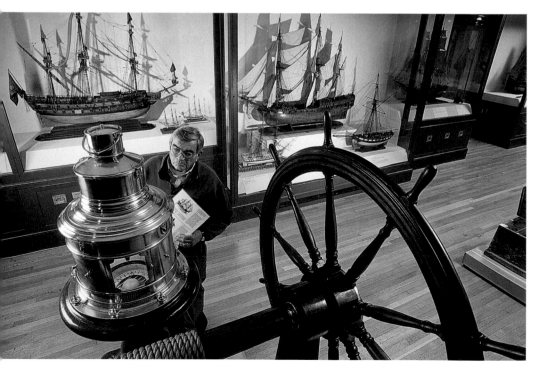

Use of the Guide

One of the great pleasures of a book like this is that it enables the Museum to share many of its great works in one place at one time. Not every work in this book will be on view in the Museum at all times. Some will be on loan to other museums. Some will be undergoing conservation treatment. Textiles, photographs, and other works on paper are particularly sensitive to exposure to light; in the interest of preserving them for future generations, these works are exhibited only for brief periods.

For the convenience of the reader, dimensions of objects in the guide have been kept to a minimum. For two-dimensional works, height precedes width. For furniture, three dimensions are given: height, width, depth. For other three-dimensional works, only one dimension (height or diameter, unless otherwise indicated) has been provided.

Accession numbers (shown at the end of the last line of captions, after the credit line) reflect the date of acquisition. In the case of objects acquired during the first century of the Museum's history (1870–1969), the final two digits of the year are the first two digits of the accession number: Gilbert Stuart's portrait of George Washington, for example (42.543) was the five hundred and forty-third object acquired by the Museum in 1942. For the Museum's second century, beginning in 1970, the full four-digit date is used. For example, the accession number for *Numbers*, Jasper Johns's work on paper, is 1996.362.

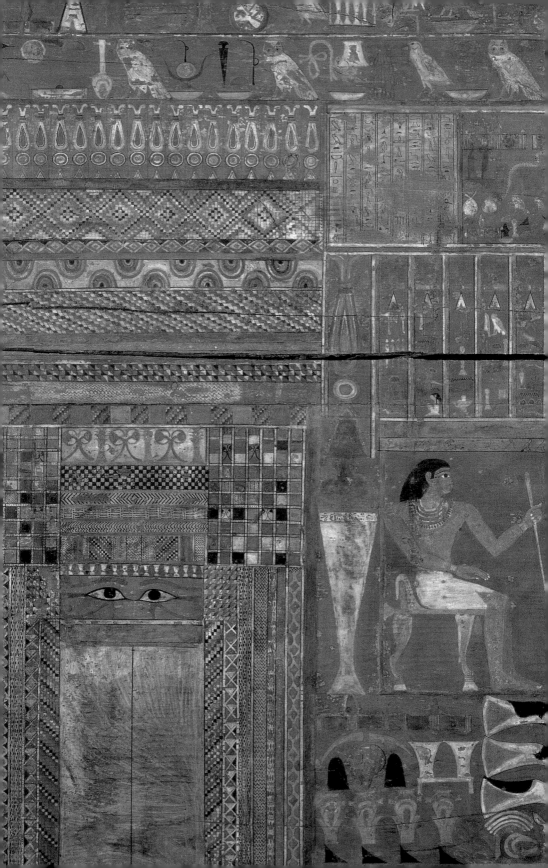

ART OF EGYPT, NUBIA, AND THE ANCIENT NEAR EAST

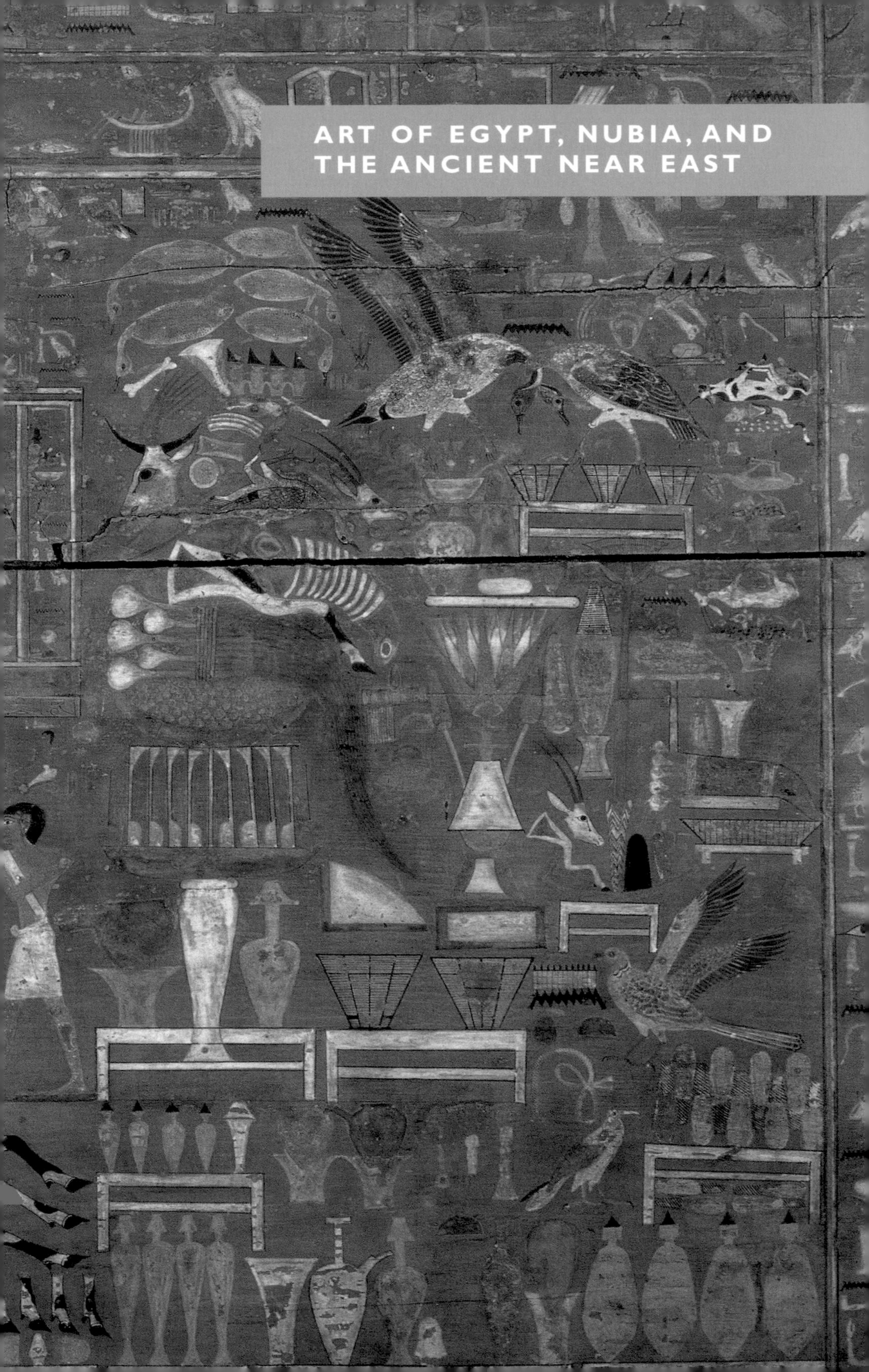

The Valley Temple at Giza, just outside Cairo, was part of the pyramid complex of King Mycerinus, which also included one of the three great pyramids. It was excavated by George Andrew Reisner and the Harvard University–Museum of Fine Arts Expedition between 1908 and 1910 (see page 30), and as Reisner noted in his journal, it was here that the extraordinary statue of Mycerinus and his queen (opposite) was unearthed on January 18, 1910: "In the evening, just before work stopped, a small boy . . . appeared suddenly at my side and said 'come.' . . . the female head of a statue (¾ life size) of bluish slate had just come into view in the sand . . . immediately afterward a block of dirt fell away and showed a male head on the right—a pair statue of a king and queen. A photograph was taken in failing light and an armed guard of 20 men put on for the night."

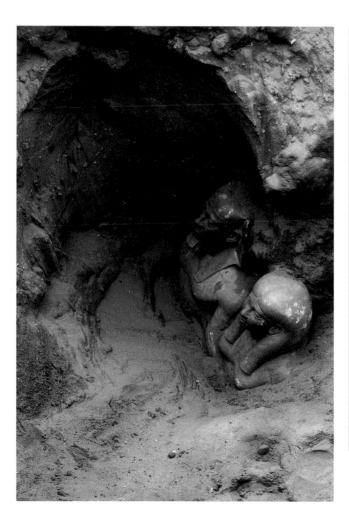

Egyptian Kingdoms, Periods, and Dynasties

Working with ancient texts and archaeological evidence, scholars have constructed a chronology from about 3100 B.C. to the country's conquest by Alexander the Great in 332 B.C. Egyptian history is subdivided into Kingdoms (times of strong central government and political stability) and Intermediate Periods (times when central authority collapsed). These divisions are further broken down into thirty-one dynasties, each comprising a series of reigning pharaohs.

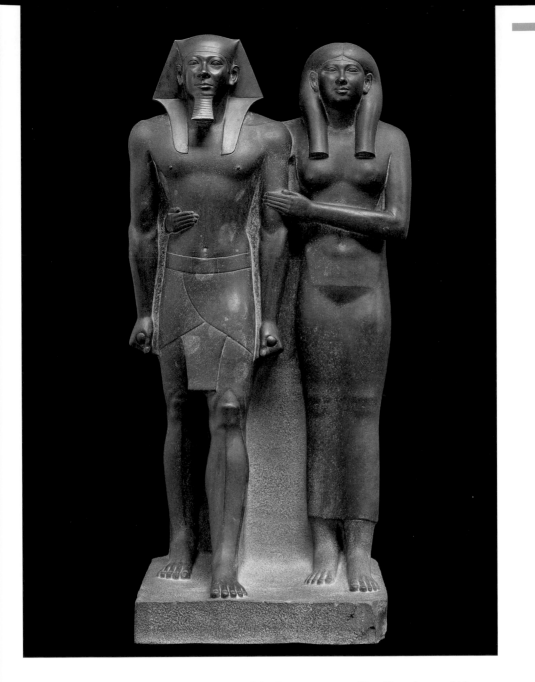

This serene and idealized royal image is one of the finest pieces of Egyptian sculpture known. Made of stone, its surface is subtly modeled and gives a very real sense of bodily form and structure. Mycerinus assumes the classic pose for men in Egyptian art, striding forward, his left leg advanced, arms rigid by his sides. He wears the royal headcloth *(nemes)*, kilt, and false beard. The queen also steps forward, clasping Mycerinus in a traditional gesture of intimacy and respect.

King Mycerinus and his queen (possibly Kha-merer-nebty II)
Egypt (found at Giza, Valley Temple of Mycerinus)
Old Kingdom, Dynasty 4, reign of Mycerinus, 2548–2530 B.C.
Greywacke
Height: 54⅞ in. (139.5 cm)
Harvard University–Museum of Fine Arts Expedition 11.1738

Ptah-khenui and his wife
Egypt (Giza, tomb G 2004)
Old Kingdom, mid- to late
Dynasty 5, 2488–2400 B.C.
Painted limestone
Height: 27⅝ in. (70.1 cm)
Harvard University–Museum of
Fine Arts Expedition 06.1876

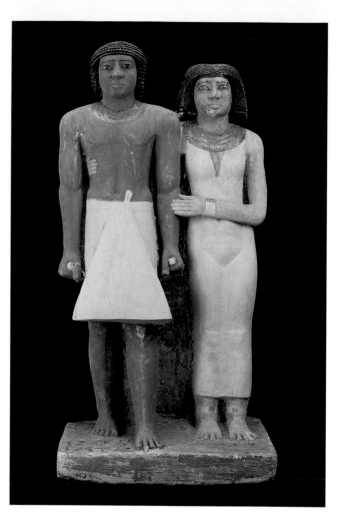

Woman grinding grain
Egypt (Giza, tomb G 2185)
Old Kingdom, Dynasty 5,
2524–2400 B.C.
Limestone
Length: 12¼ in. (30.9 cm)
Harvard University–Museum of
Fine Arts Expedition 12.1486

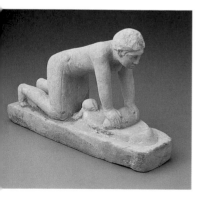

Statuettes of servants engaged in such domestic tasks as baking, weaving, and brewing were occasionally placed in tombs in the belief that they would magically become real to provide for the *ka* (that part of the human spirit that needed to be fed and sheltered) and to ensure the well-being of the deceased in the afterlife. This kneeling woman grinding grain for bread wears a kilt tied up at the side and a cloth to cover her hair. Flour spills over the front of the grindstone, while behind the stone is a partempty sack of grain. Carved from limestone, this figure would originally have been covered with a fine layer of plaster and then painted.

Although most Egyptian sculptures were originally painted, the color rarely survives. However, this statue is exceptionally well preserved. Ptah-khenui and his wife, wearing wigs and beaded collars, are painted in colors standard in Egyptian art: red for the skin of men and yellow for that of women. They stand in a pose very similar to that of King Mycerinus and his queen on page 23, but they are not royal: the inscription on the statue's base identifies Ptah-khenui as "supervisor of palace retainers"; his spouse (whose name is indecipherable) is termed "his beloved wife." This statue was found in a *serdab*, a hidden chamber within the tomb that had a window through which the figures could "see" into the adjacent chapel, where gifts of food and drink were left for them.

Triad of King Mycerinus with the goddess Hathor and the deified Hare nome
Egypt (Giza, Valley Temple of Mycerinus)
Old Kingdom, Dynasty 4, reign of Mycerinus, 2548–2530 B.C.
Greywacke
Height: 32 ¾ in. (83.5 cm)
Harvard University–Museum of Fine Arts Expedition 09.200

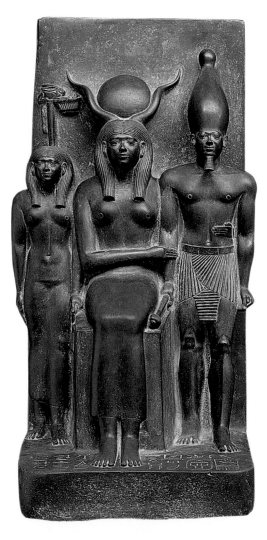

Found in one of the temples dedicated to the cult of Mycerinus, this magnificent sculpture of gray stone demonstrates the close relationship that the Egyptians perceived between their gods and their kings, whom they also believed to be divine. The central figure is the cow-goddess Hathor, identified by the horns surrounding a sun disk on her head. Expressing her devotion to the pharaoh (on her left, wearing the crown of Upper Egypt), Hathor circles his waist with one hand and lightly touches his arm with the other. The third figure personifies a nome, or province, and her symbol, the hare, rises above her head. In her left hand she carries the *ankh,* symbol of life, as a gift to the king. On the base of the sculpture, an inscription reads: "The Horus (Ka-khet) King of Upper and Lower Egypt, Men-kau-re [Mycerinus], beloved of Hathor, Mistress of the Sycamore. Recitation: I have given you all good things, all offerings, and all provisions in Upper Egypt, forever."

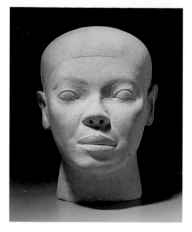

The purpose of the "reserve heads" that were placed in Egyptian tombs remains a mystery, although many scholars believe they were regarded as potential substitutes for the mummy. If the mummy or its head (essential for continued existence in the afterlife) were damaged, the spirit of the deceased could inhabit the "reserve head" and live on. Most of the thirty surviving "reserve heads" were discovered at Giza, in the vast cemetery used for courtiers and high officials of the Fourth Dynasty. There are six of these sculptures in the Museum, and no two are alike. They are modeled in broad, simplified forms, but in each case the sculptor has captured the individual's essential, identifying features. Such naturalism is rare in Egyptian art, where figures tend to be generalized and the subjects identified by inscriptions.

"Reserve head" of a woman
Egypt (Giza, tomb G 4440)
Old Kingdom, early Dynasty 4,
2630–2524 B.C.
Limestone
Height: 11 3/4 in. (30 cm)
Harvard University–Museum of Fine
Arts Expedition 14.719

This portrait bust is one of the most remarkable creations in all Egyptian art. It is a true likeness, more naturalistic than the "reserve heads" that, as portraits, are more simplified and summarizing. Here, the sculptor has captured the irregularities of Ankh-haf's skull, the lines beside his nose, the soft bags under his eyes—creating an indelible and very specific impression of maturity and intelligence. These telling details are modeled in a coat of plaster that covers the limestone core.

Ankh-haf was among the most important men of his time, serving as vizier, or senior administrative official, under King Chephren. The bust was found in Ankh-haf's tomb chapel, but its function is unknown. Although it was never part of a larger statue, it may have stood on a separately carved base that included arms stretched forward to receive offerings.

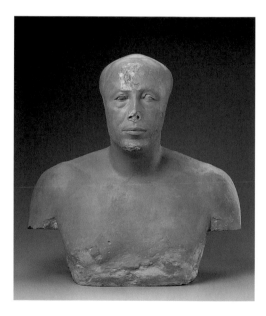

Bust of Prince Ankh-haf
Egypt (Giza, tomb G 7510)
Old Kingdom, Dynasty 4, reign of
Chephren, 2575–2550 B.C.
Limestone and plaster
Height: 19 7/8 in. (50.6 cm)
Harvard University–Museum of Fine
Arts Expedition 27.442

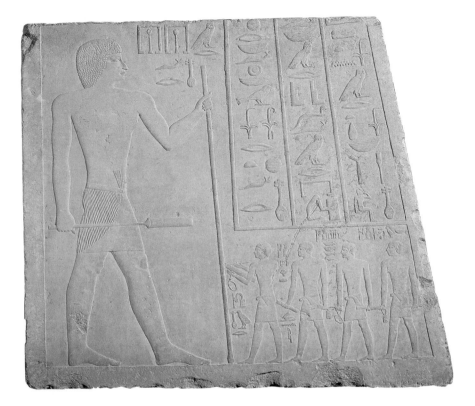

The stone walls of Egyptian tombs were often decorated with carvings that provide much fascinating information about the life of the deceased and about Egyptian society in general. This relief was placed just inside the entrance to the tomb chapel of Nofer, a government official who was buried near the great royal pyramids at Giza. Nofer is depicted on a scale befitting his importance; his distinctive aquiline nose and firmly set lips are also evident in the "reserve head" (below) that was found in his tomb. To the right of Nofer, three columns of hieroglyphs list his administrative duties and titles, which included overseer of the treasury. Below the hieroglyphic inscription is a procession of four scribes, the first one taking dictation. Civil servants like Nofer and scribes, who recorded the details of governmental affairs, were crucial to the complex, centralized administration of the Egyptian state.

Relief of Nofer
Egypt (Giza, tomb G 2110)
Old Kingdom, early Dynasty 4,
2606–2575 B.C.
Limestone
37 3/8 × 43 1/8 in. (95 × 109.5 cm)
Harvard University–Museum of
Fine Arts Expedition 07.1002

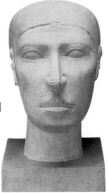

"Reserve head" of Nofer
Egypt (Giza, tomb G2110)
Old Kingdom, early Dynasty 4,
2606 2575 B.C
Limestone
Height: 6 3/4 in. (17.2 cm)
Harvard University–Museum of
Fine Arts Expedition 06.1886

Interior face of the outer coffin of Djehuty-nakht
(detail)
Egypt (Deir el-Bersha, tomb of Djehuty-nakht, no. 10A)
Middle Kingdom, late Dynasty 11, 2061–1991 B.C.
Painted cedar
45 ¼ × 103 ½ in. (115 × 263 cm)
Harvard University–Museum of Fine Arts Expedition 20.1822

Four thousand years ago, a provincial ruler named Djehuty-nakht was buried in a tomb cut into dry, limestone cliffs on the east bank of the Nile. His mummified body was placed within two nested coffins made of thick, cedar boards covered on both sides with paintings and inscriptions that would magically provide for his needs and protection in the afterlife. Exquisitely adorned with vibrant color and a wealth of detail, the interior of the outer coffin is perhaps the finest surviving example of Middle Kingdom painting. It depicts Djehuty-nakht seated before an attendant who brings a dish of incense. Neat rows of offerings, including the legs of spotted cows, are arranged below. Behind Djehuty-nakht is a representation of the "false door" through which his spirit could leave the coffin and come into the tomb chapel to receive the food and drink left there for him. The eyes on the door were painted so that the mummy, laid on its side to face them, could look out of the coffin.

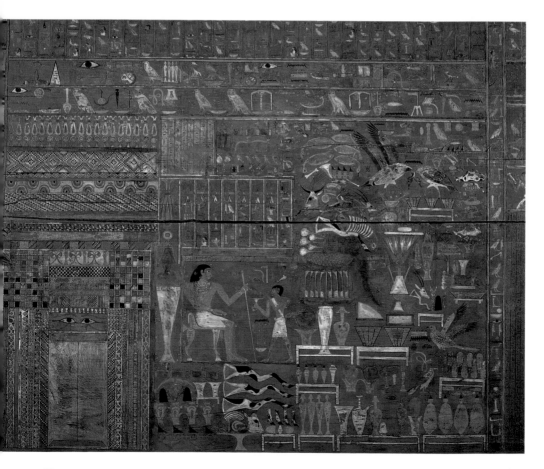

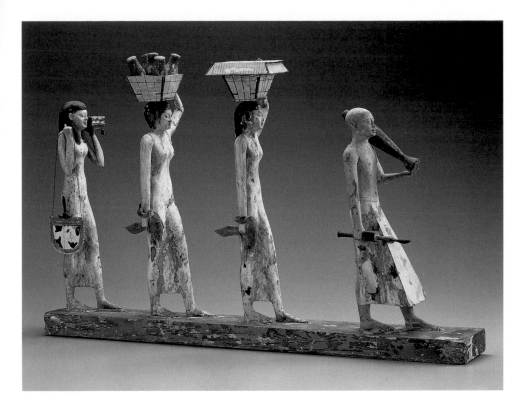

Procession of offering bearers
Egypt (Deir el-Bersha, tomb of Djehuty-nakht, no. 10A)
Middle Kingdom, late Dynasty 11, 2061–1991 B.C.
Painted wood
Length: 26⅛ in. (66.4 cm)
Harvard University–Museum of Fine Arts Expedition 21.326

In antiquity, Djehuty-nakht's tomb was plundered by thieves searching for jewelry and precious materials. When Museum archaeologists opened the tomb in 1915, they found complete chaos—the coffins disassembled, the mummies torn apart, and more than one hundred wooden models violently thrown aside and shattered. These models, like the coffin paintings and texts, were intended to ensure that the deceased would enjoy for eternity the comforts of his earthly life. Most such models are crudely made, but this is one of the finest wood carvings from any period of Egyptian history. It represents a procession, led by a priest carrying an incense burner and a ritual vase. Behind him, two women bring ducks and baskets of provisions, and a third carries a small chest and a mirror in a patterned case. In this small sculpture, ancient Egypt comes vividly to life.

Uncovering Ancient Egypt

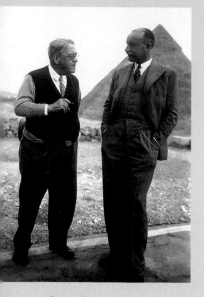

George Reisner with George Edgell, the Museum's director, at Giza (Egypt) in 1938.

The Museum's first Egyptian artifacts were accessioned in 1872, giving the collection an early start. By the turn of the century, however, high prices and the limited supply of artifacts made it clear that the only way to build an important collection was to dig. So the Museum's trustees decided to sponsor an expedition to Egypt.

Their timing was good. Unregulated digging had flourished during the nineteenth century, and in the 1890s an alarmed Egyptian government decided to monitor the excavations, authorizing teams and allowing them to keep a portion of their finds. In 1903 the government opened for excavation Giza, site of the three great pyramids. Sponsored at first by the University of California at Berkeley, an American expedition was led by George Andrew Reisner (1867–1942), who explained the compromise reached: "The division of the pyramids was easily arranged, as the Italians wanted the First pyramid, the Germans wanted the Second, and I was willing to accept the Third. But we all wanted the great cemetery west of the First pyramid. So that was divided into three strips, … for which we drew lots." In 1905 Berkeley ended its sponsorship, and the Museum allied with Harvard University to sup-

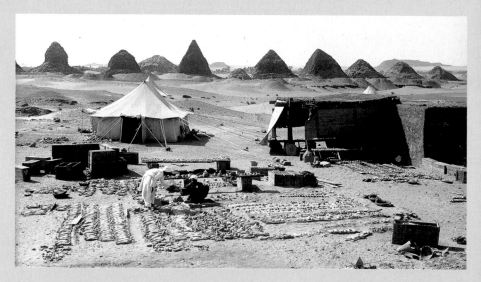

Sudanese workmen organizing the *shawabti*s of King Taharka at Nuri (Sudan) in 1917.

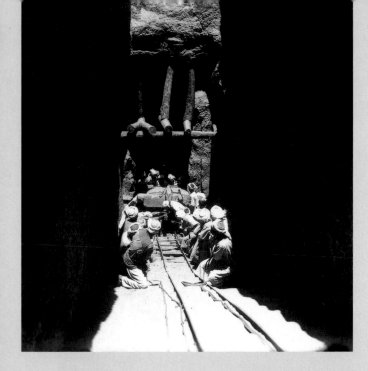

Removing the Anlamani
sarcophagus at Nuri in 1917.

port Reisner. Over the next thirty years Reisner's team rarely
stopped digging, and many of the Museum's most famous
objects, including the statue of the pharaoh Mycerinus and his
wife (page 23) and the bust of Prince Ankh-haf (page 26),
were uncovered during those years.

A man of formidable energy, Reisner did not restrict
himself to Giza. He dug his way up and down the Nile, from
the Mediterranean coast to the Sudan, excavating sites from
nearly every period of Egyptian history. His work in the Sudan
was particularly important, as it revealed for the first time the
history and culture of Nubia, ancient Egypt's rival, imitator, and
sometime conqueror (see page 42).

Reisner was an exceptionally careful archaeologist: his
methods—particularly his use of photography to document
the excavations—helped revolutionize the profession, and the
expedition's published reports are unmatched for their thor-
oughness. Today, although it no longer brings artifacts back to
Boston, the Museum continues to lead expeditions in Egypt
and the Sudan, following in Reisner's footsteps.

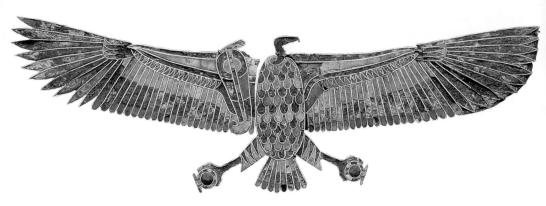

Sennuwy
Egypt (Kerma, Sudan,
royal tumulus K III)
Middle Kingdom, Dynasty 12, reign
of Sesostris I, 1971–1928 B.C.
Granite
Height: 67 3/4 in. (172 cm)
Harvard University–Museum of
Fine Arts Expedition 14.720

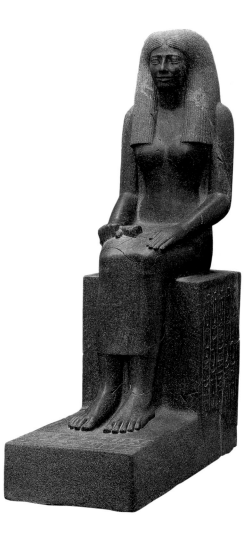

This serene image of Sennuwy, the wife of a provincial governor, is a masterpiece of Egyptian sculpture. Worked in hard, black granite, the rounded forms of Sennuwy's body are beautifully proportioned, and the smooth planes of her face are strikingly framed by the ribbed patterning of her heavy wig. Sennuwy and her husband were buried at Assiut, in central Egypt, in an elaborate tomb for which this funerary statue was probably made. However, the statue was found far to the south of Egypt, in the burial of a Nubian ruler of Kerma. Apparently, the statue was removed from the tomb in Egypt and taken to Nubia several hundred years after Sennuwy's death.

Avid for the great wealth buried with the pharaohs, tomb robbers systematically and thoroughly plundered the royal tombs of Egypt—often, very soon after they were closed. Thus, few pieces of ancient jewelry have survived into modern times; this pectoral (chest ornament) is not only extremely rare but a splendid, skillfully crafted work of art. Composed of more than four hundred pieces of inlaid glass and carnelian (a reddish stone), the pectoral was probably made for a royal burial and attached to a gilded mummy case. It represents a vulture grasping two coils of rope, symbols of the universal power of the king. To the left of the bird's body is the stylized representation of a cobra, rearing up as if to strike. Together, the vulture and the cobra signify the union of Upper and Lower Egypt and were standard symbolic attributes of the pharaoh.

Ancient Egyptians identified the lion-headed goddess Sekhmet (her name means "The Powerful One") with tempestuous weather, scorching heat, pestilence, and war. Priests constantly strove to calm her destructive and unpredictable nature with ceremonies and offerings. Sekhmet was believed to be especially threatening at the time of New Year (mid-July), for if she was not pacified, the Nile might not rise, the new year could not begin, and the cycle of life would cease. This image of the goddess, brought to Boston from Egypt in 1835, is probably one of 730 erected by King Amenhotep III in the temple precinct of the goddess Mut, Sekhmet's pacified alter-ego.

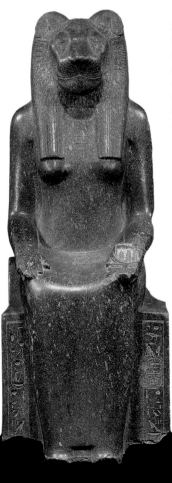

Stela of Ahmose
Egypt
New Kingdom, early Dynasty 18,
1570–1504 B.C.
Painted limestone
19 1/2 × 11 5/8 in. (49.5 × 29.5 cm)
Egyptian Special Purchase Fund
1981.2

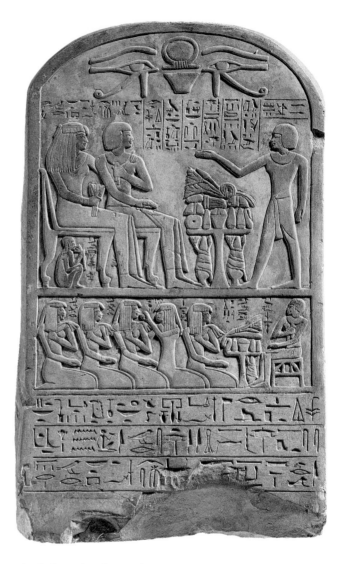

Seated in a carved chair, Ahmose, chief of metalworkers, is honored by members of his family with written prayers for the well-being of his spirit and offerings of food and flowers. Beside him sits his wife, Werel, resting her hand on his shoulder; his son Meny (called "true of voice") recites a prayer, his arm raised in a gesture of invocation. Lively details bring a sense of ordinary human experience to this ritualized image: the boy Tjer sniffs a lotus flower as he crouches beside his father's chair; one of the kneeling women turns to offer her companion a piece of fruit. This stela (a carved stone slab) was probably placed in Ahmose's tomb chapel, and the hieroglyphic text at the bottom is an offering formula that visitors recited for the benefit of his spirit.

Bes image

Egypt
New Kingdom, Dynasty 18,
probably reign of Amenhotep III,
1386–1349 B.C.
Glass frit ("Egyptian blue")
Height: 1½ in. (3.8 cm)
Pierce Fund, Purchased of E. P.
Warren 98.942

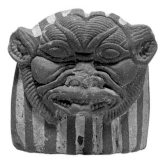

This tiny object, which may have been the pommel of a dagger, represents the dwarf god, variously known as Bes or Aha ("Fighter"), whose ferocious demeanor belies his kindliness. Bes was primarily a household god who protected the sleeping and kept the bedroom free of snakes, scorpions, and other unseen dangers, such as the evil spirits that threatened pregnant women and children. He was also the god of dance and music and performed before the great goddesses, who needed constant entertainment to prevent them from becoming angry and unleashing terrible disasters. Popular at every level of society, images of Bes were carved in temples, painted on bedroom walls, and placed on furniture and many utensils of daily use.

The powerful Hatshepsut, who ruled for more than twenty years, was one of very few women in Egyptian history to become "king," and ultimately pharaoh. She even had herself represented in sculpture with a male torso. This sarcophagus, originally designed for Hatshepsut, was reinscribed for her father, Thutmosis I, with the interior enlarged to hold his mummy and coffin. (Hatshepsut then ordered a matching sarcophagus, inscribed for herself as "king.") Made of a very hard stone, the sarcophagus is a fascinating historical document as well as an object of high artistic quality.

Sarcophagus of Queen Hatshepsut, recut for King Thutmosis I

Egypt (Thebes, Valley of the Kings, tomb 20)
New Kingdom, Dynasty 18, reign of Hatshepsut, 1498–1483 B.C.
Painted quartzite
88⅝ × 32¼ × 34¼ in.
(225 × 82 × 87 cm)
Gift of Theodore M. Davis 04.278

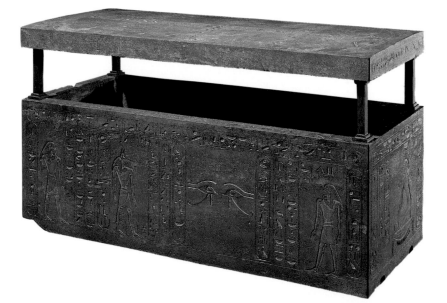

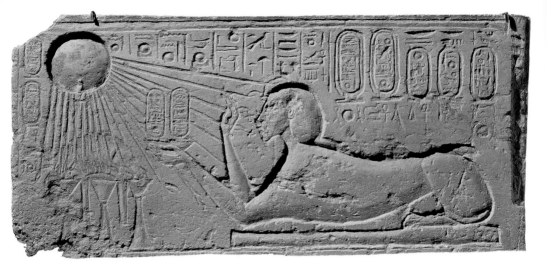

King Akhenaten as a sphinx
Egypt
New Kingdom, Dynasty 18, reign
of Akhenaten, 1350–1334 B.C.
Limestone
20⅛ × 41½ in. (51 × 105.5 cm)
Egyptian Curator's Fund 64.1944

From the Great Hymn
to the Aten, inscribed on
the wall of a tomb at
Akhetaten:

Earth brightens when you
  dawn in lightland,
When you shine as Aten of
  daytime;
As you dispel the dark,
As you cast your rays,
The Two Lands are in
  festivity.
Awake they stand on their
  feet,
You have roused them;
Bodies cleansed, clothed,
Their arms adore your
  appearance.

A true individualist among the pharaohs, Akhenaten established, for seventeen years, his own, essentially monotheistic religion, something previously unknown in the ancient world. He rejected not only the supreme state god, Amen, but the whole, age-old pantheon of Egyptian gods—ordering their images to be smashed, their temples closed, and even suppressing the plural form of the word for god. Akhenaten's one god was a manifestation of the sun called the Aten ("Disk"), and in Middle Egypt, he built a new capital named Akhetaten, the "Horizon of the Aten" (modern Tell el-Amarna). This relief, probably from a palace wall at Akhetaten, depicts the king as a sphinx lying before a table of offerings and presenting to the Aten oval tablets inscribed with the god's names. Overhead, the disk of the Aten sends down its lifegiving rays. After Akhenaten's death, one of his successors, Tutankhamen, returned the royal residence to Memphis and reinstated the old religion. The richly decorated temples, palaces, public buildings, and homes of Akhetaten were razed, and the city returned to the desert.

King Tutankhamen
Egypt (Thebes)
New Kingdom, Dynasty 18, reign
of Tutankhamen, 1334–1325 B.C.
Sandstone
Height: 11 ¾ in. (29.6 cm)
Gift of Miss Mary S. Ames
11.1533

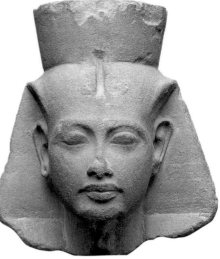

Tutankhamen, possibly the son of Akhenaten,
reigned only from his ninth to his nineteenth year,
but the discovery in 1922 of his largely undisturbed tomb caused a sensation throughout the
world. Although hastily assembled following the
unexpected death of the young king, the vast array of
sumptuous gold and jeweled objects that accompanied
Tutankhamen's burial gave archaeologists a realization of just
how magnificent must have been the funerary treasures of the
royal tombs that had been plundered. This sandstone head,
although not inscribed with his name, almost certainly represents Tutankhamen, its sensuous features strikingly similar to
those on the famous gold mummy mask from his tomb.

Pendant on a chain
Egypt
New Kingdom, Dynasty 19, probably
reign of Ramesses II, 1279–1212 B.C.
Gold with glass inlays
Height: 2 ¾ in. (7.2 cm)
Gift of Mrs. Horace L. Mayer in
memory of Horace L. Mayer 68.836

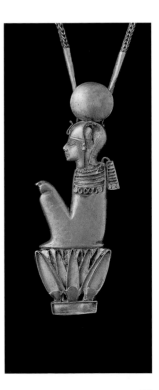

An Egyptian creation story tells of the emergence of the sun
god—the first living being—from a lotus flower growing in the
receding waters of the primeval ocean called Nun. This pendant illustrates that story and shows the newborn sun god in
the form of the pharaoh Ramesses II as a child. It is made of
hammered sheet gold, is carefully worked on both sides, and
still retains its chain of interlocking gold loops. The front was
originally inlaid with colored glass. The long reign of Ramesses
II was marked by wars against foreigners and by the construction of monumental buildings; nearly half of the temples that
remain in Egypt today were built in his reign.

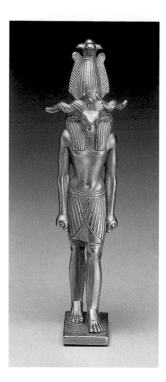

This tiny amulet of solid cast gold represents the fertility god Harsaphes, depicted as a man with the head of a long-horned ram. He wears a royal kilt, and on his head is the Atef crown that associates him with the powerful Osiris, god of the Underworld. In hieroglyphs on the underside of the base, the statuette is inscribed with the name of Neferkare Peftjauawybast, ruler of the city of Herakleopolis (modern Ehnasya, Egypt). Neferkare is recorded as a subject prince on the victory stela of the Nubian king Piye who, "raging like a panther," conquered Egypt "like a cloudburst" about 724 B.C. With its delicate sculpting of muscles and bone and its fine, linear patterning of kilt, horns, and crown, this image of Harsaphes is a superb example of the goldsmith's art.

The god Harsaphes
Egypt (Ehnasya)
Third Intermediate Period,
Dynasty 25, 767–656 B.C.
Gold
Height: 2 3/8 in. (6 cm)
Gift of Egypt Exploration Fund
06.2408

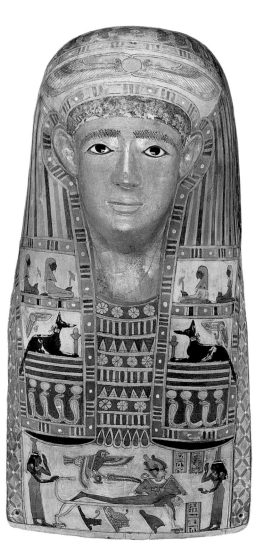

Only four inches high, the so-called "Boston Green Head" is admired throughout the world as one of the finest of all portrait sculptures from ancient Egypt. It is a masterpiece of naturalism—rare in Egyptian art, which tends to idealize—and is stamped with a remarkable humanity. Note the wrinkled forehead, the deep lines around nose and mouth, the crow's-feet, and such individual-izing details as the mole on the left cheekbone. The subject is probably a priest, identified by his shaven head. On the back of the head is an inscription with the name of the god Ptah-Sokar, suggesting that the statue (of which this head is a fragment) was originally placed in a temple dedicated to that god.

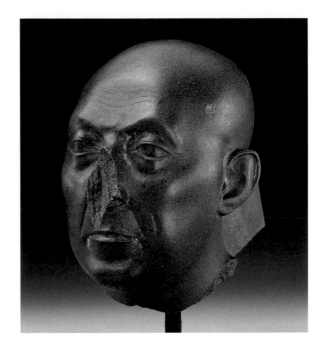

Head of a priest
Egypt (probably Sakkara)
Late Period, Dynasty 30,
380–343 B.C.
Greywacke
Height: 4 in. (10.2 cm)
Purchased of Edward P. Warren,
Pierce Fund 04.1749

Mummy mask
Egypt (possibly Meir)
Early Roman period, first half of
the 1st century A.D.
Painted and gilded cartonnage,
inlaid glass
Height: 22½ in. (57.2 cm)
Gift of Lucien Viola, Horace L. and
Florence E. Mayer Fund, Helen and
Alice Colburn Fund, Marilyn M.
Simpson Fund, William Francis
Warden Fund, and William
Stevenson Smith Fund 1993.555

To help preserve the features of the mummified head and upper body of the deceased, ancient Egyptians often covered these parts with a separate wooden mask. Long after the Romans conquered Egypt in the first century A.D., traditional Egyptian religious beliefs and funerary rituals persisted. This mask, from the Roman period, is constructed of cartonnage—a material, similar to papier maché, made of layers of linen coated with plaster. Its rich gilding signifies the status of its owner and also evokes the golden flesh of the gods, with whom the deceased hoped to be united. The mask is painted with mourning and protective figures. Across the bottom, the god Osiris, reclining on a funerary bier above the crowns of Egypt, is shown being brought back to life by the goddess Isis in the form of a bird holding a feather and the *shen*-ring of eternity.

The Art of the Afterlife

**Tomb group of
Nes-mut-aat-neru**
Egypt, (Deir el-Bahri)
Dynasty 25,
about 700–675 B.C.
Wood, plaster, linen, pigment
Outer coffin length: 80¼ in.
(204 cm)
Second coffin length: 73¼ in.
(186 cm)
Inner coffin length: 66½ in.
(169 cm)
Mummy length: 59½ in.
(151 cm)
Gift of Egypt Exploration Fund
95.1407

Nes-mut-aat-neru, the wife of a high-ranking Theban priest, died sometime around 700 B.C., and her tomb remained undisturbed for over 2500 years until it was excavated in 1894. Her mummy was contained within three wooden coffins, all decorated with inscriptions and depictions of the gods and goddesses who guaranteed protection in the afterlife. The vaulted lid and four corner posts of the outermost, rectangular coffin (shown below) are meant to imitate the tomb of Osiris, god of the Underworld. This first coffin held the smaller one (at right) shaped roughly like a human body and painted with a face and wig. Within this lay a third coffin in the shape of the mummy itself, every inch covered with inscriptions and devotional images, including one of Nes-mut-aat-neru worshipping Osiris as he lay on his funeral bed.

This elaborate housing was designed to protect the mummy—the preserved body of the deceased—for the ancient Egyptians believed that in the afterlife, the spirit or *ba* continued to use the body as a home, and that the dead had the same physical needs as the living. To ensure the integrity of the body, they employed the process of mummification—

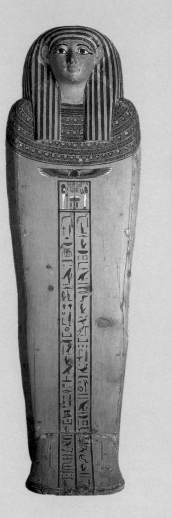

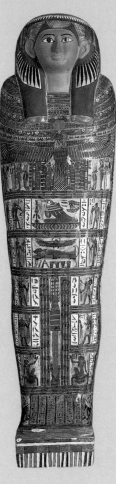

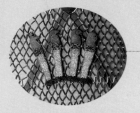

removing the internal organs of the deceased (which were preserved and stored separately), dehydrating the corpse with salts, and wrapping it in linen cloth. These procedures were accompanied by elaborate rituals and took nearly three months. Central as mummification was to the afterlife, it was only one way in which care was taken to provide for the next world. Indeed, the majority of the objects in the Museum's Egyptian collection were buried in tombs for the comfort of the deceased—and many others were ritual objects used by the living on behalf of the dead.

Protective amulets of deities were sometimes sewn onto the outside of the mummy or incorporated into the bead net, as seen above.

Nubia

Ancient Nubia—a region encompassing modern-day southern Egypt and northern Sudan—provided a major trade route over which gold, ivory, ebony, incense, and spices traveled between central Africa and the lands around the Mediterranean. Nubia's history was closely intertwined with that of its neighbor, Egypt: social, political, religious, and artistic ideas moved back and forth as each country conquered or was conquered by the other. Nevertheless, both Egypt and Nubia retained their unique characteristics, and with intensified archaeological exploration of Nubia over the past decades, scholars have recognized its importance as a distinct culture. This has greatly enhanced our understanding of ancient Africa as a complex community of nations.

Stela of the Nubian soldier Nenu
Egypt (Jebelein)
First Intermediate Period,
2250–2035 B.C.
Painted limestone
14 5/8 × 17 3/4 in. (37 × 45 cm)
Purchased by A. M. Lythgoe
03.1848

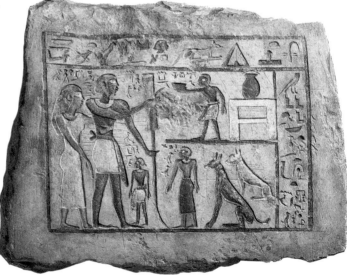

The ancient Egyptians called Nubia Ta-Sety ("Land of the Bow"), and Egyptian kings often hired the renowned archers of Nubia for their armies. Many of these mercenary soldiers settled in Egypt, married Egyptian women, and were buried in the Egyptian manner, but they still proudly maintained their Nubian identity. This limestone grave marker from Jebelein in Upper Egypt depicts a Nubian soldier named Nenu holding his bow and arrows; beside him is his wife, wearing the close-fitting linen dress typical of Egyptian women. Nenu has a short, curly, Nubian hairstyle and close-cropped beard and wears a kilt tied with a characteristically Nubian leather sash. In the upper right, an Egyptian servant presents a bowl of beer. Dogs are often included on the stelae of Nubian soldiers, suggesting the great affection they had for these pets.

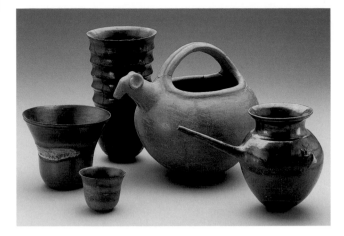

Beakers
Sudan (Kerma)
Kerma culture, 1700–1550 B.C.
Ceramic
Height of rilled beaker: 8 7/8 in.
(22.5 cm)
Harvard University–Museum of
Fine Arts Expedition 13.4080,
SU 778, 20.2006, 20.1714,
13.4102

Nubian ceramics are among the earliest and most sophisticated of the ancient world. About 1700 B.C., as Egypt declined, the great Nubian kingdom of Kush rose to power, its capital built on a fertile bend of the Nile where the modern town of Kerma now stands. A hallmark of the Kerma culture is its extraordinarily fine "black-topped red-polished" pottery, which came in a variety of elegant, inventive shapes. Remarkably thin and delicate, this pottery was not thrown on a wheel but made entirely by hand. Much of it was produced to be included in burials along with furniture, household equipment, dress, and jewelry. The unusual shape of the tall ribbed, or "rilled," beaker here suggests the nested stacks of individual cups that were often placed in Kerma tombs so that the thirst of the dead might be satisfied in the afterlife.

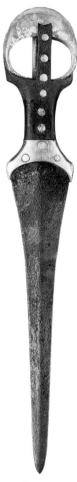

In 1913 George Andrew Reisner and the Harvard University–Museum of Fine Arts Expedition (see page 30) began a twenty-year excavation of major Nubian sites in the northern Sudan, among them the walled city and cemetery of ancient Kerma, capital of the kingdom of Kush. Sudanese authorities allowed the expedition to keep many of the objects found, and the Museum of Fine Arts now houses the finest and most extensive collection of Nubian art outside Sudan. Although many objects discovered in Kerma burials were either influenced by Egyptian art or were Egyptian in origin (see the statue of Sennuwy, page 32), exquisitely crafted miniature daggers like this one, found in the grave of a young boy, are entirely Nubian.

Miniature dagger
Sudan (Kerma, cemetery M, grave 48)
Early Kerma culture,
1900–1700 B.C.
Gold, bronze, ebony, and ivory
Height: 6 5/8 in. (16.7 cm)
Harvard University–Museum of Fine
Arts Expedition 21.11796b

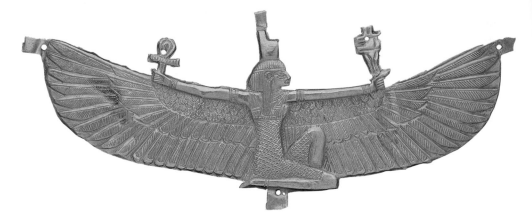

Winged Isis pectoral
Sudan (Nuri, pyramid of King
Amani-nataki-lebte)
Late 6th century B.C.
Gold
Width: 6⅝ in. (16.7 cm)
Harvard University–Museum of
Fine Arts Expedition 20.276

This gold pectoral, overlooked by the thieves who plundered the royal tombs at Nuri, represents the winged goddess Isis, holding an *ankh* (symbol of life) in her right hand and what may represent the hieroglyph for a sail (symbol of the breath of life) in her left. Twenty Nubian kings and fifty-four queens were buried at Nuri between the mid-seventh and the late-fourth centuries B.C. The mummified bodies were placed within nested sets of gilded wooden coffins inlaid with colored stones. The mummies wore gold amulets, gold finger and toe caps, and probably gold face masks. This pendant would have been sewn onto a bead net draped over a king's mummy. Cut into the bedrock beneath the pyramids, the royal tombs were excavated by the Museum expedition between 1917 and 1920.

Pendant with head of Hathor
Sudan (el Kurru)
Dynasty 25, reign of King Piye,
753–713 B.C.
Rock crystal and gold
Height: 2⅛ in. (5.3 cm)
Harvard University–Museum of
Fine Arts Expedition 21.321

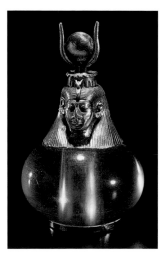

Surmounted by a gold head of the goddess Hathor (see page 25), this rock-crystal pendant—illustrated here at its actual size—served as a protective amulet. Worn by the living and buried with the dead, amulets were believed to have special powers, embodied both in their sacred imagery and in the precious materials of which they were made. This example has a gold cylinder enclosed within the crystal globe. Comparable cylinders have been found containing sheets of papyrus or metal inscribed with magical texts; however, x-rays have shown that this one is empty. The pendant was found in the tomb of a queen of the Nubian king Piye, ruler of both Nubia and Egypt. The head of Hathor is Egyptian in style, and the pendant was probably part of the tribute paid to King Piye by Egyptian princes.

**Vessel in the shape of a
bound oryx**
Sudan (Meroe)
Early 7th century B.C.
Calcite (alabaster)
Length: 6 3/4 in. (17.2 cm)
Harvard University–Museum of
Fine Arts Expedition 24.879

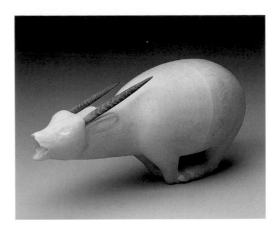

In a grave excavated at Meroe, a hundred
miles from the modern city of Khartoum,
the body of a young woman was found
surrounded by jewelry, amulets, mirrors,
pottery, bronze vessels, and three alabaster
jars in the form of bound oryxes. At once lifelike and ingeniously functional, these elegant jars were containers for
expensive perfume and ointments, which could be poured
out through the open mouth. The bound legs made a practi-
cal handle. Since calcite is a stone found in Egypt, it is likely
that the vessel—with its contents—was exported to Nubia
from Egypt. The wooden horns are modern reproductions of
the original slate ones.

Leg from a funerary bed
Sudan (el Kurru)
Dynasty 25, reign of Shebitku,
698-690 B.C.
Bronze
Height: 22 1/8 in. (56.1cm)
Harvard University–Museum of Fine
Arts Expedition 21.2815

In traditional Nubian burials, the unmummified body of
the deceased was laid out on a wooden bed. Later, in the
period when Nubian kings ruled Egypt, mummification in
the Egyptian fashion was introduced although the wooden
funerary beds were retained. This bronze leg from such a wood-
en bed (long since decayed) incorporates the figure of a goose.
In funerary texts from Old Kingdom Egypt, the deceased
expresses his desire to rise to heaven as a goose, and from the
time of the New Kingdom, the goose was one of many forms
taken by Amen, the principal Egyptian god.

Shawabti figures of King Taharka
Sudan (Nuri)
Dynasty 25, reign of Taharka,
690–664 B.C.
Granite, alabaster, and other stones
Height: 4–13¾ in. (10–35 cm)
Harvard University–Museum of Fine Arts Expedition

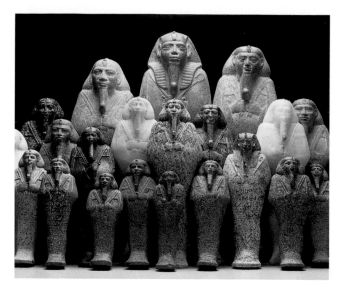

About 740 B.C. the Nubian king Piye invaded Egypt and established his family as Egypt's 25th Dynasty. Many Egyptian practices were adopted in Nubia during this period, including the construction of pyramids for royal tombs that contained _shawabti_ figures intended to perform manual labor for the deceased in the afterlife. These _shawabti_s are some of more than one thousand that were discovered standing in neat rows in the burial chamber of King Taharka's pyramid tomb at Nuri. Taharka, a son and third successor of King Piye, was the greatest of the Nubian pharaohs. His empire stretched from Palestine to the confluence of the Blue and White Niles. It was conquered by the Assyrians in 667 B.C., at which time Nubia lost control of Egypt.

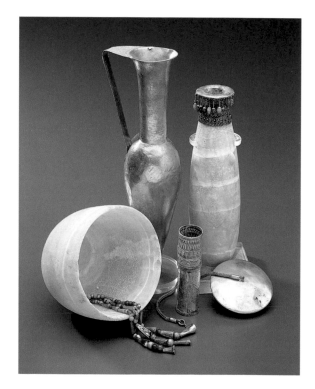

King Aspelta
Sudan (Jebel Barkal), 600–580 B.C.
Black granite
Height: 130 ¾ in. (332 cm)
Harvard University–Museum of
Fine Arts Expedition 23.730

This monumental striding statue of King Aspelta, wearing
the royal Nubian headdress, originally stood in the Great
Temple of Amen at Jebel Barkal, the foremost religious center of Nubia. Eleven feet tall and weighing eight tons, the
colossal image is smoothly polished except for the surfaces
representing dress and jewelry, which were left rough to hold
a thin layer of gold leaf. In 1916 this statue, which had
probably been broken in 598 B.C. by members of an invad-
ing Egyptian army, was discovered in pieces by Museum
archaeologists in a pit outside the temple entrance. The statue was reassembled at the Museum in 1924.

< **Tomb treasure of King Aspelta**
Sudan (found at Nuri, pyramid of
Aspelta), about 600–580 B.C.
Silver, gold, alabaster, carnelian,
turquoise, and steatite
Height of gold vase: 12 ⅜ in. (31.5 cm)
Harvard University–Museum of Fine
Arts Expedition 20.340, 20.1070,
20.334, 21.339, 20.339, 20.1072

The splendid pyramid tomb of King Aspelta (probably
the great-grandson of King Taharka) was the least-plun-
dered of all the royal burials at Nuri. Within it, Museum
archaeologists discovered a wide array of precious grave
goods buried in soil littered with gold beads and pieces of
gold foil (in which the objects may originally have been
wrapped). Included in the treasure were the objects illustrated here, among them a graceful gold vase and an
alabaster perfume or ointment jar from whose gold cap
beads of semiprecious stones hang on woven gold-wire
chains.

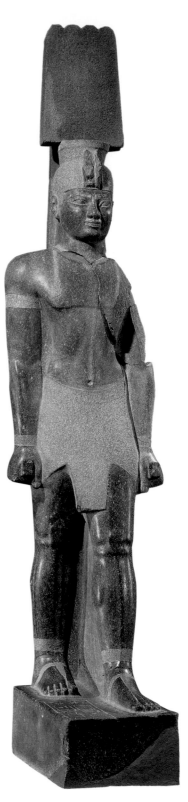

Shrine
Sudan (Jebel Barkal)
Meroitic period, 2nd century B.C.
or later
Stuccoed and painted sandstone
Height: 24 5/8 in. (62.5 cm)
Harvard University–Museum of
Fine Arts Expedition 21.3234

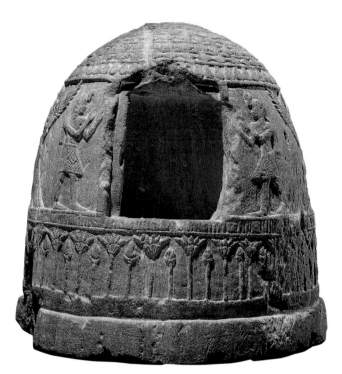

This sandstone shrine, found in the great Temple of Amen at Jebel Barkal, originally housed a statue of the god Amen hidden behind a sealed doorway. Once thought to imitate the form of a traditional African house, the shrine actually is a model of Jebel Barkal itself, the three-hundred-foot, sacred "Pure Mountain" behind whose cliff Amen was believed to dwell. On either side of the opening of the shrine are carved images of a Nubian king and a winged goddess, standing above a stylized papyrus swamp. Nubians believed that Jebel Barkal was the "primeval hill" of Egyptian mythology, where the creator god first gave himself form and, amid the primordial swamp, caused the sun to rise on the first day of time.

About 270 B.C. the royal court of Nubia was established at Meroe, a manufacturing center that traded objects of copper, ivory, glass, and ceramic as far away as Italy and Greece. Influences from central Africa, Egypt, and the Greco-Roman world combine in the distinctive art and culture of this period, and Meroitic ceramics are renowned for their quality and variety. This vessel for wine or beer is decorated with both indigenous and imported motifs—native crocodiles and twining grapevines derived from Greek art.

Funerary stela
Sudan
Meroitic period,
2nd–3rd centuries A.D.
Sandstone
Height: 33½ in. (85 cm)
Gift of Horace L. and Florence E.
Mayer, C. Granville Way, Denman
Ross, the Hon. Mrs. Frederick
Guest, Bequest from Charles H.
Parker, and Anonymous Gift, by
exchange 1992.257

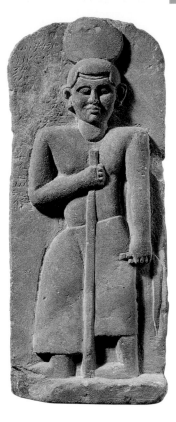

This fine stela, or grave marker, represents a high-ranking Meroitic official with his characteristic long skirt, fly whisk, and staff. The cut in his forehead represents a decorative scar that some Sudanese still wear today to identify their community affiliation, and the sun disk above his head indicates that he has died and become divine. To the left of the figure, a Meroitic inscription probably gives his name and title. However, scholars are still unable to decipher this ancient language (composed of an alphabet of twenty-three letters) which appeared in the second century B.C.

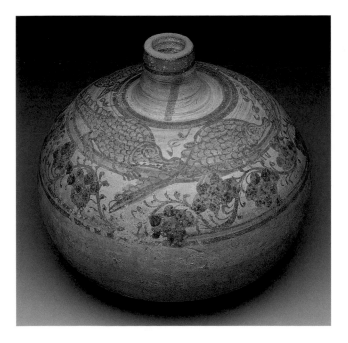

Pot
Sudan (Kerma)
Meroitic period, 2nd century A.D.
Painted ceramic
Diameter: 11 in. (28 cm)
Harvard University–Museum of
Fine Arts Expedition 13.4038

Female and male figurines
Syria (Tell Judeideh)
Early Bronze Age, about
3200–2800 B.C.
Low-tin bronze with silver
Height female: 7½ in. (19 cm)
Height male: 7 in. (17.8 cm)
Gift of the Marriner Memorial
Syrian Expedition 49.118, 49.119

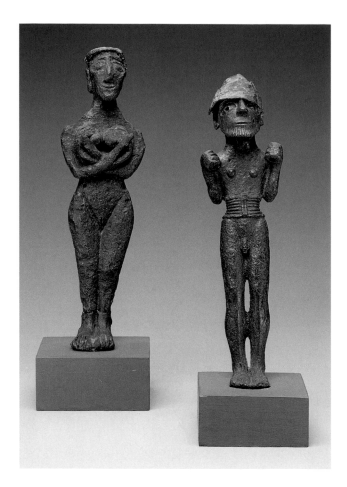

Among the oldest surviving metal sculptures from the ancient Near East, these figurines were excavated at an Early Bronze Age site in northern Syria, along with four similar figures that all appeared to have been wrapped in cloth before burial. Cast in an unusual bronze alloy, these lively figures are nude; the woman (who once had silver jewels and curls) holds her breasts, and the man, who wears only a wide belt and a silver helmet, originally grasped small bronze weapons. Such figures may have been intended to magically enhance fertility and virility.

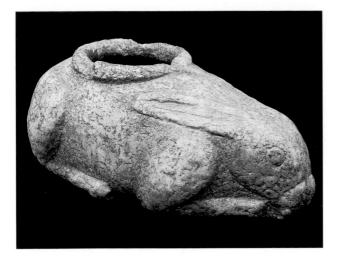

Vessel in the form of a hare
Syria
Neolithic period, about
6400–5900 B.C.
Gypsum
Length: 7¼ in. (18.5 cm)
Egyptian Curator's Fund and
Partial Gift of Emmanuel Tiliakos
1995.739

Carved about eight thousand years ago, this amazingly well-preserved vessel in the form of a hare is among the oldest works of art on view in the Museum. Simply shaped and economically detailed, the hollow vessel nevertheless vividly captures the essential hare—its round-eyed face resting on its paws and its long ears laid tightly against the body. An almost identical vessel was discovered in the 1970s at the Neolithic village site of Bouqras, on the Euphrates River in northern Syria.

Mountain goat
Iran
Proto-Elamite period, about
3000–2800 B.C.
Silver and sheet gold
Length: 2¾ in. (7 cm)
J. H. and E. A. Payne Fund   59.14

The artist who made this exquisite miniature mountain goat created an image of great dignity and naturalism, even incising its rear leg and tufted tail on the bottom of the sculpture. A fragmentary loop on the animal's back suggests that it may have been worn as an amulet. The sculpture dates from the brilliant Proto-Elamite period that saw the dawn of literacy in Iranian civilization.

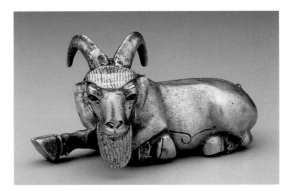

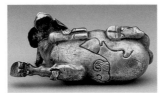

**Fragment of a
victory stela**
Iraq
Akkadian period, reign of
Naram-Sin, about
2254–2218 B.C.
Calcite (alabaster)
Height: 13 ¼ in. (33.5 cm)
Gift of the Guide Foundation
and Mrs. Hilary Barrat-Brown
66.893

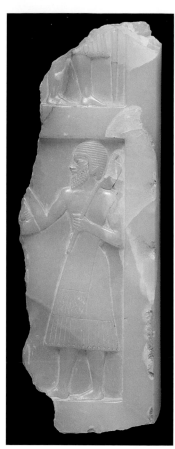

During the Akkadian dynasty, established by Sargon the Great about 2350 B.C., all of Mesopotamia and even parts of Anatolia (modern-day Turkey) were united under one ruler for the first time. The commemorative relief of which this is a fragment most likely dates from the reign of Naram-Sin, mightiest of Sargon's successors, and was originally composed of several registers carved with scenes of Akkadian soldiers leading prisoners and carrying away booty. The warrior in this fragment wears a ribbed or quilted helmet, a fringed sash, and a long skirt. He holds a battle ax and rests his right arm on the shoulder of the last man in a line of bound, nude captives (preserved in fragments in the Iraq Museum in Baghdad).

Appliqué
Southern Turkey
Neo-Hittite period,
10th–8th centuries B.C.
Silver
Length: 1 ⅝ in. (4 cm)
Marilyn M. Simpson Fund 1996.61

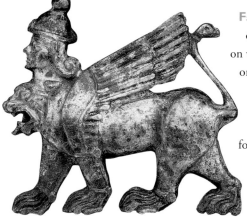

Fantastic composite creatures appear throughout the art of the ancient Near East. Painted on walls, carved on furnishings, and embroidered onto textiles, they were believed to provide protection against evil supernatural forces. This intricate silver ornament, which probably once adorned a rich garment, represents a four-legged beast with a helmeted human head above the creature's snarling head of a lion. The curling tail terminates in yet another head, perhaps that of a griffin.

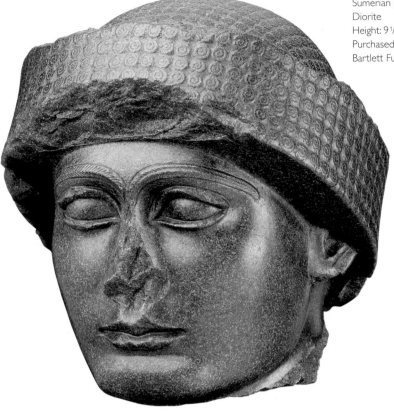

Head of Gudea
Iraq (probably Tellah)
Sumerian period, about 2200 B.C.
Diorite
Height: 9 1/8 in. (23 cm)
Purchased from the Francis
Bartlett Fund 26.289

During the turbulent era following the collapse of the Akkadian empire, Gudea governed the small state of Lagash on the Persian Gulf. Ironically, most major known pieces of late-Sumerian art represent this quite minor ruler, who filled the temples of his local gods with statues of himself. These images are mostly carved from diorite—a hard, black stone that Gudea claimed to have brought by sea from "Magan," a distant land now believed to be somewhere on the Arabian coast. Like the majority of surviving images of Gudea, this one was vandalized in antiquity, the head lopped from the body and the nose broken. Nevertheless, it remains a superb work of art, the remarkable surfaces of smooth, polished stone emphasizing dramatically large eyes beneath sweeping eyebrows and a wool crown formed of tight, stylized curls.

Most ceramics from the ancient kingdom of Phrygia in Anatolia (modern-day Turkey) were painted with geometric designs. This highly unusual pitcher, however, was decorated with figures, probably reflecting the influence of Greek art. Many scholars consider it the most important surviving late-Phrygian ceramic. It seems to have been equally valued in antiquity, when it was carefully repaired with lead clamps (visible here). The decoration shows a huntress shooting at a leopard; an ibex stands behind her. The huntress is Kubaba or Cybele (known as Artemis by the Greeks), the powerful Anatolian mother goddess and mistress of the animals. This vessel may have been used in rituals at one of the goddess's shrines.

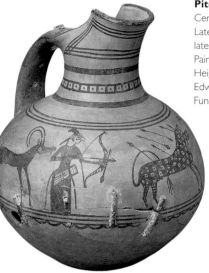

Pitcher
Central Turkey
Late Phrygian period,
late 7th century B.C.
Painted ceramic
Height: 11 ¾ in. (30 cm)
Edward J. and Mary S. Holmes
Fund 1971.297

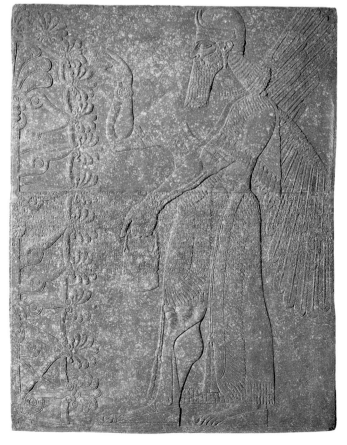

Relief
Iraq (Northwest Palace at Calakh)
Assyrian, reign of Assurnasirpal II,
883–859 B.C.
Gypsum
87 ¼ × 69 ⅜ in. (221.7 × 176.3 cm)
Charles Amos Cummings Fund
35.731

54

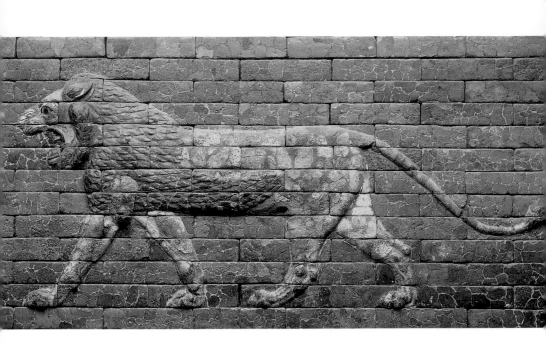

Lion
Iraq (Babylon)
Neo-Babylonian period, reign of
Nebuchadnezzar II, 604–561 B.C.
Glazed bricks
41 ¾ × 91 in. (106 × 232 cm)
Maria Antoinette Evans Fund
31.898

In 1899 German archaeologists excavating the ancient site of
Babylon found hundreds of thousands of glazed brick fragments—all that was left of the massive Ishtar Gate and the Processional Way that once led to the great temple of Marduk, chief
deity of the city. The lion was sacred to the goddess Ishtar and
on both sides of the Processional Way, the walls were adorned
with multicolored tiles depicting some 120 lifesized lions striding toward the temple in what must have been one of the most
spectacular ensembles in antiquity.

< In the belief that they were constantly threatened by a host of
malignant supernatural forces, the Assyrians surrounded themselves with images of protective deities, often represented as
mighty, winged men. In the palace of Assurnasirpal II at Calakh
(modern-day Nimrud), huge carved reliefs such as this one covered the walls of throne rooms, banquet halls, bedrooms, and even
lavatories. The deity depicted in this sculpture pollinates a sacred
tree with a cone and *situla*, or pail. Across the middle of this and
every similar relief—all of which were once painted—is the "standard inscription" of Assurnasirpal II, in which he describes himself
as "the strong man who treads on the necks of his foes . . . who
shatters the alliance of the rebels; the king who with the help of
the great gods . . . has mastered all the mountain regions and has
received their tribute."

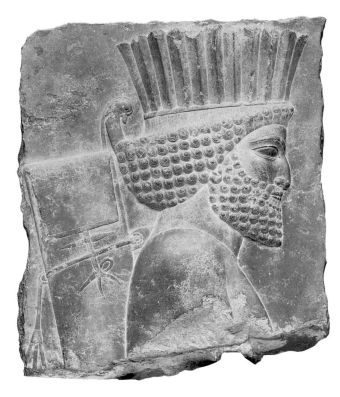

A Persian guard
Iran (Persepolis, Palace of Xerxes)
Achaemenid period, reign of
Xerxes, 486–464 B.C.
Limestone
20⅞ × 18¼ in. (53 × 46.5 cm)
Archibald Cary Coolidge Fund
40.170

This noble figure was a member of the elite guard of the Persian kings, called the "Ten Thousand Immortals" because if one fell in battle another would immediately step forward to take his place. The fragment was once part of a long frieze, portraying a single file of the Immortals, that decorated the palace of Xerxes at Persepolis, a royal residence of the Achaemenid Persian kings. With a quiver and bow case over his shoulder, the soldier wears a high, fluted helmet, and his beard and hair are rendered in rows of tight, spiraling curls. Traces of pigment on similar reliefs suggest that the figure was once painted in shades of yellow, blue, and purple.

The Greek historian Herodotus described the "Ten Thousand Immortals" in his chronicle of the wars between the Persians and the Greeks, written about the time this relief was carved.

Of all the troops, these were adorned with the greatest magnificence, and they were likewise the most valiant. Besides their arms, they glittered all over with gold, vast quantities of which they wore about their persons. They were followed by litters, carrying their concubines, and a numerous train of attendants handsomely dressed. Camels and pack animals carried their provisions apart from those of the other soldiers.

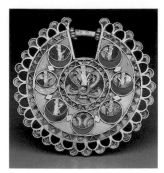

Earring
Iran
Achaemenid period, 525–330 B.C.
Gold with inlays of turquoise,
carnelian, and lapis lazuli
Diameter: 2 in. (5 cm)
Edward J. and Mary S. Holmes
Fund 1971.256

This sumptuous gold earring is decorated on both sides with a dense web of inlaid, semiprecious stones (originally 460 individual pieces) that create a brilliant and complex composition. Around a central roundel featuring a bearded regal figure, seven smaller roundels contain six male figures and a lotus blossom. The design closely parallels one carved over the royal tombs at Persepolis, and it probably represents simultaneously the king revered by the six Great Houses of the empire, the land of Persia surrounded by the six world regions, and the god Ahuramazda surrounded by the six Bounteous Immortals. The lotus blossom may identify the king as the sun, as it does in Egypt, or it may symbolize a seventh world region, the ocean.

Bowl
Iran
Sasanian period, 5th–7th
centuries A.D.
Silver with mercury-gilded details
Diameter: 8¼ in. (21.2 cm)
J. H. and E. A. Payne Fund 1971.52

The nimble mountain sheep on this silver bowl picks his way daintily across flower-covered peaks to sniff a magical blossom. A symbol of royalty, and more specifically of Ardashir, founder of the Sasanian dynasty—the last to rule Persia before the empire fell to the Arabs in the mid-seventh century—the sheep wears a studded bell-collar with the fluttering ribbons often depicted streaming from the king's crown and royal vestments. On this exquisite bowl, the blossom and the animal's body, head, and horns were made separately, attached to the surface, and then gilded.

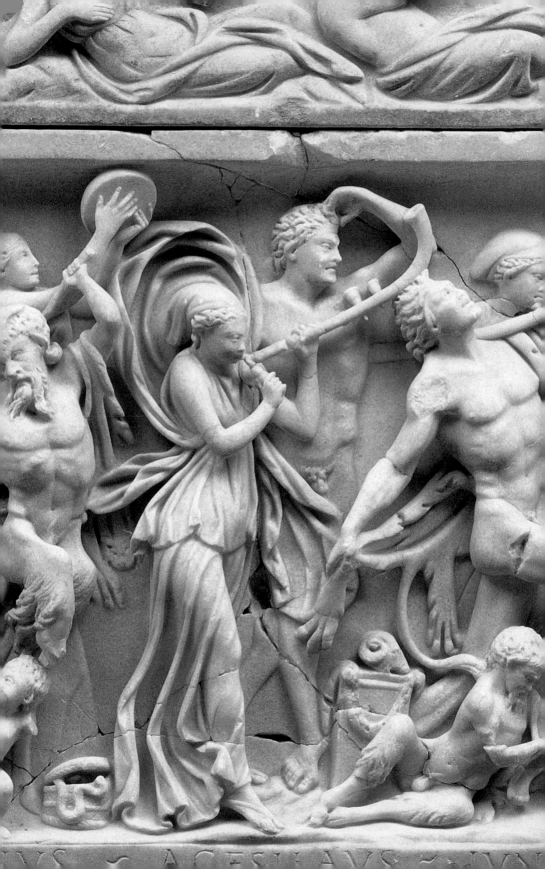

ᏚᎥᏚ ᛫ ᎪᏔᎬᏚᏆᏞᎪᏙᏚ ᛫ ᏔᏙ

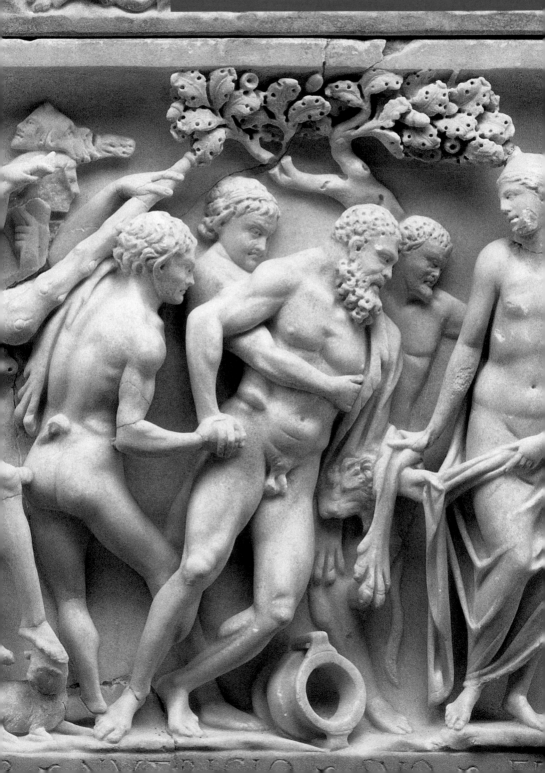

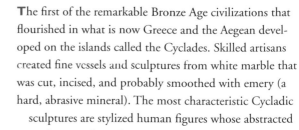

The first of the remarkable Bronze Age civilizations that flourished in what is now Greece and the Aegean developed on the islands called the Cyclades. Skilled artisans created fine vessels and sculptures from white marble that was cut, incised, and probably smoothed with emery (a hard, abrasive mineral). The most characteristic Cycladic sculptures are stylized human figures whose abstracted forms and timeless serenity are particularly attractive to the modern eye. Most of the figures represent women and were found in tombs; this one belongs stylistically with those from Chalandriani, on the island of Syros. Were they intended as images of a deity? Portraits of the deceased? Fertility symbols? Although their meaning remains a mystery, Cycladic figurines stand as the earliest examples of the classical world's extraordinary tradition of shaping stone into works of art.

Female figurine
Greece (Cyclades)
Early Cycladic,
about 2300–2000 B.C.
Marble
Height: 7¾ in. (20 cm)
Gift of Mr. and Mrs. J. J. Klejman
61.1089

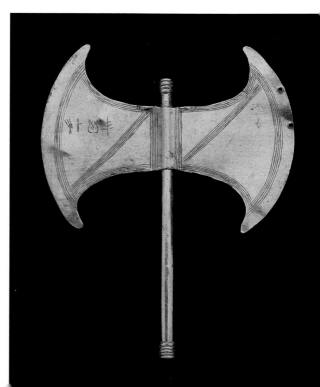

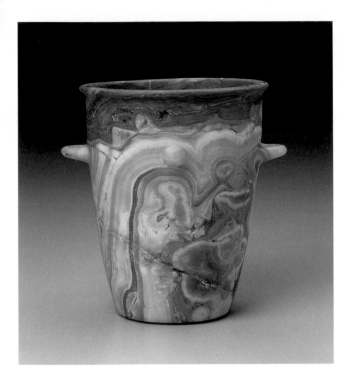

Spouted jar
Greece (Crete, Mochlos)
Early Minoan,
about 2600–2000 B.C.
Banded travertine
Height: 4¼ in. (11 cm)
Gift of Mrs. T. James Bowlker
09.18

The prosperous and sophisticated Bronze Age civilization on the island of Crete is called Minoan after the legendary King Minos, who ruled a mighty, seafaring empire. More than four thousand years ago, high-ranking families on the island of Mochlos, off Crete, built tombs in the shape of simple houses as eternal dwellings for the deceased. Graceful containers worked from local stone—perhaps inspired by vessels imported from Egypt and the Cyclades—were symbols of wealth and status, buried with the dead as offerings or for use in the afterlife. The basic form of this thin-walled jar, shaped to take advantage of the travertine's color and swirling pattern, was painstakingly worked with a bronze chisel or stone hammer, then drilled out using hollow reeds and emery powder.

< **Votive double ax**
Greece (Crete, the Arkalokhori
Cave)
Late Minoan, about 1550–1500 B.C.
Gold
Height: 3½ in. (9 cm)
Theodora Wilbour Fund in memory
of Zoë Wilbour 58.1009

Only three inches high, this delicate and exquisitely worked miniature ax was found in the sacred cave of Arkalokhori on Crete. The cave was first discovered in 1912 by local residents who collected and sold for scrap metal the many pounds of ancient bronze weapons they found there. Alerted to the find, archaeologists excavated hundreds of bronze, gold, and silver weapons from the site. This ax, made of thin sheet gold mounted on a hollow gold shaft, seems to have been a religious offering, although its precise significance is unknown. On the left blade is a very rare inscription in the early, still-undeciphered script called Linear A.

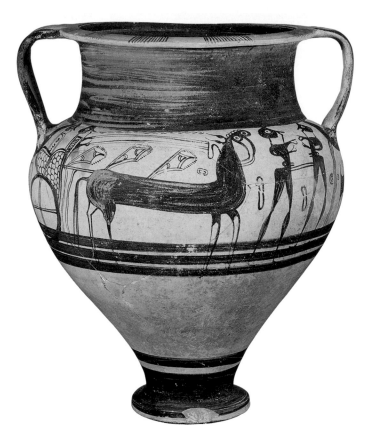

Wine vessel *(krater)*
Greece (found in Cyprus)
Late Bronze Age, 1350–1250 B.C.
Ceramic
Height: 17¼ in. (43.6 cm)
Henry Lillie Pierce Fund 01.8044

Large ceramic vases, painted with scenes of aristocratic pursuits, testified to their owner's wealth and status and were often placed in tombs. This vase is decorated with horse-drawn chariots and an unusual representation of an athletic contest: the two men standing in front of the horse are belt-wrestling, trying to pull each other off balance while bound together at the waist. Found on the island of Cyprus, the vase was probably imported from mainland Greece. The abstract and exaggerated painting style is typical of the art associated with Mycenae, the brilliant Bronze Age civilization of Greece whose influence spread throughout the Aegean and into the eastern Mediterranean.

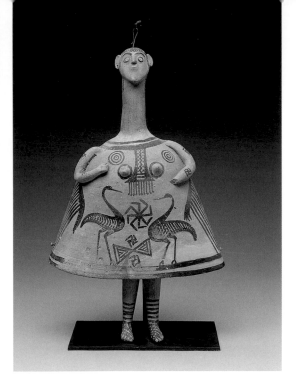

This is one of a small group of similar objects that most likely came from Boiotia on mainland Greece. The context in which they were found is unknown, and their original purpose and use remain a mystery. However, it has been suggested that this doll-like figure may have served as an offering to a deity and been hung from a tree at one of the outdoor sanctuaries typical of this early period. Because the legs were made separately and attached beneath the skirt, the figure might have appeared to "dance" in the wind and ring like a chime.

Fragile legs braced, this slender doe stands nursing her fawn. A bird perches on her rump, and her body is decorated with concentric circles. Her antlers are those of a male deer, and although inaccurate, these give added weight to the upper portion of the sculpture and enhance its distinctive silhouette. This tiny and appealing cast-bronze figure is among the most accomplished early Greek sculptures, both in design and technique. Like the ceramic "doll" above, it was probably made as an offering to a deity and placed in an outdoor sanctuary—perhaps by a hunter hoping that the deer on whom his livelihood depended would thrive and multiply.

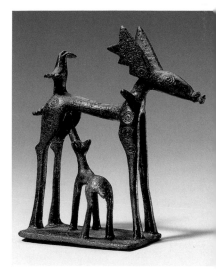

Apollo
Greece (Boiotia)
Geometric period,
about 700–675 B.C.
Bronze
Height: 8 in. (20.3 cm)
Francis Bartlett Donation 03.997

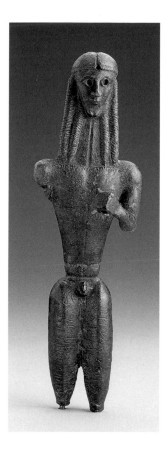

This powerfully expressive figure comes from an important transitional moment in the development of Western art. The simplified, elongated forms and emphatic symmetry (the torso is even bisected with an incised line) typify the conventions for depicting the human figure in this period. However, the artist reached beyond this tradition toward a greater naturalism, and the figure projects a striking new sense of mass and volume, particularly in the heavy coils of hair and the rounded curves of shoulders, thighs, and chest. It almost certainly portrays Apollo and possibly once held a silver bow in the left hand. On the thighs, a metrical inscription in ancient Greek characters states that the statuette was dedicated to Phoebus (Apollo) by a man named Mantiklos: "Mantiklos donated me as a tithe to the far-shooter, the bearer of the Silver Bow. You, Phoebus, give something pleasing in return."

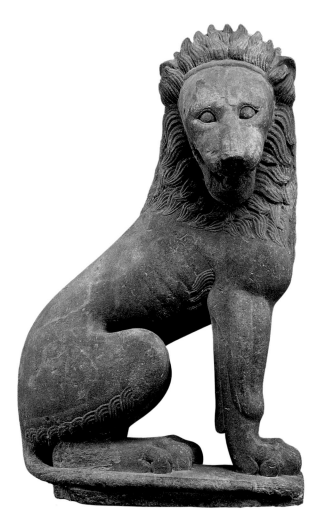

Vase painters in the port city of Corinth were celebrated for their decoration of tiny *aryballoi*, containers for the precious perfumes and oils that were exported from Corinth throughout the Greek world. Corinthian painters invented a technique, now called "black-figure," that was well suited to the rendering of detail on a miniature scale. First, the artist painted black, silhouetted forms on the unfired vessel, then incised anatomical or decorative details so that the light-colored clay beneath showed through. Influenced by the art of the Near East, Corinthian painters developed a repertoire of animals and human figures; the latter had rarely been seen in Greek art before this time. This *aryballos* is a very early example of Greek narrative painting.

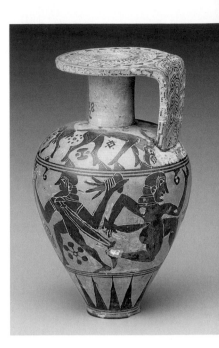

< Lion
Greece (Perachora, near Corinth)
about 550 B.C.
Red limestone
Height: 37½ in. (95.3 cm)
Catharine Page Perkins Fund
97.289

Perfume flask (*aryballos*)
Greece (Corinth)
Protocorinthian period,
675–650 B.C.
Ceramic
Height: 2¾ in. (7.4 cm)
Catharine Page Perkins Fund
95.12

For the Greeks, the lion was a symbol of success in battle and the hunt, and an embodiment of courage, intelligence, and danger. This stone lion (once coated with smooth plaster and painted) was probably part of a funerary monument and set on a low pillar. With its muscular forelegs tensed and jaws open to roar, the lion would have served as a protective emblem of strength and ferocity, eternally vigilant to guard the dead from both earthly and supernatural marauders. Although lions were extinct in central and southern Greece by the sixth century B.C., they are frequently represented in art. On grave markers, they are sometimes accompanied by such inscriptions as: "Tell me, lion, what dead man's tomb are you guarding between your legs? Bull-eater, who was worthy of your power?"

More information on Greek vase-painting techniques can be found on page 74.

Science in the Service of Art

Snake goddess
Crete, about 1600–1500 B.C.
Gold, ivory
Height: 6¼ in. (16.1 cm)
Gift of Mrs. W. Scott
Fitz 14.863

Among many other tests, carbon 14 analysis was performed on fragments of the ivory; the results of the tests were inconclusive as the statuette was initially restored in the nineteenth century using hide glue, and later reassembled using bees' wax. These organic materials, which permeate the ivory, can affect the results of the analysis.

Before the mid-twentieth century, guesswork, hearsay, and wishful thinking often played significant roles in the identification, attribution, and dating of works of art. Over the years, archival research, the systematic study of art history, and collective debate gave art historians a much better sense of changing styles and historical context. Today, scholars also benefit from methods of scientific examination that have answered questions that could never be answered by the naked eye alone.

In 1893 Henry Lee Higginson, founder of the Boston Symphony Orchestra, gave the Museum Rogier van der Weyden's *Saint Luke Drawing the Virgin and Child* (see right and page 178). It is one of several versions of the work, and at the time of acquisition there was much unresolved debate as to which was the original. But by using analytical methods such as x-rays, and, more recently, infrared reflectography, it became certain that the Museum's version is the original on which van der Weyden based his later copies.

However, science does not have all the answers. One of

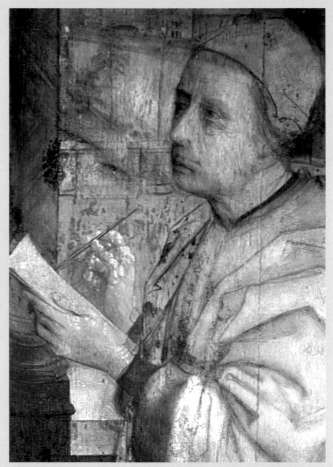

Infrared reflectography (IRR) uses low energy infrared radiation (basically heat) and an infrared-sensitive video system to reveal the underdrawing or preparatory sketch hidden below a painting's surface. As shown at right, tests revealed that van der Weyden redrew the head of St. Luke many times before settling on the final composition. The other versions of the painting do not have this evidence of developing ideas, indicating that they were derived from the Museum's example.

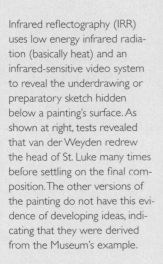

the Museum's most famous objects, the small ivory and gold statuette of a Minoan snake goddess at left, has been controversial for decades. Since the sculpture arrived at the Museum in 1914, it has been surrounded by a fog of romantic stories about its purchase. Those stories and the sculpture's uniqueness (for some time this was the only known ivory sculpture of its type) have long raised questions as to its authenticity. Opinion has see-sawed for decades. Connoisseurship has no answers, and all scientific tests have proved inconclusive. In the future, new or improved tests may provide an answer; for now, the goddess remains an enigma.

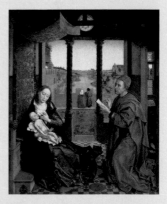

Wine jar (amphora)
Greece (Athens),
about 540–530 B.C.
Close to the style of **Exekias**
Ceramic
Height: 20 ¼ in. (51.4 cm)
Henry Lillie Pierce Residuary Fund
and Bartlett Collection 63.952

Dionysos was the Greek god of wine and its attendant pleasures—intoxication, physical delight, and the banishment of care. In the sixth century B.C. the cult of Dionysos became extremely popular at all levels of society, and in Athenian art, representations of this god outnumber those of any other. Dionysos was, of course, a natural subject for the decoration of vessels used in the production, storage, and drinking of wine. On this magnificent, black-figure storage jar, the god sits on a folding stool sipping wine from a *kantharos* (see facing page). In the huge, laden grape vine, diminutive satyrs appear to be diligently harvesting the fruit (closer inspection reveals that they are all at play). The satyr above Dionysos' head, lolling back with his arm hooked around a vine, leisurely examines the ornamental border. The scene is idyllic, humorous, and masterfully organized. The ivy that trails over Dionysos' shoulder is echoed on the handles of the vase, and the whole image is energized by the rhythm of the vine that twists across the surface.

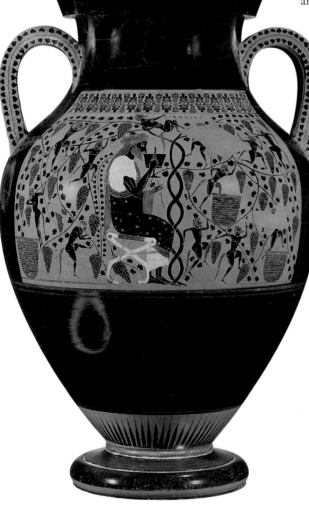

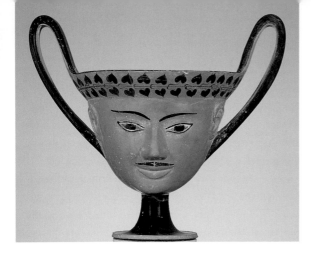

Wine cup (kantharos)
East Greece, about 530 B.C.
Ceramic
Height: 6¾ in. (17.3 cm)
Henry Lillie Pierce Fund 98.925

The *kantharos*, a stemmed wine cup with high, looped handles, was particularly associated with Dionysos, god of wine (he drinks from one on the preceding page). Cups of this sort were made in molds and painted in different ways; three other cups taken from the same mold as this one survive, all painted with the faces of women. This example, however, features on each side the face of a man with finely drawn eyebrows and a dapper moustache. These cups were probably made on the island of Samos, one of the prosperous Greek centers in the eastern Aegean. Such East Greek pottery was widely exported, much of it destined for the Etruscan market. The Etruscans, who lived in central Italy, admired Greek ceramics, and many of the finest and best preserved Greek vases have been found in Etruscan tombs.

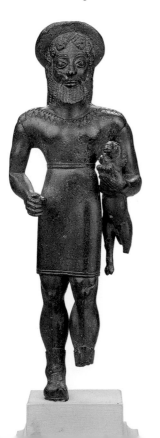

Hermes Kriophoros
Greece (Arcadia), 520–500 B.C.
Bronze
Height: 6⅝ in. (16.7 cm)
Henry Lillie Pierce Residuary Fund
04.6

In Greek mythology, the god Hermes takes many guises: protector of travelers and thieves, quick-witted trickster, and messenger for the gods who dwelt on Mount Olympus. Here, however, he is represented as Hermes Kriophoros (the ram-bearer), guardian of shepherds and their flocks. He wears the short tunic, brimmed hat, and low boots of a herdsman, and with one hand supports the front legs of the lamb tucked under his arm. In his other hand, Hermes probably once held the snake-entwined staff (*kerykeion* in Greek, *caduceus* in Latin) that identifies him as the emissary of the gods. With its huge eyes, taut contours, and lively surface patterning, this cast bronze statuette (probably created as an offering to the god) captures Hermes' fabled alertness and intensity.

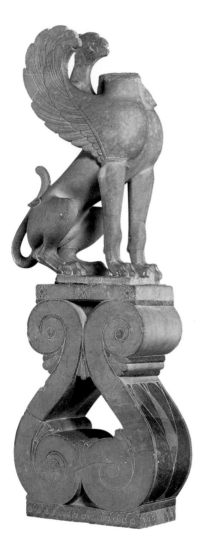

The sphinx, like the lion (see page 64), was favored as a guardian figure and often placed on grave monuments to protect the deceased from malevolent forces in this world and the next. This sphinx, crouching on a capital that originally surmounted a tall shaft, is all taut curves; her wings and haunches are lifted, her body ready to spring. The sculpture is expertly carved of warm, golden marble and traces remain of its original painted decoration—the hair was black, for example, and the wing feathers alternately green, black, red, and blue. Grave monuments of this quality and complexity could only have been afforded by the rich, and sometime after the mid-sixth century B.C., laws against ostentatious display put an end to their production. Almost every surviving example was deliberately broken in antiquity, possibly during a period of civil unrest; the Museum's sculpture is in unusually good condition.

Upper part of a grave stela
Greece (Athens), about 530 B.C.
Marble
Height: 55 3/4 in. (141.7 cm)
1931 and 1939 Purchase Funds
40.576

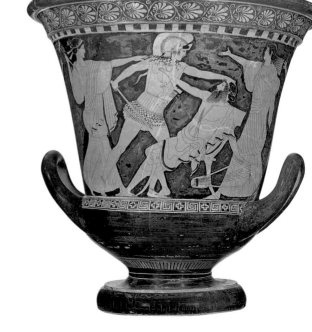

The Trojan War was a favorite subject among Greek vase painters (see page 79). This *hydria* depicts the harrowing story of the Greek hero Achilles, whose best friend Patroklos was killed in battle by the Trojan prince Hector. Distraught and thirsting for revenge, Achilles killed Hector and defiled the body by dragging it behind his chariot. The painter has abridged the story, compressing two locations and the events of three days into a single image. Achilles (holding a round shield) mounts the chariot to which Hector's body is bound. Hector's grieving parents stand in a portico at left. At the far right, beyond the horses, is Patroklos's tomb. The winged female figure is Iris, sent by the gods to urge Hector's father to offer ransom for his son's body and so end its brutal violation. The whole composition—packed with detail and the vigorous movement of overlapping forms—is anchored in the center by the stern, anonymous figure of the charioteer.

Water jar (hydria)
Greece (Athens), about 520 B.C.
Attributed to the **Antiope Group**
Ceramic
Height: 22 ¼ in. (56.6 cm)
William Francis Warden Fund 63.473

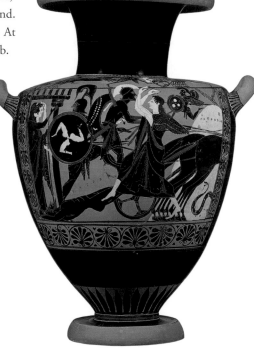

< **Bowl for mixing wine and water
(calyx krater)**
Greece (Athens), about 470 B.C.
Attributed to the **Dokimasia Painter**
Ceramic
Height: 20 ⅛ in. (51 cm)
William Francis Warden Fund 63.1246

On his return from the Trojan War, Agamemnon, commander of the victorious Greek army, was murdered by his wife, Clytemnestra, and her lover, Aegisthus. On this vase, Aegisthus, grasping Agamemnon's head, has plunged his sword into his victim's body and prepares to strike again. Clytemnestra, bearing an ax, is close behind. The sense of urgency and drama is conveyed in the swing of draperies and the bold gestures that resonate against the empty spaces of the background. The figure of Agamemnon is extraordinary, naked and helpless in a snare made of sheer and costly fabric. In Aeschylus's play *Agamemnon* (first presented in 458 B.C., soon after this vase was painted), Clytemnestra describes this moment:

> *He had no way to flee or fight his destiny—*
> *our never-ending, all embracing net, I cast it*
> *wide for the royal haul, I coil him round and round*
> *in the wealth, the robes of doom. . .*

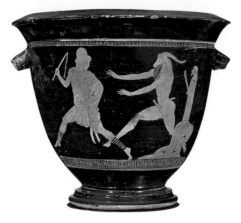

Bowl for mixing wine and water (bell *krater*)
Greece (Athens), about 470 B.C.
Attributed to the **Pan Painter**
Ceramic
Height: 14⅝ in. (37 cm)
James Fund and by Special
Contribution 10.185

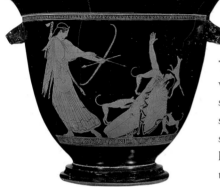

This *krater* is among the greatest of all Athenian painted vessels. The image illustrated above is one of the first representations in Greek art of Pan, the goat god. Across the vessel's broad surface, Pan pursues a frightened young shepherd; the god's impressive erection is echoed in the herm, a kind of pillar with the head of the god Hermes that marked the intersections of roads.

The image on the other side of the *krater*, although inherently more brutal, is as lyrical as the depiction of Pan and the shepherd is explosively energetic. It shows the death of Aktaion at the hands of Artemis, goddess of the hunt. Aktaion had angered Artemis, and she caused his own hounds to turn on him and tear him to pieces. As Artemis leans back to draw the arrow she will not need, Aktaion falls before the onslaught of the dogs.

Both the form and decoration of this cup are extremely unusual. The cover, seen here from above, was not designed to open. The cup was filled through a hollow in its stemmed base, and libations were poured out through the opening in the cover. Most Greek vessels were painted either in the black-figure or red-figure technique (see page 74). This cup, however, is decorated with the white-ground technique, in which a layer of white slip (a thin mixture of fine clay and water) was applied to all or part of a vessel. The figures were drawn in outline on the unfired clay and painted with a range of delicate colors. Because many of these colors were subject to deterioration, white-ground vessels were primarily reserved for ritual or funerary use. This one depicts the god Apollo opening his cloak to reveal himself (both actually and metaphorically) to one of the nine Muses, goddesses of the arts, whom he led and inspired.

This monumental sculpture forms the front of a three-sided marble structure that probably served as a windbreak to protect sacrifices being burned on an altar. It depicts Eros, god of love, weighing two small spirits on a balance (the lost arm of which was secured in the three rectangular holes). On the right is Demeter, goddess of agriculture, and on the left is Aphrodite, goddess of love, fertility, and fate.

Three-sided relief
Greece (found in Rome),
470–440 B.C.
Marble (Greek island of Thasos)
37 3/4 × 63 3/8 in. (96 × 161 cm)
Henry Lillie Pierce Fund 08.205

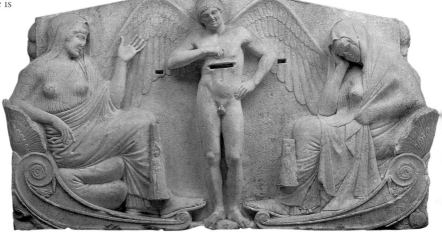

The sculpture is closely related to the so-called Ludovisi relief, found in Rome in 1887, and it has been challenged as a forgery inspired by the Ludovisi sculpture. However, recent scientific examination has shown that both reliefs are made of the same, rather rare marble, and that the Boston relief shows evidence of ancient weathering. It is likely that both sculptures were brought to Rome years after they were carved and placed in a sanctuary dedicated to Venus (Aphrodite) near the place where they were ultimately excavated.

Covered wine cup (kylix)
Greece (Athens), about 450 B.C.
Attributed to the
Carlsruhe Painter
Ceramic
Diameter: 6 1/2 in. (16.6 cm)
Henry Lillie Pierce Fund 00.356

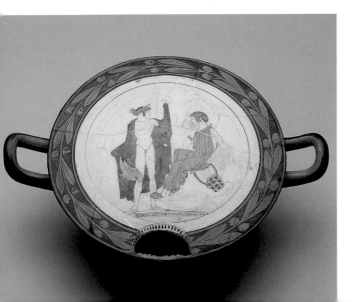

Painting in Red and Black

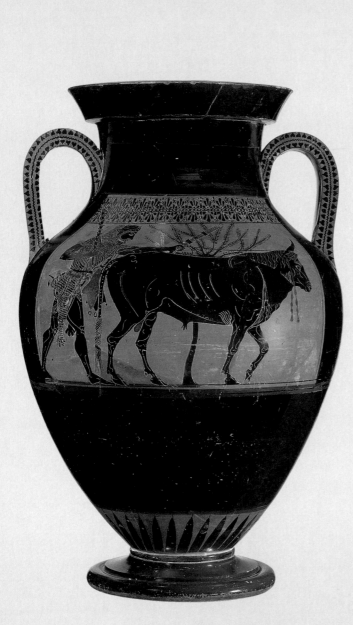

Both of the vase paintings shown here depict the legendary strong man Hercules driving a bull. In design the scenes are almost identical, but in other ways they are completely different. Their differences illustrate the two main styles of Greek vase painting, known, appropriately enough, as black-figure and red-figure. Black-figure vases were made by painting a design on an unfired pot with slip (a thin, paint-like mixture of clay and water). The artist then scratched in the details of the design, such as the ribs on the bull's flank, revealing the main body of the vase underneath. Although they were the same color when wet, the slip and the clay of the vase took on different colors (red and black) when baked in the kiln. Red-figure vases were made in exactly the *opposite* way. The artist painted the whole vase with slip except for the design, which was left unpainted. Details such as Hercules' lion skin were then drawn with slip.

These paintings are excellent examples of two styles; what makes them really remarkable is that they are on opposite sides of the *same* vase.

By law, Athenian potters all worked in the same part of town, creating ample opportunity for artistic exchange. Bilingual vases such as this one, dating from about the time of the introduction of the red-figure technique, were most likely made to show the strengths of each style, the old and the new, perhaps as an advertisement to potential customers.

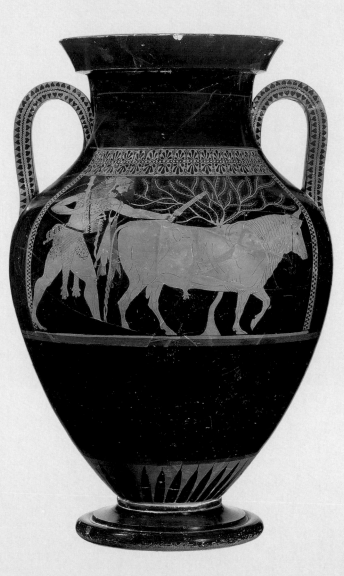

Bilingual *amphora*
Greece (Athens), about 525 B.C.
Ceramic
Height: 20⁷⁄₈ in. (53.2 cm)
Henry Lillie Pierce Fund 99.538

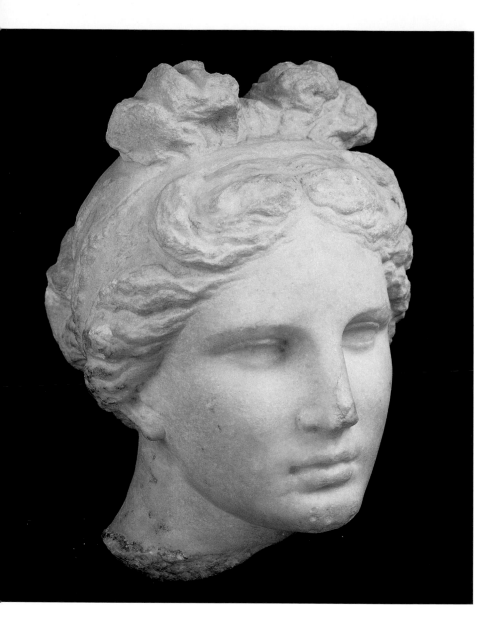

Head of Aphrodite
Greece (found in Athens),
about 330–300 B.C.
Marble (Greek island of Paros)
Height: 11 ¼ in. (28.8 cm)
Francis Bartlett Donation 03.743

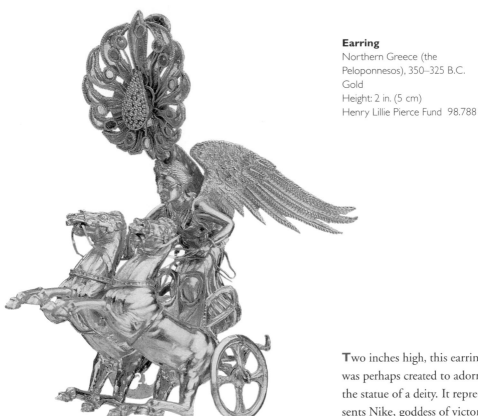

Earring
Northern Greece (the Peloponnesos), 350–325 B.C.
Gold
Height: 2 in. (5 cm)
Henry Lillie Pierce Fund 98.788

Two inches high, this earring was perhaps created to adorn the statue of a deity. It represents Nike, goddess of victory, a symbol of success in war and other contests. She is depicted driving a chariot, her face focused and determined, her wings sweeping behind her. She holds her horses on a tight rein, and they rear sharply, muscles tensed. Every detail of Nike's costume and the harness of her horses is minutely rendered—hundreds of tiny pieces of gold soldered together with marvelous precision to create a harmonious whole.

< **T**his sensuous and beautiful head is one of the finest surviving Greek sculptures of the late Classical period. It represents Aphrodite, goddess of love, and was originally set into a full-length statue. The sculpture's idealized grace, subtle modeling, and contrasting textures of skin and hair recall the workmanship and revolutionary style of Praxiteles, among the most celebrated of all classical sculptors. Greek sculptures of this period and quality are very rare, and most are known today primarily through later, Roman copies.

After a year of dalliance with the beautiful sorceress Circe on the island of Aeaea, Odysseus, hero of Homer's *Odyssey*, journeyed to the Underworld to consult the spirit of the prophet Teiresias. There, Odysseus sacrificed two rams so that their blood would call forth the spirits of the dead. Many spirits came, including that of Odysseus' young companion Elpenor, who had broken his neck in a drunken fall from Circe's roof and been left unmourned and unburied in the haste of departure. The central figure on this elegantly painted *pelike* is Odysseus, solemn and unafraid. Beyond the dead rams, Elpenor climbs up out of the black background (evidence of a new interest in illusionistic effects in vase painting of this period). According to Homer, Elpenor begged Odysseus to bury him properly, and Odysseus promised, reflecting: "So we two sat there, exchanging regrets, I with my sword held out stiffly across the blood-pool and the wraith of my follower beyond it, telling his tale."

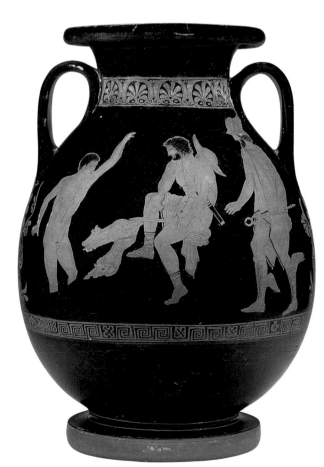

Storage jar (pelike)
Greece (Athens), about 440 B.C.
Attributed to the **Lykaon Painter**
Ceramic
Height: 18 3/4 (47.4 cm)
William Amory Gardner Fund
34.79

The Greek colonists who settled on the coast of Italy maintained close contact with their homeland, and South Italian vases derive from Greek models. Indeed, early examples were often made by immigrant Greek craftsmen. This sumptuously ornamented *krater* is among the finest (and largest) South Italian vases and is painted with a complex, multi-figured composition that emphasizes dramatic expression and gesture. The subject is an event of the Trojan War. The Greek hero Achilles, seated within a pavilion, has just beheaded Thersites, the Greek soldier whom Homer called "the most obnoxious rogue who ever went to Troy." All around, mortals and deities are identified by neat inscriptions. The size of this *krater* suggests that it was probably made for burial in the tomb of an important person, rather than for actual use.

Vessel for mixing wine and water (volute *krater*)
Southern Italy (Apulia, Ceglie del Campo, near Bari),
about 340 B.C.
Ceramic
Height: 49 ⅛ in. (124.6 cm)
Francis Bartlett Donation   03.804

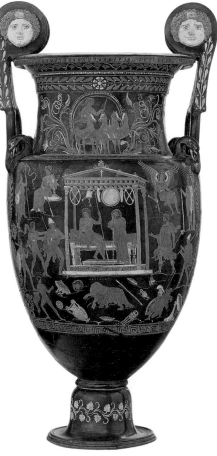

The body of this vessel depicts the birth of the goddess Aphrodite (Venus) from the sea. Framed by the scallop shell in which, according to legend, she sailed to the island of Cyprus, she is accompanied by two Cupids, their wings lifted to catch the ocean breezes. At once delicate and extravagant, this vessel—appropriately decorated with the goddess of love and beauty—probably held precious perfumes or oils.

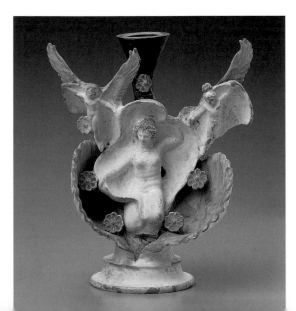

Oil bottle (*lekythos*)
Greece (Athens), about 350 B.C.
Ceramic
Height: 7½ in. (19 cm)
Gift of Mrs. S. T. Morse   00.629

79

The Etruscans

Long veiled in mystery because no literary or religious documents survive, the Etruscans are now believed to have been indigenous people of the central Italian peninsula. Their civilization lasted from 900 to 89 B.C., when they were absorbed by the Roman Republic. The Etruscans were a wealthy and powerful seafaring people living in politically independent, densely populated cities. The region's "metal-bearing hills" were mentioned frequently by ancient writers, and Etruscan bronzes were traded throughout the Mediterranean world and as far as northern Europe and Russia. The connection with Greece was particularly close; Etruscan pottery has been found in Greece, and many of the finest surviving Greek ceramics were excavated from Etruscan tombs.

In their sculptures, the Etruscans often exaggerated and distorted the human form for decorative and expressive effect. The artist who created this charming bronze dancer emphasized her delicate and lively silhouette. The curves of her elongated hands and the sharp points of her swinging sleeves and flaring hem provide a counterpoint to the softer lines of her body, which shows clearly beneath a clinging dress sprinkled with incised patterns. This statuette was probably placed in a tomb.

Dancer
Central Italy, about 500 B.C.
Bronze
Height: 5 ¼ in. (13.3 cm)
Purchase by Contribution
01.7482

Bowl for mixing wine and water (calyx *krater*)
Central Italy, about 370 B.C.
Attributed to the
Nazzano Painter
Ceramic
Height: 19 ¼ in. (49.1cm)
John H. and Ernestine A. Payne
Fund 1970.487

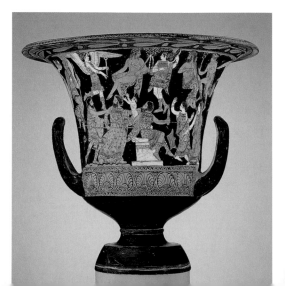

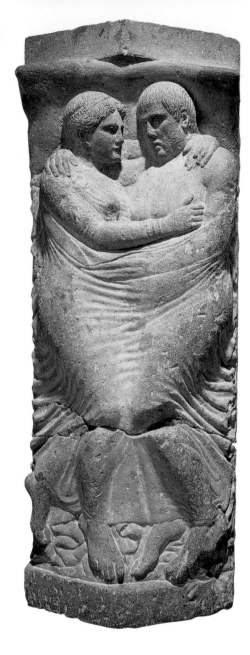

Sarcophagus lid
Italy (Vulci), about 300–280 B.C.
Peperino
85¾ × 30¾ in. (218 × 78 cm)
Gift of Mr. and Mrs. Cornelius C.
Vermeule III 1975.799

This stone sarcophagus lid is carved with the image of a married couple whose affectionate embrace conveys the continuation of their love for all eternity. Only the woman's name, Ramtha Visnai, is inscribed on the sarcophagus, and she may have been buried alone in it. However, it is possible that the body of her husband was interred later and his name added in paint that has since worn away. This type of sarcophagus lid, which would originally have been painted, is uniquely Etruscan, and very few examples survive. Two are in the Museum collection; the other was apparently made for this couple's son, Larth Tetnies, and his wife.

< **A**lthough clearly indebted to Greek examples, this enormous and unusually fine *krater* is typically Etruscan in its dense decoration and aggressive figures. It was apparently made by the Faliscans—a culture centered in the city of Falerii (modern-day Città Castellana) that was linguistically distinct from, but artistically very close to, that of the Etruscans in this period. The painting style suggests the work of an artist known as the Nazzano Painter, who may have been a Greek immigrant or trained in Athens. The scene depicted is from *Telephos* (a lost play by Euripides) in which the Mysian king Telephos threatens the infant Orestes; Orestes strains toward his father, Agamemnon, while a host of mortals and deities react to the event.

Portrait of a man
Italy (Cumae), late Roman
Republican period, about 50 B.C.
Terra-cotta
Height: 14⅛ in. (35.7 cm)
Purchase by Contribution
01.8008

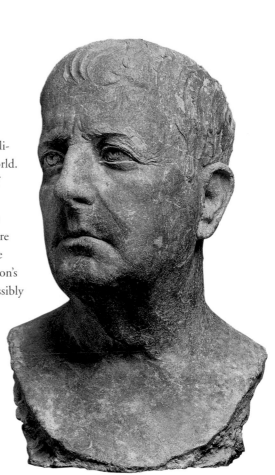

The striking naturalism that emerged in Roman portrait sculpture of the late Republican period is unparalleled in the ancient world. Nevertheless, it does reflect the influence of other civilizations, particularly that of the Etruscans, whose impact on Roman culture ranged from funerary customs to architecture and city planning. Such portraits as this one expressed the Roman conviction that a person's individuality was seen solely in the face. Possibly a preparatory study for a sculpture in bronze or marble, this terra-cotta bust unflinchingly records signs of aging that would have been appreciated as marks of experience and wisdom. Interestingly, only mature individuals seem to have been considered subjects worthy of major portraiture in this period.

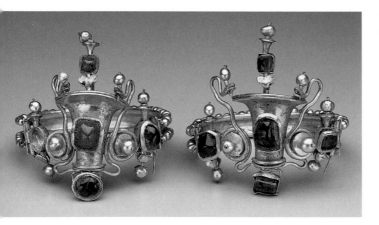

Bracelets
Possibly Egypt, late Hellenistic or early Roman Imperial period, about 40–20 B.C.
Gold, with pearls and emeralds
2¾ × 2½ in. (6.4 × 6.2 cm)
Classical Department Exchange Fund 1981.287, 1981.288

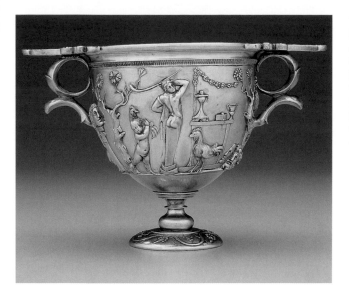

Two-handled cup (skyphos)
Italy (Rome), early Imperial period,
A.D. 1–30
Silver with traces of gold leaf
Height: 4 ⅜ in. (11.1 cm)
William Francis Warden Fund,
Frank B. Bemis Fund, John H. and
Ernestine A. Payne Fund, and
William E. Nickerson Fund
1997.83

This silver wine cup was probably made during one of the most extravagant periods of Roman history—the reigns of the emperors Augustus and Tiberius. Such superbly made and expensive objects were avidly collected, and this taste for luxury could be carried to excess; the historian Pliny noted that the Roman governor of Lower Germany carried "12,000 pounds weight of silver plate with him when on service with an army confronted by tribes of the greatest ferocity."

The cup is decorated with scenes showing the preparations for a sacrifice in honor of Bacchus (Dionysos), god of wine, fertility, and good times. The plain background sets off the poses of the figures, and the outdoor setting is filled with sacrificial equipment—a portable altar and offering table, an incense burner, cups for wine—all rendered with precision and delicate detail. Two thousand years after its creation, the cup is in remarkable condition.

< **A**lthough it is not known where these opulent bracelets were made, they may be from Egypt; similar examples are painted on representations of the deceased on mummy shrouds of Egypt's early Roman period. The gold bands are studded with two rows of pearls and hinged to a central projecting ornament surrounded with emeralds and coiling snakes crowned with pearls. In the classical imagination, snakes were beneficent creatures associated with Asklepios, god of health, and with the revels of Bacchus (Dionysos), god of wine and nature. In Egypt, the snake was an emblem of the creator god, Atum, and the green color of emeralds was associated with Osiris, god of the Underworld, and with the concept of rebirth.

The playwright Menander
Italy (Rome, found near Torre
Annunziata)
Late Roman Republican or early
Imperial period, about 40 B.C.
Marble
Height: 20¼ in. (51.5 cm)
Catharine Page Perkins Fund
97.288

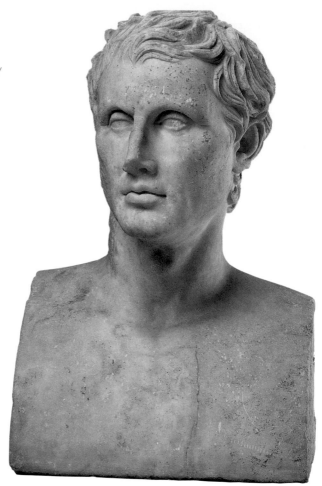

The Roman conquest of Greek colonies in southern Italy and ultimately of Greece itself led to a passionate appreciation and emula-
tion of Greek culture, of which this bust is evidence. It represents
the playwright Menander and was probably based on a statue that
stood in or near a theater in Athens. The Greek sculptures that
Roman armies brought back to Rome were set up in public places
throughout the city, and wealthy Romans commissioned local
artists to make the copies and adaptations to which we owe much
of our knowledge of lost Greek masterworks.

This idealized image of a somber, handsome man in the prime
of life was found near Torre Annunziata on the Bay of Naples. It
takes the form of a herm—a roadside marker often found in the
Greek countryside—and has holes in the sides of the shoulders for
wooden inserts designed to be hung with garlands.

Roman glass was widely produced and universally admired in ancient times. Many richly colored glass objects were made in the city of Alexandria, in Egypt, which was a major center for the production of luxury goods during the Roman Empire. The mosaic bowl below was made by assembling slices or spirals of multicolored glass canes into molds that were then placed into a furnace for slow fusing. The covered box at right was constructed of ribbons of variegated glass, also placed in a mold and fused. After the discovery of the technique of glassblowing in the mid-first century B.C., glass became readily available and affordable. Nevertheless, objects made by such complex and labor-intensive techniques continued to be highly prized. Very little ancient glass has survived unaffected by the moisture and acids of the soil in which it was buried.

Box with cover
Probably Egypt (Alexandria)
or Italy
Roman Imperial period, late 1st
century B.C. to early 1st century A.D.
Glass
Height: 2⅝ in. (6.6 cm)
Henry Lillie Pierce Fund 99.454 a,b

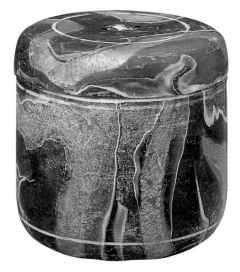

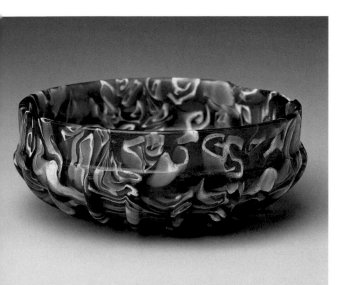

Mosaic bowl
Probably Egypt (Alexandria)
or Italy
Roman Imperial period, late 1st
century B.C. to early 1st century A.D.
Glass
Height: 1¾ in. (4.4 cm)
Henry Lillie Pierce Fund 99.442

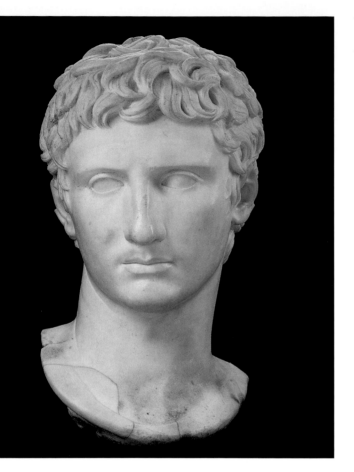

The emperor Augustus
Italy (Rome), Imperial period,
about A.D. 40
Marble (Italy)
Height: 17 in. (43.3 cm)
Henry Lillie Pierce Fund 99.344

Augustus (63 B.C.–A.D.14), the designated heir of his great-uncle Julius Caesar, was Rome's first emperor and began a long imperial tradition of commissioning art as a form of political propaganda. In the previous, late Republican period, young people were seldom considered deserving of political or artistic consideration (see page 82). Therefore, when Augustus became emperor at the age of thirty-two, artists looked for inspiration to fifth-century Greece, a time when youthful beauty was much admired. Until his death at seventy-six, Augustus was always represented as a handsome young man with a full head of thick curls. As imperial icons, these idealized portraits continued to be made long after the emperor's death. This superb example, which was probably inserted into a full-length statue, may have been created for a private villa at Ariccia, near Rome, during the reign of the emperor Claudius (A.D. 41–54).

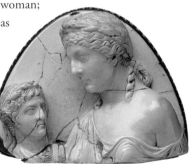

In Roman times, high officials and members of the imperial family often commissioned carved gemstones as private or official gifts. This cameo—a stone carved in relief on one layer against the background of a lower, contrasting layer—depicts the marriage of Cupid (Eros) and Psyche. Venus (Aphrodite), goddess of love and beauty, was so jealous of the beautiful Psyche that she sent Cupid to make Psyche fall in love with some insignificant man. Predictably, Cupid fell in love with Psyche himself, and after many tribulations, the enamored couple was brought to heaven and married. This cameo, which bears a signature ("Tryphon made it"), once belonged to the celebrated Flemish artist Peter Paul Rubens (see page 206), a self-proclaimed "lover of antiquities."

Cameo

Italy (Rome), Greco-Roman
period, mid-1st century B.C.
Layered onyx
1 ¾ × 1½ in. (4.5 × 3.7 cm)
Henry Lillie Pierce Fund 99.101

To promote imperial power and political ideology, images of the emperor Augustus and his family were disseminated throughout the vast Roman empire. Coins placed such images in the hands of Roman citizens of every class (see page 88), but precious cameos were special gifts. This exquisite example depicts Augustus's widow, Livia, holding a bust of her deceased husband. Although created late in her life, the cameo shows the empress as a lovely young woman; indeed, she is represented as Venus (Aphrodite)—an acknowledgment of the fact that, in his will, Augustus declared his wife a member of the family of Julius Caesar, whose patron goddess was Venus.

Cameo

Italy (Rome), Greco-Roman
period, A.D. 14–19
Turquoise
Height: 1 ¼ in. (3.1 cm)
Henry Lillie Pierce Fund 99.109

The carving of tiny images on precious stones was a Greek art form that was later enthusiastically adopted by the Romans. In the first century, the Roman scholar Pliny wrote in his *Natural History:* "Very many people find that a single gemstone alone is enough to provide them with a supreme and perfect aesthetic experience of the wonders of Nature." Pliny went on to list ways of assuring that a particular stone was genuine: "The most effective test is to knock off a piece of the stone so that it can be baked on an iron plate, but dealers in precious stones not unnaturally object to this."

Heads or Tails: The Meanings of Money

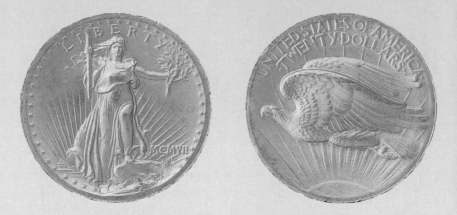

Twenty dollar coin ("Double Eagle")
United States (Philadelphia), 1907
Designed by **Augustus Saint-Gaudens,** American (born Ireland), 1848–1907
Gold
Diameter: 1 ⅜ in. (3.42 cm)
Gift of Dr. William Sturgis Bigelow
13.2918

Coins throughout their history have always been more than money: if these little pieces of metal were simply currency, they could be blank (or nearly so). However, coins are ambassadors, and the symbols they bear matter. The personification of Liberty and the eagle displayed on the United States twenty-dollar coin say a great deal about how the country wanted to represent itself at home and abroad as a nation that was free and powerful. Commissioned from one of the greatest American sculptors, this coin also evokes the distinguished style of the ancient coins of Greece and Rome.

Greek city-states began issuing coins decorated with local gods and symbols as early as the seventh century B.C. The Syracusan ten-drachma piece illustrates a format still seen on most modern coins: a head on one side (the nymph Arethusa, associated with a famous spring in Syracuse) with a more complicated scene on the other: Nike, goddess of Victory (see page 77), crowning the horses of a victorious racing team.

Around the time of Alexander the Great (356–323 B.C.), kings and emperors began celebrating their reigns by issuing coins bearing their own image. The Roman emperors took up the habit with enthusiasm. The coin from the city of Laodiceia in Phrygia (now central Turkey), bears the head of the Roman emperor Caracalla on one side and on the other a scene in which he addresses a crowd in the city's main square. Laodiceia had only recently come under Roman rule; thus, the coin served to remind citizens that Caracalla brought with him not only the dignity and eloquence of Rome, but also the power of the Empire.

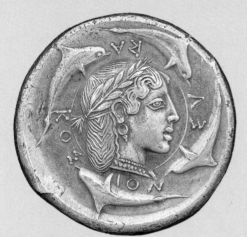

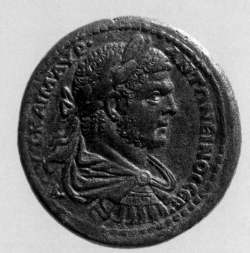

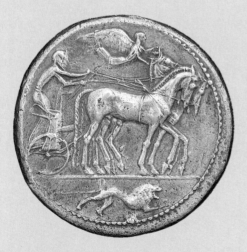

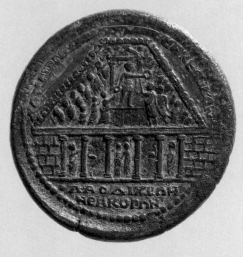

Ten drachma coin
Italy (Syracuse), about 480 B.C.
Silver
Diameter: 1⅜ in. (3.5 cm)
Theodora Wilbour Fund
in Memory of Zoë Wilbour 35.21

Coin showing the Emperor Caracalla
Turkey (Laodiceia), A.D. 211–17
Bronze
Diameter: 1⅝ in. (4.5 cm)
Theodora Wilbour Fund
in Memory of Zoë Wilbour 1971.45

Athena Parthenos
Italy (Rome), about A.D. 150–230
Marble (Attica)
Height: 60 5/8 in. (154 cm)
Classical Department Exchange
Fund 1980.196

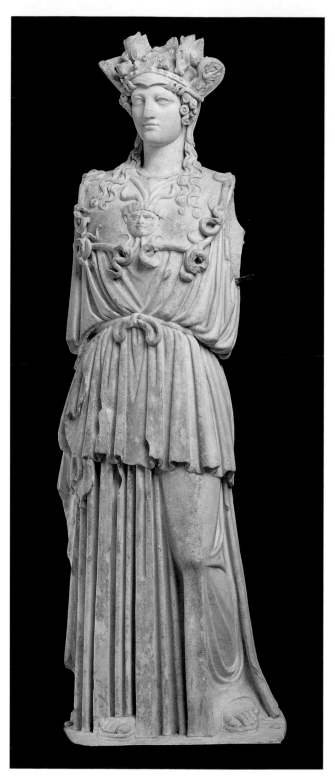

A monumental figure of Athena Parthenos, the masterpiece of the sculptor Pheidias, was the principal image in the Parthenon, the temple dedicated to Athena that still crowns the Acropolis in Athens. Made between 447 and 438 B.C., Pheidias's statue of the goddess of wisdom was sheathed in ivory and gold and stood almost forty feet high. It was gone from the Acropolis by about A.D. 450 (possibly destroyed by fire), but before that time, numerous copies had been made for export throughout the Mediterranean world.

This small replica is one of the most accurate known, preserving details—found in no other copy—that match a description of the original written about A.D. 150 by the Greek traveler and writer Pausanias. Athena's aegis— a breastplate emblematic of majesty—is adorned with twining snakes and an image of one of the Gorgons, fearsome sisters of Greek mythology whose glance turned men to stone.

Although the ancient Greeks believed that the great epics, the *Iliad* and the *Odyssey* (see page 78), were the work of the poet Homer, reliable information about the poet's life was as elusive then as it is today. This sculpture, therefore, is not a real portrait but a conceptual image of creative genius: the unruly hair and knitted brow suggest intensity and passion; the worn, furrowed face reflects experience; the eyes, sightless in accordance with ancient tradition, reflect the belief that Homer and other great bards saw into the future and beyond this world.

Probably once set into a seated statue, this head is the best of many Roman copies of a lost Greek sculpture from the Hellenistic period, a time in which art was characterized by an interest in expressiveness, naturalistic detail, and technical virtuosity.

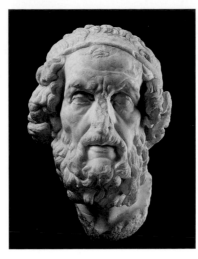

Homer
Italy (Rome), A.D. 90–120
Marble
Height: 16 1/8 in. (41 cm)
Henry Lillie Pierce Fund 04.13

Portrait of a woman
Italy (Rome), A.D. 100–125
Marble
Height: 13 3/4 in. (35 cm)
Gift of Samuel and Edward Merrin, William Francis Warden Fund, Benjamin and Lucy Rowland Collection, and Gift of Barbara Deering Danielson, by exchange 1992.575

This unknown woman's full lips and sweet expression suggest portraiture, but the sculpture is really about the extravagant hairstyle, made up of tight curls twisted into a great crest. Behind this "facade," the hair is wound into a wide, flat bun. Such a coiffure may have been inspired by the masks worn by actors, although in a more subdued form, it had been made popular decades earlier by women of the imperial family. With great skill, the artist used a drill to create the strong contrasts of light and shadow that give substance and vitality to the marble curls.

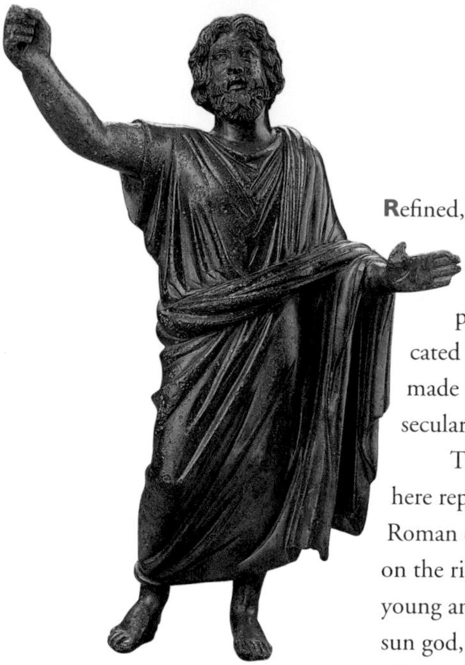

Refined, superbly worked bronze statuettes have been found throughout the extensive territory that was once the Roman Empire, and like so much Roman art, they perpetuate Greek traditions. Although some were dedicated to gods and placed in public sanctuaries, many were made for household shrines that often contained a variety of secular images as well as religious ones.

The finely detailed bronzes shown here represent the highest standards of Roman craftsmanship. The figure on the right is the young and powerful sun god, Helios. Beams of light originally radiated from his lionlike mane of hair (only one remains). The god above may have held a scepter in his right hand; his left is extended outward in a gesture of salutation or prayer. There is nothing idealized about the third figure—a professional athlete who would have fought heavily armed opponents with only a net and pronged spear. With a battered face and strong, muscular body, he stands in an aggressive, striding pose, his left arm wrapped with protective leather straps.

Male deity, probably Jupiter
Roman Empire (possibly Spain),
1st century A.D.
Bronze
Height: 7 in. (17.8 cm)
Frank B. Bemis Fund 1989.191

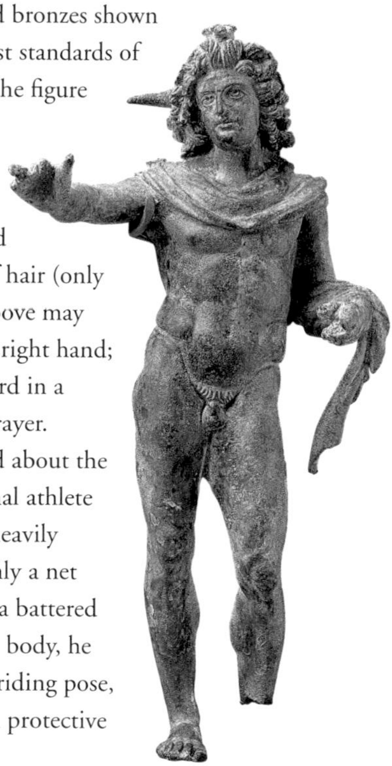

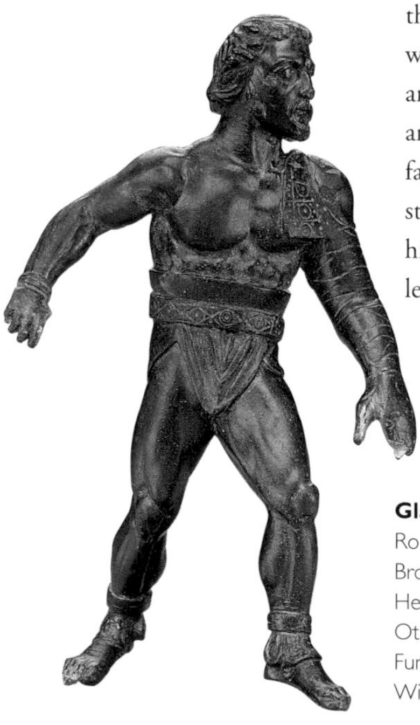

Gladiator
Roman Empire, mid-2nd century A.D.
Bronze
Height: 5 7/8 in. (15 cm)
Otis Norcross Fund, Frank B. Bemis
Fund, William F. Warden Fund, and
William Nickerson Fund 1993.682

Helios
Roman Empire (possibly Asia
Minor), about A.D. 150–190
Bronze
Height: 7 3/4 in. (18.9 cm)
Frank B. Bemis Fund, William E.
Nickerson Fund, Otis Norcross
Fund, and Helen B. Sweeney Fund
1996.3

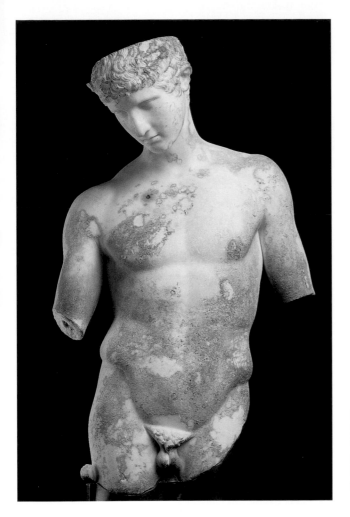

Mercury
Italy (Rome), about A.D. 30–40
Marble
Height: 28¼ in. (72 cm)
Catharine Page Perkins Fund
95.67

The Greek sculptor Polykleitos, working in the fifth century B.C., established a new concept of the ideal proportions for an athletic body. This Roman sculpture emulates the Polykleitan model. However, the head and neck are more slender, the hair is textured in a more naturalistic way, and the body is slightly fleshier, giving this Roman interpretation a distinctively youthful and sensuous elegance. The figure represents the god Mercury (Hermes) in his role as divine messenger and conductor of souls to the Underworld. Much of the sculpture's polished marble surface was stained by deposits in the soil in which it was buried. Long before the sculpture came to the Museum, attempts were made to remove this deposit with acid, resulting in a waxy, discolored effect on parts of the surface.

Grave monument
Syria (Palmyra),
about A.D. 150–200
Limestone
Height: 21 ¾ in. (55 cm)
Gift of Edward Perry Warren in
memory of his sister
22.659

The Syrian city of Palmyra was a major commercial hub for the merchants that traded between the Persian Gulf and the Mediterranean. There, the cultures of east and west met and fused, creating an artistic style unique in the Roman world.

This Palmyrene funerary monument is inscribed in Greek: "Aththaia, daughter of Malchos, Happy One, Farewell." Adorned for eternity, Aththaia wears jewelry that reflects the taste and craftsmanship of the Greek, Roman, and Near Eastern cultures that shaped her city—elaborate pendant earrings, a large circular pin, two signet rings on her left hand, a betrothal or wedding ring on her right, bracelets made of twisted gold or silver, and two necklaces. All this jewelry has been rendered with such precision that this relief, and others like it, are invaluable resources for charting the fluctuations of fashion among the prosperous residents of ancient Palmyra.

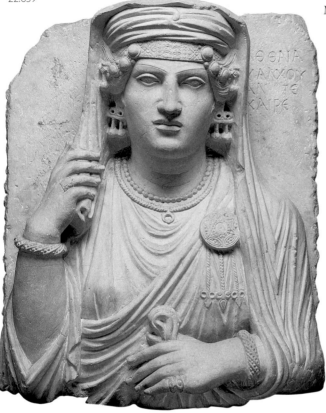

This remarkable and moving portrait presents a dreamy boy with a soft, rounded face and lips at once childish and sensual—a boy who was also an emperor. Elagabalus (A.D. 203–222) ascended to the throne at the age of fifteen and as hereditary high priest of the Syrian sun god Elah Gabal, from whom he took his name, he was determined to bring the worship of Elah Gabal to Rome. The aristocracy, however, was enraged by religious practices it considered both ludicrous and obscene, and before his twentieth birthday, Elagabalus was murdered by members of his imperial guard and his body dumped in the river Tiber.

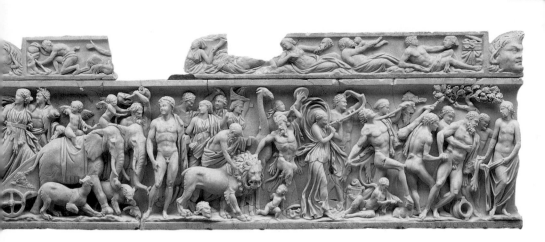

The scene that sweeps along the side of this sarcophagus depicts the triumphant return of the god Bacchus (Dionysos) from India, where he had been spreading his cult of joyous physical abandon. On the left edge, Bacchus steps into a chariot drawn by two Indian elephants. Before him, his merry-making attendants (many part-human, part-beast) celebrate with wine, dance, and music. At the far right is Hercules, who has lost a drinking contest to Bacchus and staggers toward a coyly welcoming maenad, one of Bacchus' lustful female followers. Almost every inch of the relief is covered with figures of astonishing variety and vitality, carved in such high relief that some are almost free of the block.

Sarcophagus
Roman Empire (probably Asia Minor), about A.D. 215–25
Marble
30½ x 81⅞ in. (77.5 x 208 cm)
William Francis Warden Fund
1972.650

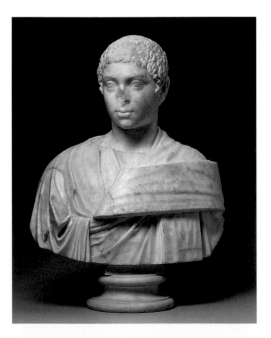

The emperor Elagabalus
Italy (Rome), A.D. 218–22
Marble
Height: 28 in. (71 cm)
Mary S. and Edward J. Holmes Fund 1977.337

A dancer sits on a stool, massaging her tired foot and perhaps preparing to put on the slipper that rests on the sculpture's rectangular base. Images of seated figures adjusting a sandal or slipper had a long history in ancient Greek sculpture. The artist who created this figurine hundreds of years later, in the late Roman period, clearly was still attracted by classical ideals of grace and beauty. The sculpture is exquisitely worked, cast in silver with lion-headed supports at the corners of the base and details of hair, costume, and jewelry picked out in gold.

Seated dancer
Roman Empire (the eastern Mediterranean),
late 4th century A.D.
Silver with gold details
Height: 4¾ in. (12 cm)
Frederick Brown Fund 69.72

A saint
Egypt, 5th century A.D.
Wool, tapestry weave
7 x 9 in. (18 x 23 cm)
Charles Potter Kling Fund
1976.743

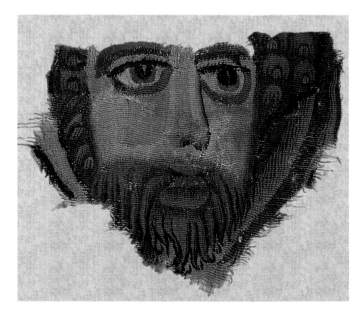

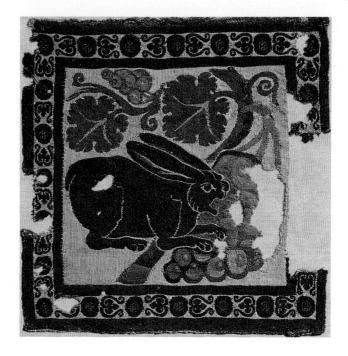

Hare feeding on a vine
Egypt, 4th century A.D.
Wool and linen; tapestry weave
8½ × 8 in. (22 × 21 cm)
Denman Waldo Ross Collection
96.343b

Ancient Egyptian culture changed course dramatically when Alexander the Great conquered the country in 332 B.C. and founded the city of Alexandria—a magnet for thousands of Greek immigrants. Three hundred years later, in 31 B.C., Egypt became a Roman province, and along with the rest of the Roman Empire, eventually adopted Christianity as its official religion. Gradually a new and original civilization known as Coptic (a word derived from the Greek for "Egyptian") developed in Egypt, incorporating Greek, Roman, and Christian influences.

Following the Roman ban on mummification at the end of the fourth century A.D., the inhabitants of Egypt began to bury their dead clothed and wrapped in woven wool and linen; thousands of these fragile textiles were preserved in the dry, desert sands of Egypt. The two examples here are highlights of one of the most extensive American collections of Coptic textiles. In ancient Greece, the hare was associated with the goddess Aphrodite (Venus) and often presented as a gift of love; the little hare above, hungrily attacking a bunch of oversized grapes symbolizes fertility and abundance. Even though Christianity was the official religion, the fragment at left depicting a Christian saint—with large, dark-ringed eyes that seem to gaze beyond the world of the viewer—is very unusual among weavings from this period of late antiquity.

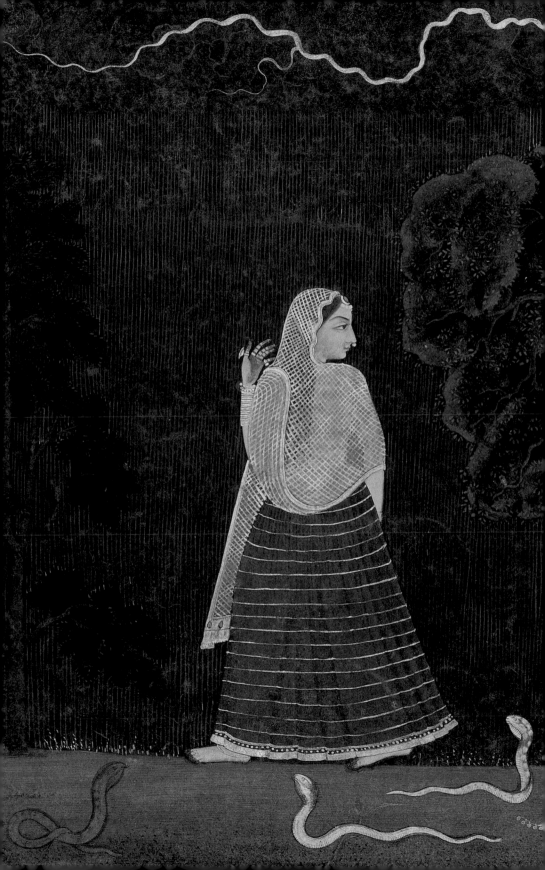

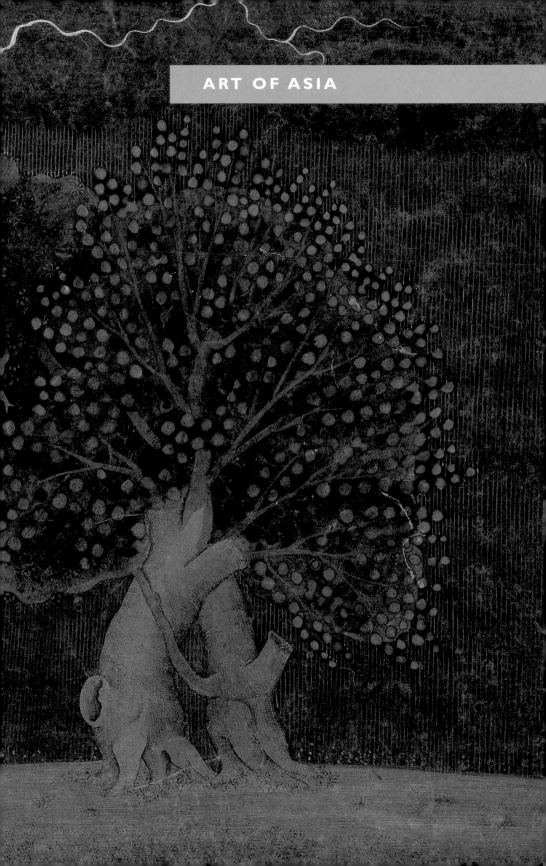

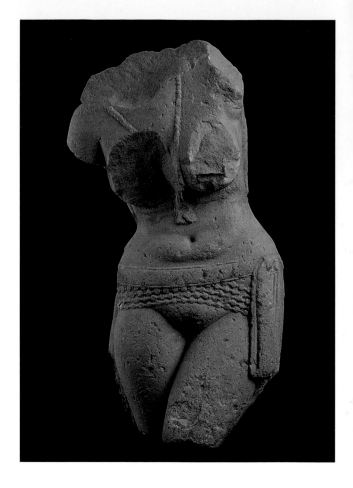

Torso of a fertility goddess (yakshi)
Central India (Sanchi), from a gateway of the Great Stupa, 25 B.C–A.D. 25
Sandstone
Height: 28 ³⁄₈ in. (72 cm)
Denman Waldo Ross Collection 29.999

Prior to the development of Buddhism in India (see page 116), *yakshi*s were honored as semidivine nature spirits believed to bring good luck, wealth, and other blessings such as the birth of children. Incorporated into the early imagery of Buddhism, *yakshi*s and their male counterparts, *yaksha*s, were placed at the entrances to religious monuments to provide protection and welcome the faithful. This sensuous sculpture comes from a gateway at one of the oldest and most important Buddhist monuments in India, the Great Stupa at Sanchi. Like figures still found on gateways at the site, this *yakshi* stood beneath a tree, her left arm raised to hold a branch. Since it was believed that the touch of a beautiful woman would cause a tree's sap to run, making that tree flower and bear fruit, such figures were powerful symbols of fertility and abundance.

Bodhisattva

Northwestern Pakistan
(Gandhara), late 2nd century A.D.
Gray schist
Height: 43 1⁄8 in. (109.5 cm)
Helen and Alice Colburn Fund
37.99

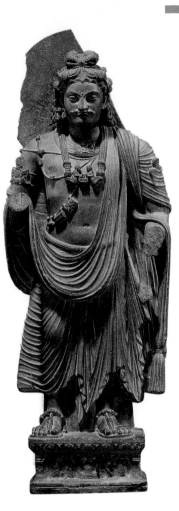

A bodhisattva is an enlightened being who postpones his own entry into nirvana and remains on earth to assist other beings in their quest for salvation. This is an extremely important concept in Buddhism, a religion that stresses altruism and compassion. Reflecting the origins of the historic Buddha, who was born a prince, bodhisattvas wear elaborate jewelry and layers of rich garments. Details of this sculpture, such as the stiff folds and ridges of the heavy drapery, reflect the Gandharan region's contacts with the contemporary Greco-Roman world and Gandharan artists' knowledge of Western sculptural traditions (see page 90).

Male spear thrower or dancer

Pakistan (Sindh, Chanhudaro),
Indus Valley civilization,
2600–1900 B.C.
Copper
Height: 1 5⁄8 in. (4.1 cm)
Joint Expedition of the American
School of Indic and Iranian Studies
and the Museum of Fine Arts,
1935–1936 Season   36.2236

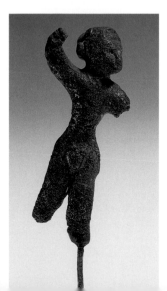

The pose of this tiny, fragmentary figure suggests that he is either dancing or throwing a spear. Many similar male figurines with their hair tied back in buns have been found at Indus Valley sites in modern-day Pakistan, but their function and meaning are unknown. The metalworking techniques of this early civilization, however, were remarkably sophisticated, and this sculpture was probably cast using the lost-wax process. In this process, a wax model is encased in clay that is heated until the wax melts; the wax is then poured out and replaced with molten bronze or copper. When cool, the clay casing is broken away from the metal cast, which is then smoothed and finished.

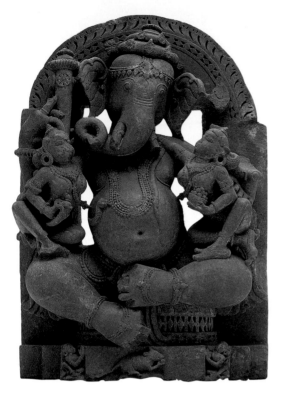

Ganesha with his consorts
Northern India (Madhya Pradesh
or Rajasthan), early 11th century
Sandstone
Height: 41 ⅜ in. (105.2 cm)
John and Ernestine A. Payne Fund,
Helen S. Coolidge Fund, and Keith
McLeod Fund 1989.312

Ganesha is a Hindu god represented with
the body of a boy and the head of an elephant. Elephants are symbols of royalty and
very auspicious animals in Indian culture,
and part of Ganesha's function is to help
clear obstacles from the worshiper's path to
enlightenment. Sculptures of Ganesha, like
this one, are often placed on the exterior
wall of temples so that they are the first
images encountered by the reverent visitor,
who circles the temple before entering. In
this lively sculpture, Ganesha is shown with
his consorts, Siddhi (Success) and Riddhi
(Prosperity). Below him is a rat, his traditional means of transportation.

This exquisitely carved ivory sculpture may have been designed
to ornament a piece of furniture—perhaps the throne of a king
or a deity. The sensual interplay of intricate jewelry and softly
rounded flesh reflects the eastern Indian origin of the sculpture.
Such images of lovers *(mithuna)* are often found in Indian art
as part of the decoration on both Buddhist and Hindu monuments; they symbolize the union between the male and female
principles—the equal yet opposing forces of nature. With the
sense they convey of fertile energy and infectious optimism,
they are also prized as good luck charms. Stylistically, this
object is very close to the erotic stone sculptures on the sun
temple at Konarak in Orissa, built in the thirteenth century.

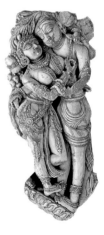

Lovers *(mithuna)*
Eastern India (Orissa),
13th century
Ivory
Height: 6 ¼ in. (15.9 cm)
Keith McLeod Fund and Seth K.
Sweetser Fund, by exchange
1987.622

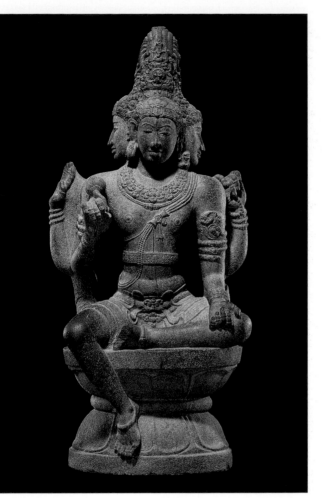

Shiva
Southern India (Tamilnadu region),
late 10th century
Green schist
Height: 63¾ in. (162 cm)
Gift of Mrs. John D. Rockefeller, Jr.
42.120

Hindu gods are often depicted in human form but with super-human attributes such as multiple heads and eyes that symbolize enhanced knowledge and vision. This figure's many heads are associated with Brahma, the god of creation, but the third eye in the forehead and the tall, matted hair indicate that he is, in fact, Shiva—the god of destruction who also embodies the life force. With five faces (a fifth, looking upward, is implied), this image represents the god as supremely powerful and would probably have been placed in a niche on the outside of a temple wall. Hindu temple sculptures function both as representations and physical embodiments of the gods; they are there to be seen by and also to see the worshipers.

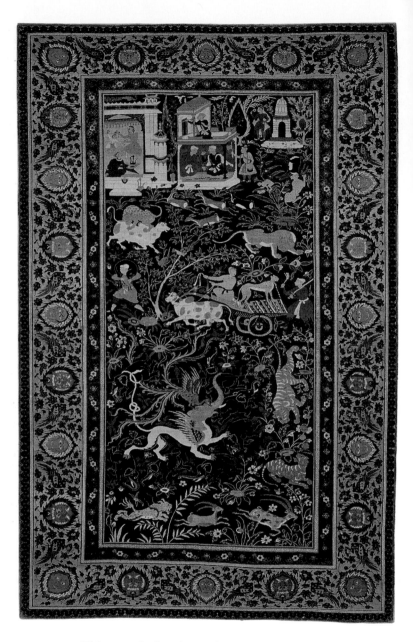

Pictorial carpet

Northern India (Lahore),
about 1590–1600
Cotton warp and weft, wool pile
95⅝ × 60⅝ in. (243 × 154 cm)
Gift of Mrs. Frederick L. Ames in
the name of Frederick L. Ames
93.1480

This carpet brilliantly translates into knotted pile the lively painting style of the court of the Mughal emperor Akbar, where it was probably made. The wealth of imagery includes scenes of palace life, hunting, and fabulous beasts in combat and a border filled with glowering monster masks. The celebrated nineteenth-century American architect Henry Hobson Richardson selected this carpet for the house of an important client, Boston businessman Frederick L. Ames.

Seventeenth-century Mughal painting is one of the great glories of Indian art. This vivid, meticulously executed image of courtly life is probably a page from a manuscript illustrating the life of the Mughal emperor Jahangir, son of the great emperor Akbar, and may depict his birth. The infant's jewel-encrusted crib is placed near the bed of his mother who is surrounded by female attendants, musicians, eunuchs, and Akbar's other wives. Male attendants bring platters of presents, the court astrologers (at bottom center) forecast the child's future, and the entrance to the harem (at left) is garlanded with flowers in honor of the festive occasion. The painting is attributed to Bishan Das, one of the most celebrated Mughal painters, whom Jahangir called "unequaled in his age for making likenesses."

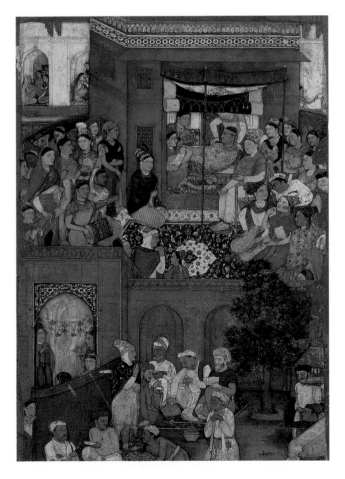

Attributed to
Bishan Das
Indian, about 1570–1630
Birth of a Prince, about 1620
Opaque watercolor on paper
10 3/8 × 6 1/2 in. (26.4 × 16.4 cm)
Francis Bartlett Donation of 1912
and Picture Fund 14.657

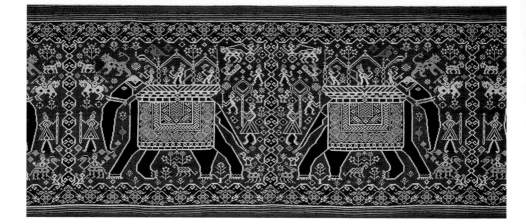

Patola
Western India (Gujarat),
late 18th or early 19th century
Silk; double ikat (resist-dyed warp
and weft yarns)
43 × 191 in. (109.2 × 485 cm)
Marshall H. Gould Fund 1985.709

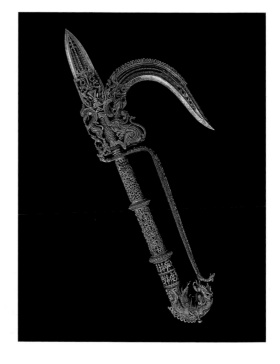

Elephant goad (ankus)
Southern India, probably early
17th century
Steel
Height: 27 5/8 in. (70.2 cm)
Keith McLeod Fund 1995.114

Elephant goads such as this one, made for steering the giant animals, are found in armories and temples across India, where elephants march in religious processions and serve as laborers for the military. This goad was probably made for ritual use and is richly engraved with images of deities, animals, and mythical creatures. In the middle section are elaborate depictions of the ten earthly incarnations of the Hindu god Vishnu, while the god Shiva and his family are shown along the spine. In southern India it is believed that Vishnu, representing the preservation of the universe, and Shiva, representing its destruction, complement each other, and they are often shown together in the same artistic setting.

Ikat is a Malay-Indonesian word for an intricate cloth-making process in which threads are patterned by repeated binding and dyeing before they are placed on the loom and woven. *Patola*—Indian silk textiles richly patterned in the exacting double-ikat technique—were prized as heirlooms and luxury trade goods. Valued also for their spiritual potency, fragments of *patola* were even powdered and mixed with medicines. Many of these textiles were made for the Indonesian export market and have survived in excellent condition because their use was reserved for religious and ritual functions. Their superb quality and vibrant color inspired the Indonesian name *patola,* which means "gifts from the sky." This example was probably given to an Indonesian ruler by officials of the Dutch East India Company as a mark of special esteem.

Gateway (detail)
India (Delhi area), Mughal period, about 1677
Red sandstone
120 × 120 in. (305 × 305 cm)
Keith McLeod Fund 1983.386

The elaborately carved floral-and-leaf designs of this monumental sandstone gateway are characteristic of late-seventeenth-century architecture of the Mughal empire. A stone slab found with the gateway is inscribed with the Muslim date corresponding to 1677. This year falls during the reign of the emperor Aurangzeb whose father, Shah Jahan, had built the Taj Mahal—the masterpiece of Mughal architecture—as a mausoleum for his wife. In fact, the decoration of this gateway shares some motifs with the Taj Mahal, including the juxtaposition of both naturalistic and stylized depictions of flowers.

Attributed to
Manaku of Guler
Indian, about 1700–1760
***Ravana Facing His Demon
Army,*** 1730–40
Opaque watercolor and gold paint
on paper
32½ × 25⅝ in. (82.5 × 60 cm)
Ross-Coomaraswamy Collection
17.2740

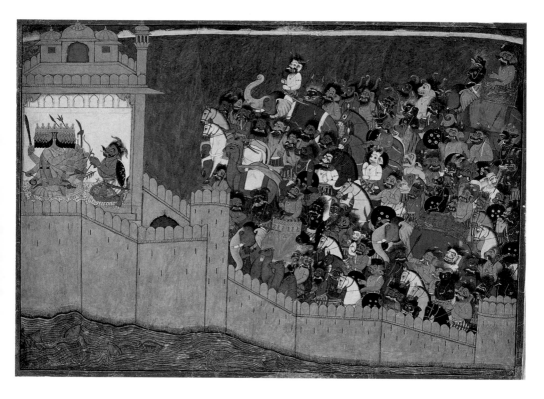

Remarkable for its vivacious draftsmanship and flat expanses of
intense color, this page is from an oversized manuscript of the
Ramayana, the Indian epic that recounts the life of the warrior-
king Rama. A reincarnation of the god Vishnu, Rama descends
to earth to vanquish the demon king Ravana and restore the
balance of the universe. This page illustrates an incident from
"The Siege of Lanka" in which Rama attempts to rescue his
wife who has been abducted by Ravana and imprisoned in his
garden on the island of Lanka (modern-day Sri Lanka). A great
battle ensues between Ravana's demon soldiers and Rama's
armies of monkeys and bears; Rama eventually kills Ravana and
is reunited with his wife.

Long-necked lute *(tambura)*
Northern India, early 19th century
Jackfruit wood, gourd, ivory,
black mastic
Height: 53⅝ in. (135 cm)
Mary L. Smith Fund 1992.259

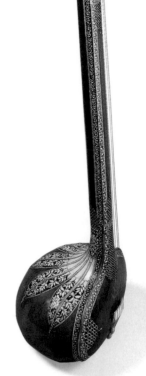

An essential component of classical Indian music, the *tambura* provides a drone accompaniment to the human voice or solo instruments such as the sitar. The strings are plucked slowly in repeated sequence, and a prolonged buzzing tone is achieved by tying silk thread around the strings where they contact a wide bridge. In this splendid example, the bridge is ivory and the instrument, undoubtedly created for a wealthy patron, is finely decorated with ivory inlay.

Paintings from the state of Kangra are celebrated for their delicacy of detail, juxtapositions of brilliant and muted colors, and evocation of complex emotions. The word *nayika* in the title of this page refers to the female personification of the notion of human love. Here, the heroine ignores the perils of the night—darkness, lightning, beating rain, snakes—as she hurries to meet her lover. The storm symbolizes her passion, and the trees represent intertwined lovers. Paintings of such secular subjects were popular among painters at the Hindu Rajput courts of Rajasthan and the Punjab Hills, which prospered in close proximity to the Muslim Mughal courts of northern India.

Heroine Rushing to Her Lover
(Abhisarika nayika)
Northern India (Punjab Hills, Kangra), late 18th century
Opaque watercolor and gold on paper
6⅜ x 9⅞ in. (16.2 x 25 cm)
Ross-Coomaraswamy Collection 17.2612

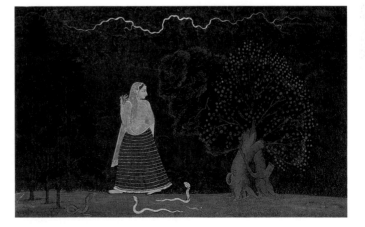

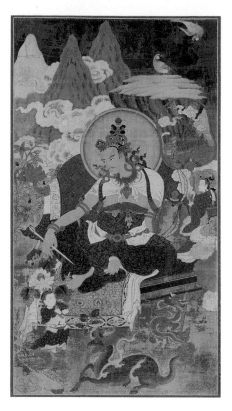

The Fifth King of Shambhala
Tibet or China, second half of the
17th century
Opaque watercolor on cotton
13⅞ × 17 in. (80.9 × 43.3 cm)
Denman Waldo Ross Collection
06.324

This painting is one of a set portraying the pious kings of Shambhala, a mythical region in Central Asia. These kings were believed to have transmitted from one generation to the next an esoteric spiritual system that is an essential part of Lamaism, the Tibetan form of Buddhism. Although the brilliant colors of this painting are characteristically Tibetan, the work may have been created in neighboring China—the scrolling clouds are Chinese in style and the oversized fan held by the servant at right is decorated with a Chinese landscape that echoes the painting's mountainous setting.

In Buddhism, wrathful deities serve as protectors of the faith and the faithful. Vajrabhairava, the subject of this beautifully worked small sculpture, is a form of the Bodhisattva of Wisdom, and he represents the anger that destroys attachment to the ego. Here, he embraces his consort, the female embodiment of wisdom; the union of the two achieves enlightenment. The figures are sexually joined—anatomically complete and separable—and Vajrabhairava's body was filled with such offerings as incense and Buddhist relics through a small door located between his legs. The animals, demons, birds, and Hindu gods crushed beneath the deity's feet symbolize the destruction of the ego, while his many legs, arms, and heads represent his all-encompassing ability to take action.

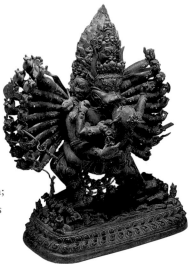

Vajrabhairava and his consort
Tibet, 17th century
Copper with pigment
Height: 8⅝ in. (22 cm)
William Sturgis Bigelow Collection
21.2168

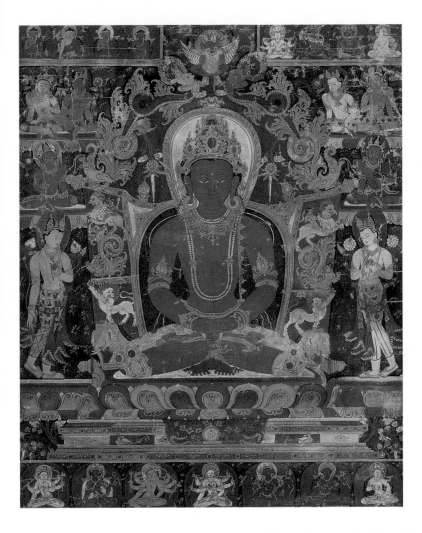

Seated on an elaborate peacock throne with typically Nepalese
architectural elements, the Buddha of Eternal Life is encircled
by elephants, snakes, lions, flying goats, boys, and—at the peak
of the throne—the bird deity Garuda. Around the Buddha are
eight bodhisattvas, enlightened beings who remain on earth to
assist others to salvation. Other Buddhist deities are ranged
across the top and bottom of the painting. Known as *thangka*s,
painted textiles such as this were displayed in Buddhist temples
throughout the Himalayan region. This extraordinary example,
probably painted by a Nepalese artist working in an important
Tibetan monastery, belonged to a set of five, each depicting one
of the Five Transcendental Buddhas.

**Buddha of Eternal Life and
eight bodhisattvas**
Tibet, 11th century
Opaque watercolor on cotton
16¼ x 13 in. (41.3 x 33 cm)
Gift of John Goelet 67.818

Temple hanging (pidan)
Cambodia (Phnom Penh),
late 19th century
Silk ikat; resist-dyed warp
33¾ × 62⅞ in. (85.7 × 159.7 cm)
Gift of the Textile and Costume
Society 1993.694

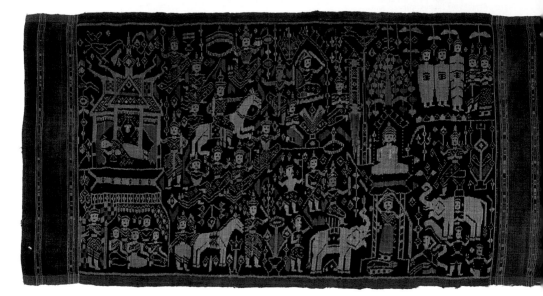

Figural textiles, *pidan,* were presented to Buddhist temples and monasteries for use as ceremonial hangings and as canopies for statues. They were also hung in houses to celebrate marriages and provide comfort to the dying. Woven in an ikat technique (see pages 107 and 154), *pidan* depict scenes from the life of the Buddha. In this composition, the plain, saffron-colored robes of the monks are contrasted with the traditional ikat clothing worn by the secular figures. These images of lively activities in elaborate palace settings convey a sense of the richness of the social and ceremonial life of the Khmer people of Cambodia.

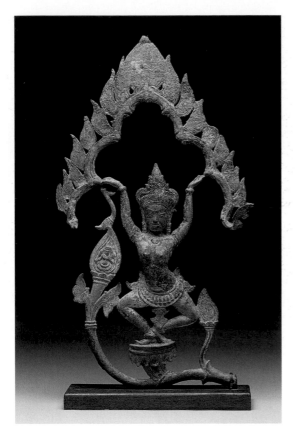

Dancing celestial figure (apsaras)
Cambodia, late 11th century
Bronze
Height: 15½ in. (39.3 cm)
Denman Waldo Ross Collection
22.686

Sprightly female *apsarases* appear on temples throughout southern Asia. Heavenly beings, they are usually shown dancing or playing musical instruments as they entertain and pay homage to the gods. In this example, the elegant figure is framed by a flamelike arch and dances on a lotus flower whose branch sprouts two additional buds. The sculpture was originally part of an incense burner or a hanging lamp whose flickering light would have enhanced its sense of graceful movement. This is one of the most exquisitely worked and best preserved of the very few fragments of such fragile bronzes that have survived from Cambodia.

Ewer
Vietnam, late 12th–early 13th centuries
Stoneware with crackled ivory glaze
Height: 4⅞ in. (12.5 cm)
Anonymous gift 1991.969

Ceramics from Vietnam often reflect that region's role as a bridge between eastern and southern Asia. This ewer was probably made for royal patrons or temple officials in Thang Long (modern-day Hanoi). The vessel's rolled lip and collar of modeled lotus petals are typical of Vietnamese ceramics, but the creamy, crackled glaze recalls Chinese wares. The ewer's dramatic silhouette may have been inspired by metal vessels that originated in India but were used in Buddhist and Hindu rituals throughout southern Asia.

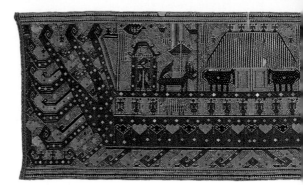

Bhairava or Mahakala
Indonesia (eastern Java),
14th century
Volcanic stone (andesite)
Height: 78 in. (198 cm)
Frederick L. Jack Fund
1972.951

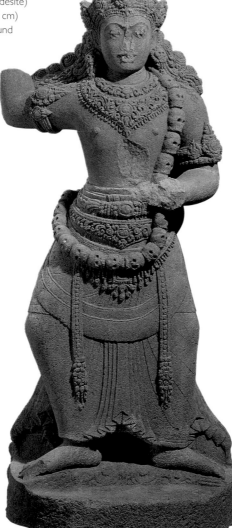

Striking a pose from traditional Javanese dance, this large, stone sculpture may represent either Mahakala (a Buddhist deity) or Bhairava (a Hindu deity); Hinduism and Buddhism coexisted in Javanese culture and often shared imagery. Wearing royal attire—an ornate crown, belts, necklaces, earrings, and armbands—this figure may have been intended as an idealized portrait, combining the representation of a deceased royal personage with that of a deity. The rope of skulls indicates that this is a wrathful deity, representing the power to overcome fears and frightening only to those who are not part of the faith.

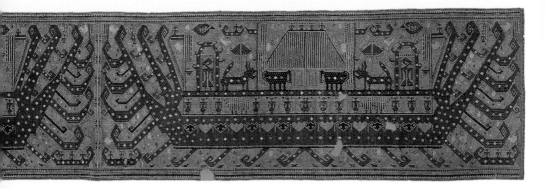

**Ceremonial hanging
(palepai)**
Indonesia (Sumatra, southern
Lampong region), 1825–75
Cotton; discontinuous
supplementary pattern wefts on
plain-weave ground
29 × 150 in. (74 × 382 cm)
William E. Nickerson Fund No. 2
1980.172

Depictions of ships have appeared on Southeast Asian artifacts for millennia; long associated with funeral rites, ship imagery in the culture of Sumatra stands not only for death but also for the transition from one social or spiritual state to another. Owned and displayed only by the aristocracy, large *palepai* or "ship cloths" of Sumatra, like this one, were hung as backdrops for the important ceremonies of initiation into adulthood, marriage, and the attainment of rank. The fabulous sailing vessels depicted on *palepai* have elaborately curled bows and sterns, multiple decks with royal pavilions and banners, and cargos that include elephants—creatures associated with royal power.

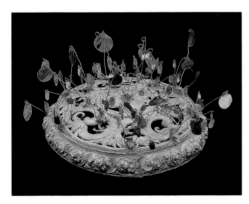

Crown
Indonesia (eastern Java),
13th century
Gold
Diameter: 5 in. (12.7 cm)
Keith McLeod Fund 1982.141

This delicate golden crown, which would have been attached to a cloth cap, is formed in the shape of a lotus pond. Lotuses are found at the center of the crown and at the base of the wired spangles, which themselves suggest flowers emerging from the pond. Made of very thin, beaten gold, the spangles would have shimmered as the wearer moved. The flowers, water creatures, and snakes that also decorate the crown are auspicious symbols that appear frequently in the religious and courtly arts of Southeast Asia.

Buddhism: A Journey through Asia

Over the last twenty-five centuries Buddhism has grown and flourished—and sometimes declined and disappeared—all over southern and eastern Asia. In each country and era, the religion has taken on new ideas, practices, and institutional structures; still, all Buddhism's many variations grow out of the central belief that in northern India, sometime around 500 B.C., a member of the socially prominent Gautama clan named Siddhartha found the secret to happiness. Profoundly disturbed by the traumas and troubles of the human condition, Siddhartha gave up the luxuries and rights of his station, and lived the wandering life of an ascetic holy man, meditating on the eternal suffering and disappointment of life. After a long period, he achieved Enlightenment, and became the Buddha (the "awakened one"), with the realization that escape from the human condition can come only with an escape from desire, since it is desire—for power, for pleasure, even to live—that brings suffering. Escape can come only through right and moderate living and meditation. When an individual achieves rightness, he or she also achieves nirvana—escape from the physical world.

Buddhism spread quickly outward from northern India, aided both by its appeal and by the active proselytizing of its adherents. Already by the third century B.C., Buddhism had spread throughout the Indian subcontinent and the island of Sri Lanka, eventually reaching Southeast Asia and Indonesia. It also traveled north and east, through central Asia, arriving in China some time around the first century A.D. China already possessed sophisticated religious and philosophical traditions of its own, which both affected and were affected by Buddhist ideas. Still, Buddhism was successful enough that it became the official state religion beginning in the Sui Dynasty (A.D. 581–618). From China, missionaries brought the religion to Korea and then to Japan by the mid-sixth century. In both countries, but particularly in Japan, Buddhism became the dominant reli-

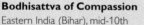

Bodhisattva of Compassion
Eastern India (Bihar), mid-10th
century A.D.
Gray schist
Height: 35 in. (88.9 cm)
Marshall H. Gould and Frederick
L. Jack Funds 63.418

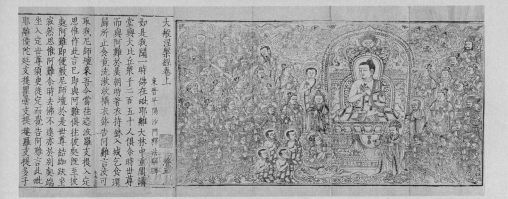

如是我聞一時佛在毗耶離大林中重閣講
堂與大比丘眾千二百五十人俱僉時世尊
而與阿難於晨朝時著衣持鉢入城乞食還
歸所止食竟洗漱收攝衣鉢告阿難言汝可
取我尼師壇來吾今當往逝波羅支提入定
思惟作此言已即與阿難俱往彼敷既至彼
處阿難即便敷尼師壇於是世尊結跏趺坐
寂然思惟阿難亦於不遠亦別敷端
坐入定世尊須更從定而告阿難言此毗
耶離樓陀延支提羅髻支提
菴羅支提多子

大般涅槃經卷上
東晉平陽沙門釋法顯譯
澄五

Buddhist *sutra* with illustration
China, Yuan Dynasty, about 1301
Woodblock print
11 7/8 × 4 3/8 in. (30.2 × 11.2 cm)
Marshall H. Gould Fund 1984.415

gious and philosophical system; in Japan, Buddhism almost immediately became intertwined with the political system, and took on a particular local flavor.

By the twelfth century Buddhism was in decline in India, and has now almost completely disappeared from India, overshadowed by Hinduism, Jainism, and Islam, but the artistic forms that were developed early on in India became influential wherever Buddhism traveled. Like the religion itself, the artistic forms reflect their Indian origins, yet are distinctly local as well.

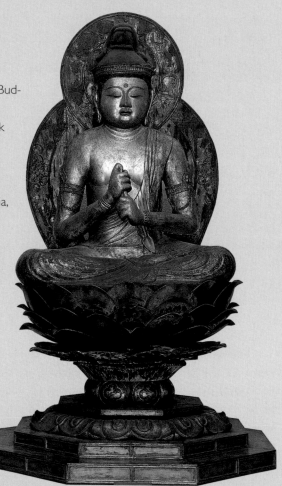

Buddha of eternal radiance
Japan, late Heian period, 1189
Wood, gilt
Height: 55 3/4 in. (141.6 cm)
Denman Waldo Ross Collection
09.531

Granary jar
China, Neolithic period, Machang
type, late 3rd millenium B.C.
Earthenware with painted and
applied decoration over slip
Height: 15½ in. (39.5 cm)
E. Rhodes and Leona B. Carpenter
Foundation Grant and Edwin E.
Jack Fund 1988.29

Human images seldom appear on ancient Chinese ceramics, and this vessel is extremely unusual in that its decoration includes a three-dimensional human head with a painted body below. The tattooed face, hairstyle, and clothing indicate that the figure represents a shaman or priestly official who practiced the rites of ancestor worship and could communicate with the spirit world. Made to hold rice, the jar may have been buried in the tomb of a chieftain or a high priest. Its brush-and-ink decoration represents one of the earliest surviving examples of the Chinese tradition of brush painting.

Throughout the Bronze Age in China (about 2000 B.C. to A.D. 220), bronze vessels were prized symbols of power, authority, and wealth. Each of the more than fifty different types of bronze ritual vessels had a specialized function; this *you* was a ceremonial container for wine. Stylized horned creatures (possibly water buffaloes) dominate the design, and the eight-character inscription on the interior of the body and on the lid indicates the vessel's use in the practice of ancestor worship. It reads: "Dui Cheng had this ritual vessel made for his accomplished late father Ding."

Chinese bronzes of this early period were created by a process quite different from lost-wax casting (see page 101). Sectional clay molds, carved on the inside with designs, were placed around a solid clay core, and molten bronze was poured into the space between them. After the bronze cooled, the mold sections and core were removed, revealing the completed vessel.

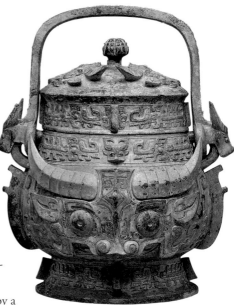

Ritual vessel with cover *(you)*
China, Western Zhou dynasty,
11th–10th centuries B.C.
Cast bronze
Height: 9⅞ in. (25 cm)
Anna Mitchell Richards Fund
34.63

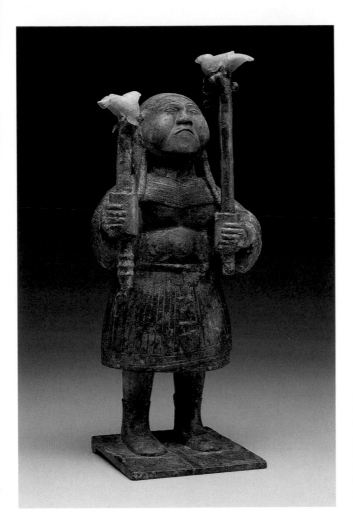

Standing youth
China, Eastern Zhou dynasty,
Warring States Period, early 4th
century B.C.
Cast bronze with applied jade
Height: 11 ¾ in. (30 cm)
Maria Antoinette Evans Fund
31.976

The Eastern Zhou period was marked by a new interest in
more accurate and specific portrayals of the human figure. This
young man's facial features, braided hair, jewelry, dagger, and
boots suggest that he represents a member of a nomadic group
that inhabited China's northern border regions until the first
century B.C. The figure gazes intently at two jade birds on top
of sticks, and, although larger than most, belongs to a group of
early bronze sculptures of lamp-bearers and other performers
that were placed in a tomb to provide eternal light and entertainment in the afterlife.

Guanyin
China, Northern Zhou or Sui
dynasty, about A.D. 580
Limestone with traces of paint
and gold
Height: 98 in. (249 cm)
Francis Bartlett Fund 15.254

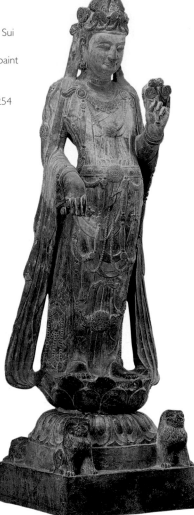

Guanyin, the Boddhisattva of Compassion and the divine figure that responds most directly to human prayers, became the most beloved Buddhist deity after the religion reached China from India in the first century A.D. (see page 116). Guanyin stands on a lotus throne and holds a cluster of lotus pods—this plant, which rises from the mud to release a white flower, is a Buddhist symbol of spiritual purity. Surviving traces of paint and gilding indicate that this monumental sculpture was once richly decorated. The figure's lithe, elongated body and flowing garments are characteristic of sculpture of both the Northern Zhou and Sui periods.

Tray
China, Tang dynasty, first half of the 8th century A.D.
Marbleized stoneware
Height: 3 ¼ in. (8.3 cm)
Charles B. Hoyt Collection
50.1979

Chinese marbleized ceramics of the Tang dynasty (A.D. 618–906) were probably inspired by Roman marbleized glass (see page 85) at a time when trade between China and the Roman Empire was conducted along the so-called Silk Road, a four-thousand mile route linking China with the civilizations on the Mediterranean Sea. On this tray, the patterns imitating veins of marble were created by pressing together two different colors of clay, which was then molded into shape and covered with a transparent glaze.

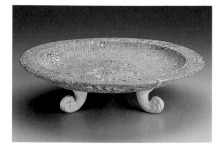

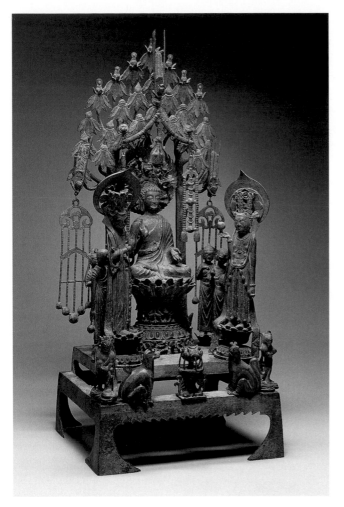

Altarpiece
China (Zhaozhou, Hebei Province)
Sui dynasty, A.D. 593
Cast bronze
Height: 30⅛ in. (76.5 cm)
Gift of Mrs. W. Scott Fitz 22.407
Gift of Edward Jackson Holmes in
Memory of his mother,
Mrs. W. Scott Fitz 47.1407–1412

At the center of this serenely beautiful altarpiece stands the
Amitabha Buddha, whose good favor ensured rebirth after
death into a Western Paradise "full of sweet smells, clouds of
music, showers of jewels, and every other beauty and joy." The
altarpiece was commissioned by eight women of the Chinese
Buddhist Pure Land sect to guarantee their own rebirths and
those of their children and ancestors. Before the meditating
Buddha, surrounded by his attendants, is an incense burner
flanked by lions and images of the Guardian Kings. The altarpiece was discovered in a pit in the late nineteenth century.
The incense burner, lions, and Guardian Kings, removed and
sold separately in 1922, were finally reunited with the altar
twenty-five years after it came to the Museum.

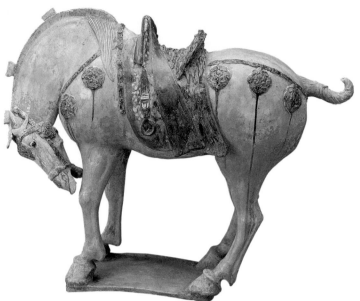

Horse
China, Tang dynasty,
early 8th century A.D.
Molded earthenware with
three-color glaze
Height: 23 ¼ in. (59.2 cm)
Gift by contribution, chiefly from
Mrs. Gaston Smith's Group 27.2

Chinese military strength was dependent upon strong and stalwart horses acquired from the border area of Samarkan. These "heavenly horses" were adopted as the preeminent symbol of the Chinese military, and their beauty and vitality were celebrated in numerous sculptures, paintings, and poems of the Tang dynasty (A.D. 618–906). This sculpture probably came from the tomb of a prince or high official; the three rectangular protrusions of its well-groomed mane indicate that the horse belonged to the imperial stables.

During the decline of the Tang dynasty, the Khitan, a nomadic people from northern Manchuria, conquered northern China and became rulers of the succeeding Liao dynasty. In China, the Khitan maintained their traditional dress, laws, and language. The gold and silver objects found in Khitan tombs were both symbols of status and intended for use by the dead in the afterlife. These silver boots, modeled after actual leather examples and decorated with gilt phoenixes, were most likely part of the tomb treasure of a Khitan Tartar princess.

Boots
Northern China, Liao dynasty,
early 11th century
Silver with engraved design and
parcel gilding
Height: 11 ⅝ in. (29.5 cm)
Charles Bain Hoyt Fund
1994.115 a,b

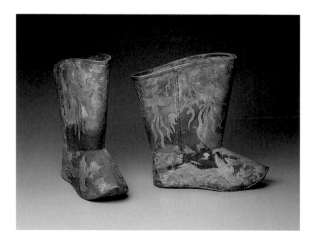

Emperor Huizong
Chinese, 1082–1135
The Five-Colored Parakeet (detail),
early 12th century
Northern Song dynasty
Handscroll; ink and color on silk
21 × 49¼ in. (53.3 × 125.1 cm)
Maria Antoinette Evans Fund 33.364

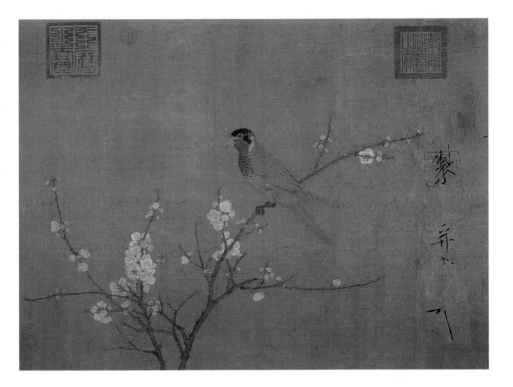

This handscroll by Emperor Huizong (reigned 1101–25) may have originally been part of a large album that he compiled to record rare birds and flowers, exquisite objects, and important events. In the poem inscribed on it, the emperor describes the exotic parakeet that perched one spring day on an apricot branch in the imperial garden. He depicted each feather of the bird and every petal of the apricot blossoms in the meticulous style of academic court painting he established. Huizong's paintings were often copied by court painters; this is one of few surviving works in which the distinctive style of the calligraphy and painting clearly identifies it as by the emperor's own hand.

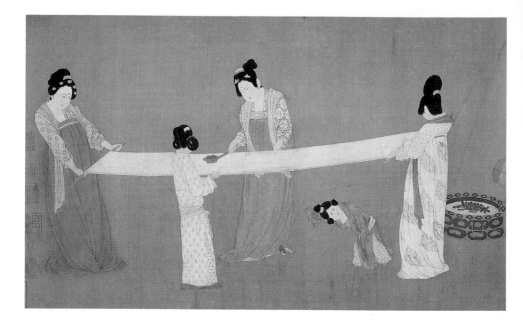

Attributed to
Emperor Huizong
Chinese, 1082–1135
Ladies Preparing Newly Woven
Silk, early 12th century
Northern Song dynasty
Handscroll; ink, color, and gold
on silk
14⅝ x 57¼ in. (37 x 145.3 cm)
Special Chinese and Japanese Fund
11.1697

Painting on silk is among the most highly treasured art forms in China. This celebrated handscroll—one of the great masterpieces of Chinese painting—depicts three scenes of elegant court ladies beating, sewing, and ironing new silk. The engagement of these aristocratic women in domestic labor may reflect a traditional, springtime event in which the empress led her attendants through the ancient ritual of producing silk. In the detail above, the women stretch a long piece of newly woven silk near a charcoal fire kindled to heat the iron.

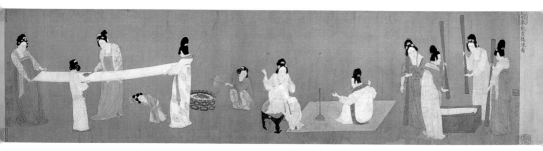

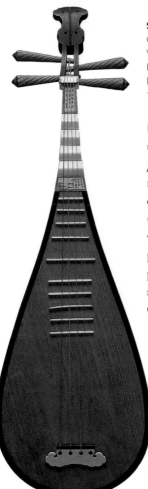

Short-necked lute (pipa)
China, Qing dynasty, 1891
Wutong, other woods, ivory
Height: 41 in. (104 cm)
Leslie Lindsey Mason Collection
17.2049

Probably originating in Central Asia, the four-stringed *pipa* was a favorite instrument at Chinese court banquets since the Tang dynasty (A.D. 618–906). The *pipa* was originally played with a pick, but in later periods, performers plucked the strings with their fingernails. Carved at the head of this *pipa* is the tail of a phoenix, a mythological bird that symbolizes the cycle of rebirth.

Elegantly simple ceramic tea bowls such as this one are unique to the kilns of Jizhou in the southern Chinese province of Jiangxi. To create them, potters dipped a mulberry leaf in wax and placed it inside the glazed bowl before it was fired in the kiln. The leaf itself disintegrated in the heat of the firing, leaving a delicate, yellow-ochre pattern. When the bowl is filled with green tea, the leaf design seems to float within the liquid.

Tea bowl
China (Jiangxi Province), Southern Song Dynasty, 12th–13th centuries
Jizhou glazed stoneware
Diameter: 5⅞ in. (14.9 cm)
Charles Bain Hoyt Collection
50.2014

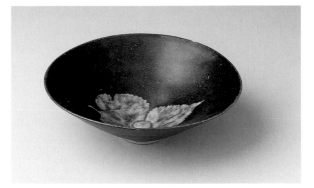

Chen Rong
Chinese, active mid-13th century
Nine Dragons (detail), 1244
Southern Song dynasty
Handscroll; ink with touches of red
on paper
Entire scroll: 18 1/4 x 431 2/3 in.
(46.3 x 1,096.4 cm)
Francis Gardner Curtis Fund
17.1697

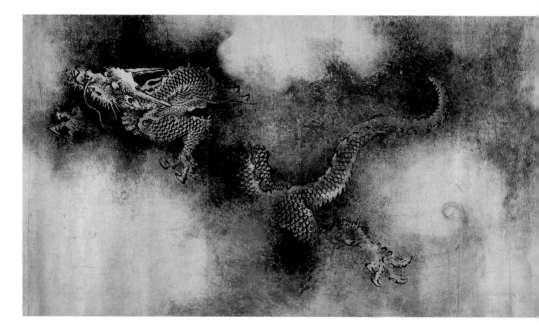

Arguably the greatest of all Chinese dragon paintings, this handscroll—almost thirty-six feet long in its entirety—is the work of Chen Rong, an impoverished painter, poet, and scholar from south China's Fujiang province. He treats the dragon as a manifestation of the principles of Daoism, a Chinese philosophy that explores the relationship of people and the natural world. The dragons in his painting, hidden and then revealed amidst mist, waves, and clouds, may symbolize the Great Dao itself—a mysterious, natural force.

Few ceramic wares have been as widely admired as the porcelain commonly known as Chinese blue-and-white. It was traded throughout the Near and Far East and to Europe, where it was imitated widely (see page 130). This jar is an early example of Jingdezhen porcelain, decorated in underglaze cobalt blue, from the Yuan period (1279–1368). Unlike other Yuan blue-and-white wares, this jar was made for the domestic market and not for export. It is decorated with a scene from *Yuchi Gong Defeats Shan Xiongxin With His Iron Whip,* a historical event frequently reenacted in the popular theater of the Yuan period. The jar's robust form, the brilliance of the cobalt blue, and the vigorous brushwork all contribute to its exuberance and vitality.

Jar
China, Yuan dynasty, 14th century
Jingdezhen porcelain, painted in
underglaze blue
Height: 11 in. (27.8 cm)
Charles Bain Hoyt Collection
50.1339

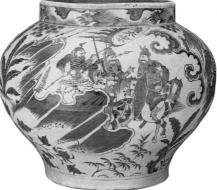

Two-tiered stand
China, Ming dynasty, early
16th century
Hardwood, lacquered and inlaid
with mother-of-pearl
Height: 18 in. (45.7 cm)
Anonymous Gift and Charles Bain
Hoyt Fund 1986.513

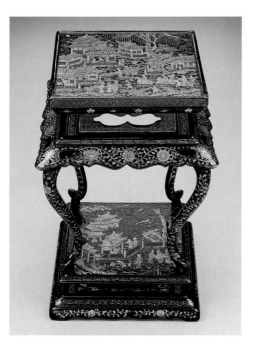

Incense burners and other objects were placed upon precious lacquered stands, such as this one, that formed part of the domestic furnishings of scholars and members of the nobility. This example is decorated in lacquer and intricately inlaid with mother-of-pearl to create two narrative scenes, one on each tier. The top scene shows a family greeting a young scholar who has just returned home after being awarded a prestigious degree for civil service; below, three men in a garden admire a scroll painting.

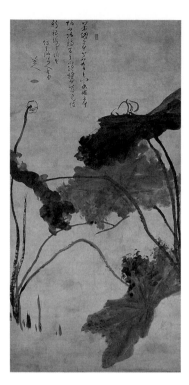

Zhu Da
Chinese, 1626–1705
Lotus: Homage to Xu Wei,
1689–90
Qing dynasty
Hanging scroll; ink on paper
72 7/8 × 35 3/8 in. (185 × 89.8 cm)
Keith McLeod Fund 56.495

One of the four great monk painters of the early Qing dynasty, Zhu Da is renowned for his highly individual, monochrome ink paintings. To escape political persecution after the fall of the Ming dynasty in 1644, he spent more than thirty years as a Buddhist monk. Eventually, disillusioned with the faith, he returned home and painted for the rest of his life disguised as a madman. Here, in a work created in the style of the Ming dynasty scholar-painter Xu Wei, Zhu Da masterfully manipulated thin and thick, dry and wet brushstrokes to paint a lotus-flower plant, symbol of spiritual purity. This lotus seems to falter and wilt, however, suggesting the artist's disillusionment with Buddhism and his grief for his country, now in the hands of Manchu conquerors.

Scholar's rock
China, 19th–early 20th centuries
Lingbi-type natural rock form; wood stand
Height: 58 in. (147.3 cm)
Gift of Richard and Nancy Rosenblum in Memory of Marianna Pineda 1997.218

From the Song period (960–1279) onward, rocks of unusual form have been collected and displayed by connoisseurs, reflecting the Daoist belief that they radiated the pure essences of nature and the cosmos. Some rocks are admired for their abstract forms, textures, and colors; others are prized for their resemblance to people, plants, animals, or landscapes. This rock, which may suggest a fantastic cave, is an example of the highly desirable rocks found in the Lingbi county of south China's Anhui Province.

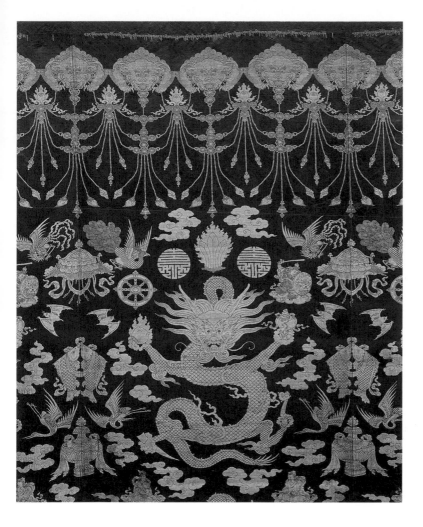

This splendid hanging was produced during the last great period of silk weaving in China. According to the Tibetan inscription across the top edge, it was woven in the imperial workshop
in Nanking and presented by the abbot of the most prestigious
Buddhist monastery in China to the abbot of a temple in Tibet.
The design is dominated by nine sinuous, five-toed dragons,
symbols of the emperor and his royal power. Buddhist emblems
such as wheels and conch shells intermingle with Chinese
motifs of auspicious clouds, bats, and cranes. Above these are
ferocious masks with jewels dangling from their mouths.

Temple hanging (detail)
South China (Nanking),
Qing dynasty, 1768
Blue silk and gilt paper lampas
140 × 91 in. (355.6 × 231.1 cm)
Keith McLeod Fund 1984.526

Not All China Is from China

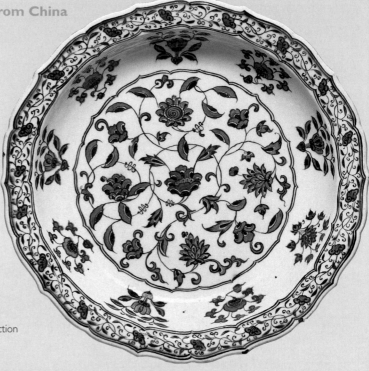

Dish in Chinese style
Turkey (Iznik), Ottoman
period, 1500–25
Composite body (quartz,
clay, and glass frit) with
underglaze cobalt blue
decoration
Diameter: 15 3/8 in. (39 cm)
John Pickering Lyman Collection
19.1196

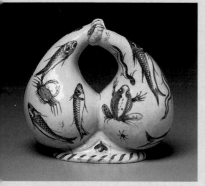

Cruet for oil and vinegar
Italy (Florence), about 1575
Earthenware
Height: 4 1/2 in. (11.4 cm)
Gift of the Estate of Henry
Williamson Haynes through Miss
Sarah H. Blanchard 12.717

Around the year 1200, Chinese potters possessed the most advanced ceramics technology of their day. They had the best and hottest kilns; access to high-quality, white clay called kaolin; and a technique using a binding agent called petuntse to create extremely hard, dense, and waterproof ceramics. At some point in the late thirteenth or early fourteenth century, potters began to exploit the pure white of the clay, producing the blue-and-white ceramics still associated with Chinese porcelain to this day (see page 127).

The beauty and durability of Chinese blue-and-white wares made them precious objects in the West, creating a market for their import as well as their imitation. By the end of the fifteenth century, potters at Iznik (in modern-day Turkey) were producing very elaborate blue-and-white wares, and in the late 1500s, Francesco I de'Medici, the grand duke of Tuscany, oversaw a state-funded attempt to unveil the secret of Chinese porcelain. In both Iznik and Florence, potters recognized that there was something fundamentally different about Chinese ceramics, but despite much experimentation with materials and kilns, the secret remained hidden.

Attempts to reproduce Chinese wares in Europe continued throughout the seventeenth century. It was not until the beginning of the eighteenth century that two German alchemists hit upon the formula. Sponsored by Augustus II, elector of Saxony and King of Poland (an obsessive collector of Asian porcelain), their success came from the slow process of testing different binding agents and building better kilns, but also from the lucky discovery of a deposit of kaolin. The first European porcelain factory opened at Meissen in 1710, producing wares with appropriately Asian forms and motifs.

The irony is that, in the end, it was "soft-paste"—the not-quite porcelain of the early experiments—that gained prominence in Europe. "Soft-paste" is more flexible and easier to work than "hard-paste" porcelain; this malleability encouraged the flights of fancy seen throughout the Museum's collection of eighteenth- and nineteenth-century ceramics (see pages 226 and 301).

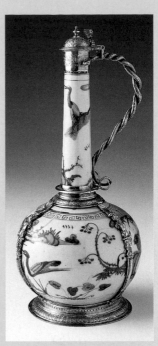

Flagon
England (probably London)
Silver-gilt mounts: England, about 1600
Porcelain with underglaze blue decoration: China, Ming Dynasty, 1573-1619
Height: 13⅛ (34.5 cm)
Theodora Wilbour Fund in memory of Charlotte Beebe Wilbour 67.601

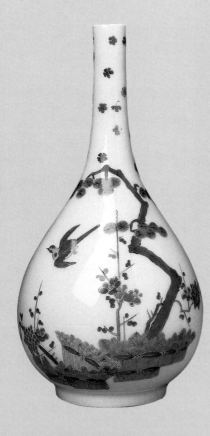

Bottle
Germany (Meissen), about 1730
Made at the **Meissen Factory**
Hard-paste porcelain
Height: 8⅛ (20.5 cm)
Gift of Rita and Fritz Markus
1993.231

Buddha of Medicine
Korea, Unified Silla dynasty,
about 8th century A.D.
Gilt bronze
Height: 14⅛ in. (36 cm)
Gift of Edward J. Holmes in
memory of his Mother,
Mrs. W. Scott Fitz 32.436

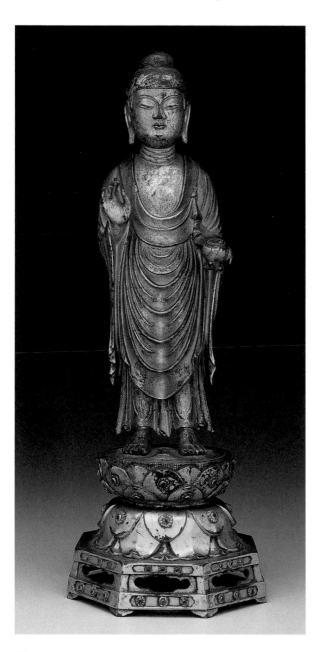

The Chinese monks who first brought Buddhism to Korea provided medical care as well, and the Buddha of Healing has always been popular there. Known as *Yaksa yorae,* he is identified by the medicine jar in his hand. This small figure of the deity may originally have been placed in a household shrine or it may have been displayed with similar statues at a temple. It is closely related to a group of more than fifty gilt bronzes once placed on the branches of an ancient elm tree in a temple in the Diamond Mountains of North Korea. A masterpiece of Korean Buddhist sculpture, it reflects the influence of Tang-dynasty China, although the rather heavy proportions, large head and hands, and octagonal base are all typically Korean.

Korea is well known in the West for its fine ceramics, particularly those with the subtle, grayish-green glaze known as celadon. This vase, with its sensuous shape and delicate design of cranes and other birds in bamboo bushes, is an early example of inlaid celadon, a technique perfected in the course of the twelfth century. No other *maebyong* of this same design is known.

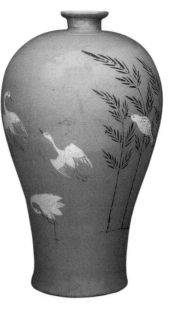

Vase (maebyong)
Korea, Koryo dynasty,
late 12th century
Glazed stoneware; inlaid
decoration
Height: 12¼ in. (31.1 cm)
Charles Bain Hoyt Collection
50.989

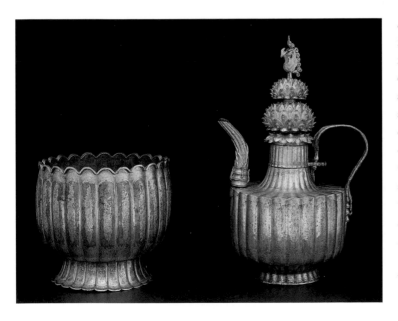

Ewer and basin
Korea, Koryo dynasty,
11th–12th centuries
Silver with parcel gilt and engraved
decoration
Height: 15 in. (38 cm)
George Nixon Black Fund 35.646

Although similar in form and decoration to ceramic examples, this sumptuous ewer and basin are made of silver partially covered with gold. Commissioned by a wealthy patron, they were used to serve wine or other liquids in a domestic setting; the ewer was placed inside the basin where hot water kept its contents at the desired temperature. Bamboo inspired the basic shape of both pieces as well as the handle and spout of the ewer. The cover to the ewer consists of three stylized lotuses surmounted by a phoenix—both auspicious symbols in Buddhist art.

133

Historically, mirrors have had special significance in Japan where, particularly in this early period, they were thought to possess magical properties and were associated with the power of the sun goddess. Mirrors with highly decorated backs, such as this one, were often buried with important officials as emblems of their authority. Here, in the broad band of decoration inside the raised rim, are symbols of the four points of the compass: the Tortoise and the Snake for the North, the Red Bird for the South, the Green Dragon for the East, and the White Tiger for the West.

Mirror
Japan, Tumuli period,
5th century A.D.
Bronze
Diameter: 9 1/4 in. (23.5 cm)
Gift by Special Contribution
08.160

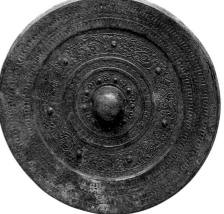

Shaka, the Historical Buddha Preaching on Vulture Peak
Japan, Nara period, 8th century A.D.
Panel; ink, color, and gold on hemp
42 1/8 x 56 1/2 in.
(107.1 x 143.5 cm)
William Sturgis Bigelow Collection
11.6120

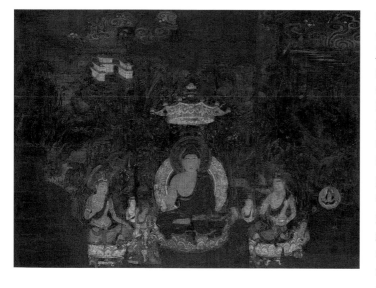

One of few surviving examples of eighth-century Japanese painting, this panel depicts the Historical Buddha surrounded by his disciples and bodhisattvas. He is preaching the *Lotus Sutra*, a highly influential text that promises salvation to both men and women. The painting has suffered greatly over time and was repaired as early as the twelfth century. Despite surface abrasion and other losses, craggy mountain peaks and deep ravines can be discerned in the background and swirling clouds representing mystical energy at the top. This painting was once installed in the Hokkedō (Lotus Hall) at the celebrated temple Tōdai-ji in Nara. In 1884, at a time when many Buddhist temples were selling their treasures because of financial hardship, it was acquired by Bostonian William Sturgis Bigelow.

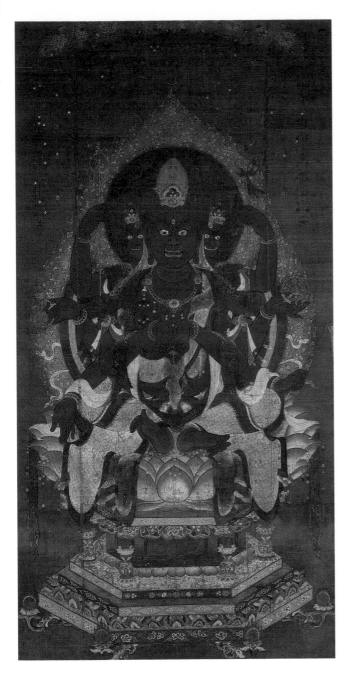

Batō Kannon, the Horse-Headed Bodhisattva of Compassion

Japan, Heian period, 12th century
Panel; ink, color, gold, and silver
on silk
65 3/8 × 32 1/2 in. (166.1 × 82.7 cm)
Fenollosa-Weld Collection
11.4035

Years of training were required to master the complicated tenets and rituals of the sect known as Esoteric Buddhism, and art was an important means of communicating the complexities of its theology and pantheon of deities. During the Heian period, the Esoteric Buddhist deity Batō Kannon, identified by the horse's head in his crown, was believed to look after those individuals reborn as animals. He was also revered as the protector of horses, cattle, and warriors. This painting was executed in the sumptuous style—featuring the lavish use of gold and silver (here darkened with age)—that dominated Japanese art during the twelfth century. Batō sits under a floral canopy festooned with strands of jewels. With some of his hands, the bodhisattva performs the ritual gestures, or *mudra*s, essential to Esoteric Buddhist practice; in others he holds symbolic objects.

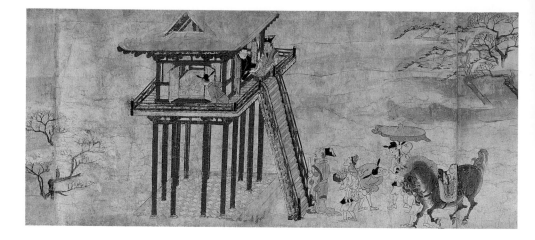

Minister Kibi's Adventures in China (detail)
Japan, Heian period,
late 12th century
One of a set of four handscrolls;
ink, color, and gold on paper
Entire scroll: 12⅝ × 961½ in.
(32.2 × 2442 cm)
William Sturgis Bigelow Collection,
by exchange 32.131

This celebrated handscroll depicts the legends that grew up around Kibi no Makibi, a Japanese courtier who served as ambassador to the imperial court of China in A.D. 753. In scene after scene, the scroll illustrates and describes Kibi's progress as he matches wits with Chinese bureaucrats determined to belittle his (and, by extension, Japan's) scholarly accomplishments. Locked into a haunted tower, Kibi impresses the resident ghost—that of the previous Japanese ambassador, Abe no Nakamaro—with his integrity and upright demeanor. Assisted by Abe, Kibi outwits the Chinese using magic, artifice, and his native cunning. Remarkable for its vigorous, often humorous, narrative style and its elegant calligraphy, this scroll was originally over eighty feet long; it has been divided into four sections to facilitate handling and ensure its preservation.

Buddhist scriptures give detailed accounts of eight main hells, each of which is subdivided into sixteen minor hells. Narrative handscrolls such as this one were frequently employed by priests in their efforts to encourage believers to lead virtuous lives. The scene shown here illustrates the hell known as "the place of the copper cauldron," where those who torment human beings or animals in life are boiled for eternity. The illustration vividly depicts the leaping flames and anguished sinners attended by a fearsome demon.

The Burning Cauldron, a >
section from The Hell Scrolls
Japan, Heian period, 12th century
Handscroll; ink and color on paper
10⅛ × 20½ in. (25.6 × 52 cm)
William Sturgis Bigelow Collection
11.6254

Kaikei
Japanese, active 1189–1223
Miroku, the Bodhisattva of the
Future, 1189
Kamakura period
Japanese cypress with gold and
inlaid crystal; split-and-joined
construction
Height: 42 in. (106.6 cm)
Special Chinese and Japanese
Fund 20.723

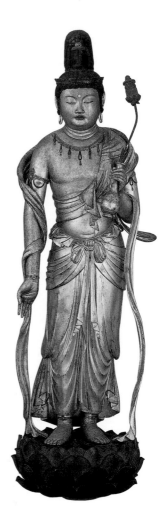

At the end of the twelfth century in Japan, the military
class ascended to power in a series of bloody civil wars.
During the rebuilding of temples destroyed in the conflict, the Kei school—of which Kaikei was a founder—
produced most of the major sculptural commissions,
creating a new, naturalistic style that dominated Japanese
sculpture for over five hundred years. In this extraordinary carved and gilded image (Kaikei's earliest dated
work), emerging naturalism is evident in the proportions
of the body, the fall of the drapery, and the use of inlaid
crystal for the eyes. The figure represents Miroku, the
Bodhisattva of the Future, who will become the next
Buddha. A scroll found inside the sculpture explains that
it was made in 1189 for the repose of Kaikei's deceased
parents and teacher.

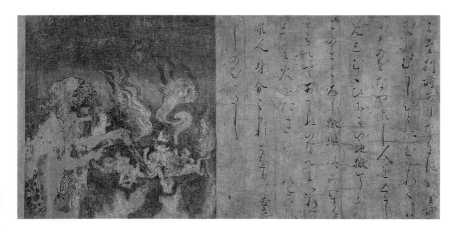

Bishamonten, the Guardian of the North
Japan, Kamakura period,
12th–early 13th centuries
Panel; ink, color, gold, and silver on silk
46⅞ × 26⅞ in. (119.1 × 68.1cm)
Special Chinese and Japanese Fund
05.202

Possibly because he is guardian of the North, the traditional source of malevolent forces, Bishamonten is the only one of the four celestial guardians of the cardinal directions who is worshiped as an independent Buddhist deity. In this highly dramatic painting, tall flames rise behind the head of Bishamonten, who wears armor embellished with the heads of demons and wields a silver-edged sword. The painting is remarkable for its vivid details and for the range of supernatural beings who surround the deity, including (to his right) his voluptuous consort Kichijōten, the Goddess of Good Fortune.

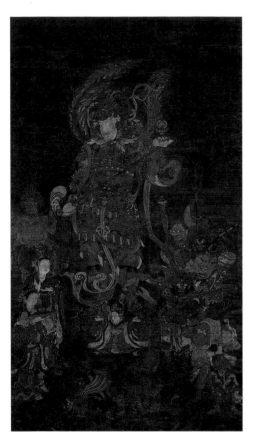

Saichi
Japanese, dates unknown
Shō Kannon, the Bodhisattva of Compassion, 1269
Kamakura period
Gilt bronze; cast from piece molds
Height: 41⅞ in. (106.5 cm)
William Sturgis Bigelow
Collection 11.11447

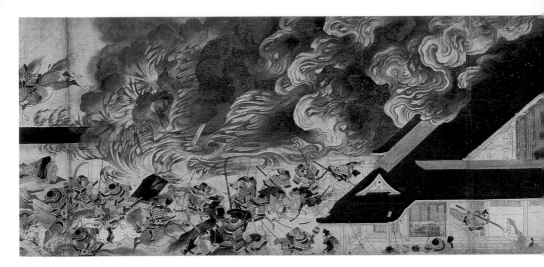

Night Attack on the
Sanjō Palace (detail)
Japan, Kamakura period, second
half of the 13th century
Handscroll; ink and color on paper
Entire scroll: 16 1/4 × 275 1/2 in.
(41.3 × 699.7 cm)
Fenollosa-Weld Collection
11.4000

The bloody civil war between the Taira and Minamoto clans in the twelfth century was a perennial source of inspiration for later artists. The earliest surviving images are three scrolls and some isolated fragments known as *The Illustrated Handscrolls of the Events of the Heiji Era*. First in the series, this scroll powerfully recreates the Minamoto's attack of 1159 on the Sanjō Palace, from which they abducted the influential retired emperor, Goshirakawa. The brilliant flames of the burning palace dominate the composition, swirling above crowds of combatants who are rendered in minute and brutal detail. Several artists were probably involved in the production of these paintings, but none of their names is known.

The white lotus symbolized purity throughout Asia because it perches above the water on its long stem as if growing miraculously out of the mud. Here, the Bodhisattva of Compassion is shown holding a lotus bud and seated on a lotus blossom throne that indicates his divinity. His distinctive halo is decorated with floral designs and eleven disks on which appear Sanskrit letters representing his name and that of the Cosmic Buddha. Cast in separable parts, this intricate sculpture is one of the finest surviving examples of thirteenth-century Japanese bronze work. It was originally enshrined in the main hall of Kongonrin-ji, a Buddhist temple west of Kyoto.

Sword blade with scabbard
Tempered steel blade: Japan, late
Kamakura period, early 14th century
Lacquered wood scabbard with gold,
silk, silver, *shakudō*, ray skin, and *suaka*:
Japan, Edo period, mid–19th century
Length of sword blade: 10¼ in.
(26.1 cm)
William Sturgis Bigelow Collection
11.11252

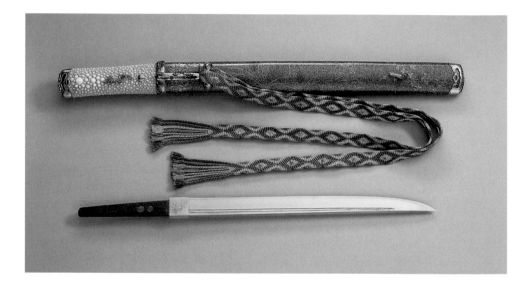

The sword possesses a unique spiritual and cultural significance
in Japan. For 1500 years it has been a part of the imperial
regalia and venerated as a symbol of the nation. The craftsmanship of Japanese sword blades marks them as among the finest
examples of metalworking in the world. The process was time-
consuming and labor-intensive, with the steel folded together
and hammered out countless times in the forging process to
remove impurities and ensure a high level of both strength and
sharpness. Eight months were often required to finish a single
blade. This sword blade, thick and without curvature, is of the
so-called armor-piercing type. It was made during the Kamakura period, when Japan was a feudal society ruled by warlords.
The sheath, crafted centuries later, is finished with gold lacquer
and a design of autumn grasses rendered in high relief.

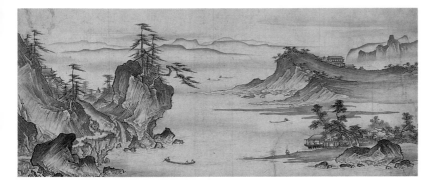

Shōkei, an artist-monk at a temple in Kamakura, was one of the most accomplished practitioners of the style of ink painting that flourished in and around that city in the late fifteenth century. Like that of Bunsei (see below), Shōkei's work reflects the admiration of Japanese artists of the Muromachi period for Chinese art and culture. This delicate and expansive landscape—rendered with precise, incisive line and soft, flowing washes—is essentially Chinese in character and in its use of the monochrome-ink technique.

Kenkō Shōkei
Japanese, active late 15th–early 16th centuries
Landscape
Muromachi period
Hanging scroll; ink on paper
15 3/8 × 36 in. (39.2 × 91.4 cm)
Fenollosa-Weld Collection
11.4127

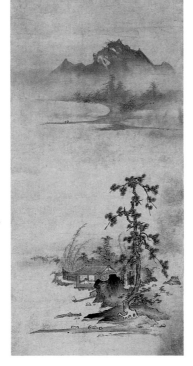

This depiction of a hermit's cottage nestling beneath a twisted pine tree is one of only two surviving landscapes by Bunsei, one of the early Zen Buddhist artist-monks whose explorations of the subtle, monochrome-ink technique of Chinese painting refined and expanded the tradition in Japan. Zen Buddhist temples were centers for the study and practice of Chinese art and learning in this period, and both the type of imaginary landscape here and the style in which it is painted are fundamentally Chinese.

Bunsei
Japanese, active mid–15th century
Landscape
Muromachi period
Hanging scroll; ink on paper
28 7/8 × 13 in. (73.2 × 33 cm)
Special Chinese and Japanese Fund   05.203

Kano Shōei
Japanese, 1519–1592
Birds and Flowers, 16th century
Muromachi period
Six-panel folding screen; ink and
light color on paper
59⅝ × 146½ in. (151.5 × 372 cm)
Fenollosa-Weld Collection
11.4347

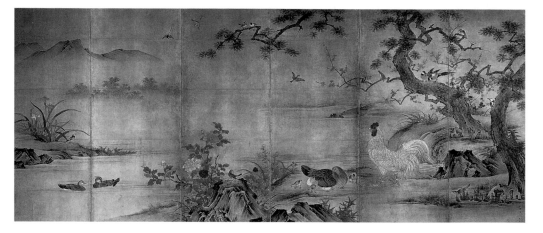

The delightful painted decoration of this folding screen places meticulously rendered birds and flowers within a soft, evocative landscape. The signature in the lower right corner is that of Kano Tanyō, who attributed this work to his great-grandfather, Kano Shōei, son of Kano Motonobu—one of the early leaders of the highly influential Kano school (see facing page). In this screen, Shōei achieved a synthesis of *kanga* (the subtle, mono-chrome ink painting of China) and *yamato-e* (the traditional bright and decorative painting of Japan). It is a style well suited to large-scale compositions such as screens and sliding doors and was popular into the modern period.

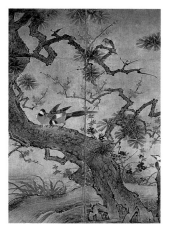

In lacquer work, the resin or sap of a lacquer tree is colored with pigments and applied over a wooden understructure in many thin layers—sometimes more than forty. The result of this painstaking process is a smooth, strong, and lustrous surface that was often inlaid with designs in precious metals. This shallow tray made to hold clothing combines bold designs and naturalistic detail. The tray is a particularly fine, large-scale example of Kōdai-ji ware, the most popular type of lacquerwork of the Momoyama period. The crests of paulownia flowers and chrysanthemums found throughout the tray's decoration associate it with the patronage of the clan of Toyotomi Hideyoshi, one of the three great warlords of Japan during this period.

Clothing tray
Japan, Momoyama period, end of the 16th century
Lacquer with gold, silver, and other metal inlays
20⁵/₈ × 22³/₈ × 2⁷/₈ in. (52.4 × 56.8 × 7.2 cm)
Keith McLeod Fund and Charles Bain Hoyt Fund 1998.58

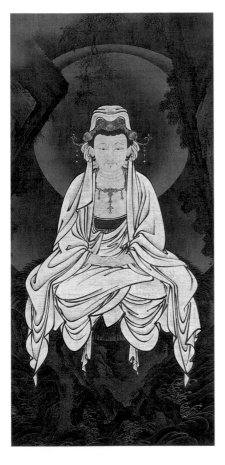

Kano Motonobu
Japanese, 1467–1559
Byaku-e Kannon, the White-Robed Bodhisattva of Compassion, 1500–50
Muromachi period
Hanging scroll; ink, color, and gold on silk
61⁷/₈ × 30¹/₈ in. (157.2 × 76.4 cm)
Fenollosa-Weld Collection 11.4267

This striking image represents one of the most revered Buddhist deities, the Bodhisattva of Compassion. The artist, Motonobu, was an early leader of the Kano school of painting favored by Japan's military rulers and the established, official style from the sixteenth to the nineteenth centuries. Kano school painting reflects the influence of Chinese art—seen here in the bold outlining of the bodhisattva's robe, the jagged contours of the rocks, and the stylized, decorative rendering of the waves below.

Hishikawa Moronobu
Japanese,1618–1694
Scenes from the Yoshiwara
Pleasure Quarter and the
Nakamura Kabuki Theater,
about 1675–85
Edo period
One of a pair of six-panel folding
screens; ink, color, and gold on paper
Each screen: 55 × 271 ½ in.
(139.8 × 689.6 cm)
Gift of Oliver W. Peabody 79.468-469

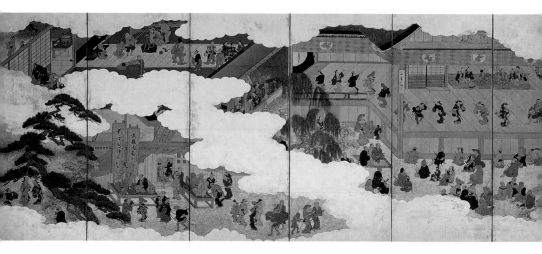

This screen is a vivid, early example of *ukiyo-e,* "images of the floating world." As a subject for art, the pleasures of the entertainment world became highly popular in the seventeenth century when members of the prosperous middle class increasingly frequented kabuki theaters as well as the brothels and teahouses of "pleasure quarters" such as the Yoshiwara in Edo (modern-day Tokyo). This screen shows three areas of the Nakamura-za, a famous kabuki theater. In the lower left, men and women of varied occupations and social levels walk along the street in front of the theater. Depicted above is a backstage area where actors and musicians prepare for a performance. The right half of the screen shows the stage and the area for the audience. On stage, costumed figures dance to the lively rhythms of the *shamisen* and drums.

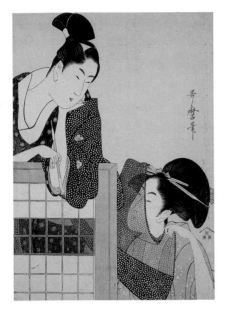

One of the most original and popular forms of *ukiyo-e* was the woodblock print—an art form that emphasized flowing outlines, simplified forms, and the patterning of flat areas of color. Among *ukiyo-e* printmakers, Utamaro is most celebrated for his images of women who worked in the brothels and tea houses of the urban pleasure quarters. His imaginative compositions, such as this one, feature idealized figures who are given character and individuality through pose, gesture, and dress. In their time, *ukiyo-e* prints were inexpensive, produced in great numbers, and collected by members of the middle class whose lives and interests they depict.

Kitagawa Utamaro
Japanese, 1753–1806
Lovers, about 1797
Edo period
Published by **Moriya Jihei**
Color woodblock print
14½ × 10¼ in.
(37.2 × 26 cm)
Gift of Captain John C. Phillips
18.308

Summer robe (*katabira*)
Japan, Edo period, 18th century
Ramie, silk, and gilt paper; plain weave with resist and stencil dyeing, hand-painting, and embroidery
Height: 64 in. (162.4 cm)
William Sturgis Bigelow Collection
21.1134

Japanese woodblock prints profoundly influenced European and American artists of the nineteenth century (see pages 263, 266, 274, and 334).

Unlined robes made from hemp or ramie (an Asian plant fiber) were worn during the summer by upper-class Japanese women. The designs of these luxurious garments often include water motifs appropriate for times of oppressive heat, and the lower section of this robe shows aristocrats enjoying themselves on pleasure boats. The robe was decorated using a technique in which the artist outlined each part of the design with rice paste to prevent bleeding of the dyes. The dyes were applied with a brush and the rice paste washed away when the colors were set. The plum blossoms and bamboo in the upper section of this *katabira* were made by this same method and further embellished with embroidery in colored threads and gold paper.

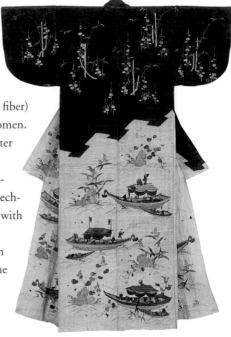

Soga Shōhaku
Japanese, 1730–1781
The Four Sages of Mount Shang
Edo period
One of a pair of six-panel folding screens; ink and gold on paper
Each screen: 61 ½ × 144 ⅜ in.
(156.2 × 366.6 cm)
Fenollosa-Weld Collection
11.4513–4514

Shōhaku's career coincided with a remarkable period of artistic innovation in Japanese art, when eccentricity and originality of vision enhanced rather than hindered a painter's reputation. An individualist in both his life and his art, Shōhaku worked almost exclusively in monochrome ink, painting in a spontaneous, expressionistic style. The energy and dexterity of his swift, broad brushwork are nowhere more fully realized than in this late work, one of a pair of screens illustrating a popular subject from Chinese legend. The Four Sages were elderly paragons of virtue who retreated to Mount Shang during the political unrest of the third century B.C., remaining there until they felt that moral rectitude had returned to the world of human affairs.

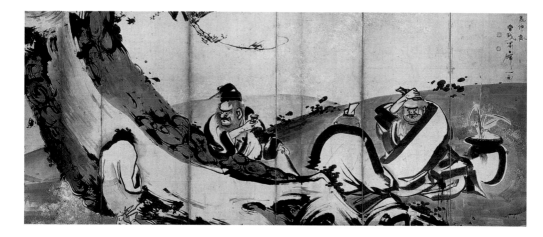

Ito Jakuchū
Japanese, 1716–1800
White Cockatoo on a Pine Branch
Edo period
15 ¾ × 21 ⅞ in. (40.1 × 55.6 cm)
Hanging scroll; ink and color on silk
Charles Bain Hoyt Collection
50.1493

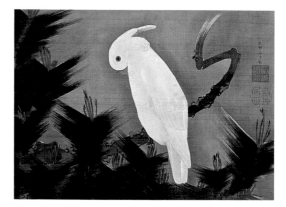

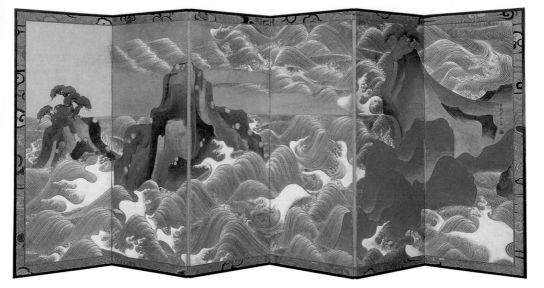

Ogata Kōrin
Japanese, 1658–1716
Waves at Matsushima
Edo period
Six-panel folding screen; ink, color,
and gold on paper
59 ⅛ × 144 ⅘ in.
(150.2 × 367.8 cm)
Fenollosa-Weld Collection
11.4584

Kōrin is the painter whose work has come to epitomize the Rimpa school of painting, a splendidly decorative art form that is considered uniquely Japanese, untouched by the influences from China that inform so much Japanese art. Characterized by the lavish use of vibrant color and gold, Rimpa school painting emerged during the Edo period and flourished for some 250 years. The subject of this screen is Matsushima, a group of hundreds of rugged, pine-clad islands in northeastern Japan that have long been regarded as one of the country's most scenic locations. Kōrin's daring and brilliant sense of design is evident in the flat, abstracted shapes of the islands and the stylized, linear patterns of the foaming waves from which they rise.

< Like his contemporary Shōhaku, Jakuchū was one of the celebrated "eccentric" painters of the Edo period whose success reflects the diminishing dominance of official styles of art at this time. Of humble origins and primarily self-taught, Jakuchū began by copying Chinese paintings preserved in the temples of Kyoto but soon found his inspiration in *shaseiga*, or painting from nature. It is said that the artist raised birds himself in order to study more closely their appearance and behavior and to sketch them from life.

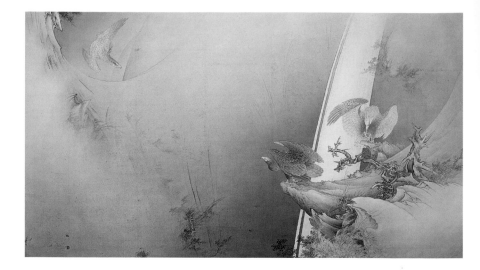

Kano Hōgai
Japanese, 1828–1888
Eagles in a Ravine
Meiji period
Hanging scroll; ink and color on paper
36½ × 65⅛ in. (92.8 × 165.5 cm)
William Sturgis Bigelow Collection
11.8740

Hōgai was first trained in the traditional, academic Kano school of painting (see page 143), but his work was considered anachronistic by the Meiji government determined to industrialize and westernize Japan. In the early 1880s, however, his paintings caught the attention of Ernest Fenollosa, an American teaching in Japan who later became the Museum's first curator of Japanese art. Encouraged by Fenollosa, Hōgai began incorporating elements of western art into his work and thus became a key figure in the transformation of Japanese painting. Hōgai retained Kano-school subject matter and technique while incorporating western-style shadows and highlights to create an illusion of volumetric form in the eagles, rocks, and branches at right. This synthesis of elements established the foundations of the modern school of Japanese painting known as Nihonga.

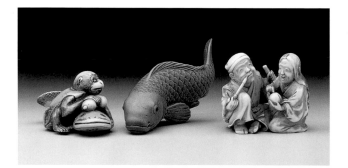

Netsuke
Japan, Edo period,
late 18th–early 19th centuries
Wood; ivory
Heights: about 1⅜ in. (3.4 cm)
Gift of Dr. Ernest G. Stillman
47.911; William Sturgis Bigelow
Collection 11.23343, 11.2359

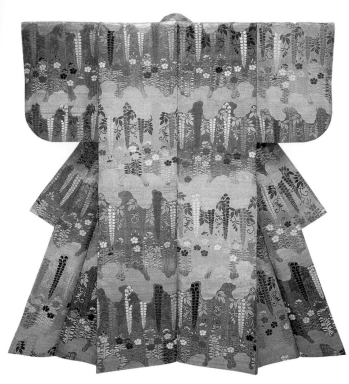

**Robe for the Nō theater
(karaori)**
Japan, Edo period,
late 18th–early 19th centuries
Silk and gilt paper; twill weave with
pattern-dyed warps and
supplementary pattern wefts
Height: 57⅞ in. (147 cm)
William Sturgis Bigelow Collection
15.1148

Silk robes woven with sumptuous floral motifs are worn by actors in the highly stylized performances of the Nō theater, which integrate speech, music, dancing, and mime. Performing on a spare stage with minimal props, the actors (who are all men) depend upon their robes and wooden masks to communicate their characters to the audience. The red color of this robe indicates that the character portrayed was a young woman. Although seen from a considerable distance by the audience (which in the Edo period was often members of the military elite), *karaori* are extremely elegant and sophisticated in materials, design, and craft.

Netsuke were used during the Edo period (1615–1868) as counterweights to secure tobacco cases, purses, and small lacquer medicine containers *(inrō)* that were suspended from the wide kimono sashes of Japan's fashionable men. At a time when the country's military rulers dictated plain, dark kimonos for men, these accessories and their netsuke permitted some expression of individual style. Netsuke were usually carved from ivory or boxwood and were generally compact in form and made to be seen from all sides. The finest are miniature masterpieces of carving and represent subjects ranging from scenes of daily life to religious and legendary figures; insects, birds, and fish are also popular subjects. Netsuke passed out of style in the late nineteenth century when Japanese men adopted Western dress, with pockets.

The Islamic World

Islam, one of the world's major religions, began along the western coast of the Arabian Peninsula in the early seventh century A.D. when a merchant named Muhammad, from the city of Mecca, received a series of divine revelations. Followers of Islam, known as Muslims, believe these revelations to be the literal word of God; together they constitute the Koran, the holy book of Islam. Through a combination of conquest and conversion, Islam quickly became the dominant religion of a huge area stretching from southern Spain to central Asia. "Islamic art" refers to the artistic output of geographic areas where Islam is the primary religion. It is sometimes but not always related to the religious practice of Islam.

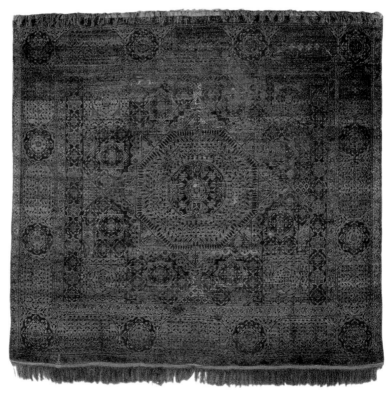

Mamluk carpet
Egypt (probably Cairo),
mid-16th century
Wool warp, weft, and pile
100 × 110 in. (254 × 279 cm)
Helen and Alice Colburn Fund
and Harriet Otis Cruft Fund
61.939

Carpets made in Egypt during the fifteenth and sixteenth centuries are unusual in their mosaic-like designs and limited palette. This carpet employs only red, green, and blue, but the weaver subtly manipulated these colors to achieve a shimmering, kaleidoscopic effect. Named for the dynasty that ruled Egypt and Syria from 1250 to 1517, Mamluk carpets were frequently exported to Europe, where they were placed on floors, draped over balconies, or used to cover tables.

Ewer
Iran, 13th century
Beaten brass inlaid with silver;
applied silver repoussé details
Height: 18 7/8 in. (47.8 cm)
Holmes Collection 49.1901

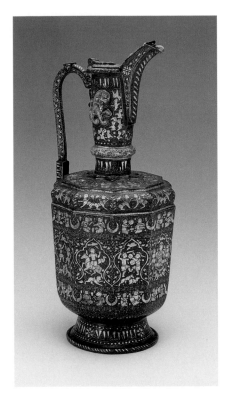

The objects produced by metalworkers in the Islamic world often have highly original shapes and intricate designs. Rendered in silver inlay on the body of this ewer are hunting scenes, musicians, banquets, gardens, and other aspects of courtly life set against a background of geometric patterns and foliate scrolls. Arabic inscriptions in several places wish good fortune to the ewer's owner. Two crouching lions on the neck were made in the repoussé technique—the artist hammered the inner surface of the silver, causing the forms to emerge in relief. The lions are amusing examples of small-scale relief sculpture, which is uncommon in Islamic art.

Bowl
Iran (Kashan), early 13th century
Composite body (quartz, clay, and glass frit) with black pigment under a translucent alkaline glaze
Diameter: 8 7/8 in. (22.5 cm)
Gift of the John Goelet
Foundation 65.231

The *karkaddan* depicted at the center of this bowl and identifiable by its single horn is among the many fabulous creatures in Islamic art. It is surrounded by large serpents whose scaly, entwined bodies give the design intricacy and strength. The bowl is painted in black under a translucent turquoise glaze and was probably produced in Kashan, a central Persian city famous for its medieval ceramic tiles and vessels.

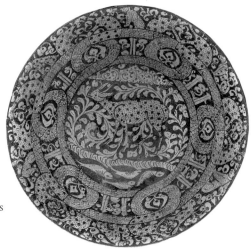

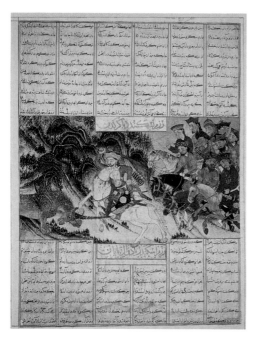

The *Shahnama* (Book of Kings) is the national epic of Persia (today's Iran) and the most frequently illustrated manuscript in Islamic art. A blend of myth and history numbering nearly sixty thousand rhymed couplets, the *Shahnama* was written by the poet Firdawsi over a period of thirty years at the turn of the eleventh century. This page shows a historical figure, Alexander the Great, slaying a fantastic, mythological beast. The mountains in the background, rendered in a distinctly Chinese manner, are typical of Eastern stylistic elements often found in fourteenth-century Persian manuscript painting. This superb page was part of a royal commission known as the "Great Mongol Shahnama"—one of the earliest surviving illustrated versions of the epic poem.

Alexander Fights the Monster of Habash
Page from a manuscript of the
Shahnama
Iran (Tabriz), Mongol period,
before 1335
Opaque watercolor, gold, and ink
on paper
23¼ × 15⅝ in. (59 × 39.6 cm)
Denman Waldo Ross Collection
30.105

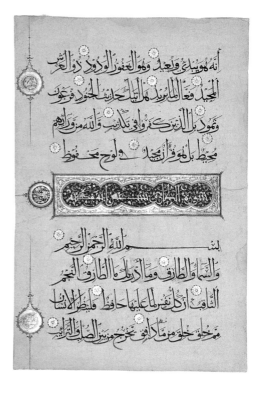

Page from the Koran
Egypt, Mamluk dynasty, about 1400
Ink, gold, and color on paper
29¾ × 19¾ in. (75.5 × 50.2 cm)
Denman Waldo Ross Collection
09.335

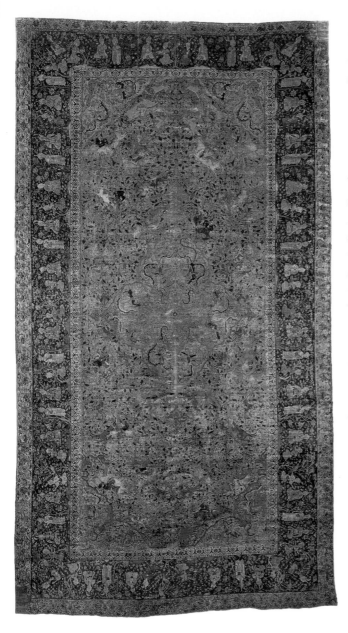

Hunting carpet
Iran, 1525–50
Silk warp, weft, and pile; silver and gilt-silver wrapped silk brocading
189 × 100¾ in.
(480.1 × 255.9 cm)
Centennial Fund, gift of John Goelet, and unrestricted textile purchase funds 66.293

This silk carpet is remarkable for its masterful design, luxurious materials, and impressive craftsmanship (more than eight hundred knots per square inch). It was woven in the royal workshops of Shah Tahmasp I, ruler of Persia from 1524 to 1576, and is filled with astonishing detail—dragons and phoenixes battling in the central medallion and corners, well-dressed courtiers picnicking in the borders, and mounted hunters in the field using a variety of weapons to bring down lions, antelopes, deer, and hares.

< Because Muslims believe that the Koran is the literal word of God, copying the text of the holy book is an act of intense religious devotion, and calligraphy is widely considered the most important of the Islamic visual arts. This page, part of a large Koran that was probably used in a mosque, is embellished with gold and luxurious colors. The main text is written in an Arabic script known as *muhaqqaq* (meticulously produced). Within each chapter, verses are separated by gold rosettes, and medallions in the margin mark every fifth verse. The horizontal band in the center contains a chapter heading written in an attenuated form of an older Arabic script called Kufic.

Woman's coat *(munisak)*
Uzbekistan (Bukhara region),
1850–1900
Silk; cut-velvet ikat; resist-dyed pile
warp
Height: 46½ in. (118 cm)
Gift in memory of Jay Abrams
58.342

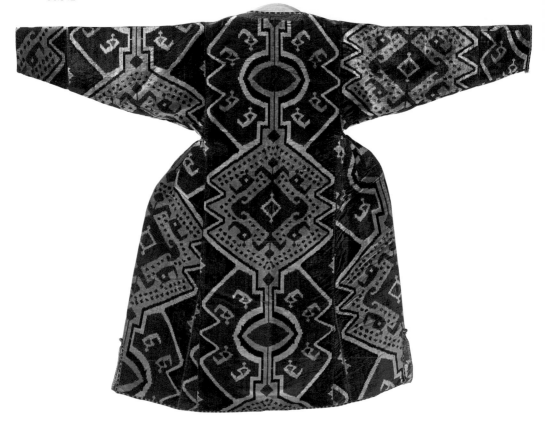

The laborious process of ikat—the repeated tying and dyeing of the threads of a cloth before weaving—has long been practiced in many parts of the world (see pages 106 and 112). The ikat textiles created in Central Asia during the nineteenth century, however, are unrivaled in their vibrant colors and explosive patterns. In such isolated desert cities as Bukhara and Samarkand (in today's Uzbekistan), sumptuous ikat wall hangings and robes brought vibrant color to life in a stark, barren landscape. Both men and women wore ikat clothing; the *munisak*, a woman's coat characterized by extra fullness at the hips, was the most costly item of a bride's dowry.

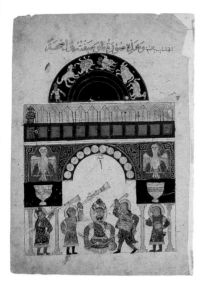

Written in 1206 by the engineer Ibn al-Razzaz al-Jazari, *The Book of Knowledge of Mechanical Devices* detailed the construction of elaborate mechanical devices ranging from clocks and locks to automated vessels for washing hands. This design for a clock is from a manuscript of al-Jazari's text created in 1354 for an official serving the Mamluk sultan of Egypt. Run by water, the clock is operated with a complex system of reservoirs, floats, and pulleys. Every hour of the day, a figure emerges from one of the twelve doorways in the arcade below the signs of the zodiac, and the two falcons on the sides come out and drop balls from their beaks. Hourly during the night, one of the twelve circles in the lower arch lights up. At the sixth, ninth, and twelfth hours, the musicians play their instruments.

Design for a water clock
Egypt (probably Cairo), Mamluk
period, 1354
Opaque watercolor, gold, and ink
on paper
15½ × 10⅞ in. (39.5 × 27.5 cm)
Francis Bartlett Donation of 1912
and Picture Fund 14.533

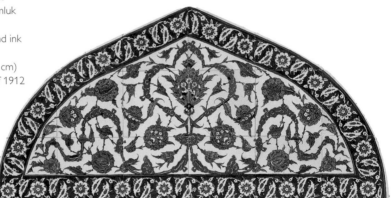

Modern-day Turkey was once the core of the Ottoman Empire that dominated large areas of the Middle East, North Africa, and southern Europe in the sixteenth century. The city of Iznik in northwestern Turkey was a center for the production of ceramic tiles used to decorate many buildings, including mosques and palaces. This panel was probably placed above a window or doorway in the palace complex at Istanbul of Piyale Pasha, grand admiral of the Ottoman fleet. Iznik ceramic artists frequently adopted designs from illuminated manuscripts and textiles. Here, the artist employed a vocabulary of Chinese-inspired plant forms known as the *saz* (enchanted forest) style, as well as Chinese cloud bands rendered in a distinctly Turkish iron-oxide red.

Tile panel
Turkey (Iznik), Ottoman period,
about 1573
Composite body (quartz, clay, and
glass frit) with colors painted on
white slip under clear glaze
Width: 57⅛ in. (145.1 cm)
Bequest of Mrs. Martin Brimmer
06.2437

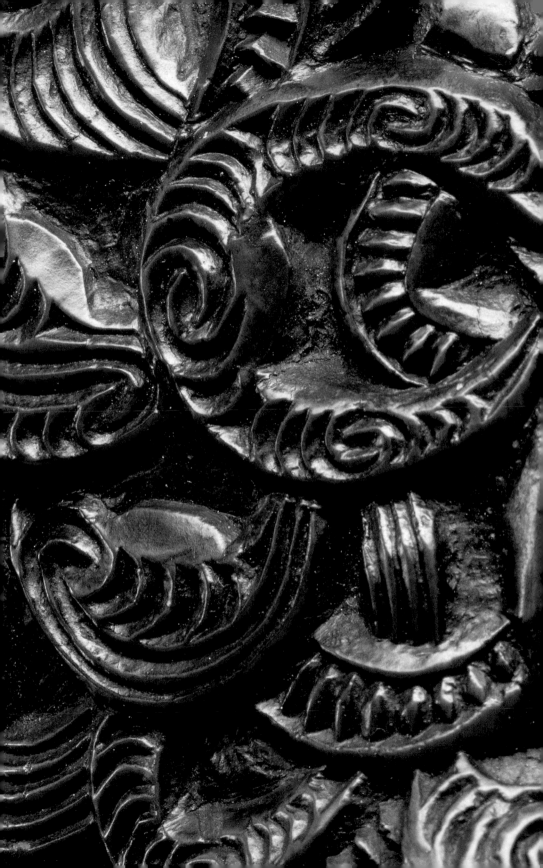

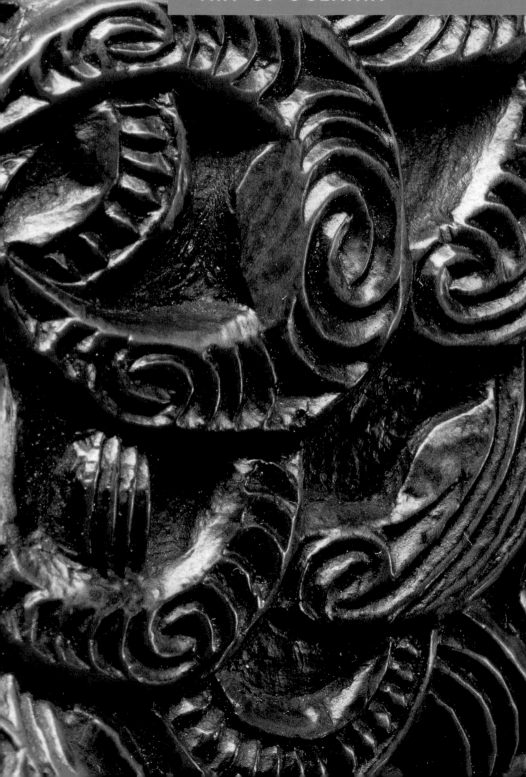

Oceania is the collective name for the thousands of Pacific islands stretching as far as New Zealand that make up Polynesia, Melanesia, and Micronesia. There, a wide range of cultures developed in almost total isolation from the rest of the world. Contact with Europeans in the late eighteenth century began the disruption of island cultures, and by the mid-1940s, most of the rituals for which these pieces were created no longer took place. Now, true ceremonial art is made in only a few remote areas.

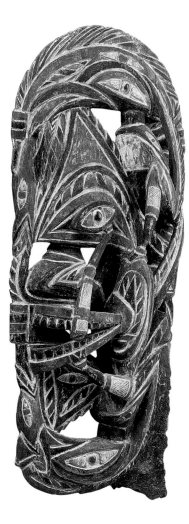

Canoe ornament
New Ireland, 19th–20th centuries
Wood, pigment
Height: 21 ½ in. (54.6 cm)
Gift of William E. and Bertha L.
Teel 1991.1073

Melanesian art is represented here by objects from just two of its many thousands of islands—New Guinea and New Ireland. However, all the myriad cultures of Melanesia shared a belief that spirit forces permeated their environment. As a result, everything from ritual objects to weapons and musical instruments were shaped and decorated to capture spiritual essence and presence. The results are highly individual and dramatic.

The richly painted wooden sculptures of New Ireland are distinguished by openwork designs that weave together representations of humans, plants, and animals. The powerfully three-dimensional form of this sculpture—created to ornament either the prow or the stern of a canoe—includes a human face, birds, feathers, and flying fish that all relate to the ancestral myths of the canoe's owner. Some hidden figures are discovered by the glint of their eyes inlaid with shell.

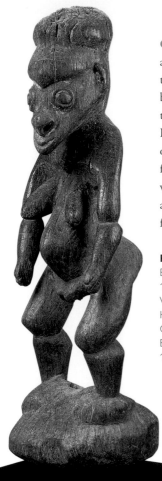

Central to the religions of Melanesia was a deep reverence for ancestors, who were believed to be more intimately connected to their descendants than any deities. Carved human images both honored ancestor spirits and served as physical hosts that they might temporarily inhabit. The ancestor figures of the Biwat people are particularly forceful, even potentially dangerous, with their characteristic hunched postures and thrusting forms. Small ones, like this, were privately owned, but they were believed to benefit both the families that possessed them and the community at large. Unfortunately, the names of the figures and their stories seldom have survived.

Female figure
Biwat people, Papua New Guinea
19th–20th centuries
Wood
Height: 20 in. (50.8 cm)
Gift of William E. and
Bertha L. Teel
1991.1079

Feeding funnel (koropata)
Maori people, New Zealand
19th–20th centuries
Wood
Height: 6½ in. (16.5 cm)
Gift of William E. and Bertha L. Teel
1991.1071

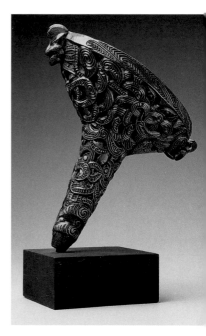

The tattoo was a mark of prestige and achievement among the Maori of New Zealand, where both men and women practiced the art of tattooing and were tattooed themselves. The practice was regulated by *tapu*—traditional rules that governed many aspects of human behavior. When the face and lips of a chief were tattooed, *tapu* forbade cooked food to touch any part of his skin. The chief was fed during this long and painful process by liquid food preferred through a wooden funnel that was both a functional object and a work of art. This example is typical of Maori workmanship in that it is completely covered with fine relief carving and then finished to bring out the intricacy of the design and the natural beauty of the wood.

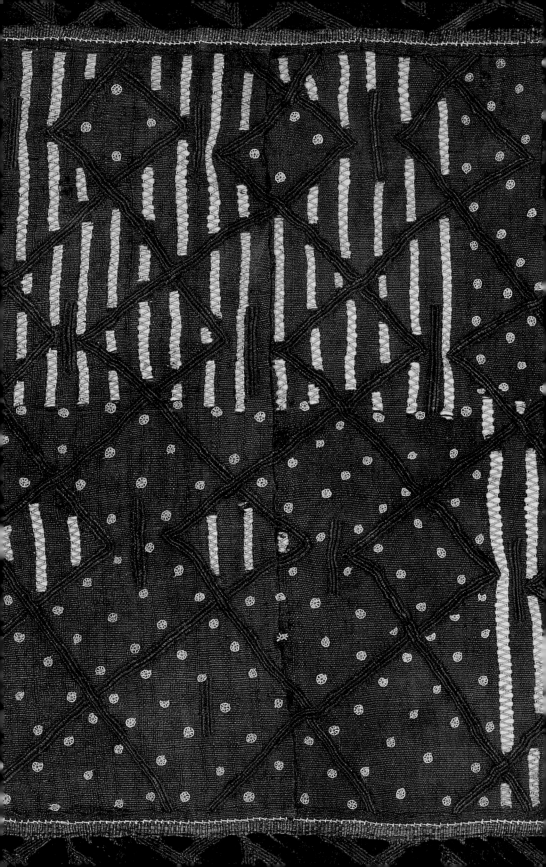

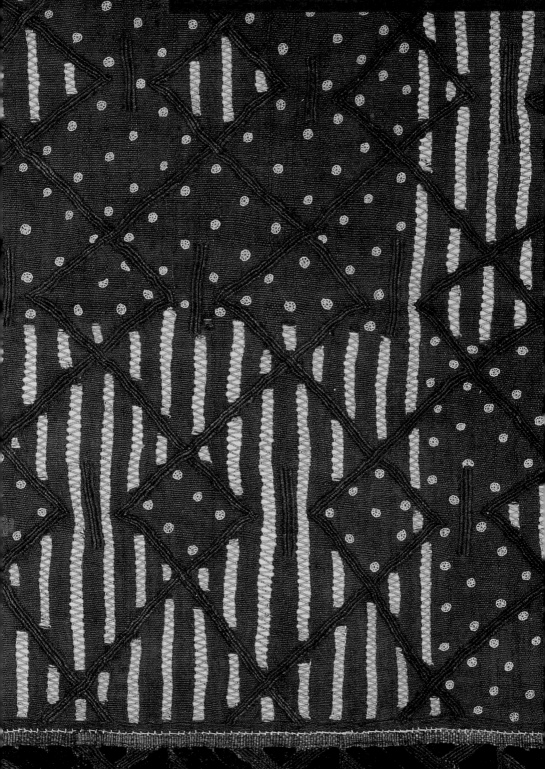

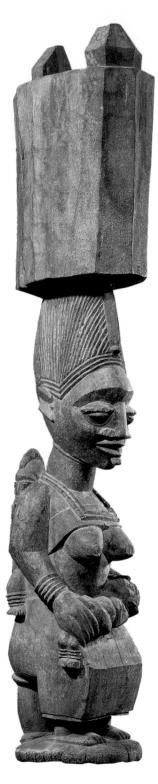

Agbonbiofe Adeshina
Nigerian, died 1945
Veranda post (opo)
Nigeria (Efon-Alaiye), early 20th
century
Wood and pigment
Height: 58 in. (147.3 cm)
Gift of William E. and Bertha L. Teel
1994.425

Carved veranda posts, representing figures that uphold the power of rulers, support the roofs around the interior court-yards of Yoruba palaces. This seated woman clasps a child; another is strapped to her back. She embodies dignity and authority and epitomizes the forces of creation and sustenance of life. The sculpture was made by a member of the Adeshina family, eminent carvers and beadworkers who worked in Efon-Alaiye, a Yoruba town in southwestern Nigeria. In 1912 a fire swept through the palace of Efon-Alaiye, and Agbonbiofe Adeshina carved twenty or more new veranda posts for its courtyards. Typical of Adeshina's sculpture, the decorative details of hair and jewelry are subdued and contained so that nothing detracts from the strength of the essential form.

Among the Igbo people, maskmakers are known >
as *ndi n'atu isi mmuo* (people who carve head spirits). As part of an intricate costume used in a ritual drama that often includes music and dance, masks represent powerful spirits. During the summer dry season, there are festivals, or mas-querades, to thank ancestors and deities for the successes of the agricultural year and to ensure their support in the future. The masquerade called *ogbodo enyi* (spirit elephant) is intended to cleanse and purify the village. In it, the performer wears this mask on top of his head; dressed in a knotted raffia costume, he moves energetically through the village—sometimes for up to six hours. The *ogbodo enyi* headdress does not specifi-cally represent an elephant but captures that crea-ture's strength and endurance.

Male figure (ikenga)
Igbo people, Nigeria, 19th–20th
centuries
Wood and pigment
Height: 43 in. (109.2 cm)
Gift of William E. and Bertha L. Teel
1994.421

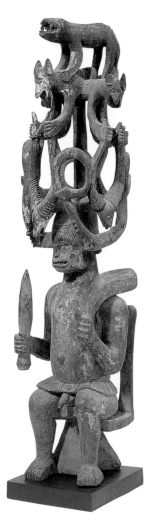

By the time an Igbo man reaches adulthood, he has usually acquired an *ikenga* figure, a symbol of masculine power and an expression of its owner's will to succeed. The *ikenga* is understood as a spirit being. The owner may "feed" it with kola nuts and wine, and he may offer it the sacrificial blood of an animal to request the ability to achieve his goals. When its owner dies, the *ikenga*'s work is over; it may be discarded or kept as a memorial by the family. Some *ikenga* are simple and abstract; others—like this example—are large and complex, their artistry indicative of wealth and social position. The facial scarification is also a mark of status, as is the prominent penis that reflects the importance of continuity through procreation.

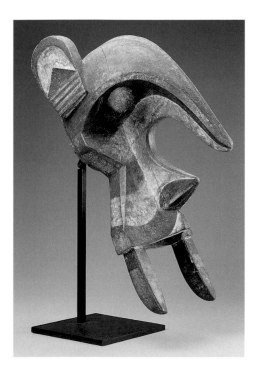

Headdress (ogbodo enyi)
Igbo people, Nigeria, 19th–20th
centuries
Wood and pigment
Height: 20½ in. (52.1 cm)
Gift of William E. and Bertha L. Teel
1992.419

163

Mask (deangle)
Dan people, Côte d'Ivoire,
19th–20th centuries
Wood, vegetable fiber, shell
Height: 16½ in. (11.9 cm)
Gift of William E. and Bertha L. Teel
1994.420

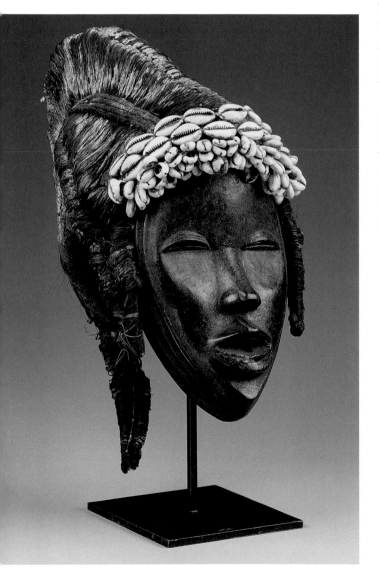

Among the Dan and other peoples of the Côte d'Ivoire, the Poro and Sande societies initiate young boys and girls into adulthood and teach them to become productive members of the community. Like the Senufo bird sculpture on the facing page, this mask was used in a ceremony of the masculine Poro society. The *deangle* represents a beautiful and gentle female spirit; the masker who wears it collects food from onlookers at dance performances and distributes it to boys of the society. Many wooden Dan masks were enhanced with materials such as feathers and shells, and this example has survived with its cowrie shells and vegetable-fiber hair intact.

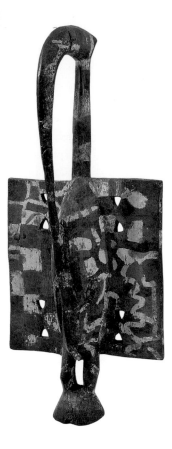

Standing bird figure (gahriga)
Senufo people, Côte d'Ivoire,
19th–20th centuries
Wood and pigment
Height: 63 in. (160 cm)
Gift of William E. and Bertha L.
Teel 1994.415

This large bird probably represents a hornbill, believed by the Senufo people to be one of the five original creatures of the earth. Thus, the figure is sometimes called "the first ancestor," its long beak and projecting belly symbolizing conception, pregnancy, and the continuity of the community. Such sculptures were used during initiation ceremonies of the secret Poro society that guides the religious and social education of boys. The base of the figure is hollow so that it could be carried on the head; cords were passed through the holes in the wings to help maintain its balance.

Power figure (nkonde)
Kongo people, Democratic
Republic of Congo, 19th–20th
centuries
Wood, pigment, metal, mirror,
sacred material
Height: 24 in. (61 cm)
Gift of William E. and Bertha L.
Teel 1991.1064

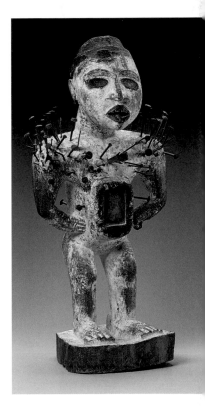

The spirits represented by these Kongo sculptures are believed to punish those who steal, swear false oaths, break treaties, cause illness, and otherwise threaten the social fabric of the community. Petitioners drove nails and blades into this figure to arouse the spirit to solve disputes and harm wrongdoers. Most *nkonde* are male, although female and animal figures exist. Every detail is significant: the pierced ears, for example, indicate attentiveness to all problems, and the placement of hands on hips signifies alertness and vigilance. The source of the *nkonde*'s power is a packet of medicinal substances (special earths and stones, vegetable materials, parts of birds and animals) that enable the image to attract the spirit. On this figure, the packet is located in the belly, behind the mirror, a symbol of mystic vision.

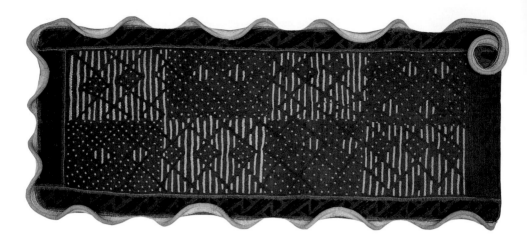

Woman's skirt (ntchak)
Kuba people, Democratic
Republic of Congo, first half of
the 20th century
Raffia and bundled reed;
embroidery on plain weave
26 ¾ x 58 ⅞ in. (68.7 x 151 cm)
Benjamin and Lucy Rowland Fund
1995.91

The Kuba people value textiles not only for their aesthetic
qualities but also as measures of rank and as prestigious political gifts; until the late nineteenth century, woven raffia cloth
also functioned as currency. This skirt, unique in its contrasting squares of positive and negative embroidered patterning,
was made for a woman of the royal Bushong group to wear on
festival and ceremonial occasions. Almost five feet long, it was
wrapped horizontally over an inner skirt that was coiled
around the wearer in a voluminous, many-layered spiral. The
skirt's wavy edging of twisted reeds undulated sensuously as the
dancer moved. Kuba men cultivate and harvest the raffia palm
and weave its fiber into squares of cloth; women hem the cloth,
pound it until soft, embroider it with dyed raffia thread, and
join the completed sections to make the skirt. The entire
process may take several years.

Lyres—on which each string sounds only one note—are among the most ancient musical
instruments. Until recently, they were the primary instruments used by East African singers
and storytellers to accompany songs that entertained and educated at wedding parties and other social events. The *ndongo* has an unusual buzzing tone, produced as the strings vibrate
against the rough, lizard skin that covers the wooden body. The tufts of goat hair that crown
the lyre are purely decorative.

Mask (kifwebe)
Songye people, Democratic
Republic of Congo, 19th–20th
centuries
Wood and pigment
Height: 20 in. (50.8 cm)
Gift of William E. and Bertha L. Teel
1992.409

The powerful and aggressive male masks of
the Songye people, their surfaces deeply
scored with grooves, are unparalleled in
African sculpture. The size of the crest is
an indication of the wearer's supernatural
strength, and the red paint is associated
with blood, flesh, and fire—a potent symbol of courage and achievement but also of
the malignant forces of witchcraft and sor-
cery. Like most masks, this one can be only
partly understood without the entire costume
that accompanied it: head covering, shirt, leg-
gings made of raffia fiber, and goat skins fastened
around the hips. The costume was worn at ceremonies designed to help leaders maintain economic
and political power, to prepare for war, and to judge and
punish wrongdoers.

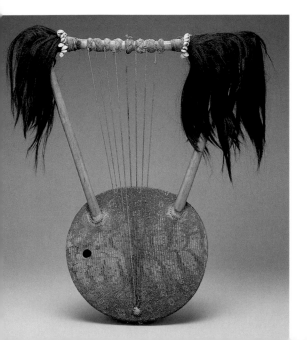

Bowl lyre (ndongo)
Ganda people, Uganda,
19th century
Wood, monitor lizard skin, goat
hair, cowrie shells, animal skin, and
twisted plant fiber
Height: 26 in. (66 cm)
Leslie Lindsey Mason Collection
17.2179

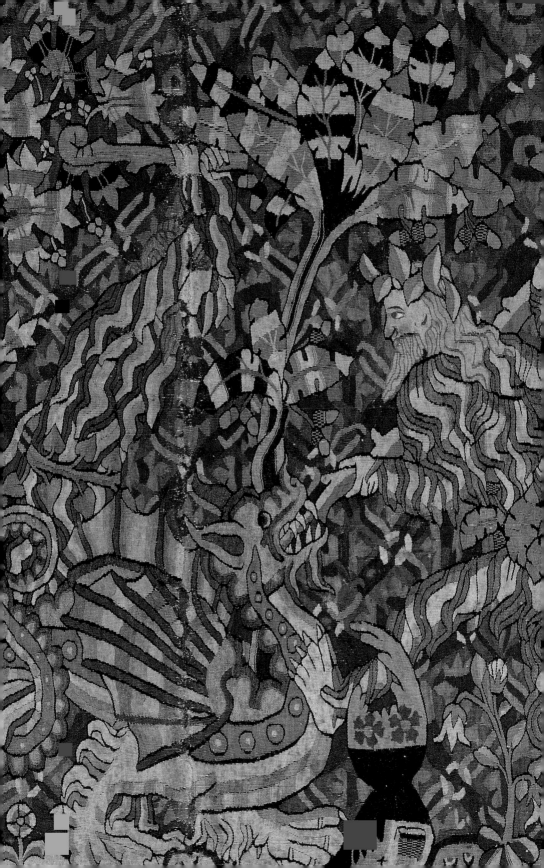

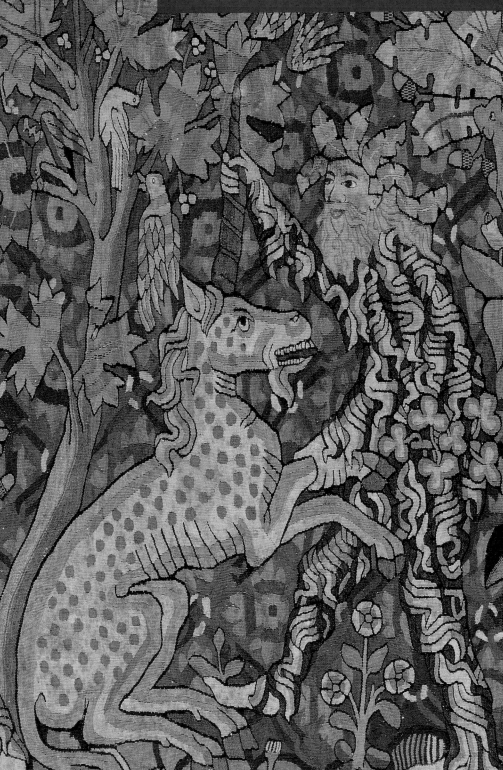

Reliquary (known as the
Emly Shrine)
Ireland, late 7th or early 8th
century A.D.
Champlevé enamel on bronze
over yew wood; gilt-bronze
moldings, inlay of lead-tin alloy
3 7/8 × 4 1/4 × 1 5/8 in.
(9.2 × 10.5 × 4.1 cm)
Theodora Wilbour Fund in
Memory of Charlotte Beebe
Wilbour 52.1396

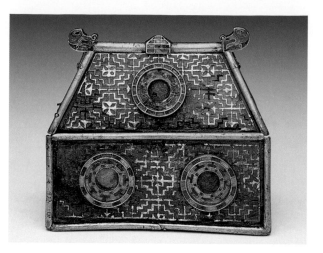

Made to hold the sacred relics of a saint (often parts of the saint's body), Irish house-shaped reliquaries have been discovered as far away as Norway and Italy—carried there by Irish pilgrims or Viking raiders. This one, however, was found in Ireland and is named for its nineteenth-century owner, Lord Emly of Limerick. It is quite tiny and was probably hung from the neck or shoulder of its owner as a source of protection and spiritual strength.

Oliphant
Southern Italy (Amalfi), about 1100
Ivory
Length: 21 in. (53.4 cm)
Maria Antoinette Evans Fund 57.581

Horns called
oliphants (from the Old
French word for elephant) were carved from elephant
tusks acquired from Islamic North Africa. Amalfi, where this oliphant was probably made, was one of several southern Italian ports that traded with Africa in the twelfth century. Although horns were used for hunting, drinking, and in battle, large and intricately carved examples such as this were prized as luxury objects and symbolic statements of wealth and status. Sometimes they were exchanged ceremonially as part of the transfer of land, which included the right to hunt on that land—a carefully guarded marker of feudal privilege, as only the nobility was allowed to hunt. Some nobles gave their oliphants to the Church, and most surviving examples were preserved through the centuries in the treasuries of cathedrals or monasteries.

Important individuals in the Middle Ages were often buried wrapped in precious fabrics, and this silk weaving brocaded with gold thread is believed to have been part of the shroud of a bishop of Burgo de Osma, a city in central Spain. Its design is Islamic and within the small circles is the Arabic inscription: "This was made in Baghdad, may God protect it." Luxury goods from Baghdad were highly prized in Europe, but this cloth was probably made in the Muslim city of Almería in Spain; the false inscription was intended to increase the value of the cloth.

Fragment of a shroud
Southern Spain (probably Almería), about 1100
Silk and metallic yarns; compound weave
17 x 19 ¾ in. (43 x 50 cm)
Ellen Page Hall Fund 33.371

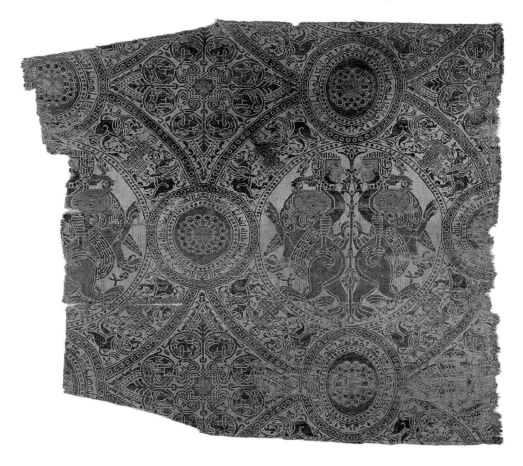

Made of stone instead of the more usual wood, and with most of its original paint intact, this sculpture of the Madonna and Child is extremely unusual. It was probably made to be used in one of the religious dramas performed throughout the Christian year. Moreover, while many twelfth-century sculptures of the Madonna are frontal and austere, this one, with its tenderly entwined figures, invites viewing from different angles. The striking depiction of Mary holding a son who is more man than baby powerfully foreshadows Jesus's death and increases the emotional intensity of this extraordinary work.

Madonna and Child
Italy (Lombardy), 1125–50
Limestone with polychromy
Height: 29 in. (74 cm)
Maria Antoinette Evans Fund
57.583

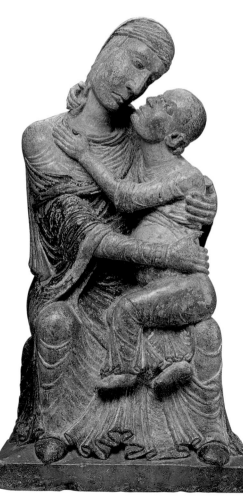

Christic in Majesty with Symbols >
of the Four Evangelists
Spain (Catalonia), 1150–1200
Fresco secco transferred to plaster
and wood
254 × 150 3⁄8 in. (645 × 382 cm)
Maria Antoinette Evans Fund
21.1285

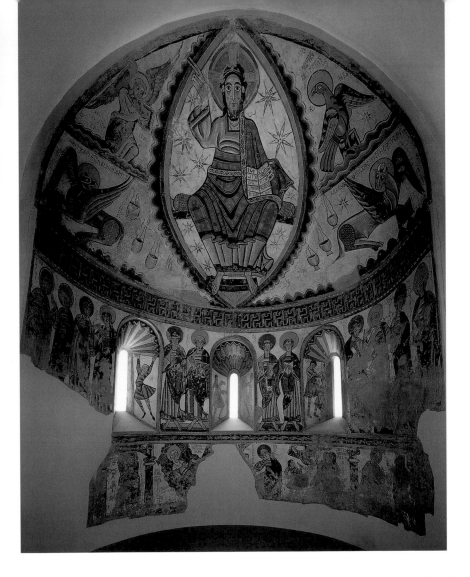

This fresco once decorated the apse of Santa Maria del Mur, a small church in the foothills of the Spanish Pyrenees. Huge-eyed and solemn, the imposing figure of Christ in Majesty dominates the composition. He is surrounded by symbols of the four Evangelists, whose writings form the core of the Bible's New Testament, and he holds a book inscribed: "I am the way, the truth, and the life; no man cometh unto the Father but by me." Below are images of Christ's original disciples, the twelve Apostles, and scenes from the Bible. More than twenty feet high, the fresco was sold from the church in 1919. The process of removing it from the wall was a delicate and difficult one. First, craftsmen glued to the front of the painting layers of cotton muslin that, when dry and hard, kept the paint in place. Next, a thin layer of plaster was chiseled away behind the fresco to separate it, in sections, from the wall on which it was painted. The fresco was then backed with canvas, waterproofed with a mixture of lime and Parmesan cheese, and transported to Barcelona, and eventually to Boston.

Three Worthies in the Fiery Furnace
The Netherlands, (Meuse region, Maastricht?), 1150–75
Champlevé enamel and gilding on copper
Height: 8¼ in. (20.8 cm)
William Francis Warden Fund
51.7

Composition, color, and technical precision place this large plaque among the finest examples of medieval enamelwork to survive. It tells the Old Testament story of the Three Worthies who refused to worship a golden image and were cast into a furnace where they "walked about in the midst of the flames, singing hymns to God and blessing the Lord. Then Azariah stood and offered this prayer: 'Blessed art thou, O Lord, God of our fathers, and worthy of praise; and thy name is glorified for ever.'" Hearing this, an angel "drove the fiery flame out of the furnace . . . so that the fire did not touch them at all or hurt or trouble them." In the Middle Ages, many Old Testament stories were viewed as precursors of New Testament ones; the Three Worthies prefigured the purity of the Virgin, as the encircling inscription here makes clear: "Neither the fury of the King nor the fire can harm the youths, nor can the birth of the Mother destroy the seal of her Virginity."

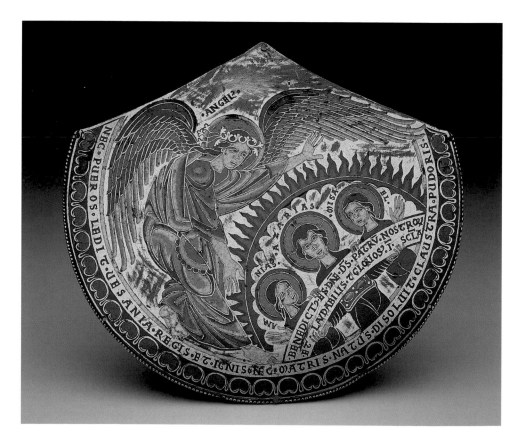

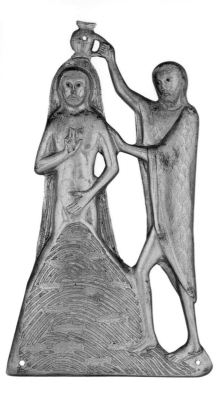

Baptism of Christ

France (Limoges),
mid-13th century
Champlevé enamel and gilding
on copper
Height: 14½ in. (36.8 cm)
Francis Bartlett Fund 50.858

This relief was originally one of several scenes from the life of Christ that were mounted on a flat plaque that decorated an altar. It is of exceptional quality, with the gilded-copper surface skillfully worked to capture the textures of hair, fur, and water. The relief is unusual in showing John the Baptist baptizing Jesus in two ways—by pouring water from a ewer over his head and by immersing him in the river Jordan. Jesus, his hand raised in blessing, stands in water whose ripples are suggested by curved segments of white enamel interspersed with shapes of swimming fish.

Aquamanile

Northern Germany (possibly Hildesheim),
mid-13th–early 14th centuries
Leaded latten (a copper alloy)
Height: 13⅜ in. (34 cm)
Benjamin Shelton Fund 40.233

In the Old Testament's Book of Judges, the young Samson met a lion that "roared against him; and the Spirit of the Lord came mightily upon him, and he tore the lion asunder as one tears a kid." Here, Samson has just leapt onto the lion's back and, with a smile, confronts its fearsome jaws. The story often appears in medieval art and literature as a prefiguration of Christ's conquest of the devil. Here, it is presented in the form of an aquamanile, a vessel used for ritual hand-washing during the Mass that was later adapted for use in wealthy homes. The aquamanile was filled through an opening on Samson's head; there is a spout below the lion's left ear and its tail makes a handle.

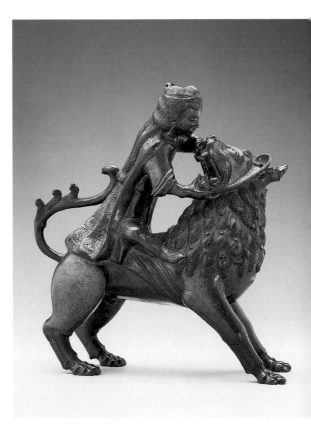

Duccio di Buoninsegna and Workshop
Italian (Siena), active by 1278, died 1319
The Crucifixion, the Redeemer with Angels, Saint Nicholas and Saint Gregory,
1311–18
Tempera on panel
Center panel: 24 × 15½ in.
(60 × 39.5 cm)
Each wing: 17¾ × 7½ in.
(45 × 19 cm)
Grant Walker and Charles Potter Kling Funds 45.880

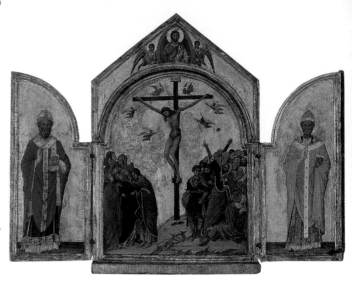

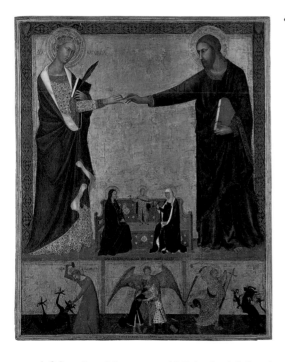

"Barna da Siena"
Italian (Siena), active mid-14th century
Mystic Marriage of Saint Catherine, about 1340
Tempera on panel
54⅝ × 43¾ in.
(138.9 × 111.0 cm)
Sarah Wyman Whitman Fund 15.1145

The legendary Saint Catherine of Alexandria had a vision in which Christ took her as his spiritual bride, placing a ring on her finger. In this painting, the union symbolized by this event is echoed in the central scenes below: the Christ Child grouped with his mother and Saint Catherine of Siena (an intercessor and peacemaker) and two enemies reconciled by an archangel. The triumph of good over evil is represented in the lower scenes to right and left by saints Margaret and Michael subduing demons. These images suggest that the donor named in the inscription, Arigo di Neri Arighetti, commissioned the painting to celebrate the end of a feud. Many aspects of the painting seem to be unique in fourteenth-century Italian art, including the representation of Saint Catherine of Alexandria with the adult rather than the infant Christ and the topical scene of enemies discarding their weapons and embracing. This is one of the largest and most unusual fourteenth-century Sienese paintings, but the identity of the artist known as "Barna da Siena" remains a mystery.

Duccio's ability to weave groups of figures into moving and compelling pictorial narratives was unprecedented in Italian painting. His jewel-like color and elegant, linear style dominated Sienese painting for two hundred years. Here, beneath the poignant, subtly modeled body of Christ, mourners gathered around the Virgin Mary melt together in shared grief; on the other side of the cross, the poses and gesticulations of soldiers and onlookers suggest confusion and disarray. This remarkably well-preserved triptych is one of Duccio's few surviving paintings. A sumptuous object for private devotion, it was undoubtedly commissioned by a wealthy individual whose patron saints were probably Nicholas and Gregory. Designed to be portable, the triptych is beautiful even when closed; the backs of the wings are painted in imitation of marble and semiprecious stones.

The same subject could be treated very differently in the artistic centers of medieval and Renaissance Italy. In spite of the similarities of their compositions, consider how distinct are the interpretations of the Crucifixion in the Sienese painting and the Florentine embroidery.

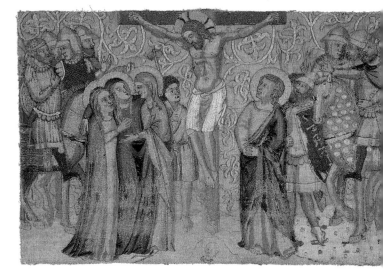

Crucifixion
Italy (Florence), late 14th century
Polychrome silk and gilded-silver
yarns on cotton and linen
11 ¼ x 16 ½ in. (28.6 x 41.9 cm)
Helen and Alice Colburn Fund
43.131

This embroidery probably was one of twelve scenes from the life of Christ that, grouped around a central panel, hung across the front of an altar. The design was first drawn on the linen cloth, possibly by a professional artist. The embroiderer then worked the design in silk and metallic yarns, achieving subtle variations of tone and texture through the use of more than twenty colors of silk and a range of different stitches. The background, with raised scrollwork across the sky, was originally covered with gilded-silver yarns, an effect that paralleled the use of gold leaf on the background of medieval paintings.

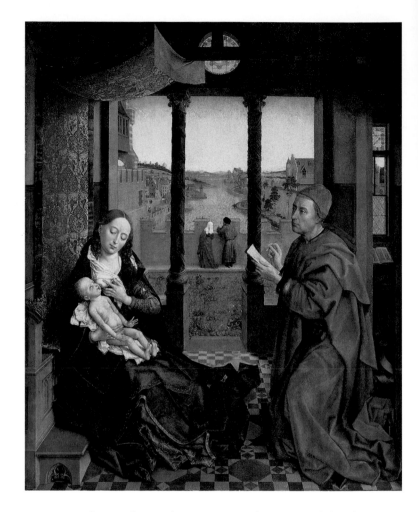

Rogier van der Weyden
Flemish, about 1400–1464
Saint Luke Drawing the Virgin and Child, about 1435
Oil on panel
54 1/8 x 43 5/8 in.
(137.5 x 110.8 cm)
Gift of Mr. and Mrs. Henry Lee Higginson 93.153

Recent scientific analysis has revealed that the Museum's version of this painting is the original (see page 66).

Saint Luke was the patron saint of painters, and this altarpiece, a masterpiece of fifteenth-century painting, may have been made for the chapel of the painters' guild in Brussels. Rogier van der Weyden made at least three full-size copies of this original version, evidence of the high regard in which the composition was held in its own time.

It was once popularly believed that Saint Luke was the first to record the Virgin's likeness, and here the saint reverently makes a preliminary drawing for his portrait of her. Among the meticulously rendered, real-world details, the enclosed garden beyond the room symbolizes the Virgin's purity, the couple gazing out at a river and a Flemish town may represent the Virgin's parents, and tiny carvings of Adam and Eve on Mary's throne allude to Christ and his mother as the new Adam and Eve, come to redeem mankind from original sin.

**Virgin and Child on the
crescent moon**
Lower Austria, about 1450–60
Poplar with polychromy and gilding
Height: 70 in. (177.8 cm)
Centennial Purchase Fund
65.1354

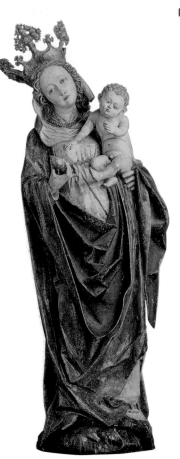

This refined and graceful sculpture was once part of an elaborate altar shrine (now lost) in the parish church of Krenstetten
in Lower Austria. It is carved from a single piece of wood, hol-
lowed out behind to prevent cracking. The quality of the carving is remarkable, as seen in the deep, looping folds of the
Virgin's mantle. Crowned as the Queen of Heaven, the Virgin
—with her gently swaying posture and delicate features—
represents the epitome of idealized beauty. Other aspects of the
sculpture are much more naturalistic, including the face of the
crescent moon on which the Virgin stands.

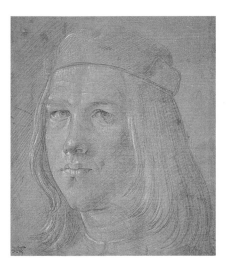

Lorenzo di Credi
Italian, 1456/59–1537
Head of a youth, about 1500
Silverpoint, highlighted with
white, on gray prepared paper
8 7/8 × 7 3/4 in. (22.5 × 19.5 cm)
Gift of Denman W. Ross
17.592

Like the one Saint Luke makes in Rogier van der Weyden's painting on the facing page, this is a
silverpoint drawing. Such drawings, common from the late fourteenth to the early seventeenth
centuries, were made with a sharp, silver instrument on paper specially coated so that the metal
would leave a mark. The son of a goldsmith, Lorenzo di Credi was a fellow pupil of Leonardo
da Vinci in the Florentine workshop of painter and sculptor Andrea del Verrocchio. Credi later
inherited and became the master of that studio, and although a fine portraitist, is best known
for his religious paintings.

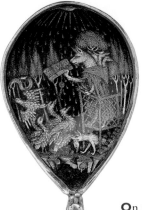

**Spoon with a fox preaching
to geese**
Southern Netherlands, about 1430
Painted enamel and gilding on
silver
Height: 6⅞ in. (17.6 cm)
Helen and Alice Colburn Fund
51.2472

On the bowl of this spoon, a fox dressed as a monk and carrying three dead geese in his cowl holds a document bearing the word "pax" (peace). He is preaching to a flock of geese, while another fox seizes one of the congregation. The perceived hypocrisy of the clergy was frequently mocked in the late Middle Ages, and the inspiration for the decoration of this spoon may have been a well-known proverb, "When the fox preaches beware your geese." Or the scene may be drawn from a Flemish version of the immensely popular *Roman de Renart*, a collection of stories (featuring Renart the fox) in which animals live in a society modeled on that of medieval France. The spoon is one of a group of luxury objects that are believed to have been made for Philip the Good, Duke of Burgundy, a great patron of the arts who amassed large collections of tapestries, paintings, metalwork, illustrated books, and jewels.

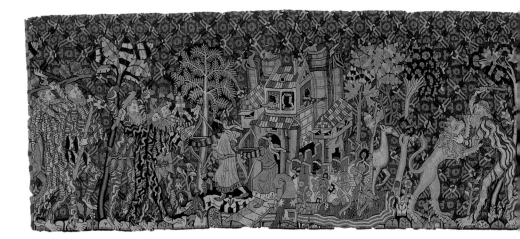

Hairy "wild men," neither entirely man nor beast, were popular subjects in medieval art and literature. On the left of this tapestry (detail), wild men attack a castle defended by Moors, whose king and queen look out from a window. In the center are wild men with a unicorn, a dragon, and a lion, and on the right, men return from the hunt and pay homage to a mother with her children. This spectacular tapestry probably hung along the back of a choir stall in a church or above a row of benches. Against the latticework background, fanciful plants and animals and the patterned, hairy coats of wild men create a magical world.

Wild Men and Moors
Southern Germany (possibly
Strasbourg), about 1440
Linen and wool; tapestry weave
39¼ × 193 in. (100 × 490 cm)
Charles Potter Kling Fund 54.1431

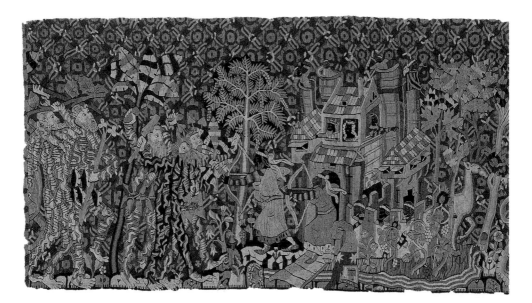

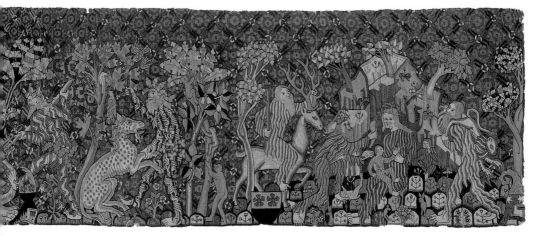

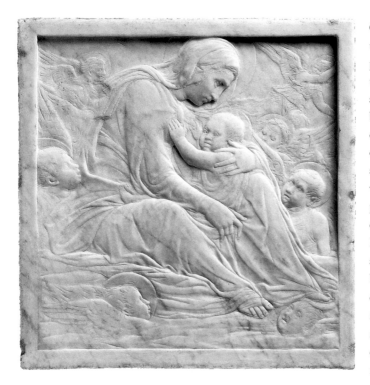

Donatello
Italian, 1386–1466
Madonna of the Clouds,
about 1425–30
Marble
13 × 12⅝ in. (33.1 × 32 cm)
Gift of Quincy Shaw, through
Quincy Shaw, Jr., and Mrs. Marian
Shaw Houghton 17.1470

One of very few works in the United States by the preeminent sculptor of the early Italian Renaissance, this exquisite marble relief was probably commissioned as an object of private devotion and originally framed in a wooden tabernacle with painted wings. The relief depicts the Madonna of Humility, surrounded by angels and seated on a bank of clouds. The extremely shallow carving, measurable in millimeters, makes the figures clearly discernible only in a soft, raking light that creates shadows to delineate the edges of the forms. This subtle and exacting relief technique is called *schiacciato* (flattened). Possibly inspired by the classical art of cameo carving (see page 87), schiacciato relief was invented by Donatello, and few other sculptors attempted it.

During the Renaissance, Florence and Venice were centers for innovation in all the arts, including textiles. Weavers perfected the complex technique of making patterned silk velvets, often in two or three heights of cut and uncut pile that produced a sculptural, three-dimensional quality. Renaissance velvets were so highly prized that worn-out robes or vestments were sometimes taken apart and their pieces reassembled, as in this case, to make a length of fabric. The popular motif of the pomegranate seen here was a symbol of immortality and fertility in Middle Eastern and Asian religions and was introduced to Italy through trade with the Ottoman Empire.

Fra Carnevale most likely painted this work as part of a monumental altarpiece for the church of Santa Maria della Bella in Urbino, and the repainted area along the top edge reveals the shape and placement of the original frame. The figures stand before a vast basilica whose facade, with its triumphal arch based on those of Constantine and Septimus Severus in Rome, is an important early instance of Renaissance fascination with classical architecture. The painting's precise spatial organization allows the viewer to gaze deep into the temple, discovering painted altarpieces and a glimpse of street. Although traditionally identified as a Presentation of the Virgin in the Temple (with the young Virgin, dressed in blue, standing in the center foreground), the painting's unusually secular aspects and lack of specific focus make it uncertain what event in the Virgin's life it actually depicts.

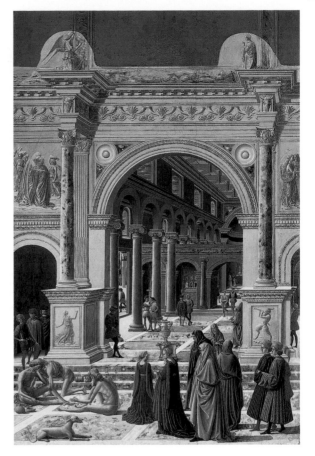

Fra Carnevale (Bartolomeo di Giovanni Corradini)
Italian (School of the Marches), active 1445–1484
Presentation of the Virgin in the Temple, about 1467
Oil and tempera on panel
57⅝ x 38 in. (146.5 x 96.5 cm)
Charles Potter Kling Fund   37.108

Panel (detail)
Italy, 15th century
Silk and metallic yarns; pile-on-pile cut voided velvet with discontinuous supplementary-pattern wefts
43¼ x 94 in. (110 x 239 cm)
Gift of Philip Lehman "in memory of my wife Carrie L. Lehman" 38.1041

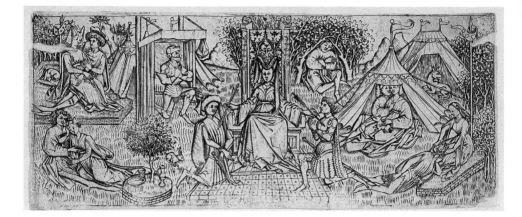

Master of the Gardens of Love
Netherlandish, active 1440–1450
The Little Garden of Love,
1440–50
3 1/4 × 7 3/4 in. (8 × 19.6 cm)
Engraving
Katherine E. Bullard Fund in Memory of Francis Bullard 65.594

The first prints from engraved plates were made in the mid-fifteenth century by armorers and other metalworkers who decorated their wares with sharp tools. To record and preserve their patterns, these craftsmen filled the indented lines with ink and printed the design onto paper. The Master of the Gardens of Love, one of the first engravers for whom a body of work can be identified, was perhaps trained as a goldsmith. This image is an allegory of courtly love: Enthroned in a pastoral and romantic setting, the Queen of Love casts her spell on a knight and a nobleman. Around her are a variety of courting couples as well as a knight who kneels reverently and a sad young man in a bower of trees, suffering pangs of love.

Saddle
Austria (Tyrol), about 1430–60
Bone over wood core lined underneath with hide covered with birch bark; polychromy
14 1/4 × 21 1/2 × 14 5/8 in. (36.2 × 54.6 × 37.1 cm)
Centennial Purchase Fund
69.944

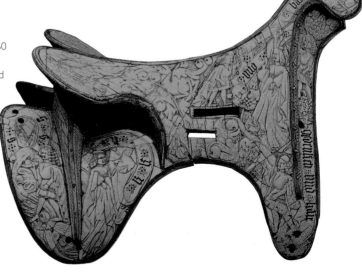

Window with eight apostles and other saints
England (West Country), 1420–35
Pot-metal glass, flashed glass, and white glass with silver-oxide stain; modern limestone tracery
221½ × 103½ in. (563 × 263 cm)
Maria Antoinette Evans Fund
25.213

This imposing stained glass window is one of the finest produced in England in the early fifteenth century. Made for an unknown location, it was moved to the chapel at Hampton Court, in Herefordshire, and sold from there in 1924. Once part of a larger window, this portion depicts eight of the twelve Apostles, the original disciples of Jesus; all but one has his name inscribed on the dais below his feet. Above their heads are long scrolls with Latin inscriptions from the Apostles' Creed, a fundamental statement of Christian belief. The figures are softly modeled and delicately detailed, silhouetted against backgrounds of deep red and blue.

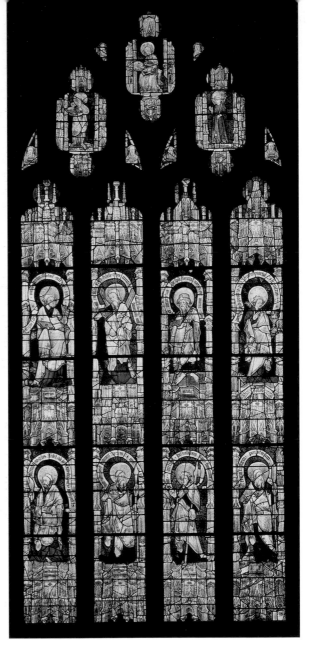

< This saddle is covered with large plaques of bone that are carved with images of Saint George and figures in courtly dress among scrolls, vines, and animals. A German inscription painted below the pommel reads *Gedench Und Halt* (Look Before You Leap, or literally, Think and Stop). The saddle is clearly a ceremonial object, probably related to some knightly order, but the carving is worn and most of the original paint is gone, indicating that the saddle may have been used, perhaps in parades. Only about twenty of these saddles have survived, all apparently made in what is now Austria and the Italian Tyrol; this one belonged to a noble Hungarian family from the early sixteenth century.

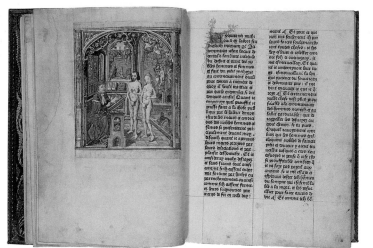

Master of the Boccaccio Illustrations
Flemish, active about 1470–1490
Adam and Eve, 1476
Engraving, hand-colored
From *Of the ruin of noble men and women* (Bruges: Colard Mansion)
Page: 14½ × 10½ in.
(36.8 × 26.6 cm)
Image: 8¼ × 6¼ in. (21 × 15.9 cm)
Maria Antoinette Evans Fund
32.458

Published in 1476 in the prosperous Flemish town of Bruges, this is the earliest known printed book illustrated with engravings, which were printed separately and pasted into the volume. In this copy (the finest and most complete surviving example), the engravings were also colored by hand. The text, written in the later fourteenth century by Giovanni Boccaccio, consists of a series of imaginary interviews with celebrated sufferers of misfortune. Translated from the original Latin into French in the fifteenth century, the book was admired throughout Europe. In the engraving illustrated here, Boccaccio sits in his study, interviewing Adam and Eve. Beyond the windows, vignettes recall events from their lives, including, on the left, the two pleading for mercy from God, who is dressed as a bishop (detail below).

Albrecht Dürer
German, 1471–1528
*Adam and Eve
(The Fall of Man),* 1504
Engraving
9⅞ × 7⅝ in. (25.1 × 19.4 cm)
Centennial Gift of Landon T. Clay
68.187

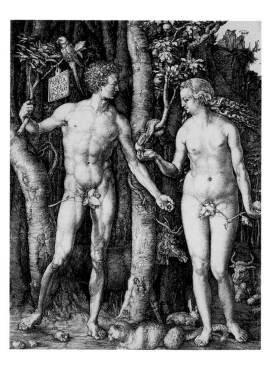

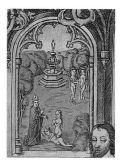

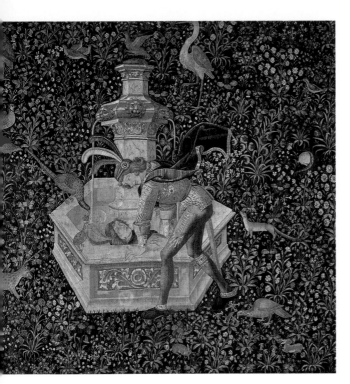

Narcissus
France or the Franco-Flemish
territories, 1480–1520
Tapestry weaving with wool warp
and wool-and-silk weft
111 × 122½ in. (282 × 311 cm)
Charles Potter Kling Fund   68.114

In the sixteenth century, prints increasingly were appreciated as works of art in their own right, and Dürer's engravings provided him with a considerable income. On one level, his *Adam and Eve,* produced shortly after his return from Italy, was intended to present the perfect human body as represented in the ideals of the Italian Renaissance. On another level, the image is dense with late-medieval symbolism. For example, the animals in the foreground represent characteristics of the four "humors"— melancholy (the elk), sensuality (the rabbit), cruelty (the cat), and sluggishness (the ox). It was believed that these "humors" had been in perfect equilibrium within the human body until Adam ate the forbidden fruit. Afterwards, this balance was destroyed, and individual men and women were controlled by different "humors," resulting in defects of character and in sin, illness, and death.

In northern Europe, tapestries were prized and costly works of art. Used to decorate walls in both religious and secular spaces, large tapestries served much the same function as fresco paintings in Italy and Spain. This example shows Narcissus admiring himself in a fountain. According to myth, Narcissus angered the goddess Juno when he spurned the love of a nymph, Echo; as punishment, Juno made him fall helplessly in love with his own reflection, staring at it until he pined away. After his death, Narcissus was changed into the flower that bears his name. The story was particularly appropriate for tapestries like this one, called "millefleurs" because their backgrounds are densely strewn with flowers.

Unidentified artist
Flemish, 1475–1500
The Martyrdom of Saint Hippolytus
Tempera and oil on panel
34½ × 99⅝ in. (87.6 × 253.1 cm)
Walter M. Cabot Fund 63.660

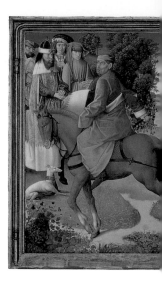

Carlo Crivelli
Italian (Venice), active 1457, died 1495
Lamentation over the Dead Christ, 1485
Tempera on panel
34¾ × 20⅞ in. (88.7 × 53 cm)
James Fund and Anonymous Gift
02.4

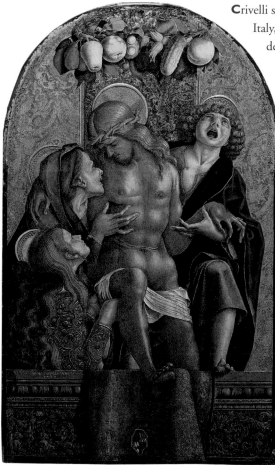

Crivelli spent his career along the Adriatic coast of Italy, away from his native Venice, and there developed a highly personal artistic style in which splendor of ornament is combined with intense emotion. In this painting, Christ's body is supported by the mourning figures of the Virgin, Mary Magdalene, and Saint John. Suffering is powerfully conveyed by the boldly fore-shortened head of Saint John and the intertwined hands of Saint John and Christ, one tense with grief, the other rigid in death. At the same time, the illusionistic swag of fruits and vegetables and the profusion of tooled and embossed gold give this devotional image the quality of a precious object. The shape of the painting and the implied point of view (well below the level of the figures) suggest that it once may have been the center of the upper tier of a large altarpiece.

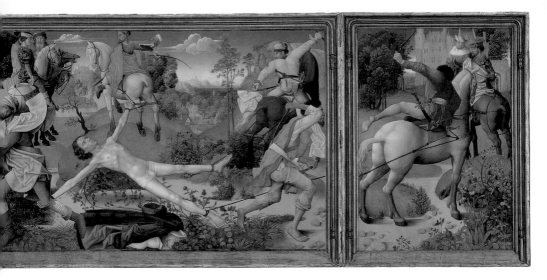

In legend, Hippolytus was a Roman soldier who was present at the martyrdom of Saint Laurence and soon after converted to Christianity. Refusing to renounce his new faith, Hippolytus was condemned to be torn apart by horses. The explosive drama of this painting is heightened by two elements not usually found in representations of the subject: the men who whip the horses to pull still harder and the way the scene is spread across all three panels, intensifying the viewer's experience of the saint's torment. The side panels of this large, exceptionally well-preserved altarpiece would have been opened or closed according to the liturgical cycle of the year; when the altarpiece is closed, these panels reveal figures of saints painted in monochrome to simulate sculpture.

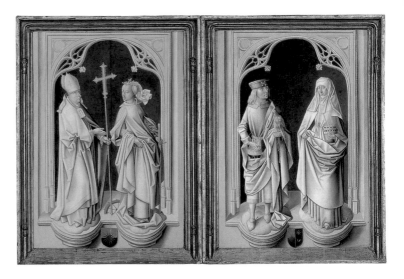

This is how the altarpiece appears when the left and right panels are closed.

Rosso Fiorentino (Giovanni Battista di Jacopo)
Italian (Florence), 1496–1540
The Dead Christ with Angels,
about 1524–27
Oil on panel
52½ × 41 in. (133.5 × 104.1 cm)
Charles Potter Kling Fund 58.527

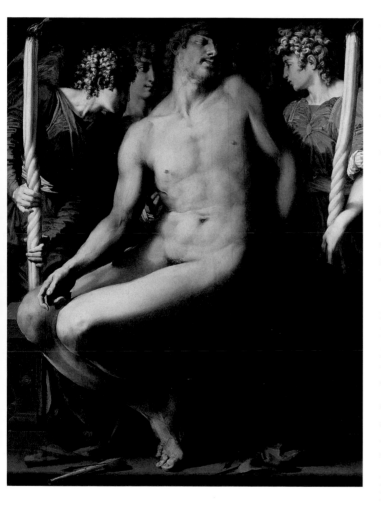

At once intensely spiritual and physical, this painting is one of few surviving works by Rosso Fiorentino, a major practitioner of the Mannerist style, characterized by the use of surprising colors, ambiguous space, and elongated figures. Most depictions of the dead Christ show him at the moment of being taken down from the cross or held by his grieving mother. Here, however, Christ's body—which seems strangely alive—is attended only by four adolescent angels.

A belligerent redhead from Florence, Rosso (red, in Italian) painted this altarpiece for the bishop of the town of Borgo San Sepolcro. The picture's relatively small size and unusual depiction of a traditional subject suggest that it was intended for the bishop's private chapel. Rosso painted the altarpiece in Rome, and his profound admiration of Michelangelo's recently painted frescoes in the Sistine Chapel is evident in the colors of the angels' garments and in the muscular body of Christ.

Plate
Italy (Urbino), about 1524
Possibly painted by
Nicola da Urbino
Tin-glazed earthenware
Diameter: 10 5/8 in. (26.8 cm)
Otis Norcross Fund 41.105

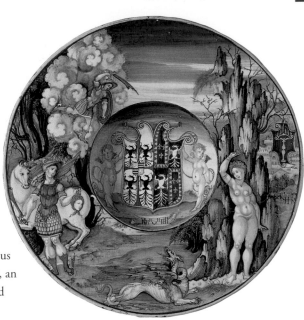

This plate is one of twenty-two surviving pieces of a splendid service
made for Isabella d'Este, duchess of
Mantua; it bears her coat-of-arms in
the center. In spite of being constantly
short of money, Isabella was an ambitious
patron of the arts with, as she admitted, an
"insatiable desire" for ancient Greek and
Roman art.

Tin-glazed earthenware, known as majolica, was often
decorated during this period with scenes from classical mythology. This plate features the exploits
of the mythological Greek hero Perseus who beheaded the snake-haired gorgon Medusa (whose
head he holds, at left) and rescued the princess Andromeda, chained to a rock by a monster. The
composition is derived from a woodcut in a 1497 edition of Ovid's *Metamorphoses*.

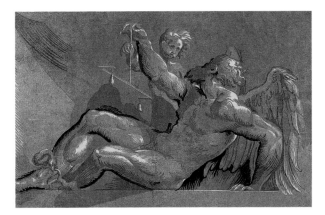

Unidentified artist
Italian, 16th century
Chronos (Allegory of Time)
After a drawing by **Pordenone,**
Italian, about 1484–1539
Chiaroscuro woodcut printed from
four blocks
12 5/8 × 17 3/8 in. (32.1 × 44.1 cm)
Bequest of W. G. Russell Allen
64.1111

Chiaroscuro (light and dark)
woodcuts are particularly effective
for reproducing wash drawings as
prints. In this technique, the
artist cuts a separate block to print each different area of tone.
The blocks are then printed in succession, one on top of the
other, resulting in a print with far more tonal variations and
sense of three-dimensional form than a traditional woodcut
could achieve. First used in Germany, the technique was introduced to Italy by Ugo da Carpi (about 1479–1532); it was
patented by the Senate of Venice in 1516 and copyrighted by
the Vatican in Rome two years later.

Albrecht Dürer
German, 1471–1528
Saint Jerome Seated near a
Pollard Willow, 1512
Drypoint
8¼ × 7⅛ in. (21.1 × 18.3 cm)
Anna Mitchell Richards Fund
37.1296

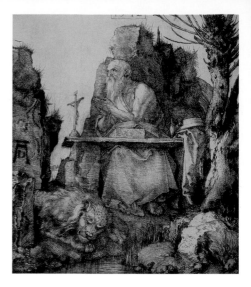

In the fourth century A.D., Saint Jerome renounced his passion for ancient Greek and Latin literature in favor of the Bible and an ascetic, Christian life. He spent many years translating the Old and New Testaments into Latin, and Dürer shows him in a mood of intellectual and religious intensity, seated with his books in a harsh landscape. The lion sleeping at his feet became his lifelong companion after Saint Jerome pulled a thorn from the animal's paw.

Dürer excelled in the uncommon medium of drypoint, in which a sharp metal instrument is used to scratch lines directly into the copper plate from which the image will be printed. This process raises, along the incised line, a ragged edge of copper called burr that holds ink and thus gives softness and depth to the print's tonal range. Because the burr is very delicate and usually wears away after fewer than twenty printings of the plate, drypoint impressions of this superb quality are extremely rare.

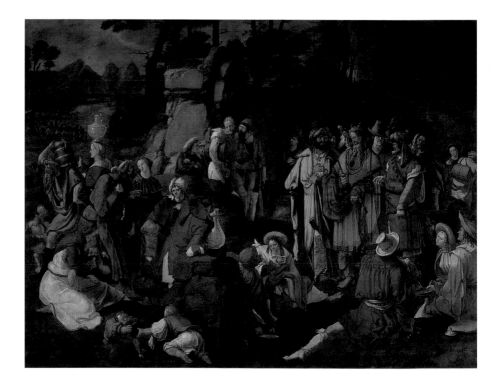

Vibrant colors and deep, atmospheric landscapes are hallmarks of the work of Lotto, a Venetian contemporary of Titian, who worked both as a portraitist and a religious painter. Here, in a characteristically clear and straightforward way, Lotto presents a visual statement of fundamental Christian beliefs. The table that supports both the Christ Child and his mother represents the altar. The small coffin beneath the Child foretells his death, as does the crucifix held by the weeping Saint Jerome. But the Child turns away from the cross and toward the lily that evokes both the Annunciation, when Mary learned she was to bear a child, and Christ's triumphant Resurrection after his death.

Lorenzo Lotto
Italian (Venice), about 1480–1556
Virgin and Child with Saints Jerome and Nicholas of Tolentino, 1523–24
Oil on canvas
37 1/8 × 30 5/8 in. (94.3 × 77.8 cm)
Charles Potter Kling Fund 60.154

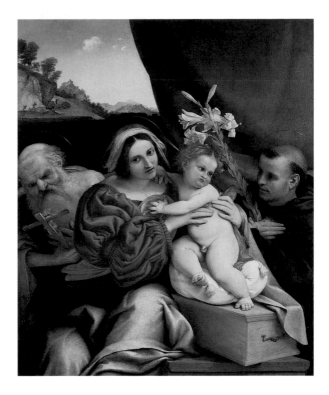

Lucas van Leyden
Dutch, 1494–1533
Moses and the Israelites after the Miracle of Water from the Rock, 1527
Glue tempera on linen
71 5/8 × 93 1/2 in. (182.5 × 237 cm)
William K. Richardson Fund 54.1432

In the Old Testament, as Moses led the Israelites through the desert, they complained: "Why have you made us come up out of Egypt, to bring us to this evil place? It is no place for grain, or figs, or vines, or pomegranates; and there is no water to drink." Advised by God, Moses struck a rock with his staff, bringing forth a spring of water. This painting depicts the aftermath of the miracle, as the Israelites eagerly quench their thirst.

Like Albrecht Dürer, Lucas van Leyden is best known as a printmaker although he was also a painter of distinction. This dramatic composition is his only work painted in tempera on linen, instead of the more usual panel. Canvases of this large size may have been intended to decorate rooms as a less expensive alternative to woven tapestries.

El Greco
Greek (worked in Spain),
1541–1614
***Fray Hortensio Felix
Paravicino,*** 1609
Oil on canvas
44 1/8 × 33 7/8 in. (112.0 × 86.1 cm)
Isaac Sweetser Fund 04.234

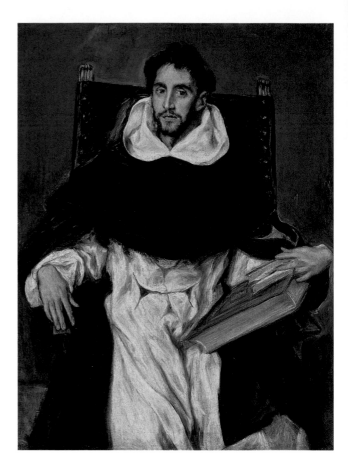

Fray Hortensio Felix
Paravicino loved this portrait and wrote El Greco
a sonnet praising it. The
poem begins:

*O Greek divine! We wonder
not that in thy works / The
imagery surpasses actual
being / But rather that, while
thou art spared, the life that's
due / Unto thy brush should
e'er withdraw to Heaven /
The sun does not reflect his
rays in his own sphere / As
brightly as thy canvases.*

Born on the Greek island of Crete, Domenikos Theotocopou-
los spent most of his career in Spain, where he became known
as El Greco, the Greek. Celebrated for religious subjects painted in a passionate, strikingly individual style, El Greco was also
a portraitist who looked beyond likeness to probe his sitter's
inner life. The brilliant young man depicted here—a close
friend of the artist—was a monk of the Trinitarian Order, a
poet much influenced by Luis de Gongora (see page 208), and
a professor of rhetoric. In later years, Paravicino became
preacher to the king and the most celebrated orator of his time.
The painting's restrained color range and its focus on Paravicino's dark eyes, sensitive mouth, and long fingers are compelling, and the swift, broad brushstrokes give the portrait
vitality and immediacy.

Titian, the greatest Venetian painter of the sixteenth century, brought new depth of emotion and an unrivaled sense of color to the Renaissance mastery of rationally depicted space. He painted this somber and meditative work—most likely intended for private worship—when he was nearly eighty years old. Within a vast and splendid architectural interior, Saint Catherine of Alexandria kneels reverently before a crucifix. More frequently portrayed in her symbolic marriage to Christ (see page 176), the saint is shown here with the attributes of her martyrdom—a piece of the spiked wheel (broken by divine intervention) on which she was to be executed and the sword with which she was eventually decapitated. The painting's flickering light, muted color, and uneven brushwork are typical of Titian's late work.

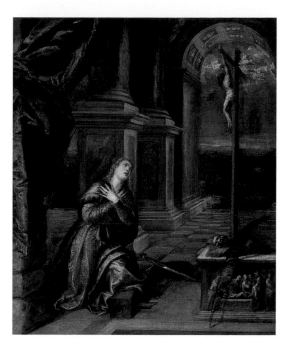

Titian
Italian (Venice), 1488/89–1576
St. Catherine of Alexandria at Prayer, about 1567
Oil on canvas
46⅞ × 39⅜ in. (119.2 × 100.0 cm)
1948 Fund and Otis Norcross Fund 48.499

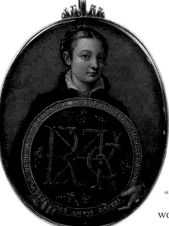

Sofonisba Anguissola
Italian, about 1532–1625
Self-Portrait, about 1555
Oil on parchment
3¼ × 2½ in. (8.2 × 6.3 cm)
Emma F. Munroe Fund 60.155

Sofonisba Anguissola was one of six sisters, all painters, from a wealthy Italian family. Because women were not permitted to study anatomy or life drawing, the sisters were inadequately trained to attempt complex religious or historical compositions. Therefore, they primarily painted portraits, including many of each other and themselves.

The art historian Giorgio Vasari wrote that Anguissola "has shown greater application and better grace than any other woman of our age in her endeavors at drawing . . . [and] by herself has created rare and very beautiful paintings." In this miniature self-portrait, the artist holds a medallion inscribed in Latin around the rim: "The maiden Sofonisba Anguissola, depicted by her own hand, from a mirror, at Cremona." Inside the circle is a cryptogram whose entwined letters are included in the name of Anguissola's father, Amilcare. The meaning and original purpose of this enigmatic portrait remain a mystery.

Oval dish
France, 1570–88
Attributed to **Bernard Palissy,**
French, about 1510–1589
Lead-enameled earthenware
Length: 22 in. (56 cm)
Arthur Mason Knapp Fund and
Anonymous Gift 60.8

Originally a stained-glass painter, Palissy turned to ceramics, experimenting to create subtle, naturalistic glazes that would not, as he wrote, "appear to involve any appearance or form of the art of sculpture, nor any labor of the hand of man." He made molds of actual animals and plants for such dishes as this one, preserving their intricate details through the use of translucent glazes. Here, casts of a snake, shells, fish, frogs, lizards, crayfish, and leaves are artfully assembled into a composition that is both richly decorative and almost disconcertingly realistic. Palissy was also a geologist and a philosopher and, as a Protestant in Catholic France, was arrested for heresy in 1588 and imprisoned in the Bastille, where he died.

Ewer and basin
England (London), 1567/68
Marked: L reversed; engraving
signed P over M
Parcel-gilt silver
Ewer height: 13¼ in. (33.8 cm)
Basin diameter: 19¾ in. (50 cm)
The G. H. and E. A. Payne Fund,
Anonymous Gift in Memory of
Charlotte Beebe Wilbour, and
17 other funds, by exchange
1979.261, 262

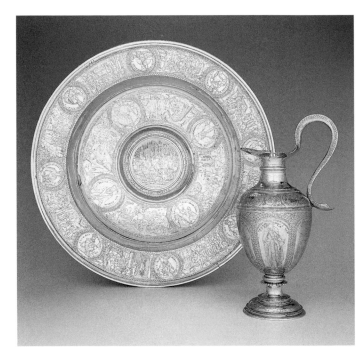

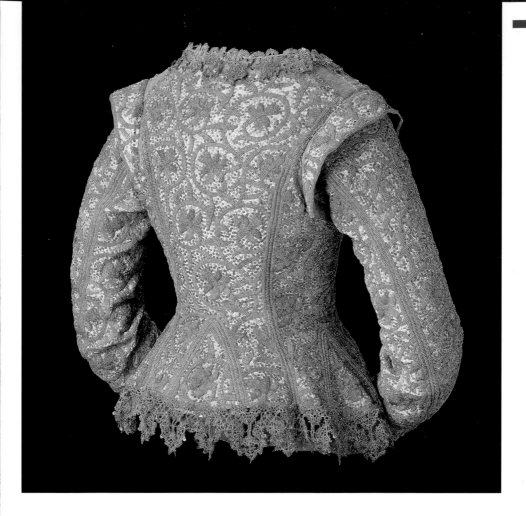

Woman's jacket
England, about 1610–15
Linen, embroidered with silk,
metallic threads, and spangles
Center back height: 17 in. (43 cm)
The Elizabeth Day McCormick
Collection 43.243

The stylized daffodils (or "daffadillies," as they were called)
exquisitely embroidered on this jacket reflect Elizabethan England's love of botany and gardening. According to family tradition, the jacket was given by Queen Elizabeth I to a member of
the Wodehouse family, following a royal visit to their estate in
1578. However, the style of the embroidery and the cut of the
jacket indicate that it was made at least thirty years later.

< The lavish display of valuable objects on a sideboard near the dining table was central to social
and ceremonial events in the courts of Europe. On occasion, this ewer and basin may also have
been passed around the table with scented water for washing hands. The set stands out among silver of the Tudor period for the quality of its engraved decoration. Finely detailed scenes from the
Old Testament are interspersed with portraits of every English sovereign from William the Conqueror to Elizabeth I, suggesting that the set may have been commissioned as a gift to or from
Queen Elizabeth herself.

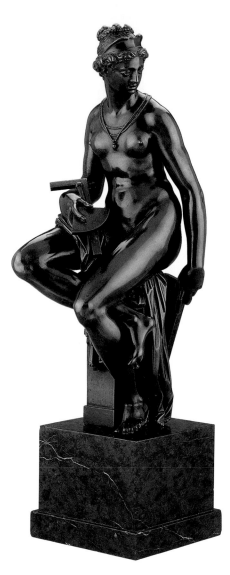

Giambologna
Flemish (worked in Italy),
1529–1608
Architecture, late 16th century
Bronze
Height: 14 in. (35.5 cm)
Maria Antoinette Evans Fund
40.23

Born in Flanders, Giambologna traveled to Italy to study sculpture and remained there for the rest of his life. By the early 1560s he was employed by the Medici grand dukes in Florence, and he soon became admired as the foremost sculptor in Europe. His bronze statuettes were exchanged as prestigious diplomatic gifts and became part of many important collections, including that of Emperor Rudolph II (see below), who owned almost thirty nudes.

This beautifully finished figure, which still bears traces of its original translucent red lacquer, was inspired by ancient Greek and Roman bronzes (see page 92). Compared to classical examples, however, this sculpture exhibits greater complexity and sense of movement in the graceful bends and turns of body and limbs. The figure, who personifies Architecture, holds a framing square, protractor, and compass. This cast is distinguished by the artist's signature, which appears on the drawing board behind her.

The flowing forms of this luxurious ivory cup are sensuous and almost abstract—the mane of a   **>**
lion, whose gaping mouth creates the vessel's rim, dissolves behind into the skull of a horse, and a winged female figure curves along the front of the cup above entwined dolphins. Clearly meant to be turned over in the hands and examined at leisure, this is the sort of object that would have been displayed in princely *Kunstkammers* (chambers for art), the private collections of exotic and precious objects that were the forerunners of modern museums. Although it is not known for certain who carved or commissioned this tiny object, the quality of its carving and design suggest the hand of a major artist, perhaps one working in Prague for the Hapsburg emperor Rudolph II, who amassed one of the greatest art collections in European history.

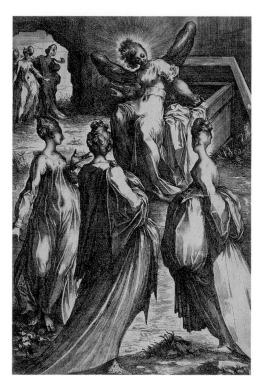

Jacques Bellange
French (active in Lorraine),
1595–1616
The Three Women at the Tomb,
about 1613
Etching and engraving
17 1/4 × 11 3/8 in. (44.1 × 28.8 cm)
Otis Norcross Fund 40.119

The New Testament's Gospel of Saint Mark describes three female followers of Christ who came, the day after his Crucifixion, to the cave where his body had been placed. There, the women found only an empty tomb and an angel who told them that Christ had risen from the dead. Bellange's depiction of this event (including another appearance of the three women entering the cave at upper left) is wonderfully artificial and theatrical, with its dramatic light effects and unsettling, tilted space. The attenuated figures, posed like modern-day fashion models with affected gestures and sweeping gowns, are characteristic of Bellange's style, which was much appreciated by the worldly dukes of Lorraine, for whom he also painted religious subjects and portraits. Working at a time when few French painters were making prints, Bellange's mastery of etching is particularly notable.

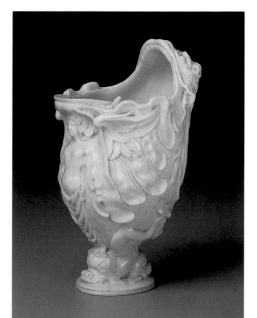

Standing cup
Possibly Prague, about 1630
Attributed to **Nicholas Pfaff,**
German, 1566–1612
Ivory
Height: 6 1/8 in. (15.5 cm)
John H. and Ernestine A. Payne
Fund, Mary S. and Edward J.
Holmes Fund, Beatrice Haines
Fund, and Frank B. Bemis Fund
1996.31

Although seventeenth-century clocks kept only approximate time, they were prized as sophisticated mechanical devices and as metaphors of cosmological organization and discipline. The astronomer Johannes Kepler wrote: "My goal is to show that the celestial machine is not like a divine being but like a clock."

The body of this German clock revolves upon its base, so that either side can be brought to the front. The face shown here is astronomical, indicating the position of the sun, moon, and planets, and the "Twelve Houses of Heaven" that astrologers used to cast horoscopes. On the other side of the clock, the disks and dials show— among other things—the time, the days and months, and the signs of the zodiac. Two overlapping disks, whose relationship changes with the seasons, record the relative hours of day and night.

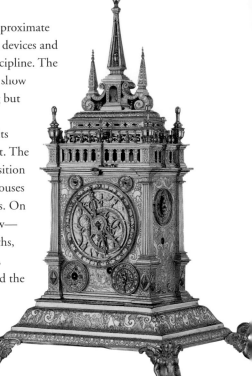

Hercules Segers
Dutch, 1589/90–about 1638
Rocky Landscape with Church Tower in the Distance, 1610–20
Etching and drypoint
5 1/8 x 7 3/8 in. (13.3 x 18.7 cm)
Kate D. Griswold, Ernest Longfellow, Jessie Wilkinson, Katherine Eliot Bullard in memory of Francis Bullard, and M. and M. Karolik Funds 1973.208

Segers's etchings are remarkable for their experimental use of color and innovative combinations of techniques. *Rocky Landscape,* for example, was printed with blue ink on paper prepared with a pink ground; after printing, the image was washed over with olive-green pigment. At a time when artists often made several hundred identical impressions from a single etched plate, each of Segers's prints is a unique work of art. Not even Rembrandt—who greatly admired Segers's work—employed so many techniques in such unprecedented ways. Etched with tangled, snaking lines, Segers's landscapes are haunting and otherworldly. The contemporary painter and theorist Samuel van Hoogstraten wrote that Segers was "pregnant with whole provinces, which he gave birth to in immeasurable spaces."

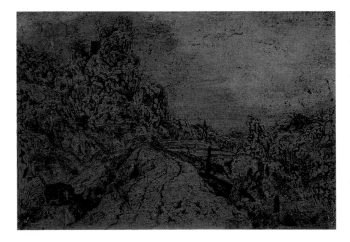

< **Clock**
Germany (Augsburg), about
1625–50
Gilded bronze and brass,
enameled silver
Height: 21 ¼ in. (54 cm)
Purchased from the Lina Franck
Hecht Fund 22.395

European admiration for
Chinese porcelains, such
as the cup in this painting,
led to their widespread
import and imitation (see
page 130).

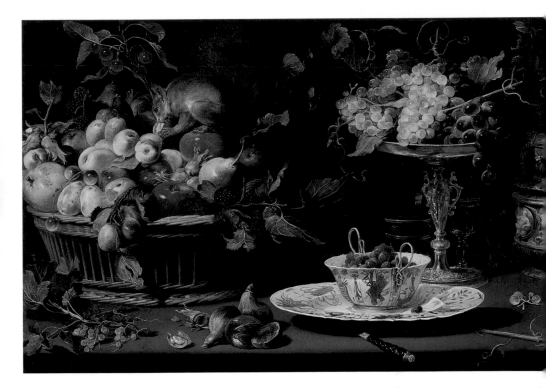

A very successful artist in Antwerp, Snyders specialized in
intricate compositions that display a wonderful sensitivity to
color, texture, and light. Here, in one of his most elaborate still
lifes, Snyders celebrated lovely creations of nature and man—a
nibbling squirrel, the rounded shapes of many fruits, a precious
Ming-dynasty Chinese porcelain cup, a gold dish on a high
foot, and a ceramic jug. The alternatingly soft and shiny fruit
and the knife handle projecting convincingly into the viewer's
space emphasize the illusionistic perfection of Snyders's technique. The artist painted this work on copper, an extremely
costly support, and the painting's coloristic brilliance and
meticulous, barely discernible brushwork are enhanced by its
hard, smooth surface.

Frans Snyders
Flemish, 1579–1657
Fruit Still Life with Squirrel,
1616
Oil on copper
22 × 38 ⅛ in. (56 × 84 cm)
M. and M. Karolik Fund, Frank B.
Bemis Fund, and other funds
1993.566

Rembrandt van Rijn
Dutch, 1606–1669
Artist in His Studio, about 1629
Oil on panel
9 ¾ × 12 ½ in. (24.8 × 31.7 cm)
Zoë Oliver Sherman Collection;
Given in memory of Lillie Oliver
Poor 38.1838

Within the cracked, plaster walls of his modest studio, an artist holds his brushes and the mahlstick he will use to steady his hand as he paints. Beside him are his palette and a stone for grinding pigments. The easel's worn rung suggests that the artist sits when he paints, resting his foot, but here he stands back, readying himself. The drama is one of thought rather than action, and it is intensified by contrasts of light and shadow and by bold juxtapositions of near and far. The painter is dwarfed by his canvas—a darkened, looming object that appears to challenge, even threaten him. This moving image transcends visual reality to explore the daunting experience of artistic creation. It is not about painting itself but about when, where, and how to begin.

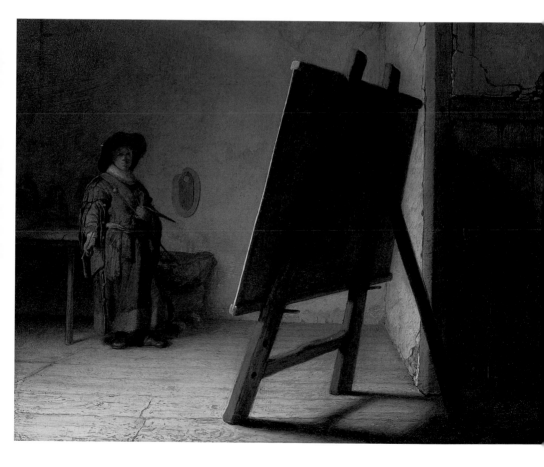

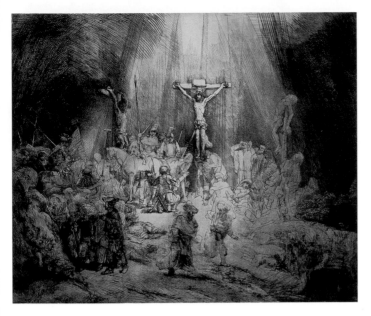

Rembrandt van Rijn
Dutch, 1606–1669
***Christ Crucified (The
Three Crosses),*** 1653
Drypoint
15 1/8 × 17 7/8 in.
(38. 5 × 45 cm)
Katherine E. Bullard Fund in
Memory of Francis Bullard
and Bequest of Mrs. Russell
W. Baker 1977.747

Rembrandt was one of the greatest printmakers of all time, and his hundreds of prints reflect his endless struggle to find new forms of graphic expression. This scene of anguish and confusion, executed in the fragile medium of drypoint (see page 192), shows his bold experimentation. It illustrates the moment when, according to the biblical account, "There was a darkness over all the earth. . . . And when Jesus had cried with a loud voice, he said, Father, into thy hands I commend my spirit." Before printing the image, Rembrandt shrouded much of the copper plate with a heavy veil of ink that would print as an almost impenetrable darkness. He then wiped the central area so that Christ appears to be illuminated by a great cone of supernatural light.

Rembrandt van Rijn
Dutch, 1606–1669
Watchdog in His Kennel, about
1638
Pen, brown ink, and wash
5 5/8 × 6 5/8 in. (14.3 × 16.8 cm)
John H. and Ernestine A. Payne
Fund 56.519

In his paintings and prints, Rembrandt brilliantly delved into the depths and complexities of human experience. In this drawing (on which he later apparently based a small etching), the artist records a much more humble subject with the same sureness and sensitivity to the potential of a few swift lines and a wash of color.

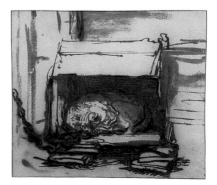

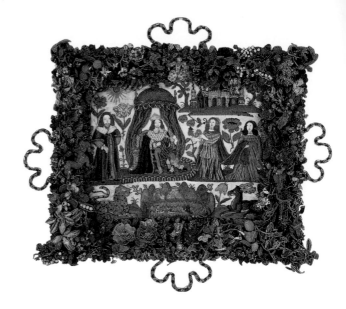

Gift basket
England, 1668
Wire, silk, wood; embroidered with
silk, glass beads, seed pearls, and
feathers; raised work
Length: 25 in. (63 cm)
The Elizabeth Day McCormick
Collection 43.530

Whimsical baskets such as
this, composed of beads
threaded on wire and embroidered on silk, were the prized
handiwork of amateur needle-
workers. Most likely presented
as gifts at weddings and chris-
tenings, they imitate silver baskets, such as the one illustrated below, made to display a child's
clothes before a christening. On this basket, the figures may depict England's king Charles II and
his queen, Catherine of Braganza. However, biblical figures were often shown in contemporary
dress on English needlework of this period, and the figures may represent King Solomon and the
queen of Sheba.

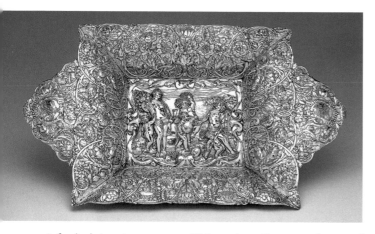

Layette basket
The Netherlands (The Hague),
1666
Marked by **Adriaen van
Hoecke,** Dutch, 1635–1716
Silver
Length: 17 in. (43 cm)
John H. and Ernestine A. Payne
Fund 1982.617

Layette baskets such as this
one—uniquely Dutch in
form—were intended for the
ceremonial presentation of an
infant's christening garments. This opulent silver example, one of only five known today, is
enriched by exquisite and varied floral decoration on the sides and handles. The central scene
depicts Venus, goddess of love, accepting gifts of wine and fruit from Bacchus, god of wine, and
Ceres, goddess of agriculture. An outstanding example of seventeenth-century Dutch silver, the
basket is worked in the embossed or repoussé technique. The forms were first shaped by hammer-
ing from the back, and the ornament was then chased—defined and finished on the front with a
sharp instrument that cut into but did not displace the metal.

Il Guercino
Italian (Bologna), 1591–1666
***Semiramis Receiving Word of
the Revolt of Babylon,*** 1624
Oil on canvas
44¼ × 60⅞ in. (112.5 × 154.4 cm)
Francis Welch Fund 48.1028

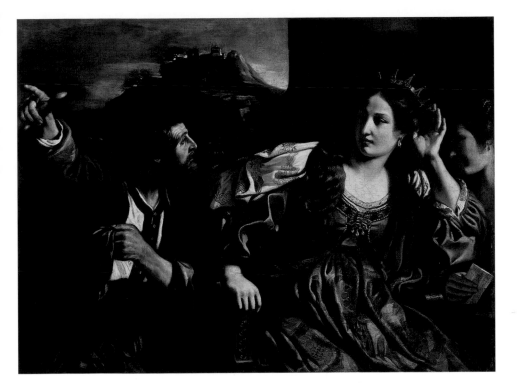

Interrupted at her toilette by a messenger bringing news of a
revolt, Semiramis, the legendary queen of Babylon, quelled the
uprising with a single command and then coolly returned to
combing her hair. In Guercino's theatrical rendering of the story, the figures appear like actors on a shallow stage, with the
maid, holding a comb, boldly cropped at one side. Gestures are
exaggerated and emphatic, particularly that of the messenger,
who seems to reach out of the painting into the viewer's space.
Gianfrancesco Barbieri (nicknamed Il Guercino because of his
squint) was greatly admired by his contemporaries. This painting, once owned by King Charles II, was a gift from the Dutch
state in 1660 on the occasion of his restoration to the English
throne after the Civil War and subsequent period of parliamen-
tary rule.

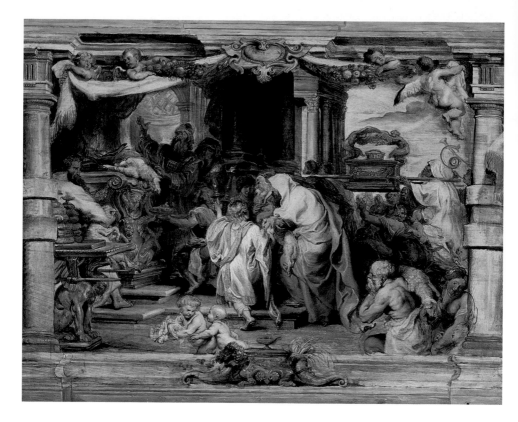

Peter Paul Rubens
Flemish, 1577–1640
***The Sacrifice of the Old
Covenant,*** about 1626
Oil on panel
27 3/4 × 34 1/2 in. (70.8 × 87.6 cm)
Gift of William A. Coolidge
1985.839

Courtier, diplomat, and among the foremost artists of his age, Rubens painted this fresh and vibrant oil sketch as a design for a tapestry in a cycle known as the *Triumph of the Eucharist*. Commissioned by a daughter of Spain's King Philip II for a convent in Madrid, the tapestries were woven in Brussels and remain in the convent today. On the left, an Old Testament priest sacrifices a lamb in a ceremony foreshadowing the sacrifice of Christ that is commemorated in the Christian sacrament of the Eucharist, or Holy Communion. The cornucopias of wheat and grapes in the foreground allude to the bread and wine of that sacrament. Delighting in pictorial illusionism, Rubens painted the scene as if it were a tapestry held up by cherubs, so that the final, woven version would suggest a tapestry within a tapestry.

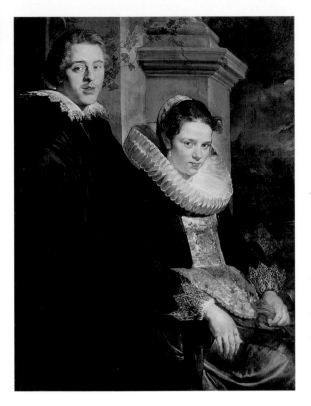

Jacob Jordaens
Flemish, 1593–1678
Portrait of a Young Married Couple, about 1621–22
Oil on panel
49 × 36⅜ in. (124.5 × 92.4 cm)
Robert Dawson Evans Collection
17.3232

Jordaens, a prolific painter and printmaker, worked for a time in the studio of Rubens and, after Rubens's death, became the leading painter of Antwerp. Although the couple in this portrait is unidentified, Jordaens's sitters were primarily members of Antwerp's prosperous middle class, and both husband and wife are handsomely and expensively dressed. Some details may have a symbolic significance, such as the ivy, an emblem of love and fidelity, that climbs over a broken column, a symbol of fortitude in adversity.

Georg Petel
German, about 1601–1634
The Three Graces, about 1624
Gilded bronze
Height: 12 in. (30.5 cm)
Gift of Mr. John Goelet in honor of Hanns Swarzenski 1976.842

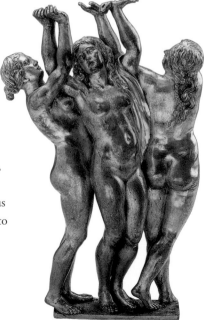

Most of Petel's brief career as a sculptor was centered in Augsburg, Germany, where he died of the plague in his early thirties. His work was strongly influenced by the paintings of Rubens, whom he first met on a trip to Flanders about 1620. Several of Petel's sculptures, including this one, translate paintings by Rubens into three dimensions. According to Calepinus, an Italian cleric writing in 1502, the Three Graces of classical antiquity represented freshness, gladness, and delight. Calepinus described them as always depicted young, cheerful, and nude "to show that kindness should be open and frank," and with their bodies intertwined in "a perpetual link of friendship." As in Rubens's painting (now in the Vienna Academy Museum), which Petel saw during a visit to Antwerp in 1624, this group originally supported a basket of flowers or fruit.

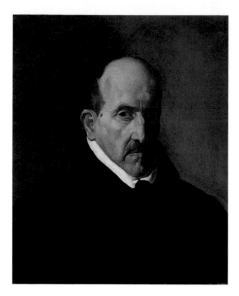

One of Velázquez's most incisive psychological studies, this portrait was painted during the artist's first trip to the court in Madrid. It was commissioned by Velázquez's teacher and father-in-law, who wanted it as a model for his own series of paintings of celebrated writers. Gongora is now considered among Spain's leading poets, but in his lifetime, although his light verse was much appreciated, his serious poetry was considered obscure and pedantic. When Velázquez painted him, the poet was sixty years old and in frail health, embittered by his long years and lack of recognition at court. This acclaimed portrait may well have led to Velázquez's appointment as a court painter at the age of twenty-four.

Diego Rodríquez de Silva y Velázquez
Spanish, 1599–1660
Luis de Gongora y Argote, 1622
Oil on canvas
19¾ × 16 in. (50.3 × 40.5 cm)
Maria Antoinette Evans Fund
32.79

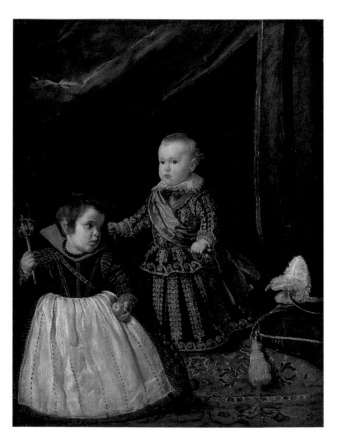

Diego Rodríquez de Silva y Velázquez
Spanish, 1599–1660
Don Baltasar Carlos with a Dwarf, 1632
Oil on canvas
50⅜ × 40⅛ in. (128.1 × 102 cm)
Henry Lillie Pierce Fund 01.104

Francisco de Zurbarán
Spanish, 1598–1664
Saint Francis, about 1640–45
Oil on canvas
81 ½ × 42 in. (207 × 106.7 cm)
Herbert James Pratt Fund 38.1617

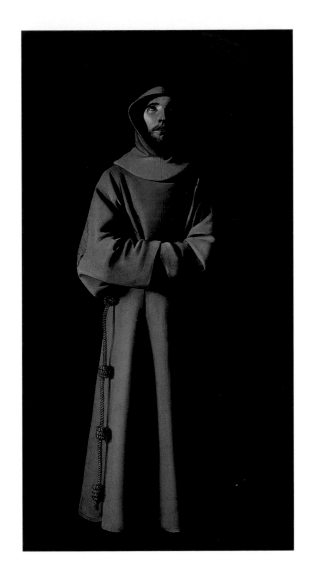

Zurbarán was renowned as a painter of austere religious images for churches and monasteries throughout Spain. Muted colors, rigorously simple compositions, and theatrical lighting give the artist's sacred figures an almost mystical presence. This painting apparently illustrates a ghostly legend invented to promote a belief that the body of Saint Francis had never decomposed. According to the story, in 1449 Pope Nicholas V visited the church where Saint Francis had been buried for more than two hundred years. There, in the darkness of the crypt, the pope came upon the upright body of the saint, standing in a shallow niche and showing no sign of decomposition. Zurbarán captures the moment when the pope first saw the body, illuminated by torchlight that throws an eerie shadow on the wall.

< **B**orn in 1629, Baltasar Carlos was the first son of King Philip IV. This portrait, at once majestic and tender, may commemorate the ceremony in which the nobility swore allegiance to the two-year-old prince as heir to the throne. The baby is dressed as he was at that ceremony, with the sash, sword, and baton of command. The lively pose of one of the dwarfs employed as companions to royal children provides a foil to the regal immobility of the infant prince. The dwarf holds an apple and a rattle, trifles that may allude playfully to the orb and scepter that Baltasar Carlos would wield as king of Spain (in fact, the young prince died at the age of seventeen, without succeeding to the throne).

Nicolas Poussin
French (worked in Rome),
1594–1665
Mars and Venus, about 1628
Oil on canvas
61 × 84 in. (155 × 213.5 cm)
Augustus Hemenway Fund and
Arthur William Wheelwright Fund
40.89

Although he spent most of his career in Rome, the French artist Poussin's intellectual, idealizing style influenced the course of painting in his native land for three hundred years. This allegory of the triumph of love over war shows Mars, god of war, enraptured by Venus, goddess of love, while her attendant cherubs make playthings of his weapons and armor. Intended for a circle of erudite collectors and connoisseurs in Rome, Poussin's paintings were inspired by the art and literature of classical antiquity and the Renaissance. *Mars and Venus* was based on a passage from the ancient Roman poet Lucretius, and many elements of the composition derive from an antique sarcophagus relief. However, in its warm color, harmonious landscape, and sensuous mood, the painting also demonstrates Poussin's early admiration for Titian (see page 195) and other Venetian painters of the Renaissance.

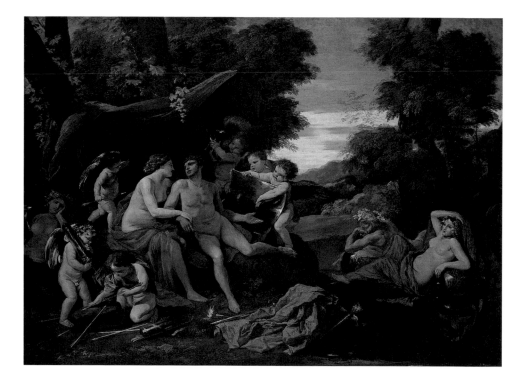

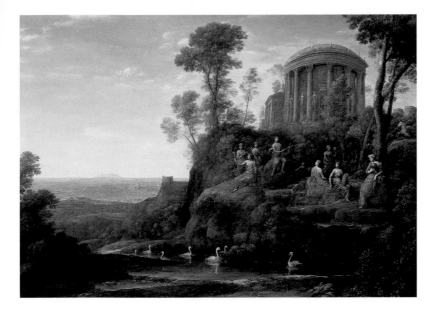

Claude Gellée, called **le Lorrain**
French (worked in Rome), 1600–1682
Apollo and the Muses on Mount Helicon, 1680
Oil on canvas
39¼ × 53¾ in. (99.7 × 136.5 cm)
Picture Fund 12.1050

Claude Gellée, born in the Lorraine region of France, lived (like Poussin) most of his life in Rome, painting the countryside—redolent with associations of classical antiquity—around the city and along the Bay of Naples. Painted when the artist was almost eighty, this work represents Apollo, god of poetry and music, surrounded by the nine Muses, embodiments of the arts. At the upper right, the winged horse Pegasus has dislodged a rock, thus releasing the waters of Hippocrene, the fountain of the Muses and the source of artistic inspiration.

Although his mythological and religious paintings present an imaginary, golden world, Claude worked a great deal outdoors, expressing his pleasure in the natural world through such keenly observed sketches as the one illustrated below. The artist sometimes used these drawings later in the composition of his finished works.

Claude Gellée, called **le Lorrain**
French (worked in Rome), 1600–1682
A Herd of Cattle, 1630–35
Red and black chalks and gray-green wash on paper
4¼ × 7 in. (10.9 × 17.6 cm)
William E. Nickerson Fund, No. 2
59.964

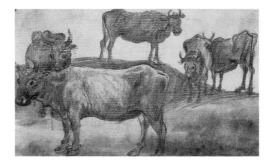

The Classics Are Never Out of Fashion

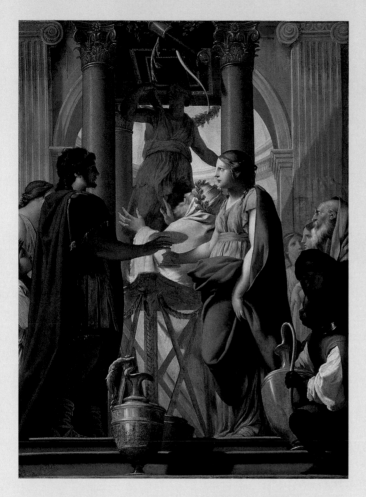

Eustache Le Sueur
French, 1616–1655
Camma Offers the Poisoned
Wedding Cup to Synorix in the
Temple of Diana, about 1644
Oil on canvas
67⅝ × 49½ in. (171.8 × 125.7 cm)
M. Theresa B. Hopkins Fund 48.16

The Roman Empire fell but never disappeared. The languages, literature, art, and architecture of the ancient world have provided Europe with models—to be imitated or rejected—for the last fifteen hundred years. Latin remained the language of religion and intellectual life through the Middle Ages, and in the fifteenth and sixteenth centuries, a wild enthusiasm for antiquities encouraged the close study and copying of Roman art. The bust of Cleopatra on the facing page, commissioned by Isabella d'Este (see page 191), is by a sculptor who became so skilled at capturing the spirit of ancient art that his contemporaries gave him the nickname "Antico."

The ancient world also provided ideas and subjects for works of art in more modern styles. The painting of Camma and Synorix looks nothing like any surviving work of classical art, but the Greek writer Plutarch (about 46–120 A.D.) provided the artist with this story of love, murder, and revenge. The climax of the tragedy takes place in a temple of Diana, goddess of the hunt; in the

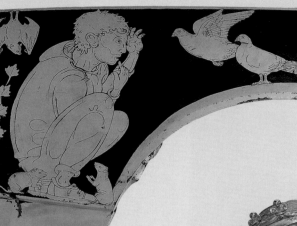

John Kindness
Irish, born 1951
Dionysus, 1992
Etched, painted steel
Height: 25 in. (63.5 cm)
Contemporary Curator's Fund
1992.531

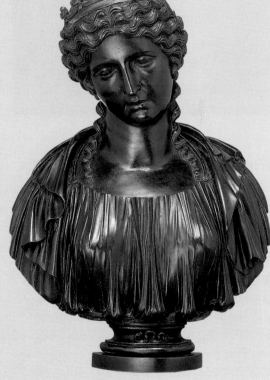

interest of authenticity, Le Sueur even included a depiction of an ancient sculpture of Diana then housed in the Louvre.

Even today antiquity retains its influence. In the early 1990s, the Irish artist John Kindness spent a year in New York, during which he created a series of works drawing on ancient Athenian red-figure vase painting (see page 74). The piece here resembles a shard of pottery; it is actually the front panel of a New York City taxicab. The subject is contemporary as well, as Kindness evokes the fragmented lives of the homeless in today's cities.

Pier Jacopo Alari Bonacolso,
called **"Antico"**
Italian (Mantua), about 1460–1528
Cleopatra, about 1519
Bronze
Height: 25 ⅜ in. (64.5 cm)
William Francis Warden Fund
64.2174

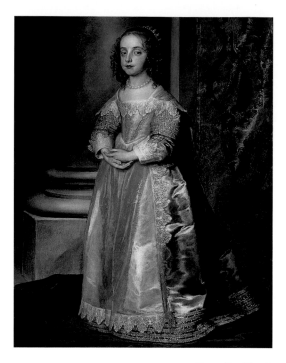

Anthony van Dyck
Flemish, 1599–1641
Princess Mary, Daughter of
Charles I, 1641
Oil on canvas
53 x 41⅞ in. (134.5 x 106.3 cm)
Given in Memory of Governor
Alvan T. Fuller by the Fuller
Foundation 61.391

This portrait of Mary, Princess Royal, (the daughter, sister, and eventually mother of kings of England) was probably a gift to her bridegroom, the Dutch prince William of Orange, on the occasion of their marriage in 1641. Poised beyond her years, ten-year-old Mary is richly dressed, her gown densely ornamented with embroidery and lace, although still with her child's leading strings hanging down behind.

Described by Peter Paul Rubens as "the best of my pupils," van Dyck was in the service of James I of England by the age of twenty and later became court painter to James's son and Mary's father, King Charles I. He produced a series of portraits of the king, his family, and the court that are of almost unparalleled elegance and distinction.

The provincial potteries of Staffordshire grew dramatically in the late seventeenth century and eventually became famous throughout Europe and beyond for the production of lead-glazed earthenware. The finest seventeenth-century Staffordshire wares were decorated with slip (clay diluted to a creamy consistency and poured out of a spouted jug—or through a quill inserted in the jug) and then covered with a lead-based glaze and fired. Although most slipware was utilitarian, such elaborately decorated examples as this one were made for special occasions— births, betrothals, and weddings. The royal figure with the letters C and R flanking his crown represents England's King Charles II, whose restoration to the throne in 1660 was commemorated in many of the decorative arts (see page 204).

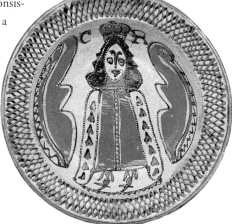

Glove
England, early 17th century
Leather, embroidered with silk,
metallic threads, and spangles;
metallic bobbin lace
Height: 15 in. (38 cm)
Gift of Philip Lehman in memory
of his wife, Carrie L. Lehman
38.1356

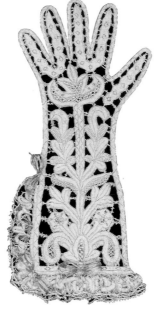

Glove
England, early 17th century
Leather, embroidered with silk,
seed pearls, metallic threads, and
spangles; metallic bobbin lace;
woven silk and metallic ribbon
Height: 13 in. (33 cm)
Gift of Philip Lehman in memory
of his wife, Carrie L. Lehman
38.1351

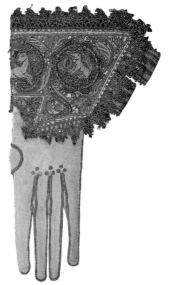

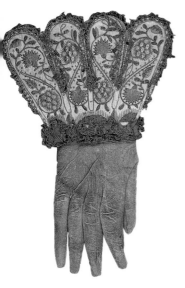

Glove
Italy, late 17th century
Linen bobbin lace, silk ribbons
Height: 15 in. (38 cm)
Gift of Philip Lehman in memory
of his wife, Carrie L. Lehman
38.1271

An Italian visitor to London in 1618 observed: "The fashion of gloves is so universal that even the porters wear them very ostentatiously." Indeed, throughout Europe, delicate lace or splendidly decorated leather gloves (sometimes perfumed at extra expense) were a mark of wealth and style and frequently presented as prestigious gifts. Most gloves were made in one size, and the extremely long fingers reflect fashion more than the actual size of the wearer's hands. Although these gloves show signs of occasional use, the fact that they have survived is evidence of the esteem in which they were held.

< Dish
England (Staffordshire), 1670–75
Lead-glazed, slip-decorated
earthenware
Diameter: 14 in. (35.6 cm)
Gift of Dr. and Mrs. Lloyd E. Hawes
1986.974

Landscape painting traditionally had as its subject either imaginary >
views or picturesque scenes of Italy and other foreign lands. But
seventeenth-century Dutch artists invented a new form of landscape painting that captured without embellishment the low horizons and expansive skies of their native country. Understood as
proud emblems of the prosperous Dutch republic, such paintings
were eagerly purchased by people of all social classes. An English
visitor wrote in 1641: "The faires are full of pictures, especially
Landscips." However, even though Dutch painters enjoyed the
most active patronage in Europe, they often had to supplement
their income with other occupations; Jan Steen worked as a brewer
and an innkeeper, and it is believed that Ruisdael was a doctor.

View of Alkmaar is dominated by a towering, cloud-filled sky
that patterns the countryside below with sun and shadow.
Although modest in size, the painting's effect is monumental.

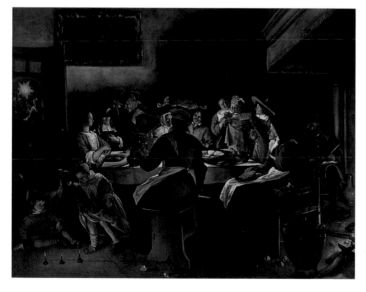

Jan Steen
Dutch, 1625/26–1679
Twelfth-Night Feast, 1662
Oil on canvas
51 ⅛ × 64 ¾ in. (131 × 164.5 cm)
1951 Purchase Fund, 1954 54.102

Twelfth Night, the sixth
of January, was the day
when the three kings, led
by a star, are believed to
have arrived in Bethle-
hem to honor the birth
of Jesus. Although the
celebration of this and
other Catholic holidays
was condemned in the
Protestant Netherlands,
many people continued
to observe it at home
with festive gatherings.
Steen was a gifted and
lively storyteller, and this
painting, originally owned by a Catholic family in Leiden, is
crowded with convivial detail. A baby (wearing a paper crown)
has been chosen by lottery to be king. Children play a jumping
game over candles symbolizing the three kings, and in the background, a servant greets the "star singers" who traveled from
house to house. The revelers are individualized and yet drawn
together by the light (whose source we do not see) emerging
from the table.

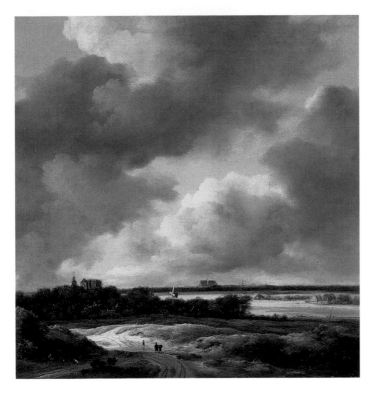

Jacob van Ruisdael
Dutch, 1628/29–1682
View of Alkmaar, 1670–75
Oil on canvas
17 1/2 × 17 1/8 in.
(44.4 × 43.4 cm)
Ernest Wadsworth
Longfellow Fund 39.794

Dirck van Baburen
Dutch, 1590/95–1624
The Procuress, 1622
Oil on canvas
40 × 42 3/8 in. (101.5 × 107.6 cm)
M. Theresa B. Hopkins Fund
50.2721

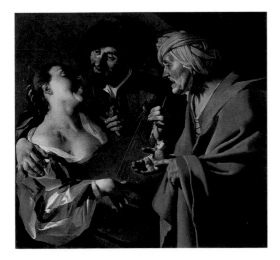

The city of Utrecht was the center of Catholic life in the otherwise Protestant Dutch republic, and Baburen was one of a group of Utrecht painters who, unlike most of their Dutch contemporaries, had studied in Catholic Rome. Influenced by the Italian master Caravaggio, these artists specialized in painting large, half-length figures, brought close to the picture surface and solidly modeled in strongly contrasting light and shadow. In this spirited image of mercenary love, an amorous client bargains with a procuress (one who solicits clients for a prostitute) for the favors of a voluptuous young woman. The figures' colorful costumes suggest street entertainers or characters in a play. A lute, symbol of love, occupies the center of the composition and the gestures of the hands that surround it tell the painting's story.

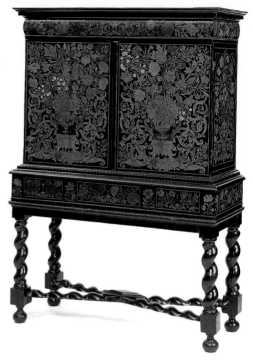

Small cabinets placed on tables to hold works of art and other rare objects were the precursors of this luxurious cabinet-on-stand. Ornamented with intricate marquetry (an applied design composed of wood veneers and other materials), such cabinets were themselves prized as works of art. The floral marquetry on this example is of unusually high quality and covers the front, sides, and interior—which contains twelve drawers surrounding a central door.

Dutch and German cabinetmakers pioneered the technique of marquetry in the early seventeenth century, but it is difficult to determine where individual objects were made as marquetry soon became the speciality of hundreds of craftsmen migrating throughout northern Europe. This cabinet was probably made in England or the Netherlands following the accession of the Dutch prince William of Orange to the English throne in 1689.

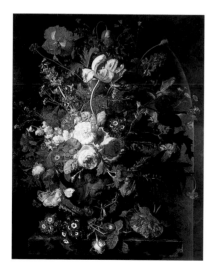

Jan van Huysum
Dutch, 1682–1749
Vase of Flowers in a Niche,
about 1735
Oil on panel
35 × 27½ in. (88.9 × 70 cm)
Bequest of Stanton Blake 89.503

Although flowers had traditionally enlivened portraits and other paintings, Dutch artists of the seventeenth century invented the independent flowerpiece. This speciality reached its peak in van Huysum's exuberant paintings, which are unsurpassed in their illusionism and dazzling color. Each flower provides a precise, permanent record of a living specimen, and the artist traveled every summer to Haarlem, a center of flower cultivation, to make studies of such rare flowers as the hybrid striped tulip depicted here. Although apparently real, this composition is an imaginary one, combining flowers that bloom in different seasons. Van Huysum's determination to paint blossoms from life could delay a work's completion; in 1742 he wrote to an impatient client: "The flowerpiece is very far advanced; last year I couldn't get hold of a yellow rose, otherwise it would have been completed."

Cabinet-on-stand
England or the Netherlands,
about 1690
Ebony, boxwood, yew, and other
woods; ivory veneered on oak
67 7/8 × 46 3/4 × 19 1/4 in.
(172.5 × 118.7 × 48.9 cm)
Gift of Mr. and Mrs. Graham Gund
1987.467 a,b

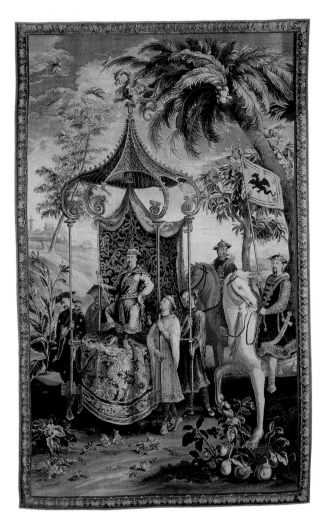

During the reign of Louis XIV, the French tapestry industry enjoyed a brilliant period. At this time, there was a passion for what has come to be called "chinoiserie"—depictions of Asian life and landscape that reflect a little knowledge and a great deal of imagination. For many years, the manufactory at Beauvais wove a series of chinoiserie tapestries called *The Story of the Emperor of China,* perhaps inspired by the accounts of a French Jesuit priest who returned from China in 1697. On this panel, the emperor—enthroned beneath a fanciful canopy with his feet on a Near Eastern rug—is probably Kang Xi, who reigned from 1661 to 1721. The tapestry has survived in particularly fine condition, with its vibrant colors intact.

The Emperor on a Journey
France (Beauvais), late 17th or
early 18th century
Designed by **Guy Louis
Vernansal, Jean-Baptiste
Belin de Fontenay,** and
"Batiste" (probably **Jean-
Baptiste Monnoyer**)
152 × 94 in. (386 × 239 cm)
Wool warp; wool and silk wefts;
tapestry weave
Gift of Mr. and Mrs. Henry U.
Harris in the name of Mrs. Edwin
S. Webster and Mr. and Mrs. Henry
U. Harris 65.1352

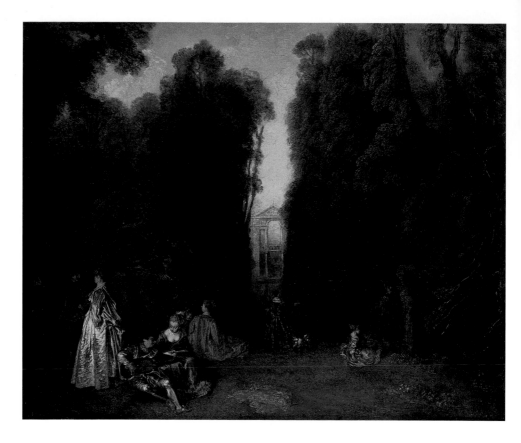

Jean Antoine Watteau
French, 1684–1721
View through the Trees in the
Park of Pierre Crozat,
about 1715
Oil on canvas
18⅜ × 21¾ in. (46.7 × 55.3 cm)
Maria Antoinette Evans Fund
23.573

Watteau was famous for a specific type of painting called the *fête galante,* in which ladies and gentlemen converse, flirt, and make music in idyllic landscapes. This is Watteau's only *fête galante* with an identifiable setting: the Château de Montmorency near Paris, home of Watteau's patron, the art collector and financier Pierre Crozat. The artist often visited Montmorency where he observed at first hand the aristocratic delight in artifice and ambiguity that his paintings capture with such perfection. Here, the marble facade of the house (originally built for Charles Le Brun, First Painter to King Louis XIV) appears in the distance beyond a reflecting pool. Seamlessly blending reality and fantasy, Watteau transformed Crozat's park into a dreamlike world where fashionably gowned women and men in costumes are arranged like actors on a stage framed by towering trees.

Jean Antoine Watteau
French, 1684–1721
Studies of a woman, about
1717
Red, black, and white chalks on tan
paper
13⅜ x 9½ in. (34.1 x 24.1 cm)
Bequest of Forsyth Wickes;
Forsyth Wickes Collection
65.2610

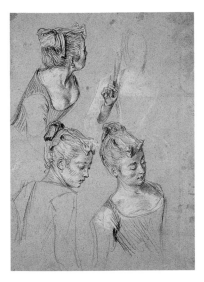

Drawing from life, Watteau made sheets of figure studies that he often incorporated into paintings, bringing
a sense of naturalness and spontaneity to his romantic
and idealized canvases. Such sheets, however, are also
harmoniously composed works of art in their own
right, as in this example with its three views of a young
model and her hand holding a fan. Watteau used red
chalk (his favorite drawing medium) to shape and
model the figures, combining it with black to define
and emphasize the forms and white for the planes of
eyelids, cheeks, and chest.

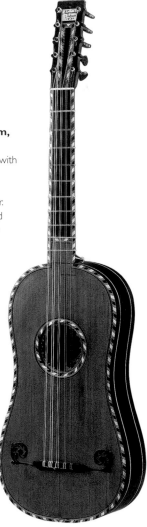

Guitar
France (Paris), 1680
Made by **Alexandre Voboam,**
French, active 1652–1680
Yew, spruce, and ebony; inlaid with
ebony and ivory
Height: 36¼ in. (91.9 cm)
Otis Norcross Fund, Gift of Mr.
and Mrs. Richard M. Fraser, and
Bequest of Gertrude T. Taft, by
exchange 1993.576

King Louis XIV played the guitar, and the instrument was a
feature of aristocratic French social gatherings. (Note the man
in the foreground in Watteau's painting on the facing page.)
One contemporary observed: "Everyone at court wanted to
learn, and God alone can imagine the universal scraping and
plucking that ensued." Enjoyed both as solo instruments and to
accompany singers, many guitars were beautifully decorated.
Here, the graceful outline of the instrument's body is accentuated with a border of inlaid ivory and ebony that contrasts handsomely with the spruce top. Guitars made by the Voboam
family, active in Paris between 1650 and 1730, were much in
demand, but only about thirty examples survive today.

Ewer
France (Paris), 1706
Possibly made by **Jean Ecosse**
Silver
Height: 11 ¾ in. (29.9 cm)
Elizabeth Parke and Harvey S.
Firestone Collection 1993.357

Impressive ewers such as this, paired with a matching basin, were "sideboard plate" intended for display on a tiered sideboard rather than for use at the dining table. The ewer's inverted-helmet shape, the acanthus leaves around its domed foot, and the boldly modeled masks on handle and lip reflect the period's great admiration of classical art.

In order to fund foreign wars, King Louis XIV of France often required noble households to surrender their silver objects to be melted down for the value of the metal. Therefore, surviving examples of high-quality French silver from this period are very rare.

Like his French contemporary Chardin, Meléndez favored arrangements of everyday objects painted with sober yet sensuous realism. He savored shapes, surfaces, and colors—from the webbed rind of the melon to the glint of a wine bottle cooling in a cork bucket—and despite the profusion of objects, his paintings convey a satisfying sense of balance and measure. This still life may be from a series of forty-five, said to represent "every species of food produced in Spain," that Meléndez created for the king's summer residence outside Madrid. Ironically, many were painted at a time when poor harvests had produced severe food shortages. The artist himself had no money to buy food, claiming that his brush was his only asset.

Luis Meléndez
Italian (worked in Spain),
1716–1780
*Still Life with Melon and
Pears,* about 1770
Oil on canvas
25 ⅛ × 33 ½ in. (63.8 × 85 cm)
Margaret Curry Wyman Fund
39.41

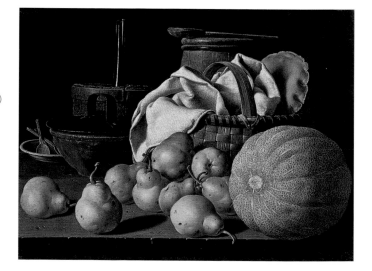

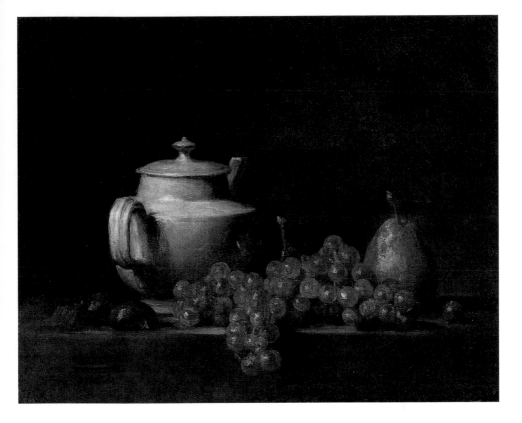

Chardin celebrated the commonplace. There is an air of informality and intimacy about his still lifes, as if he were working in his kitchen rather than his studio. In fact, inventories reveal that he owned most of the objects that he painted so meticulously, balancing form and texture. He also loved the pure, sensuous quality of paint, as the patch of brilliant orange brushed on the pear attests. The critic Denis Diderot enthused: "O Chardin! It's not white, red, or black pigment that you crush on your palette: it's the very substance of the objects, it's air and light that you take up with the tip of your brush and fix onto the canvas."

Giovanni Battista Tiepolo
Italian (Venice), 1696–1770
Time Unveiling Truth, 1745–50
Oil on canvas
91 × 65¾ in. (231 × 167 cm)
Charles Potter Kling Fund 61.1200

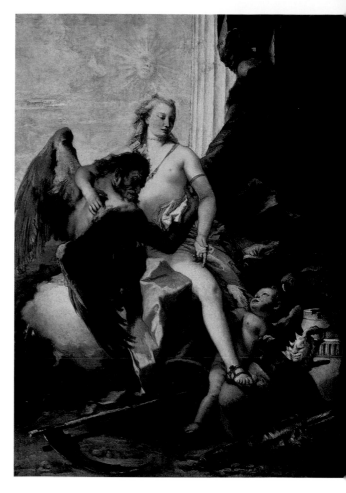

One of the last great, international court artists, Tiepolo is best known for huge frescoes that decorate the walls and ceilings of palaces in Italy, Germany, and Spain. This complex allegory is among Tiepolo's largest paintings in oil on canvas. It depicts Truth as a proud young woman whose voluptuous beauty is set off by the dark, winged figure of Time. Time's scythe denotes death, and Cupid, whose quiver of arrows remains on the ground, symbolizes earthly love rendered powerless by Time. The parrot at right represents the enemies of Truth: vanity and deceit. Truth's emblem, the sun, shines above, while earthly things, represented by the globe, lie subject beneath her foot.

A console table, supported by only two legs, was made to be placed against a wall, sometimes between tall windows. The structure of this ornately carved and gilded example features two cherubs supporting the Austrian coat of arms and a portrait of Maria Amalia, daughter of the Austrian emperor and wife of the elector (prince) of Bavaria, in Germany. It is one of a set of four (two are in the Museum's collection) most likely designed for a palace in or around Munich by Josef Effner (1687–1745), whose family had served the electors of Bavaria as gardeners for generations. Deeply enamored of French style, the elector sent Effner to Paris to learn gardening skills. There, the artist turned to architecture, and in 1724 he was appointed chief architect and interior designer to the Bavarian court.

Attributed to
Franz Martin Mutschele
German, 1733–1814
Virgin and Child, 1771
Made at the **Schrezheim
Ceramic Manufactory**
Tin-glazed earthenware with brass
halo and iron staff
Height: 44¼ in. (112.3 cm)
William Francis Warden Fund
61.1185

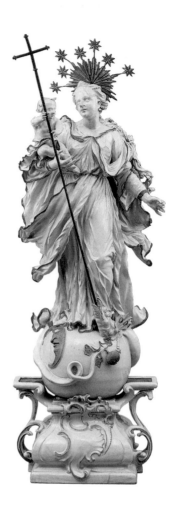

Standing on a celestial globe and treading on a serpent
(symbol of original sin), this image of the Madonna of
Victory derives from the description in the Bible's Book
of Revelation of a woman crowned with stars and
"clothed with the sun." Statues of the Madonna were
often placed outside houses to ensure heavenly protection from evil, and this one stood above the door of the
meeting house of the Teutonic Knights (originally militant crusaders bringing Christianity to eastern Europe)
in the town of Wolframs-Eschenbach in Germany.

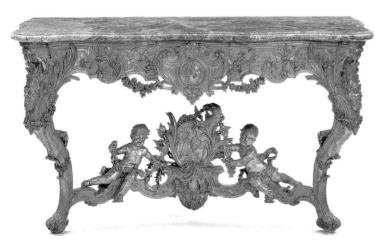

Console table
Germany (Munich), about
1730
Possibly designed by **Josef
Effner**
Gilded pine and
limewood; marble top
33¾ x 59¼ x 25⅜ in.
(85.7 x 150.5 x 64.4 cm)
Helen and Alice Colburn
Fund 57.658

Formal dress
France, about 1770
Silk and metallic threads; metallic
lace and silk flowers; brocaded
compound weave
The Elizabeth Day McCormick
Collection 43.643a, b

Opulent dress epitomized status
and taste in the eighteenth century, when textiles and decorative trims made from precious
materials were extremely costly.
This extravagant French gown
literally reshaped the body of the
woman who wore it. Tightly
laced, boned stays (corset) supported the bust and imposed an
elegant posture, while wide side
hoops (paniers) under the skirt
extended the hips by as much as
four feet.

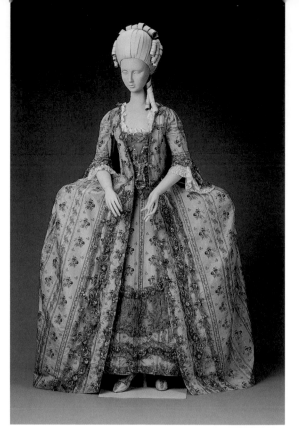

Soup tureen
England (Chelsea), about 1755
Made at the **Chelsea Factory**
Soft-paste porcelain with
polychrome enamels
Height: 10 in. (25.4 cm)
Jessie and Sigmund Katz
Collection, Gift of Mrs. Sigmund J.
Katz 1972.1081, 1082

When porcelain was introduced to Europe from China, it
inspired enormous enthusiasm among collectors and connoisseurs, but for many years, the recipe for making true, hard-paste
porcelain remained a mystery (see page 130). Many European
manufactories developed a substitute for porcelain known as
soft-paste, and in 1744 the silversmith Nicholas Sprimont established England's first soft-paste porcelain manufactory in the
London suburb of Chelsea. That year, a local newspaper
reported: "We hear that the China made at Chelsea is arriv'd
to such Perfection, as to equal if not
surpass the finest old Japan. . . . The
Demand is so great, that a sufficient
Quantity can hardly be made to
answer the Call for it." Many of
Chelsea's most successful prod-
ucts were tureens such as this
one, skillfully modeled as animals, fish, or birds, and colored
"according to nature."

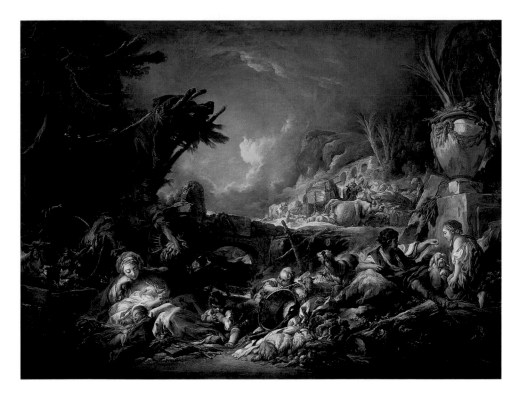

Boucher, possibly the most influential French artist of the eighteenth century, was also one of the most versatile. He not only decorated palaces and private residences, but also painted portraits, landscapes, and mythological scenes; and designed opera sets, porcelains, and tapestries. He enlarged and reworked this painting (originally a depiction of the Rest on the Flight into Egypt, with Mary, Joseph, and Jesus at left) into a fantasy of peasant life enlivened by dashing brush-work, lighthearted sensuousness, and pastel colors sparked by vibrant red. Attracted to the fanci-ful and artificial, Boucher objected to the natural world as "too green and badly lit." When this painting was exhibited in Paris in 1761, the critic Denis Diderot wrote: "What colors! what vari-ety! what richness of objects and of ideas! This man has everything except truth." Acquired in the mid-nineteenth century for a house in Boston's South End, *Halt at the Spring* and its companion, *Return from Market,* subsequently became the first European paintings to enter the Museum's collection.

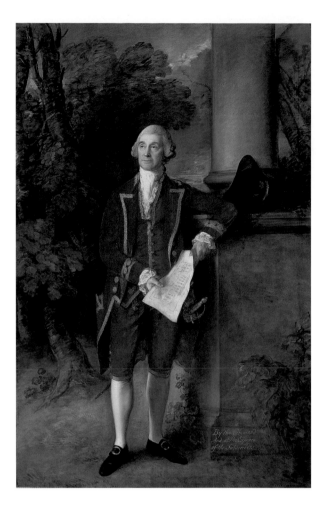

John Eld (1704–1796) was a founder of the Staffordshire General Infirmary, and this portrait was commissioned by the infirmary's trustees. It hung in the board room there until it was sold to benefit the hospital in 1912. Employing a traditional formula for fashionable portraiture, Gainsborough depicted Eld, holding a sketch of the hospital's facade, formally dressed yet at ease, and placed so that the viewer looks up at him from below. Although Gainsborough made his living with such elegant portraits, his "infinite delight" was painting landscapes, for which, at that time, there was little market. Not surprisingly, he includes a glimpse of wooded landscape in his painting of Eld.

Thomas Gainsborough
English, 1727–1788
John Eld of Seighford Hall,
Stafford, about 1772
Inscribed on base of pedestal:
"By the Command/And at the
Expence/of the Subscribers"
Oil on canvas
94 × 60¼ in. (238.6 × 153 cm)
Special Painting Fund 12.809

Best known for his moralizing scenes of middle-class domestic   >
life, Greuze also painted accomplished portraits. "I don't like faces that are painted already," Greuze declared, and this image of an unidentified young woman captures the combination of voluptuousness and innocence much admired in prerevolutionary France. The sitter's artfully dishevelled dress reflects a "natural" fashion favored by Queen Marie Antoinette, and her glowing skin is enhanced by the painting's palette of soft blues and grays. The oval shape, which Greuze often employed for images of beautiful women, is echoed in the curves of the woman's shoulder and breast—and in the remarkable feathered hat that dominates the composition.

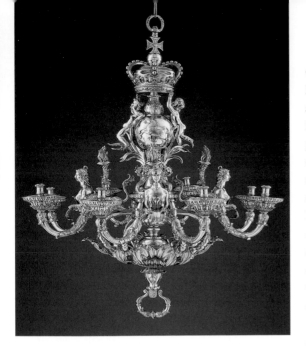

Chandelier
Germany (Hanover), 1736
Designed by **William Kent,**
English, 1685–1748; marked by
Balthasar Friedrich Behrens,
German, 1701–1760
Silver
Height: 46½ in. (118.1 cm)
William Francis Warden Fund,
Anonymous Gift in memory of
Zoë Wilbour, Gift of Henry H. Fay,
and Gift of W. K. Flint, by exchange
1985.854

George II, the second Hanoverian king of England, frequently spent his summers in Germany. This chandelier is one of five that he commissioned, probably for the Leineschloss, the ducal palace in Hanover; the figure of a horse on the globe beneath the sovereign's crown is the emblem of the House of Hanover. The chandelier was designed in England by William Kent and executed in Germany by the goldsmith of the court of Hanover, who worked from a wooden model carved after Kent's original design.

Kent was the first and most influential of the great eighteenth-century English architect-designers, and received many important commissions from the court and the aristocracy, designing not only buildings but also gardens, furniture, silver, paintings and their frames, book illustrations, and theatrical productions.

Jean Baptiste Greuze
French, 1725–1805
Young Woman in a White Hat,
about 1780
Oil on canvas
22⅜ × 18¼ in. (56.8 × 46.5 cm)
Gift of Jessie H. Wilkinson Fund,
Grant Walker Fund, Seth K.
Sweetser Fund, and Abbott
Lawrence Fund 1975.808

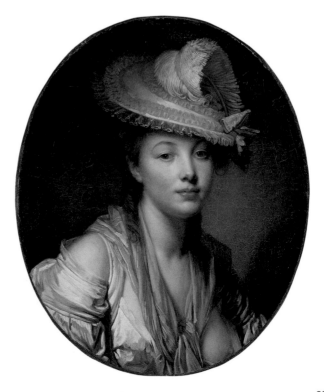

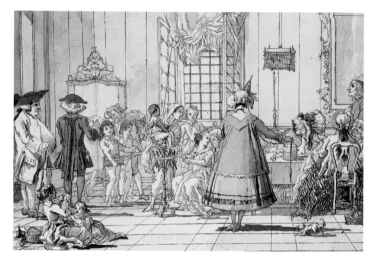

Giovanni Domenico Tiepolo
Italian (Venice), 1729–1804
The Milliner's Shop, 1791
Pen and brown ink, gray and
brown washes, yellow watercolor
on paper
11 ½ × 16 ¾ in. (32.5 × 42.5 cm)
William E. Nickerson Fund 47.2

Son and chief assistant of a famous and successful father (see page 224), Tiepolo was an accomplished artist in his own right: a masterful draftsman with a special talent for acutely observed images of Venice's upwardly mobile middle class going about their daily business. In this drawing, one in a series depicting scenes of contemporary life, employees of a fashionable shop mingle with customers and their children. Amid the bustle, the motionless woman in yellow (seen from behind) provides the composition's focal point; her sweeping gesture leads the eye to the all-important bonnet displayed on the table at right.

(clockwise from top)
Woman's shoe
Probably Italy, 1700–50
Silk and gilt-silver yarns; brocade;
metallic lace
Length: 9 ¼ in. (23.4 cm)
The Elizabeth Day McCormick
Collection 44.488a
Chopine
Italy (Venice), 1550–1650
Silk; cut and uncut velvet; gilt-silver
lace trim, wood or cork vamp
Height: 5 ¼ in. (13.8 cm)
The Elizabeth Day McCormick
Collection 46.770a
Woman's shoe
France (Paris), 1860–75
Silk; velvet, embroidered with
gilt-silver yarns and seed pearls;
leather sole
Length: 8 ½ in. (21.8 cm)
Gift of Mrs. Perry T. Rathbone
1972.69a

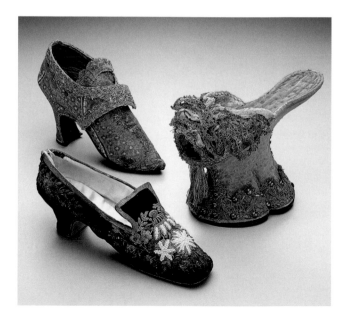

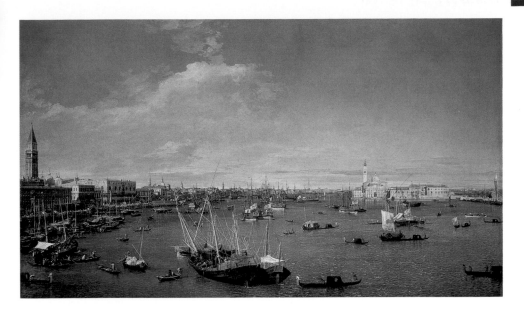

Giovanni Antonio Canal, known as Canaletto, was the fore-most painter of *vedute*, or views, of Venice, and his works were much in demand among eighteenth-century travelers on the "Grand Tour" of Europe. This painting, purchased by the Earl of Carlisle for his home, Castle Howard in Yorkshire, England, is among Canaletto's masterpieces. The expanse of the lagoon, or *bacino*, is animated with gondolas, work boats, and ships flying the flags of England, France, and Denmark. Famous landmarks include the Doge's Palace at left and the church of San Giorgio Maggiore at right. The clear light and the drifting clouds that dapple the water unite all this activity into a grand, unified whole. Canaletto composed his paintings from several viewpoints so as to encompass more buildings than actually could be seen from one place. A contemporary wrote: "He paints with such accuracy and cunning that the eye is deceived and truly believes that it is reality it sees, not a painting."

Canaletto
Italian (Venice), 1697–1768
Bacino di San Marco, Venice,
1726–38
Oil on canvas
49 × 80½ in. (124.5 × 204.5 cm)
Abbott Lawrence Fund, Seth K. Sweetser Fund, and Charles Edward French Fund 39.290

< **S**hoes have long been among the most important of women's fashion accessories. These examples, dating from three different centuries, share a use of luxurious materials and elaborate decoration that makes it clear they were not made simply to protect feet from cold and wet. The nineteenth-century shoe at lower left is Western in form, but the fabric was initially embroidered in Turkey and further embellished in Paris before being made up into a shoe. The form of the elevated shoe known as a chopine (at right) also originated in the East and was particularly favored by high-class Venetian courtesans. The perilous nature of walking on chopines—precursors of today's platform shoes—necessitated the assistance of servants.

Colonialism and the Mingling of Artistic Traditions

Cover with Chinese-influenced motifs
Peru, late 17th–early 18th centuries
Cotton, wool, silk; tapestry weave
93¾ × 81½ in. (238.1 × 207 cm)
Denman Waldo Ross Collection
11.1264

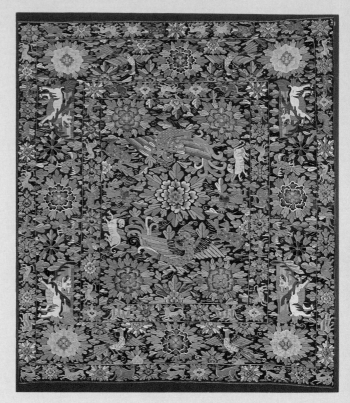

Cathedra (bishop's chair)
Mexico (possibly Puebla),
1750–1800
Spanish cedar
44 × 37 × 23 in.
(111.8 × 94 × 58.4 cm)
Gift of Landon T. Clay and Harriet
Otis Cruft Fund 1980.171

As Europeans traveled, conquered, and settled around the world, they brought with them not just their religions, governments, and diseases, but also their tastes. Through conquest and the creation of new trade routes, European imperialism fostered the invention of new decorative styles, as objects moved across cultural boundaries in ways they never had before. The chair on the left, for example, was most likely made as the seat for a Roman Catholic bishop. In taste and form it is Spanish, down to the feet carved in the shape of a claw grasping a ball, stylish in the mid-eighteenth century. In this case, however, the chair was probably made in Puebla, Mexico, for a bishop whose flock was for the most part not Spanish but of indigenous heritage.

Although the overall shape and construction of the bureau-cabinet at right is characteristic of eighteenth-century English furniture, its decoration is not. Crafted in Vishakapatam, in British-ruled India, it may have been made for export to England as an exotic, but not too exotic, piece of furniture for the British market. Alternatively, it may have been made for a wealthy Indian patron who had absorbed some English habits, but had not adopted English decorative taste. Vishakapatam had been a center of ivory carving centuries before the arrival of the British; work like this represents the adaptation of a local tradition to new conditions and new markets.

Before the European conquest, Andean weavers in South America were among the most sophisticated in the world, creating complex textiles for clothing and burial shrouds (see page 284). During the colonial period, the Spanish employed Andean weavers to create cloth for household use. The cover on the facing page mixes a generally European pattern and Andean subjects (there are llamas in the narrow interior border) with images of peonies and mythical beasts derived from Chinese silks, which came to the Andes through yet another of Spain's colonies, the Philippines. The Museum's collections of colonial art frequently demonstrate the circuitous travel of people, goods, and artistic styles during the colonial period.

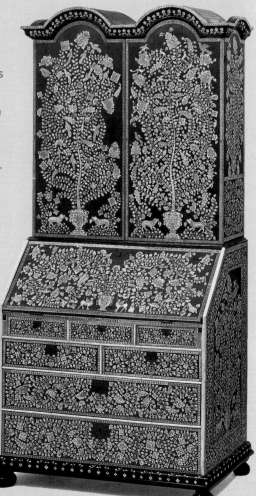

Bureau-cabinet
India (Vishakapatam), 1725–40
Teak, ebony, ivory
96 × 44½ × 26½ in.
(243.8 × 113 × 67.3 cm)
Gift of James Deering Danielson
1981.499

Giovanni Paolo Pannini
Italian (Rome), 1691–1765
***Picture Gallery with Views of
Modern Rome,*** 1757
Oil on canvas
67 × 96¼ in. (170 × 244.5 cm)
Charles Potter Kling Fund
1975.805

Pannini, like his contemporary Canaletto in Venice (see page 231), was trained as a stage designer and became extremely successful painting images of Rome for foreign visitors on the "Grand Tour." This enormous painting is one of four views of ancient and modern Rome commissioned by the Duc de Choiseul to commemorate his four years as French ambassador to the Vatican. Here, in a theatrical and totally imaginary gallery, the duke sits surrounded by plaster casts of sculptures by Michelangelo and Bernini and detailed views (all painted, of course, by Pannini) of Saint Peter's Square, the Trevi Fountain, the Spanish Steps, and other famous Roman buildings, fountains, and monuments.

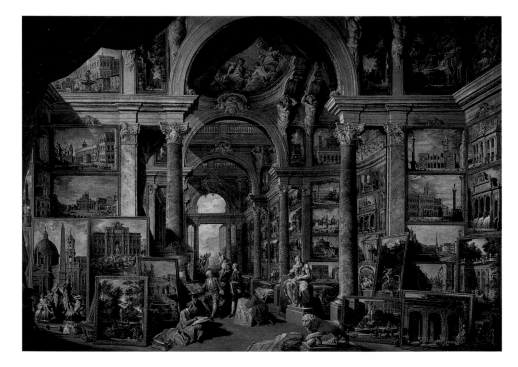

The first major English artist to make a successful career outside London, Wright painted >
portraits, landscapes, and images of contemporary life for the affluent middle class in his native Derby, who derived their wealth from the Industrial Revolution. In 1773 Wright made an extended trip to Italy where he sketched, in meticulous detail, the grottoes off the coast of Salerno, near Naples. After his return to England in 1775, he used these drawings to create paintings, like this one, that combine powerful observation and spectacular light effects with a sense of the sublime. The mysterious, moody figures (which the artist identified as "bandits") enhance this painting's haunting blend of reality and imagination.

The form and ornament of this opulent trophy reflect the enthusiasm for classical antiquity sparked by mid-eighteenth century excavations at the Roman sites of Herculaneum and Pompeii, which provided a wealth of previously unknown information about ancient architecture and decoration. It was designed by Robert Adam, whose style—inspired and shaped by two years in Rome—introduced neoclassicism to England. Commissioned by the stewards of the prestigious Richmond Gold Cup race, this trophy was won by Silvio, a horse owned by John Hutton of Yorkshire.

Richmond Race Cup
England (London), 1764
Designed by **Robert Adam,**
Scottish, 1728–1792;
marked by **Daniel Smith** and
Robert Sharp, English, in
partnership about 1763–1788
Gilded silver
Height: 19 ¼ in. (48.9 cm)
Theodora Wilbour Fund in memory
of Charlotte Beebe Wilbour, and
Frank B. Bemis Fund 1987.488 a,b

Joseph Wright of Derby
English, 1734–1797
***Grotto by the Seaside in
the Kingdom of Naples with
Banditti, Sunset,*** 1778
Oil on canvas
48 × 68 in. (122 × 174 cm)
Charles H. Bayley Picture and
Painting Fund and other Funds,
by exchange 1990.95

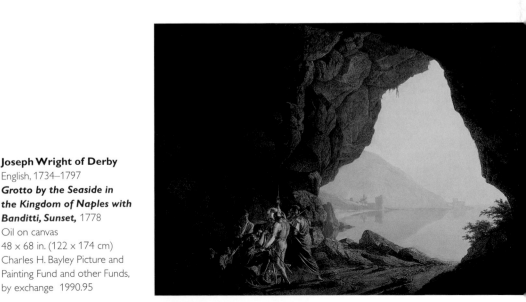

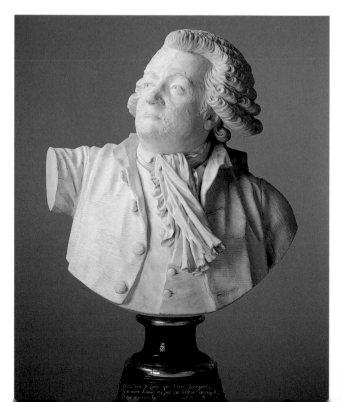

Jean-Antoine Houdon
French, 1741-1828
Thomas Jefferson, 1789
Marble
Height: 21 ½ in. (54.5 cm)
George Nixon Black Fund 34.129

One of the greatest of portrait sculptors, Houdon is most celebrated for his psychologically acute and technically superb images of famous contemporaries. Thomas Jefferson (1743–1826) had recommended the sculptor for a statue of George Washington in the Virginia state capitol years before. Jefferson was serving as American minister to France when he sat for Houdon in Paris.

Houdon first modeled the likeness in clay, and then made a plaster cast that he used as the model from which he created this marble version, the most recognizable and enduring image of Jefferson. It was the source of the presidential portrait on the 1801 Indian Peace Medal, for the Jefferson dollar (minted in 1903), and for the nickel, first issued in 1938 and still in circulation today.

Claude-André Deseine
French, 1740–1823
Honoré-Gabriel Riqueti, comte de Mirabeau, about 1791
Made by the **Manufacture des Porcelaines des Sieurs Baverstock et Compagnie,** Paris
Hard-paste biscuit (fired but unglazed) porcelain
Height: 32 ¼ in. (81.9 cm)
William Francis Warden Fund
1978.47

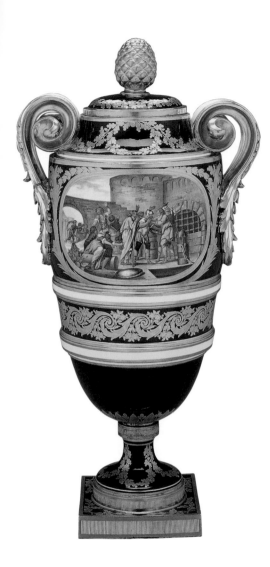

Vase
France (Sèvres), 1779
Soft-paste porcelain with
polychrome enamels and gold
Height: 28 in. (71.1 cm)
Gift of the heirs of Helen L. Jaques
38.65

This vase once stood on a marble mantelpiece in the council chamber of King Louis XVI at Versailles. The painted scene depicts an episode from the life of the sixth-century Roman general Belisarius. It is based on a popular French novel and an engraving of a painting by Anthony van Dyck. In its imposing size, lavish gilding, and vivid blue color, this vase is one of the supreme productions of the porcelain factory at Sèvres, which made porcelains for royal and aristocratic patrons from throughout Europe. A drawing and a plaster model for this vase survive in the manufactory's archives. During the French Revolution, many furnishings from Versailles and other palaces were seized by the revolutionary government and sold. This vase was acquired in Paris in the 1790s by James Swan, a Boston entrepreneur who exported basic supplies to war-ravaged France in exchange for luxury goods.

< **A** gifted orator and a fiery personality, Mirabeau (1749–1791) played a major role in the politics of revolutionary France and advocated the establishment of a constitutional monarchy rather than the deposition of the king. After his death in 1791, the political group known as the Jacobins, who shared his opinions, sponsored a competition for a memorial portrait to be displayed in the Society of Friends of the Constitution. The plaster model for this bust won that competition, but the intended marble was never carved. A number of small porcelain versions were made, but life-size porcelain busts such as this one were seldom attempted because of the technical difficulties in controlling the firing process. Deseine's sculpture is remarkable for its dramatic pose and expression, and for the unflinching realism with which the artist rendered Mirabeau's face, scarred by smallpox.

Grand piano
England (London), 1796
Manufactured by **John Broadwood and Son**
Case designed by **Thomas Sheraton**, English, 1751–1806
Satinwood, purpleheart, tulipwood, with cameos and medallions by **Josiah Wedgwood** and coin casts by **James Tassie**
97 7/8 × 43 7/8 × 35 7/8 in. (248.7 × 111.5 × 91.2 cm)
From the George Alfred Cluett Collection, given by Florence Cluett Chambers 1985.924

Unequaled in its sumptuous neoclassical ornamentation, this instrument was commissioned from England's leading piano maker by Manuel de Godoy, prime minister of Spain. It is the earliest extant piano with a range of six full octaves and the only piece known to have been specifically designed by the influential cabinetmaker Thomas Sheraton. The piano's decoration includes inlays of rare tropical woods, opaque glass-paste casts of ancient Greek coins, and cameos and medallions made of jasperware, a white porcelain invented by Josiah Wedgwood, the artist who raised English ceramics to an unprecedented level of artistic and commercial success.

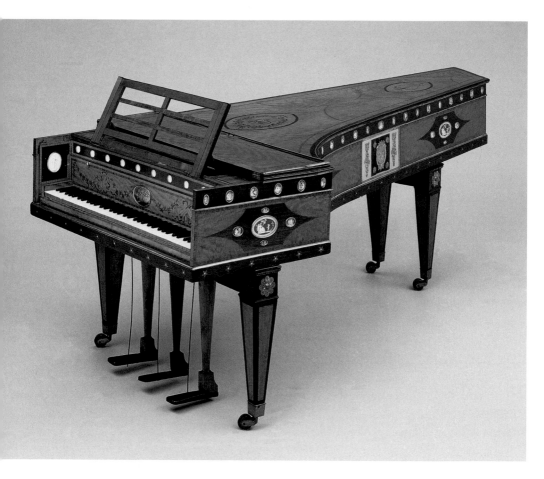

This andiron (one of a pair in the Museum's collection) evokes the splendors of prerevolutionary France. It is made of bronze, coated with a thin layer of gold, a process involving the application of mercury that burned off in the firing, unwittingly exposing workers to the deadly effects of this toxic element.

The refined technique of the andirons suggests that they are the work of Thomire, a prominent French bronzeworker. However, they may well represent the collaborative effort of many individual specialists in modeling, casting, chiseling, and gilding. The design features goats eating grapes from a basket, while below them, against a background originally covered with blue enamel, two cherubs shear a ram. The andirons may have been made for the Hameau, Queen Marie Antoinette's self-consciously rustic farm.

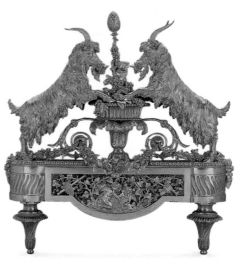

Andiron
France (Paris), about 1785
Attributed to **Pierre-Philippe Thomire,** French, 1751–1843
Gilded bronze
Height: 19 in. (48.3 cm)
Bequest of Miss Elizabeth Howard Bartol 27.521

Weisweiler was among the most skilled of many German cabinetmakers working in France in the late eighteenth and early nineteenth centuries. He specialized in exquisitely crafted luxury furniture with fine, gilded-bronze mounts—which appear here in the frieze below the marble top and along the flutes of the legs. Although this table does not bear Weisweiler's identifying stamp, the legs that swell at the top and the interlaced stretcher are hallmarks of his work. Like the andiron on this page, the table was among the furnishings acquired by Bostonian James Swan from the revolutionary government of France (see page 237).

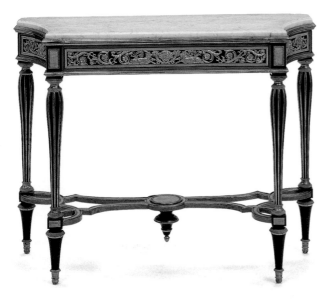

Side table
France (Paris), about 1785
Attributed to **Adam Weisweiler,** German (working in France), 1774–1820
Mahogany and satinwood veneers with gilded-bronze mounts and marble top
47 × 36⅞ × 18⅜ in.
(119.4 × 93.7 × 46.7 cm)
Bequest of Miss Elizabeth Howard Bartol 27.520

William Blake
English, 1757–1827
The Temptation and Fall of Eve, 1808
Watercolor on paper
19 5/8 × 15 1/4 in. (49.7 × 38.7 cm)
Gift by subscription 90.99

Living in a time he viewed as excessively confused and materialistic, Blake expressed his mystical, theological, and philosophical beliefs in visionary poetry, prints, and paintings. This watercolor illustrating a scene from John Milton's epic poem *Paradise Lost* is one of a set commissioned by Blake's loyal patron Thomas Butts. In the Bible, Adam and Eve were forbidden by God to eat fruit from the tree of the knowledge of good and evil. Like Milton, Blake specifically identifies the Fall of Man with the moment when Eve succumbs to temptation and takes the fruit from the mouth of the evil serpent. The sky is rent by lightning and the tree covered with thorns, as Blake expresses Milton's words: "Earth felt the wound, and Nature from her seat / Sighing through all her Works gave signs of woe / That all was lost."

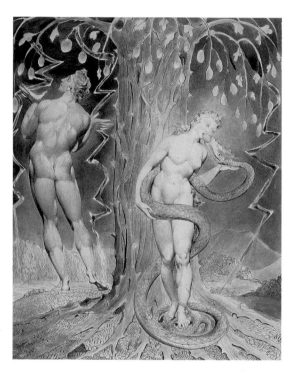

For other interpretations of the story of Adam and Eve, see pages 186, 315, and 351.

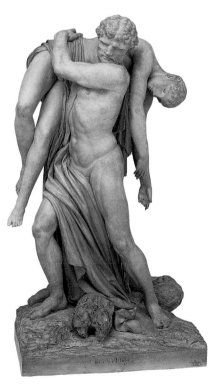

Clodion
French, 1738–1814
The Flood, 1800
Terra-cotta
Height: 21 1/2 in. (54.5 cm)
John H. and Ernestine A. Payne Fund 1981.398

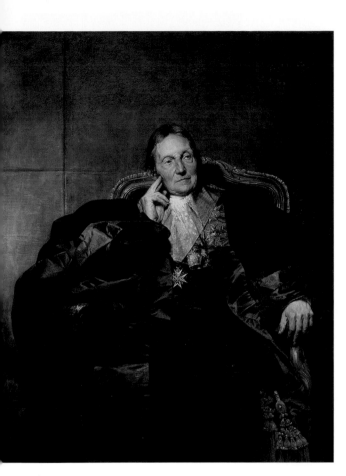

When Delaroche painted Pastoret (1756–1840) the marquis had just become Chancellor of France, the culmination of a long career in public life. Commissioned by Pastoret's son from an artist best known for his detailed paintings of highly charged historical events, this image recalls aristocratic portraits of the seventeenth century in its scale and emphasis on Pastoret's voluminous robes. The marquis wears the insignia of a Grand Officer of the Order of Saint-Esprit and two medals (the Saint Andrew Cross and the Legion of Honor) on his lapel. This opulence is strikingly contrasted with the sitter's thoughtful pose and austere, unidealized face.

About a year after his portrait was painted, Pastoret was stripped of his honors for refusing allegiance to the new constitutional monarch, Louis Philippe. The change in political climate may explain why Pastoret's coat of arms (still faintly visible in the upper left corner) was removed from the painting.

Hippolyte Delaroche
French, 1797–1856
Marquis de Pastoret, 1829
Oil on canvas
61 ⅛ × 48 ¼ in. (155.3 × 122.6 cm)
Susan Cornelia Warren Fund and the Picture Fund 11.1449

< **C**laude Michel (known as Clodion), who had benefitted from royal patronage, fell out of favor during the French Revolution. Determined to reestablish his career, the aging artist, who had previously specialized in small terra-cotta statues, exhibited at the Paris Salon of 1801 a life-sized plaster sculpture for which this superb terra-cotta was a model. Balanced on a rocky ledge surrounded by water, a man struggles to save his son; behind him (not visible here) is the half-submerged figure of a drowned woman and her child. In conceiving a human drama caused by a flood, Clodion was being deliberately "modern," for recent scientific discoveries suggested that earthquakes and floods had played a major role in the formation of the planet.

Francisco Goya y Lucientes
Spanish, 1746–1828
Reclining Nude, 1824–25
Carbon black and watercolor on ivory
3½ × 3½ in. (8.8 × 8.6 cm)
Ernest Wadsworth Longfellow Fund 63.1081

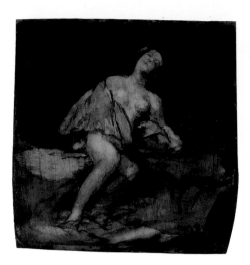

Goya's paintings, drawings, and prints—which range from official royal portraits to bitter satire on the foibles and atrocities of contemporary society—reflect the dramatically changing world in which he lived. Near the end of his life, Goya left Spain for France, arriving "deaf, old, clumsy, and weak. . . and so happy and wanting to experience life." It was during the winter of 1824 that he painted a group of tiny yet extraordinarily innovative paintings on thin sheets of ivory. According to a contemporary description, Goya "blackened the ivory plaque and let fall on it a drop of water which removed part of the black ground as it spread out, tracing random light areas. Goya took advantage of these traces and always turned them into something original and unexpected."

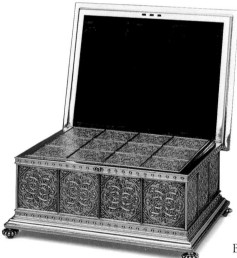

Box
England (London), 1820–21
Marked by **John Harris,** English, active after 1818
Silver, parcel gilt
5⅞ × 12⅝ × 9⅞ in.
(15 × 32.2 × 25.3 cm)
Theodora Wilbour Fund in memory of Charlotte Beebe Wilbour, and Frank B. Bemis Fund 1994.89

This box was made for William Beckford (1760–1844), an extravagant writer, collector and connoisseur, who inherited at an early age an immense fortune derived from his family's sugar plantations in Jamaica. His home in England, Fonthill Abbey, was a fanciful, Gothic-style house with a huge tower, which Beckford furnished with treasures worthy of a prince. This extraordinarily ornate silver box was a gift from Beckford to Gregorio Franchi, his agent, confidential secretary, and intimate friend. Here, the cover of the box is shown lifted to reveal a hidden inner cover with a design incorporating a monogram and the motto: *Le temps peut nous détruire mais non pas nous détacher* (Time may destroy us but cannot separate us).

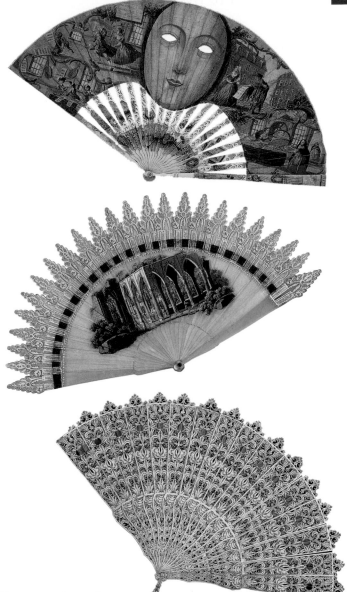

Mask fan
England, made for the Spanish
market, 1740s
Paper leaf (double), patched with
skin, etched, engraved, and painted
in watercolor; ivory sticks, pierced,
partially painted, varnished and
gilded; mother-of-pearl buttons on
brass rivet
Maximum open: 19⅛ in. (48.5 cm)
Oldham Collection 1976.179

**Fan depicting Gothic church
ruins**
England, about 1825
Brisé; horn blades, painted in
watercolor and gilded; silk
connecting ribbon; paste studs
at rivet
Maximum open: 13 in. (33 cm)
Oldham Collection 1976.317

Fan
Possibly Italy, 1810–30
Brisé; silver filigree blades with silk
connecting ribbon; silver washer
and filigree ring
Maximum open: 14⅜ in. (36.5 cm)
Oldham Collection 1976.354

The fan, more than all other fashion accessories to elegant
dress, was an essential part of the rituals of the arts of conversation and flirtation. The English
writer James Addison commented in 1711: "Women are armed with fans as men with swords and
sometimes do more execution with them." First introduced into European court circles in the late
sixteenth century, fans are wonderfully varied both in the materials of which they are made and
their decoration, which ranges from biblical scenes to famous architectural landmarks and the
words of popular songs. Some examples feature masks with eye openings and can be held to
provocatively conceal the user's identity. Brisé (broken, in French) fans, constructed without connecting leaves of paper or skin, were inspired by Japanese examples. The intricate, silver brisé fan
shown here belonged to Marie Louise, second wife of Napoleon I. It survives with its original
leather case, stamped with a crown and its owner's initials.

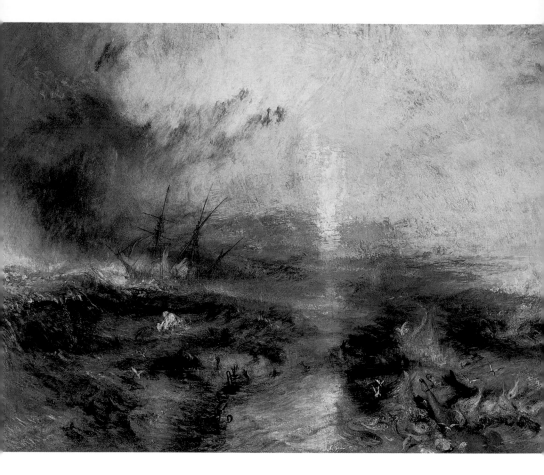

Joseph Mallord William Turner
English, 1775–1851
Slave Ship (Slavers Throwing Overboard the Dead and Dying, Typhon Coming On),
1840
Oil on canvas
35 3/4 × 48 1/4 in. (90.8 × 122.6 cm)
Henry Lillie Pierce Fund 99.22

One of Turner's most celebrated paintings, *Slave Ship* was inspired by an eighteenth-century poem and by the true story of an English ship, traveling in 1783 from Africa to Jamaica. The captain of this ship threw overboard 132 sick slaves because he could collect insurance money for slaves "lost at sea," but not for those who died from disease. Although the limbs and chains of the victims are discernible in the foreground, Turner focuses on the terrifying power of nature and the merging of churning sea and livid sky. The painting was owned for almost thirty years by art critic John Ruskin who stated: "If I were reduced to rest Turner's immortality upon any single work, I should choose this."

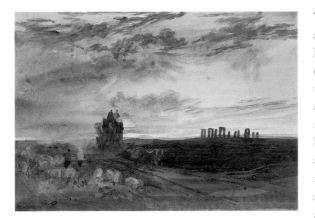

Turner had equal command of oil and of watercolor, but favored the latter when working outdoors, rendering directly and spontaneously the changing qualities of atmosphere and light. This drawing is one of many studies he made specifically to be engraved for his *Liber Studiorum,* a compilation of landscapes—long regarded as his most important achievement—which occupied the artist for over a decade. Here, dramatically silhouetted on the horizon is Stonehenge, a mysterious circle of massive, ancient stones on Salisbury Plain in southern England. Turner loved such picturesque and romantic subjects, and he captured the essence of Stonehenge's grandeur and monumentality in this small image.

Joseph Mallord William Turner
English, 1775–1851
Stonehenge at Daybreak,
about 1820
Brush and brown wash over graphite pencil on paper
7⅝ × 10⅝ in. (19.3 × 26.8 cm)
Gift of Ellen T. Bullard 59.795

Unlike his contemporary Turner, who traveled widely in search of dramatic subjects, Constable painted the ancient villages and rural landscape of his native Suffolk, in England. The resulting images are fresh, immediate, and closely observed. This painting was commissioned by Thomas Fitzhugh as a wedding present for his bride, Philadelphia Godfrey, so that she might have a memento of the countryside stretching out around her family home. In the foreground is a dunghill from which workers dig manure to fertilize the fields for next year's crops. As well as making numerous preliminary drawings and oil sketches, Constable worked on the canvas itself outdoors—rendering enthusiastically the expansive landscape early in the morning of a perfect fall day.

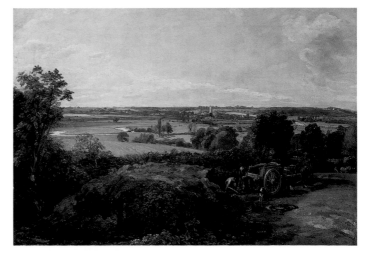

John Constable
English, 1776–1837
Stour Valley and Dedham Church, about 1815
Oil on canvas
21⅞ × 30⅝ in. (55.5 × 77.8 cm)
Warren Collection 48.266

Jean Baptiste Camille Corot
French, 1796–1875
Forest of Fontainebleau, 1846
Oil on canvas
35½ × 50¾ in. (90.2 × 128.8 cm)
Gift of Mrs. Samuel Dennis Warren
90.199

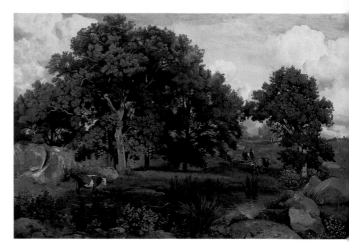

Eugène Delacroix
French, 1798–1863
The Entombment of Christ,
1848
Oil on canvas
64 × 52 in. (162.6 × 132.1 cm)
Gift by Contribution in Memory of
Martin Brimmer 96.21

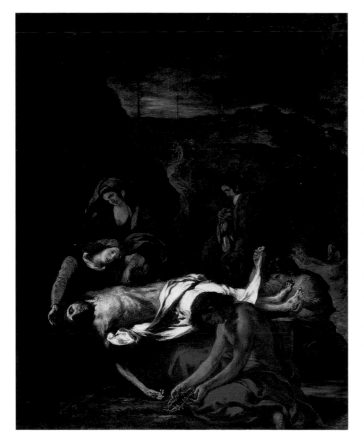

Against a deep and somber landscape, desolate mourners gather around the body of Christ. Delacroix's use of resonant color and expressive, sketchy brushwork had a profound influence on later painters, including the Impressionists. Although Delacroix constantly struggled with his personal spiritual beliefs, American writer and critic Henry James called this "the only modern religious picture I have seen that seemed to me to be painted in good faith." Delacroix himself wrote that "the whole arouses an emotion that astonishes even me."

Beginning in the 1820s, Corot spent summers sketching in the vast Forest of Fontainebleau, south of Paris. He based this painting on such informal sketches, reworking them to create a more structured composition, with the horizontals of foreground and background balanced by the verticals of trees and the cows positioned to mark recession into space. Nevertheless, as a depiction of a familiar, local site without the "justification" of a biblical or mythological subject, this painting became a key work in the development of French landscape painting when it was accepted for the Salon of 1846. Corot believed that artists "must. . . never lose the first impression that quickened our emotion." His work formed a bridge between traditional, idealizing landscapes and those of the Impressionists, to whom Corot was a mentor and an inspiration.

Gustave Courbet
French, 1819–1877
The Quarry, 1856–57
Oil on canvas
82¾ x 72¼ in. (210.2 x 183.5 cm)
Henry Lillie Pierce Fund 18.620

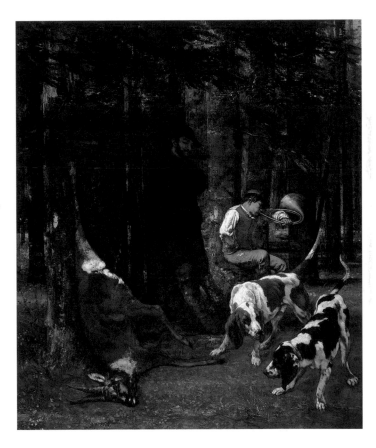

Courbet was the self-styled leader of the Realist movement in French art. Most of his paintings of modern life were condemned as offensively ordinary, but *The Quarry* was well received when it was exhibited at the Salon of 1857. Probably set in the Jura Mountains along the French-Swiss border, the painting features the artist himself, posed as a huntsman. He enlarged the original canvas as he worked, adding one piece across the top above the hunter's head and others to include the horn blower and the dogs. In 1866 when he learned that *The Quarry* had been purchased by a group of young Boston artists, Courbet exclaimed: "What care I for the Salon, what care I for honors, when the art students of a new and great country know and appreciate and buy my works?"

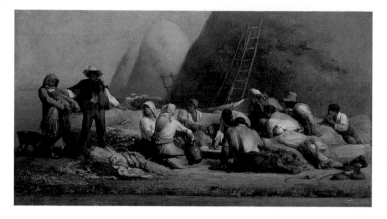

Jean François Millet
French, 1814–1875
Harvesters Resting (Ruth and Boaz), 1850–53
Oil on canvas
26½ × 47⅛ in. (62.8 × 119.8 cm)
Bequest of Mrs. Martin Brimmer
06.2421

Millet conceived this painting as a depiction of the biblical story of Ruth, a poor widow who supported herself by gathering grain left behind by the harvesters. When the artist exhibited this work at the Salon of 1853, however, he changed the title to underscore its contemporary significance. Millet has painted peasants of his own time, and the setting is the fertile plain of Chailly, breadbasket for much of France. In the 1850s rural France was increasingly owned by absentee landlords more interested in personal gain than in the welfare of the people who worked their fields. The gleaner's meager bundle contrasts poignantly with the stacks of grain behind her, and Millet's Boaz is not the landowner of the biblical story, but a sharecropper hired to work a rich man's land. In this, as in so many of his works, Millet urges respect for the hardship and dignity of humble lives.

Jean François Millet
French, 1814–1875
Dandelions, 1867–68
Pastel on buff paper
15⅞ × 19¾ in. (40.2 × 50.2 cm)
Gift of Quincy Adams Shaw
through Quincy A. Shaw, Jr., and
Mrs. Marian Shaw Haughton
17.1524

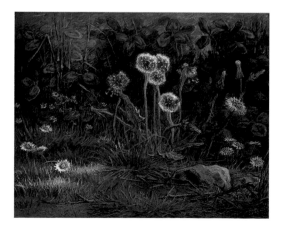

Millet frequently worked in pastel, which allowed him to combine his love of drawing and painting. Indeed, after 1865 he made almost as many pastels as oil paintings, thanks to an admiring patron, Parisian architect and financier Emile Gavet, who was prepared to buy every pastel that Millet produced. Here, against a richly variegated green background, Millet presents the life of a common wildflower, from tight buds to airy bursts of white-plumed seeds. Not a conventional still life, *Dandelions* is a landscape—a close-up view of a small patch of meadow that might otherwise be overlooked.

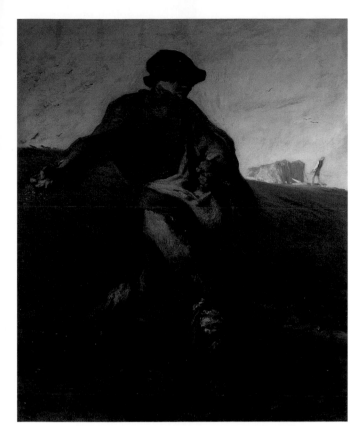

Jean François Millet
French, 1814–1875
The Sower, 1850
Oil on canvas
40 × 32½ in. (101.6 × 82.6 cm)
Gift of Quincy Adams Shaw
through Quincy A. Shaw, Jr., and
Mrs. Marian Shaw Haughton
17.1485

Striding across broken ground, a peasant sows winter wheat in the cold November twilight. Behind him, an ox-drawn harrow closes the soil over the grain. This painting's dark, heavily worked surface inspired one critic to write that the artist "seemed to paint with the very earth that is being planted." Millet said that he was "driven to make pictures that mattered," and his art was revolutionary in its assertion that the commonplace activities of ordinary people were worthy subjects for serious art. France's Revolution of 1848 had granted the vote to all male citizens, including the landless peasants who vastly outnumbered landowners. Although Millet insisted that his art was not political, many Parisians found this powerful, shadowed figure threatening when the painting was exhibited at the Salon of 1850. One writer saw the peasant as sowing not wheat but "the seeds of discord and revolution."

In the 1850s, long before Millet was widely appreciated in his homeland, Boston artists and collectors traveled to France to meet the artist and purchase his works. The Museum acquired its world-famous holdings of Millet's work through the generosity of these foresighted collectors, in particular Martin Brimmer, the Museum's first president; local artist William Morris Hunt; and collector Quincy Adams Shaw.

Cabinet
England, about 1870
Designed by **Bruce Talbert,**
Scottish, 1838–1881
Ebonized cherry and fumed oak
with exotic wood veneers
85 ⁷/₈ × 44 ¹/₄ × 24 ³/₈ in.
(218.1 × 112.4 × 61.9 cm)
John Wheelock Elliot and John
Morse Elliot Fund and Arthur
Tracy Cabot Fund 1997.188

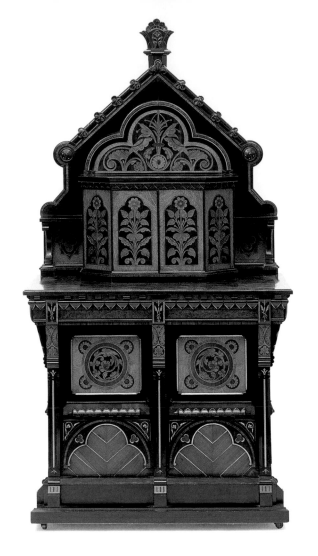

Trained as a woodcarver, architect, and cabinetmaker, Talbert was among the foremost designers of the nineteenth century to work in the Gothic-revival style. He created designs not only for furniture but also for cast iron, textiles, ceramics, stained glass, carpets, and wallpapers. Talbert worked in the Modern or Reformed Gothic style that aimed to counteract the extravagances of other revival styles with designs that were more honest and historically accurate. The form of this cabinet derives from the English court cupboard of the Tudor period; its carved, gilded, and inlaid decoration is gothic in inspiration. The design for the cabinet appeared in *Gothic Forms Applied to Furniture, Metal Work and Decoration for Domestic Purposes* (1868), the book that established Talbert's reputation in England, Europe, and America.

The early photographic process of calotype, unstable and difficult to control, was nevertheless capable of effects of great beauty. Intrigued by its possibilities, Hill and Adamson formed a remarkable collaboration, and in less than four years, they produced 3000 calotypes described by a contemporary as "the wonder of every gathering of scientific or artistic men." Their most innovative project—which effectively invented social documentary photography—was a series of photographs of the fishermen and women in the village of Newhaven, just north of Edinburgh. The fishwives, famous for their good looks and picturesque dress, cleaned the catch and carried it to market in huge baskets. In portraits like this one, where broad areas of light and dark are skillfully juxtaposed, the photographers created small works that are nevertheless monumental in feeling.

Dante Gabriel Rossetti
English, 1828–1882
Bocca Baciata (Lips That Have Been Kissed), 1859
Oil on panel
12 5/8 × 10 5/8 in. (32.2 × 27.1 cm)
Gift of James Lawrence 1980.261

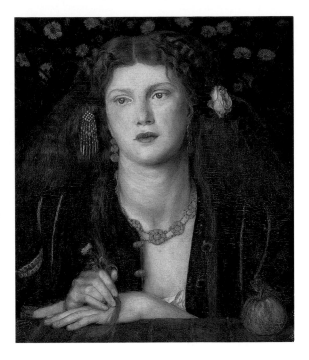

Rossetti was a founding member, in 1848, of the Pre-Raphaelite Brotherhood, which sought to counteract the eclecticism and excess of the midnineteenth century by returning to the simplicity of medieval art. His works in the new style are detailed, storytelling images drawn from the Bible, the writings of Dante, or the legends of King Arthur. This painting, however, represents a turning point in Rossetti's career—the first example of the subject that was to occupy him for the rest of his life. The painting depicts a sensual young woman with loosened hair and a distant, unfocused gaze. There is no story here, no clue to the painting's meaning. The poet Algernon Swinburne declared that *Bocca Baciata* was "more stunning than can be decently expressed," and many others recognized it as an assertion that a work of art might be only beautiful, without any obligation to moralize or instruct.

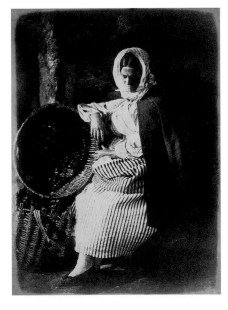

David Octavius Hill
Scottish, 1802–1870
Robert Adamson
Scottish, 1821–1848
Mrs. Elizabeth (Johnstone) Hall, Seated Newhaven Fishwife, 1843–47
Calotype
8 3/8 × 6 1/4 in. (21.3 × 15.9 cm)
Purchased with funds given by David Bakalar 1974.469

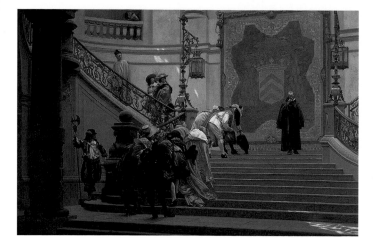

Gérôme's paintings—with their precise detail, imperceptible brushwork, and brilliant effects of color and light—epitomized the admired and officially sanctioned academic style that prevailed throughout Europe in the later nineteenth century. This wonderfully theatrical painting recreates the grand staircase of the palace of Cardinal Richelieu (the Red Cardinal) who ruled France during the

Jean-Léon Gérôme
French, 1824–1904
L'Eminence grise, 1873
Oil on canvas
27 × 39¾ in. (68.5 × 101 cm)
Bequest of Susan Cornelia Warren
03.605

childhood of Louis XIII in the early seventeenth century. Descending the staircase is Richelieu's secretary and confidant, François LeClerc du Trembly, a friar known as *l'éminence grise* (the Gray Cardinal), a term that has come to mean "the power behind the throne." Framed by a huge tapestry bearing Richelieu's coat of arms, the friar reads his prayerbook, ignoring the obsequious bows and resentful glances of the courtiers, whose opulent dress contrasts strikingly with his own sober garments.

Sir Lawrence Alma-Tadema
Dutch (worked in Brussels and London),
1836–1912
Woman and Flowers (Opus LIX), 1868
Oil on panel
19⅝ × 14⅝ in. (49.8 × 37.2 cm)
Gift of Edward Jackson Holmes 41.117

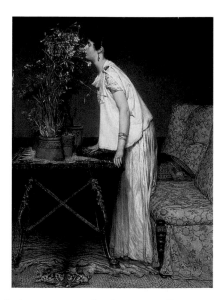

On his honeymoon in Italy in 1863, Alma-Tadema spent hours sketching among the ancient Roman ruins at Pompeii, and throughout his career, he painted numerous works inspired by classical antiquity. The smooth, polished surfaces of his romantic recreations of the past, like those of Jean-Léon Gérôme, are luminous in color and meticulous in the delineation of every material, surface, and detail. Alma-Tadema kept 168 volumes of photographs of Greek and Roman antiquities, and the objects in his paintings are scrupulously correct. Here, a young woman, probably modeled by the artist's wife, Pauline, leans on a Pompeiian bronze table, the model for which is now in the archaeological museum of Naples.

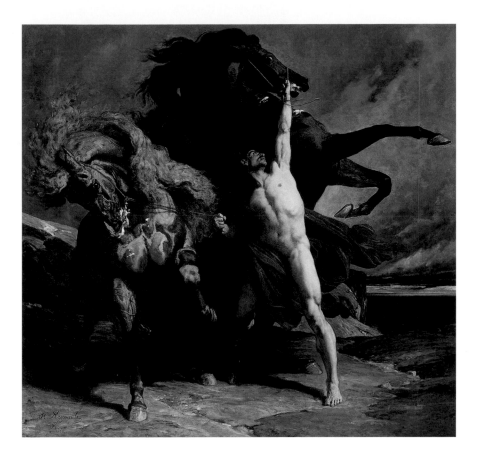

Full of youthful fire and passion, this mammoth painting—more than ten feet square—was painted while Regnault, the son of the director of the Sèvres porcelain manufactory, was a student in Rome. Several years later, the artist returned home to fight in the Franco-Prussian War and was killed during the siege of Paris at the age of twenty-seven.

Derived from Homer's epic, the *Iliad,* the painting depicts Automedon, chariot driver for Achilles, struggling to control Xanthos and Balios, the horses that will carry the Greek hero into his final, fatal battle. Exhibited around the United States in the 1870s and 1880s, the painting was called both "the grandest painting in America" and "highly seasoned and unhealthful food which renders the palette insensitive to the milder flavors of what is wholesome." Following petitions by Boston artists and art students, this work was purchased by public subscription and presented to the Museum in 1890.

Alexandre-Georges-Henri Regnault
French, 1843–1871
Automedon with the Horses of Achilles, 1868
Oil on canvas
124 × 129½ in. (315 × 329 cm)
Gift by Subscription 90.152

Prints: Out of One, Many

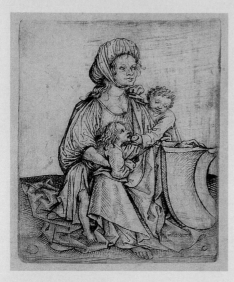

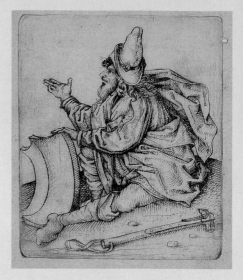

**Master of the Housebook
(Master of the Amsterdam
Cabinet)**
German, active about 1470–1500
*Gypsy Woman with Two
Children Holding a Blank
Shield* and *Gypsy Man Holding
a Blank Shield,* about 1475–80
Drypoint
3⅝ x 2⅞ in. (9.2 x 7.2 cm)
3¾ x 2⅞ in. (9.3 x 7.2 cm)
Katherine E. Bullard Fund in
Memory of Francis Bullard
66.375, 376

All encyclopedic collections of prints are measured both by the
depth of their holdings and by individual works of superb artistic quality or rarity. The drypoints above are by the printmaker
known as the Master of the Amsterdam Cabinet, one of the
first to explore the medium for artistic purposes. These images,
which demonstrate a remarkable ability to create natural poses
and a convincing illusion of three-dimensional form, are among
very few surviving examples. Similarly, the Museum's fine
impression of Goya's *The Giant* (facing page), among the most
enigmatic and compelling of the Spanish artist's graphic works,
is a highlight of the collection.

On the other hand, one of the primary characteristics of
printmaking is that many images—subtly or dramatically different—can be made by inking, printing, or otherwise altering the
same woodblock, etching or engraving plate, lithographic stone,
or silkscreen. Many printmakers value this ability to create

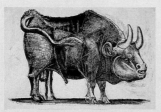

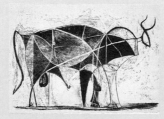

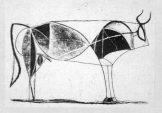

variations on a theme, printing a composition and then modifying it by adding or removing lines, or by simply changing the colors of the ink, printing the image on papers of contrasting colors or textures, or wiping the ink in different ways to alter the balance of light and dark.

From works by Dürer and Rembrandt to Jim Dine, the Museum's collection embraces this evidence of the creative process. Many examples of individual prints allow viewers to explore, evaluate, and learn by comparison. As an example, across these pages, below, are six images of a bull that Pablo Picasso created on the same lithographic stone. Each one is beautiful and interesting in its own right; together, they provide the opportunity to, in a sense, look over the artist's shoulder as he worked reductively from a detailed rendering of the animal's outward appearance to its essential structure, captured in a few, swift lines.

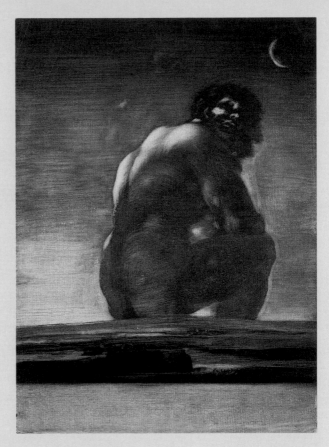

Francisco Goya y Lucientes
Spanish, 1746–1828
The Giant, by 1818
Aquatint
11 ¼ × 8 ¼ in. (28.5 × 21 cm)
Katherine E. Bullard Fund in Memory of Francis Bullard
65.1296

Pablo Picasso
Spanish (worked in France), 1881–1973
The Bull, 1945
Lithograph (6 states)
Sheets: 12 ¾–13 ⅜ × 17 ⅜–21 ⅛ in. (31–33.9 × 44–53.6 cm)
Lee M. Friedman Fund
1970.272–277

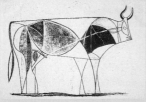

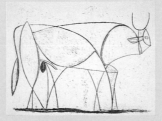

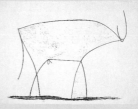

Edouard Manet
French, 1832–1883
Street Singer, about 1862
Oil on canvas
67 ³/₈ × 41 ⁵/₈ in. (171.3 × 105.8 cm)
Bequest of Sarah Choate Sears in
Memory of her husband, Joshua
Montgomery Sears 66.304

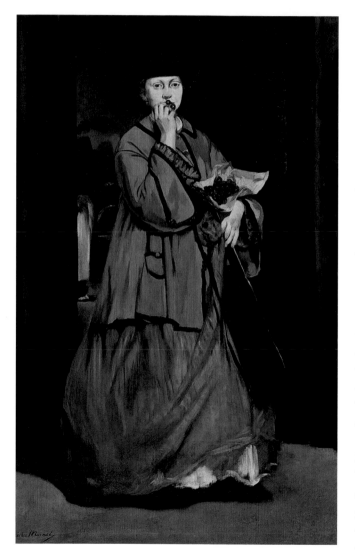

Manet was one of the first great painters of modern urban life. One day, while walking through the streets of Paris, he saw a woman with a guitar emerging from a modest café. He asked her to pose for him, but she laughed and ran away. Although *Street Singer* was ultimately created in the studio using a professional model (eighteen-year-old Victorine Meurend), it retains the impact of Manet's initial experience—including the swiftly brushed glimpse of a petticoat as the woman lifts her skirt, her enigmatic expression, and the blurred impression of an aproned waiter beyond the swinging doors.

In this large painting, Manet gave a humble member of the working class great dignity, and most contemporary critics found the work vulgar and offensive. One wrote, however, that "Had there been a touch of pathos in the treatment of the subject, the public might have overlooked its ordinariness."

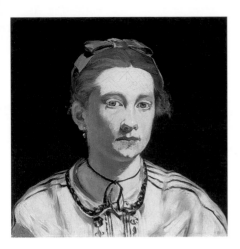

When Manet first saw Victorine Meurend, he was "struck by her unusual appearance and her decided air." She became his favorite model, posing for *Street Singer* and many other paintings of the 1860s. This small portrait clearly illustrates Manet's bold style, which was criticized for its "crude conflict of chalk whites with black tones" and for brushwork that seemed rough and unfinished. For Manet, however, this style was a means of rendering modern subject matter in an equally modern way.

In 1864 Maximilian, brother of the emperor of Austria, was installed as emperor of Mexico under the protection of the French emperor Napoleon III and a French army of occupation. In 1867, however, Napoleon suddenly withdrew his support and his troops, and Maximilian was captured and executed by Mexican forces loyal to their former government. When the shocking news reached Paris, Manet—a republican and fervent critic of the French empire—decided to immortalize this event on a scale traditionally reserved for scenes from history or the Bible. Basing his composition on photographs and eyewitness accounts, the artist worked for almost two years, producing four oil paintings and a lithograph of the subject. This immediate and impassioned painting is the first, unfinished version.

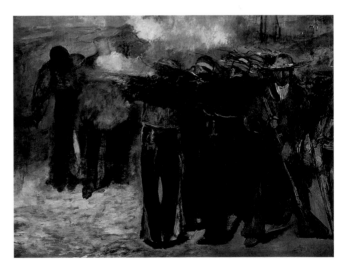

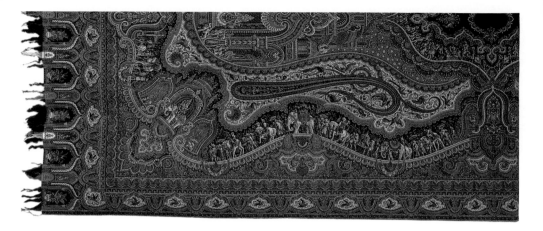

Shawl (detail)
France (Lyons) about 1867
Manufactured by **Maison Pin**
Wool, silk, and cotton; twill weave
(Jacquard woven)
140 × 63½ in. (356 × 161 cm)
Gift of Mary Bailey Derr Knox
1986.981

At the end of the eighteenth century, European textile manufacturers began to produce more affordable imitations of the handwoven Indian shawls associated with Kashmir. With the invention of the Jacquard loom, about 1800, shawls could be machine woven with increasingly complex patterns and subtle shading. Remarkable in design and execution, this example depicts a Europeanized view of a procession of dignitaries riding horses, camels, and elephants on their way to pay homage to an Eastern ruler. A shawl of this design was included in the great international exposition held in Paris in 1867.

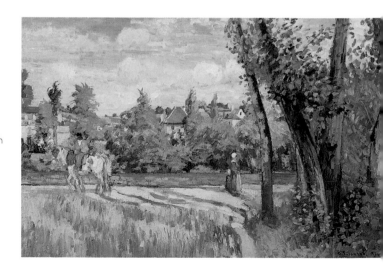

Camille Pissarro
French (born in the Danish
West Indies), 1830–1903
*Sunlight on the Road,
Pontoise,* 1874
Oil on canvas
20⅝ × 32⅛ in.
(52.3 × 81.5 cm)
Juliana Cheney Edwards
Collection 25.114

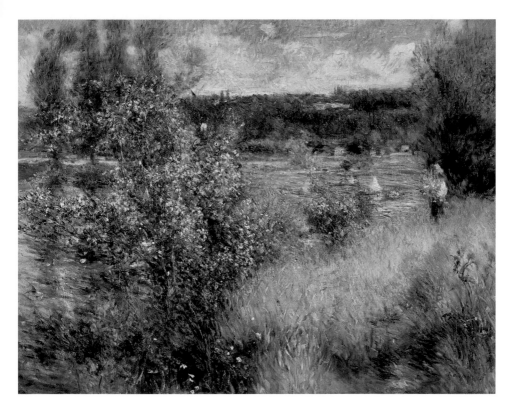

Pierre Auguste Renoir
French, 1841–1919
The Seine at Chatou,
about 1881
Oil on canvas
28 7/8 × 36 3/8 in. (73.5 × 92.5 cm)
Gift of Arthur Brewster Emmons
19.771

This is one of Renoir's most radiant landscapes, in which the edges of forms dissolve in the brilliant sunlight, and even the figure merges into the meadow. It was painted near Chatou, a town ten miles from Paris on the banks of the Seine, easily reached by train, and popular among Parisians for weekend sailing and swimming. Not surprisingly, therefore, Renoir's painting evokes a mood of idyllic escapism. Working here in the spring of 1881, Renoir postponed a trip to London with a friend, explaining, "I'm struggling with trees in flower, with women and children, and I don't want to look at anything else."

< **S**omewhat older than the other French Impressionists, Pissarro was an early leader of the group and later an important mentor to Cézanne and Gauguin. This serene view of a village near Paris, with its fresh palette and broad brushwork, exemplifies Impressionist painting at the time of the group's first exhibition in 1874. Typical of Pissarro, the painting is not only direct and spontaneous but carefully structured around a series of horizontal bands punctuated by the verticals of the trees and animated by the woman and horseman making their way along the road.

Edgar Degas
French, 1834–1917
At the Races in the Countryside, 1869
Oil on canvas
14³⁄₈ × 22 in. (36.5 × 55.9 cm)
1931 Purchase Fund 26.790

Degas's paintings were often inspired by the amusements that he enjoyed as a well-to-do Parisian: the opera, the ballet, art exhibitions, and horseracing. Like many of his compositions, this painting of a race course in Normandy, shown at the first Impressionist exhibition in 1874, is artfully structured so as to appear as casual as a snapshot. Grouped informally in the foreground are Degas's friend Paul Valpinçon, his wife, and their infant son in the arms of his wet nurse. Their carriage and horses are cut off at the edges of the canvas as if just moving out of our sight. The abrupt juxtaposition of objects near and far away and the contrast of indistinct and sharply focused forms are other features that give this painting its revolutionary effect of spontaneity.

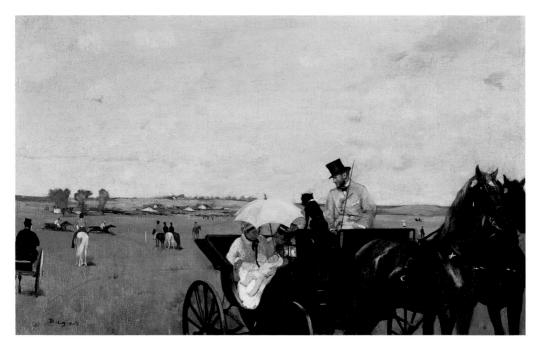

Edgar Degas >
French, 1834–1917
The Violinist, about 1879
Black and white chalk on blue-gray paper
18⁷⁄₈ × 12 in. (47.9 × 30.5 cm)
William Francis Warden Fund
58.1263

Edgar Degas
French, 1834–1917
Edmondo and Thérèse Morbilli,
about 1867
Oil on canvas
45⅞ x 34¾ in. (116.5 x 88.3 cm)
Gift of Robert Treat Paine 2nd
31.33

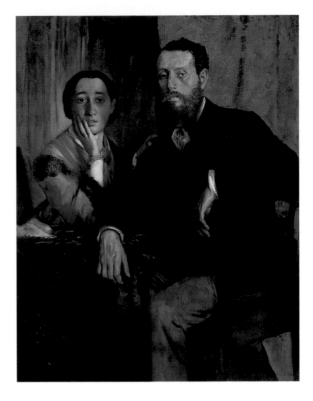

This intriguing double portrait shows Degas's sister Thérèse and her husband Edmondo Morbilli, their first cousin, whom she married in 1863. While never a professional portraitist, Degas created numerous images of family and friends in which he explored personality through pose, gesture, and the subtleties of facial expression. Here, Edmondo, self-assured and at ease, physically dominates the composition, while Thérèse, more introspective, one hand resting on her husband's shoulder, is partly in shadow, the details of her clothing a little blurred, as if out of focus. Although the composition suggests the formal, sixteenth-century portraits Degas had studied in Italy, the neutral background, shallow space, and overlapping poses are typical of contemporary daguerreotype photographs.

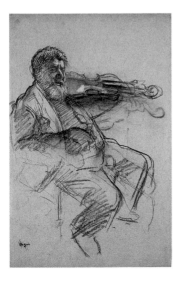

Degas's father was an accomplished organist, and the artist had a deep love and appreciation of music. During the 1870s he frequently attended rehearsals of the orchestra and ballet of the Paris Opéra, sketching the performers at work, often as preparatory studies for paintings. This study is for the violinist in *The Rehearsal,* a painting of a ballet practice now in the Frick Collection, New York. Although sketchy and spontaneous, the drawing is rich in tonal variations and bold line, the fall of light rendered with accents of white chalk. Degas captures with remarkable facility the progression of arms and instrument as they move from one position to the next.

Claude Monet
French, 1840–1926
Poppy Field in a Hollow,
Near Giverny, 1885
Oil on canvas
25 ⅝ × 32 in. (65.2 × 81.2 cm)
Juliana Cheney Edwards
Collection 25.106

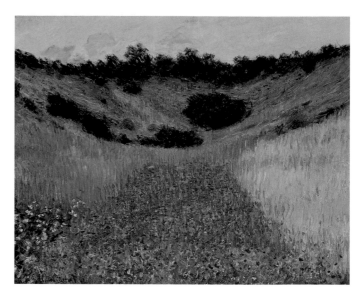

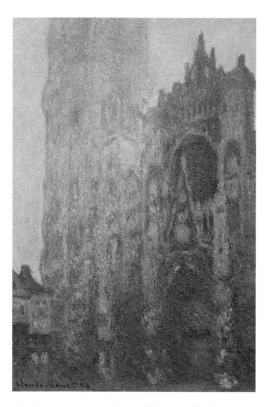

Claude Monet
French, 1840–1926
Rouen Cathedral Facade and
Tour d'Albane (Morning
Effect), 1894
Oil on canvas
41 ¾ × 29 ⅛ in. (106.1 × 73.9 cm)
Tompkins Collection 24.6

Monet's series paintings of the 1890s—multiple variations of a single motif conceived, executed, and exhibited as a group—are among his most inventive and remarkable works. In the winter of 1892 the artist spent several months studying and painting the facade of Rouen Cathedral in his native Normandy. From rooms facing the cathedral across a square, Monet concentrated on the analysis of light and its effects on the forms of the facade, changing from one canvas to another as the day progressed. Later he extensively reworked the thirty paintings of the cathedral series in his studio at Giverny. Their encrusted surfaces of dry, thickly layered paint evoke the rough texture of weathered stone, absorbing and reflecting light like the walls of the cathedral itself.

< **M**onet and his fellow Impressionists believed that art should express its own time and place and that it should do so in an appropriately modern style. In the 1860s and 1870s, working primarily outdoors, the Impressionists observed that objects seen in strong light lose definition and appear to blend into one another. No clear outlines exist in this sunny landscape. Its forms and textures are suggested by the size, shape, and direction of the brushstrokes, and the juxtaposition of complementary reds and greens gives the painting a vibrant intensity. By the mid-1880s, most members of the original group had turned away from Impressionism, but Monet declared: "I am still an Impressionist and will always remain one."

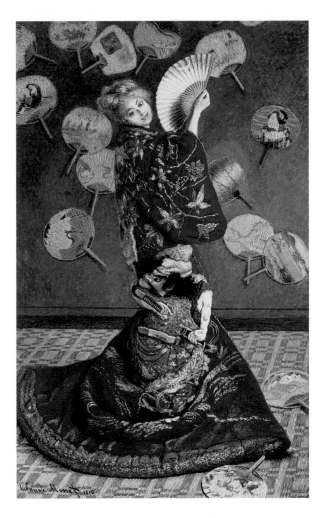

The quintessential Impressionist landscape painter, Monet executed only a handful of major figure paintings. This lifesize portrait, a great success at the second Impressionist exhibition in 1876, is a virtuoso display of color and texture as well as a witty comment on the current enthusiasm—which Monet shared—for all things Japanese. The seemingly coy model is Monet's wife, Camille, who wears a blond wig to emphasize her Western identity and holds a fan with the colors of the French flag. On one of the Japanese fans decorating the background wall, a woman in traditional costume casts the impostor a startled look, while the clever arrangement of the splendid robe animates the fierce warrior embroidered on it.

Claude Monet
French, 1840–1926
La Japonaise, 1876
Oil on canvas
91 ½ x 56 in. (231.6 x 142.3 cm)
1951 Purchase Fund 56.147

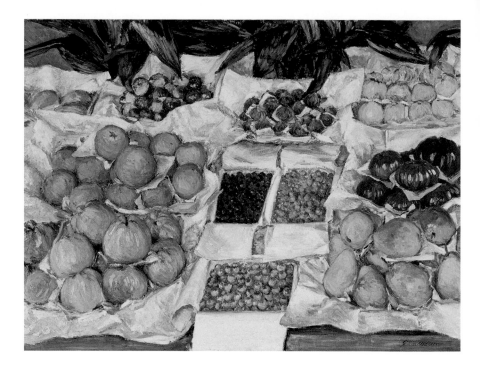

Although less well known than other French Impressionists, Caillebotte was one of the style's most original practitioners and a major promoter and collector of Impressionist art. Often attracted by unusual vantage points and innovative manipulation of space, his close-up view of a fruit vendor's wares enticingly arranged on rumpled paper was described by a contemporary critic as "still life freed from its routine." It is a memorable composition of complementary shapes and colors that gives an immediate sense of a display glimpsed along a Parisian street.

Gustave Caillebotte
French, 1848–1894
Fruit Displayed on a Stand,
about 1881–82
Oil on canvas
30⅛ × 39⅝ in. (76.5 × 100.5 cm)
Fanny P. Mason Fund in Memory
of Alice Thevin 1979.196

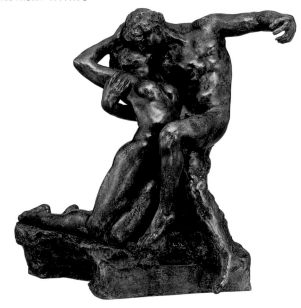

Curtain panel or *portière*
England, 1892–93
Made by **May Morris,** English,
1862–1938, for **Morris &
Company**
Silk damask; embroidered
102 × 53.5 in. (259 × 136 cm)
In Memory of J. S. and Sadye A.
Gordon from Myron K. and
Natalie G. Stone 1983.160d

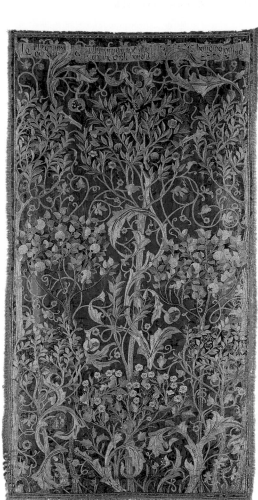

The members of the Arts and Crafts movement advocated a return to the preindustrial ideal of handmade, finely crafted works of art. William Morris, founder of Morris & Company, was the greatest single influence on this movement, and this curtain panel represents his firm's commitment to the use of fine materials and to design inspired by medieval traditions. The panel is the work of Morris's daughter May, who wrote: "Design is the very soul and essence of beautiful embroidery, as it is of every other art, exalted or humble."

The panel is one of four (all in the Museum's collection) that hung in a Brookline, Massachusetts, home. The words embroidered at the top—"Lo silken my garden and silken my sky / And silken the apple boughs hanging on high" are from a poem by William Morris.

< **Auguste Rodin**
French, 1840–1917
Eternal Springtime
Modeled about 1881; cast about
1916–17
Bronze
Height: 24 3/4 in. (62.9 cm)
Bequest of William A. Coolidge
1993.50

Rodin modeled *Eternal Springtime* while planning his monumental project *The Gates of Hell,* the bronze doors inspired by Dante's *Inferno* that were commissioned in 1880 for a planned museum of decorative arts. *The Gates of Hell* were never finished; the original plaster version is now in the Musée d'Orsay, Paris. Although Rodin ultimately did not include *Eternal Springtime* in his composition for the doors, it is among his most celebrated works, daring in the precarious pose of the figures, their lean bodies extended into space, and in the complexity of convex and concave curves as the bodies intertwine.

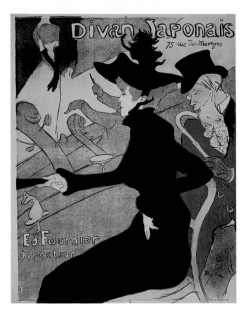

Henri de Toulouse-Lautrec
French, 1864–1901
Divan Japonais, 1893
Color lithograph on paper
32 × 24½ in. (81.5 × 62.3 cm)
Lee M. Friedman Fund 68.72

Nineteenth-century guidebooks described Paris as "the capital of pleasure," with its thousands of theaters, dance halls, cafés, circuses, racetracks, and other entertainments. Posters advertising these amusements were made possible by the development of color lithography, a process capable of producing large editions of high-quality prints. The clever, eye-catching posters of Toulouse-Lautrec—with their stylized shapes and flat areas of color—immortalized such places as the cabaret Divan Japonais. Here, seated in the audience are the popular dancer Jane Avril and the critic Edouard Dujardin. In the background, beyond the musicians, is the singer Yvette Guilbert, instantly recognizable although the artist does not show her face. A journalist described Guilbert: "She has no bosom to speak of and her chest is quite extraordinarily narrow. She has long—too long—thin arms clad in high black gloves that look like flimsy streamers."

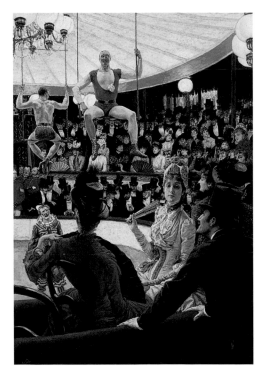

Tissot, like the Impressionists, chose his subjects from modern urban life, but his detailed and polished style is that of traditional academic painting. This is one of a series called *Women of Paris (La Femme à Paris)* that depicts women of different social classes encountered as if by chance at their occupations and amusements.

Circuses were popular entertainments in Paris and were painted by Degas and Picasso, among others. The event here is a "Cirque du High Life" in which the amateur performers were aristocrats. An early exhibition catalogue explained: "He on the trapeze facing you. . . is no less a person that the Duc de la R—, and his companion is a person of the same blue blood."

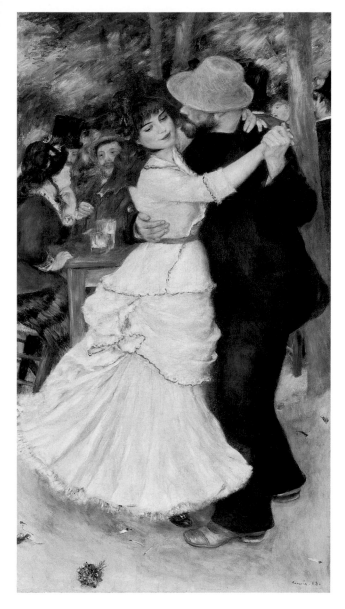

Pierre Auguste Renoir
French, 1841–1919
Dance at Bougival, 1883
Oil on canvas
71⅝ x 38⅝ in. (181.8 x 98.1 cm)
Picture Fund 37.37

One of Renoir's most ambitious and beloved works, this painting was executed in the studio but captures with delightful immediacy a sunny afternoon at Bougival. Close to Paris and frequented by city dwellers, Bougival's open-air cafés were described as "quite select and expensive, and girls go there without particular expectations." Renoir's young woman was modeled by Suzanne Valadon, a trapeze artist turned professional model who became well known as a painter and was the mother of artist Maurice Utrillo. Renoir's friend Paul Auguste Llhote, a notorious ladies' man, posed as Valadon's intent partner. The motion of the dancing couple is conveyed by the swirl of the woman's skirt and by the blurred focus of the revelers in the background. The painting is timeless in the pleasure it conveys but modern in its setting and details—Valadon's dress, bonnet, and haircut, for example, were the latest summer fashions in 1883.

James Jacques Joseph Tissot
French, 1836–1902
Women of Paris: The Circus Lover, 1885
Oil on canvas
58 x 40 in. (147.2 x 101.6 cm)
Juliana Cheney Edwards Collection
58.45

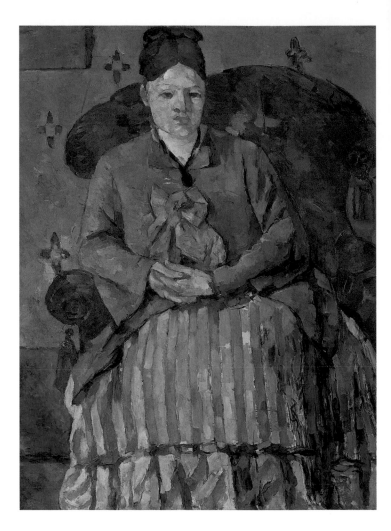

Cézanne said: "I want to make Impressionism into an art as solid and lasting as the art of the museums." Whether painting landscapes, still lifes, or people, the artist spent many painstaking hours studying and analyzing his subjects, and some of his portraits required up to 100 sittings. More than two dozen portraits exist of Hortense Figuet, who lived with Cézanne for almost twenty years before she married him in 1886. Painted in the couple's Paris apartment, this early portrait has a serene and timeless monumentality; its many small blocks of subtly varied color, describing shadows and volume, are locked into a harmonious whole. After seeing this painting in a 1907 exhibition, the German poet Rainer Maria Rilke wrote: "In this red armchair, which is a personality, a woman is seated. . . . It seems that each part [of the painting] knows of all the other parts."

Paul Cézanne
French, 1839–1906
Madame Cézanne in a Red Armchair, about 1877
Oil on canvas
28½ × 22 in. (72.5 × 56.0 cm)
Bequest of Robert Treat Paine 2nd
44.776

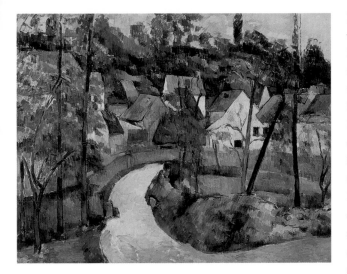

During the 1870s, Cézanne worked closely with Camille Pissarro (see page 258) who taught him to paint outdoors using the bright colors and broken brushstrokes of Impressionism. Cézanne, however, was always less interested in the changing face of nature than in its permanent aspects. Here, the artist shows his preference for clearly outlined shapes and for three-dimensional forms modeled with squarish brushstrokes of changing colors. While the road draws us back into space it exists at the same time as a flat, yellowish shape: Cézanne is asserting that, although his painting gives the illusion of recession and of depth, it is first and foremost a work of art that actually exists only on the surface of the canvas. *Turn in the Road* was owned for many years by Claude Monet.

Paul Cézanne
French, 1839–1906
Turn in the Road, 1879–82
Oil on canvas
23⅞ × 28⅞ in. (60.5 × 73.5 cm)
Bequest of John T. Spaulding
48.525

Signac was profoundly inspired by Georges Seurat (1859–1891), who developed the style of painting called pointillism or divisionism in which color and form are rendered in tiny touches of paint. Signac became the chief theorist of the new style and also devoted himself to the scientific study of optics, publishing his findings on the relationship of light and color in 1898. This austere, luminous seascape is one of a series of four paintings depicting different views of the coast of Brittany, France, that Signac exhibited in 1891 as *The Sea*. The large, simplified forms of the spare design may reflect Signac's admiration for the Japanese woodblock prints that influenced many French painters in the later nineteenth century.

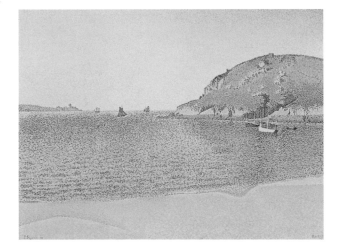

Paul Signac
French, 1863–1935
Port of Saint-Cast, 1890
Oil on canvas
26 × 32½ in. (66 × 82.5 cm)
Gift of William A. Coolidge
1991.584

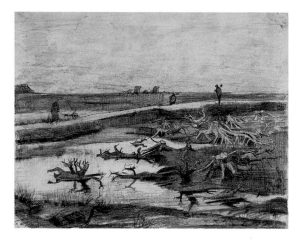

Vincent van Gogh
Dutch (worked in France),
1853–1890
Work in the Fields, 1883
Graphite pencil, pen, and brown
ink on paper
12 ⅝ × 16 ¼ in. (34.3 × 42.3 cm)
Gift of John Goelet 1975.375

Van Gogh studied for the ministry
and worked as a lay preacher among
coal miners before deciding to become
an artist. The work of his early, Dutch
period, inspired by the art of French
painter Jean François Millet (see page
248), is imbued with his intense sympathy for the harsh life of the working poor. This early drawing of workers digging peat in a bleak landscape anticipates the emotional power of van Gogh's
mature style. The artist wrote to his brother about it: "Yesterday I drew some decayed oak roots,
so-called bog trunks (that is, oak trees that have perhaps been buried for a century under the
bog. . .). Some black ones were lying in the water in which they were reflected, some bleached
ones were lying on the black earth. A little white path ran past it, behind that more peat, pitch-
black. . . . it was absolutely melancholy and dramatic."

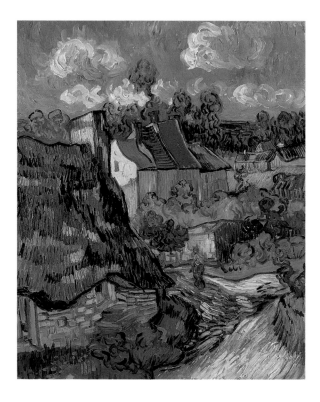

Vincent van Gogh
Dutch (worked in France),
1853–1890
Houses at Auvers, 1890
Oil on canvas
29 ¾ × 24 ⅜ in. (75.5 × 61.8 cm)
Bequest of John T. Spaulding
48.549

Vincent van Gogh
Dutch (worked in France),
1853–1890
Postman Joseph Roulin, 1888
Oil on canvas
32 × 25¾ in. (81.2 × 65.3 cm)
Gift of Robert Treat Paine 2nd
35.1982

In 1886 van Gogh left his native Holland for Paris, where he learned from the Impressionists to look closely at nature and to lighten his dark palette. Unlike the Impressionists, however, he became less interested in capturing visual reality than in exploring color and line as a means of personal expression. In 1888 he went south to Arles, where he made six portraits of the local postman, Joseph Roulin. Wanting to "paint the postman as I feel him," he rendered the figure in intense, brilliant color, the forms—notably the hands—distorted for expressive effect. The artist described his subject as "a man who is neither embittered, nor sad, nor perfect, nor happy, nor always irreprochably right. But such a good soul and so wise and so full of feeling and so trustful."

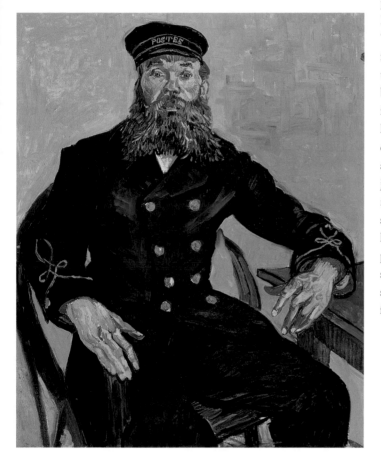

< Van Gogh moved in 1890 to the village of Auvers, near Paris, placing himself in the care of Dr. Paul Gachet, who had long been interested in both psychiatry and the arts. Here, van Gogh depicted the street not far from Dr. Gachet's house, creating a flattened tapestry of shapes in which the tiled and thatched roofs form a patchwork of texture and color. Although based on observation, *Houses at Auvers*—with its swirling, stabbing brushstrokes and sinuous contours— is a landscpe of emotions, charged with energy and passionate feeling. Soon after this painting was finished, van Gogh committed suicide at the age of thirty-seven.

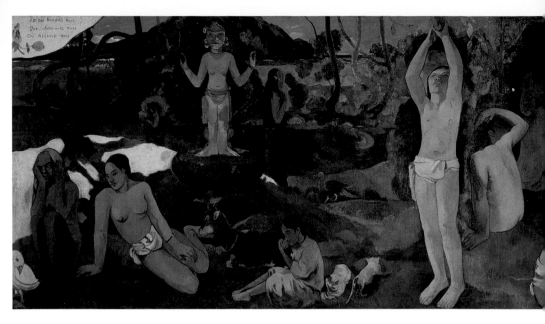

Paul Gauguin
French, 1848–1903
Where Do We Come From?
What Are We? Where Are We
Going?, 1897
Oil on canvas
54 3/4 × 147 1/2 in.
(139.1 × 374.6 cm)
Tompkins Collection 36.270

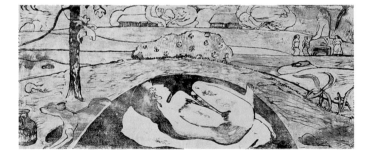

Paul Gauguin
French, 1848–1903
Watched By the Spirits of the
Dead, 1894–95
Woodcut, with hand-coloring, on
Japanese paper
9 × 15 3/4 in. (23 × 40 cm)
Gift of W. G. Russell Allen
54.1607

Gauguin made his last visit to Brittany in 1894. Obsessed with what he romantically viewed as "the primitive," the artist had already traveled once to Tahiti, in the South Pacific, and was soon to return for good. Produced during that Brittany summer but based on drawings made in Tahiti, this is Gauguin's largest woodcut. It shows a woman curled in the fetal position before a Tahitian village, but its meaning remains ambiguous.

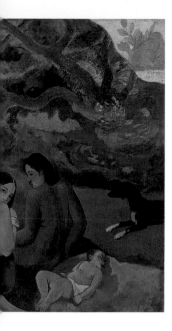

Gauguin wrote, "The Impressionists look for what is near the eye, and not at the mysterious centers of thought." He, in contrast, sought to capture an inner world of fantasy and dream and considered this enormous canvas, created in Tahiti, his masterpiece. He indicated that the painting should be read from right to left, with the three major figure groups illustrating the questions posed in the title. The three women with a child represent the beginning of life; the central group symbolizes the daily existence of young adulthood; and in the final group, according to the artist, "an old woman approaching death appears reconciled and resigned to her thoughts"; at her feet "a strange white bird. . . represents the futility of words." Yet, as so often in Gauguin's work, the whole remains mysterious: "Explanations and obvious symbols would give the canvas a sad reality," Gauguin wrote, "And the questions asked [by the title] would no longer be a poem."

Paul Gauguin
French, 1848–1903
***Be In Love and You Will Be
Happy (Soyez amoreuses vous
serez heureuses),*** 1889
Carved and painted lindenwood
47 × 38 in. (119.4 × 96.5 cm)
Arthur Tracy Cabot Fund 57.582

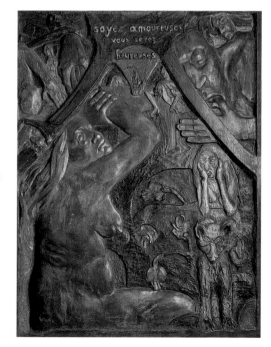

A stockbroker by profession, Gauguin began painting as a hobby in the early 1870s and soon became part of the Impressionist circle. In 1883 he lost his job and decided to become a full-time artist. Three years later he made his first trip to Brittany, in France—the beginning of his lifelong search for places untainted by the materialism of modern urban society, which Gauguin saw as "morally and physically corrupt."

Carved in Brittany, this extraordinary relief addresses the theme of love with bitterness and sarcasm. Gauguin wrote: "I have carved something. . . remarkable. Gauguin (as a monster) seizing the hand of a protesting woman and telling her: 'Be in love and you will be happy.'" The fox, an Indian symbol of perversity, reappears in the work Gauguin executed in Tahiti.

Edvard Munch
Norwegian, 1863–1944
Melancholy (Evening), 1896
Woodcut in color, printed on
paper from two blocks, each cut
into two sections
14 ¾ x 17 ⅞ in. (37.6 x 45.5 cm)
William Francis Warden Fund
57.356

Munch's first attempts at printmaking, of which this is an
example, were made in Paris, a center of experimentation in
printmaking methods. At first working in color lithography
(which required extensive collaboration with a professional
printer), Munch soon turned to woodcut, a technique that
enabled him to prepare the block himself up to the moment of
printing. In his woodcuts, the artist innovatively included the

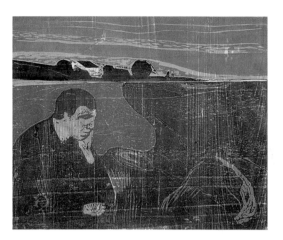

grain of the wood into his designs. He also
developed a unique jigsaw-puzzle technique of sawing the wooden blocks into
pieces, inking them individually, then
reassembling and printing them as a single
block. Composed of simplified shapes and
curving, expressive line, this image,
derived from his *Frieze of Life* paintings,
universalizes human experience while
depicting a specific subject—a friend,
infatuated with an older woman, who
mourns alone on a beach while his lover
and her husband embark on a boat trip on
a midsummer night.

Dragon vase
Hungary (Pecs), 1895–1900
Modeled by **Lajos Mack** at the
Zsolnay factory
Earthenware with luster glaze
Height: 13 ¾ in. (34.9 cm)
European Decorative Arts
Curator's Fund 1990.1731

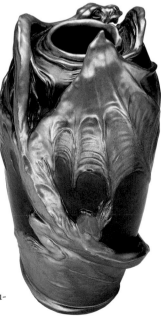

This vase molded with a winged dragon was made at the
factory founded by Vilmos Zsolnay in 1855 in Pecs, a Hun-
garian town near the Austrian border. Beginning with earthenware vessels in traditional styles, the Zsolnay factory
expanded production in the 1870s to include more refined and
decorative wares, some inspired by Turkish, Chinese, or ancient
American ceramics. Luster glazes imitating contemporary irides-
cent glass were developed at the factory in the 1890s. A range of
subtly colored luster glazes creates the rich surface effect of this
fanciful vase whose asymmetrical, curving forms and stylized naturalism typify the influential Art Nouveau style.

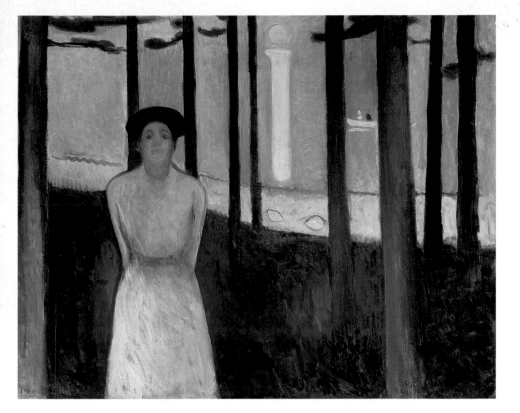

Many of Munch's most memorable paintings are from the series called *The Frieze of Life,* which deals symbolically with themes of love and death. *Summer Night's Dream* presents a gently melancholy evocation of adolescent sexual awakening, in which the still figure of the girl both offers herself to and holds back from the viewer, whom the artist has placed in the position of her anticipated lover. The setting is probably the Borre woods on the Oslo Fjord, a site of ancient Viking graves and a traditional place for courtship during Norway's softly illuminated summer nights. Munch's notes reveal that this painting recalls his first, ultimately painful love affair: "What a deep mark she left on my mind, so deep that no other image can ever totally drive it away."

Edvard Munch
Norwegian, 1863–1944
***Summer Night's Dream
(The Voice),*** 1893
Oil on canvas
34⅝ × 42½ in. (87.8 × 108 cm)
Ernest Wadsworth Longfellow
Fund 59.301

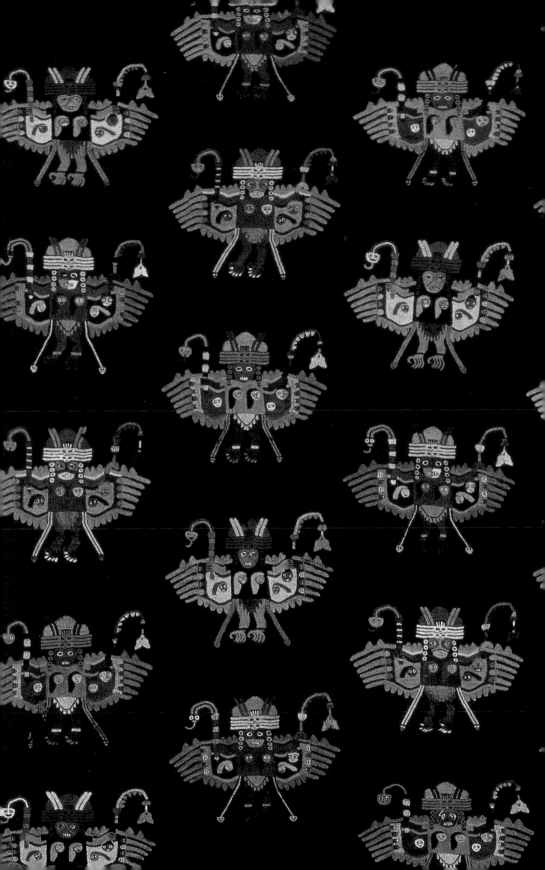

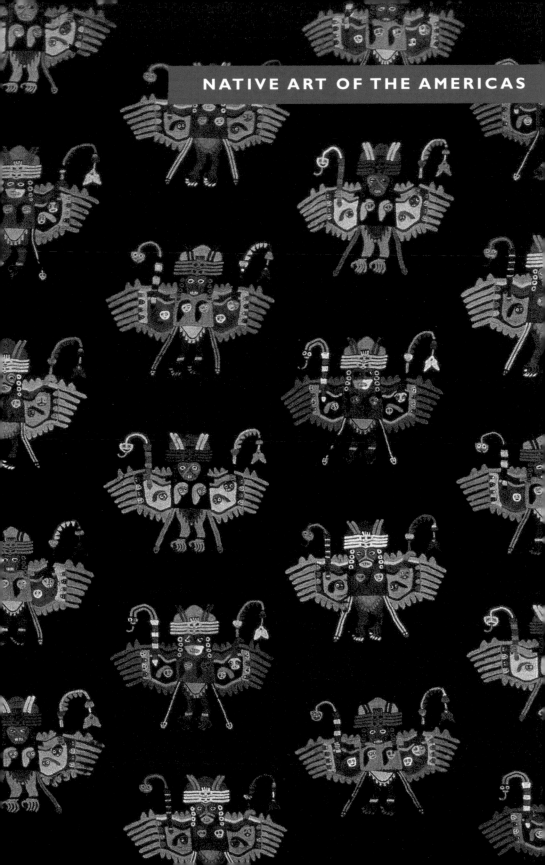

Art of the Ancient Americas

Beginning 3000 years ago in what are today Mexico, Central America, and South America, great civilizations arose, prospered, declined, and were absorbed into succeeding cultures that built upon their achievements. The art, architecture, city planning, science, religion, social structure, and political organizations that existed before the Spanish invasions of the mid-sixteenth century represent the accomplishments of societies that— along with Mesopotamia, Egypt and Nubia, India, and China—are among the cradles of civilization.

Mask
Olmec culture, Mexico,
1150–550 B.C.
Jadeite with black inclusions
Height: 8 ½ in (21.6 cm)
Gift of Landon T. Clay 1991.968

The Olmec, who lived along what is now the Gulf Coast of Mexico, were the first inhabitants of the Americas to develop a writing system, to create complex visual symbolism, and to use art as a means of embodying their beliefs. Olmec civilization influenced all subsequent societies in ancient Mesoamerica (modern-day Mexico, Guatemala, Belize, Honduras, and El Salvador). Olmec artists excelled in working precious, green jadeite that they presumably acquired through trade with distant places. Jadeite is an extremely hard stone, and the Olmec, who had no metal tools, worked it with other stones and abrasives such as crushed garnet. This powerful Olmec mask may have been displayed as a symbol of authority, worn during ceremonies, or attached to the mummified body of a deceased lord.

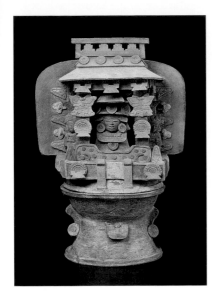

Incense burner
Teotihuacán culture, Mexico,
A.D. 450–700
Ceramic with paint
Height: 24½ in. (62.2 cm)
Gift of Landon T. Clay   1988.1229 a,b

The city of Teotihuacán in highland Mexico—the center of a mighty state—was among the world's largest cities in the fifth century. Until the completion of New York's Empire State Building, the Pyramid of the Sun at Teotihuacán was unchallenged as the tallest building in the western hemisphere. This incense burner is made in the form of a Teotihuacán temple. Inside, the figure of a deity is flanked by two attendants, probably priests, who hold bags of incense. Burning coals and incense were placed in the bottom part of the vessel, and the smoke rose through a chimney at the back of the upper half, emerging behind the "roof."

Burial urn
Maya culture, Guatemala,
A.D. 650–850
Ceramic with white, black, yellow,
and red slip paint
Height: 52 in. (132.1 cm)
Gift of Landon T. Clay   1988.1290

The K'iché Maya people of highland Guatemala buried royal and noble individuals in large, ceramic urns such as this. The body of the deceased was tightly flexed and wrapped in cloth, placed in the urn with offerings of pottery and jadeite, and then buried inside pyramids or sacred caves. The lid of this urn is sculpted as the head of a supernatural being whose open mouth may have been used to make offerings to the deceased in the afterlife. The figure on top of the lid, holding two cobs of corn (maize), is probably the Maize God.

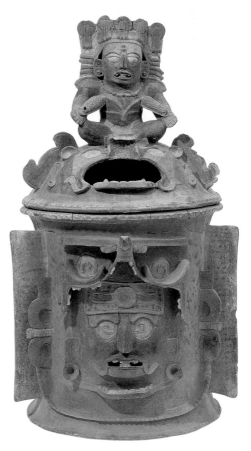

Drinking vessel

Maya culture, Guatemala,
A.D. 650–800
Ceramic with red, white, gray,
and black slip paint on cream
slip ground
Height: 8 ¾ in. (12.1 cm)
Gift of Landon T. Clay
1988.1168

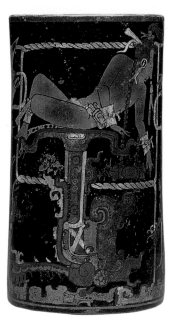

The sophisticated civilization of the Maya reached its height in the Classic period (A.D. 250–900). During this time, artists—who were highly educated members of elite society—produced extraordinary painted ceramics that served ritual functions in life and were also buried in tombs of the honored dead. This vessel is one of the masterpieces of Maya art. The artist has exploited the watercolor-like potential of slip paint (clay diluted to a watery consistency and colored with mineral pigments) to create the subtle washes on the figures' bodies. The painting depicts the birth of a supernatural being whose supple body is framed by a stylized, white, umbilical cord.

Drinking vessel

Maya culture, Mexico,
A.D. 593–830
Ceramic with red, white, and black
slip paint on yellow-cream slip
ground
Height: 8 in. (20.3 cm)
Gift of Landon T. Clay 1988.1169

The painstaking decipherment of the hieroglyphic texts and images painted on Maya ceramics is enabling scholars, for the first time, to grasp the intricacy of Maya politics, history, and religion. The figures on this vessel are identified by the large hieroglyphs above their heads as Hun Ahaw and Xbalanque, the Hero Twins. The bold escapades of these supernaturals are recounted in the *Popol Vuh*, the creation myth of the K'iché Maya people. The father of the Hero Twins had descended to the Underworld and been tricked and then killed by the lords who resided there. Later, the Hero Twins traveled in their father's footsteps and succeeded in out-foxing the Lords of the Underworld. The hieroglyphic text around the rim states that the vessel was used for a special chocolate drink, made from the sweet pulp of the cacao fruit, consumed by the elite on ceremonial occasions.

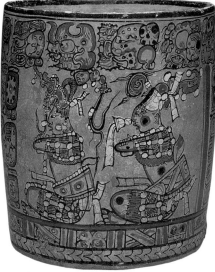

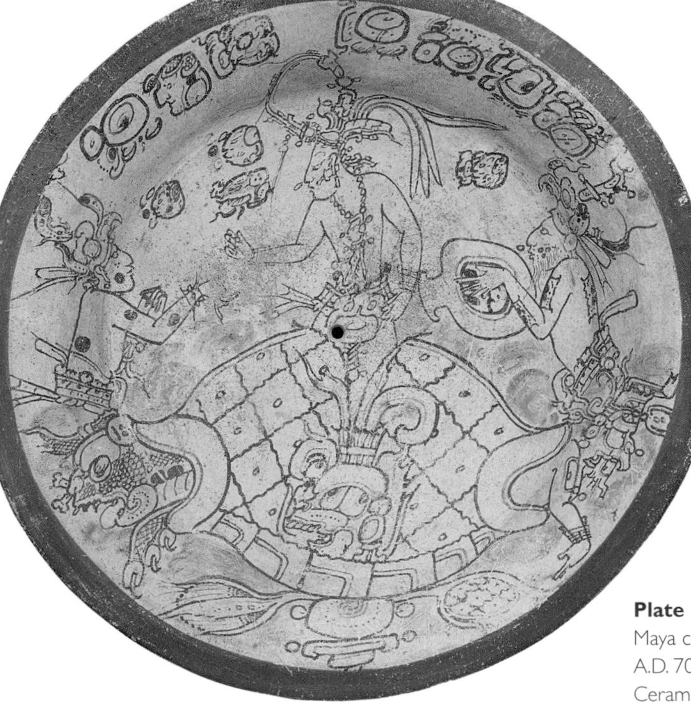

Plate
Maya culture, Guatemala,
A.D. 700–800
Ceramic with brown-black and red
slip paint on cream slip ground
Diameter: 12½ in. (31.8 cm)
Gift of Landon T. Clay 1993.565

The Maya believed that the first humans were formed from ground corn (maize), and they saw the reappearance of maize in the fields each spring as a metaphor for the resurrection of the human soul. This plate depicts the Maize God "growing" from the crack in a turtle shell, symbol of the earth. The figure also represents First Father flanked by his sons, the Hero Twins, who defeated the Lords of the Underworld, rescued their father's bones, and thus created the path of resurrection from death. The style of painting on this plate, which was used to hold corn tamales, is similar to that found in a Maya codex, or book made of folded leaves of fig-bark paper. Thousands of these books were burned by the Spanish, who believed they contained "lies of the devil," and only four fragments are known today. The scenes painted on codex-style vessels are therefore important evidence of Classic Maya religion and cosmology.

Ancient American Gold

Called "sweat of the sun" by the Inka of Peru, gold was believed by many ancient American civilizations to embody the essence of the sun. Gold ornaments were used in religious ceremonies, buried with the dead, and worn as emblems of political power and social status. Skilled artisans showed a fine sensitivity to the inherent beauty of the metal and produced an amazing variety of forms that, like all ancient American art, embodied symbolic meanings and functions.

Gold, mostly mined from riverbeds, was plentiful. Although goldsmiths worked only with stone and bronze tools, they developed most techniques known today, including cold-hammering, embossing, soldering, welding, casting, gilding, and fabricating alloys.

The Spanish who invaded Central and South America in the mid-sixteenth century were interested only in the monetary value of gold and melted down thousands of objects, sending an estimated 18,000 pounds of American gold to Spain. The vast majority of gold objects known today survive because they were hidden in burials.

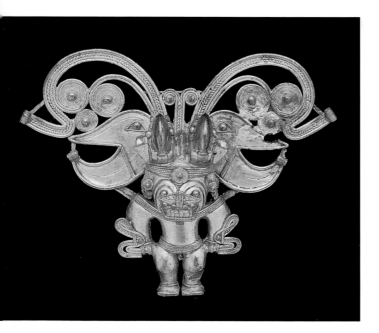

Cacique pendant
Tairona culture, Colombia,
A.D. 900–1550
Gold alloy
Height: 7⅛ in. (18.1 cm)
John H. and Ernestine A. Payne
Fund 1975.35

The Spanish invaders believed that male figures of this sort, wearing masks and fantastic headdresses and grasping ritual objects, represented caciques, or chiefs.

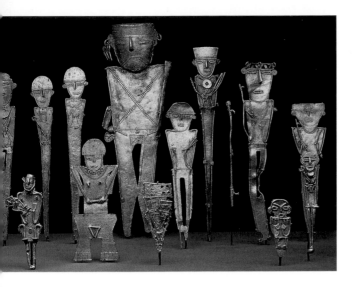

Offering figures *(tunjos)*
Muisca culture, Colombia,
1300–1550
Gold, copper, and tin alloy
Height of tallest figure: 8¹/₄ in.
(21 cm)
Gifts of Landon T. Clay, 1975 and
1993

In an isolated highland valley near modern-day Bogotá, Colombia, the Muisca people developed unique works of art in metal, including these distinctive offering figures, or *tunjos*. Many represent men with implements and headdresses indicating political, religious, or social affiliation. *Tunjos* were cast in a single mold using only one flow of metal. In their search for gold, the Spanish invaded Muisca lands three times. Enslaved and with no resistance to European diseases, the Muisca were extinct by the seventeenth century.

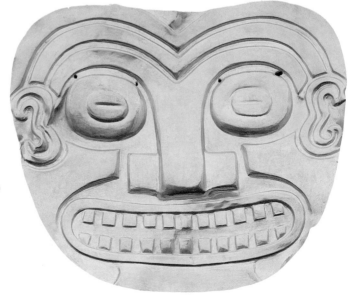

Pectoral
Coclé style, Panama, A.D. 450–900
Gold
Width: 10³/₈ in. (26.3 cm)
Gift of Landon T. Clay, 1971.1127

Burial mantle
Paracas culture, Peru,
A.D. 50–100
Camelid fiber; plain-weave ground
cloth with stem-stitch embroidery
39 3/4 × 96 1/8 in. (101 × 244.3 cm)
Denman Waldo Ross Collection
16.34a-c

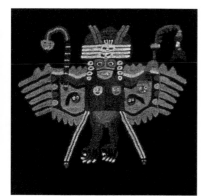

In the ancient Andean world, textiles played a profound symbolic role in sacred and secular life. Andean textiles are among the most complex ever made (some of their techniques have never been replicated), and the prestige of cloth was directly related to the extraordinary energy that spinners, dyers, weavers, and embroiderers expended to produce it.

When burials of the Paracas civilization were uncovered in the early twentieth century, the bodies were found wrapped in textiles that had been perfectly preserved in the desert sands of Peru's coastal plain for almost 2000 years. It has been estimated that all the textiles in one large mummy bundle may have taken between 11,000 and 29,000 hours to complete. The ritual figures embroidered on this mantle wear elaborate headdresses, masks, embroidered tunics, and feathered capes. They hold serpent-headed staffs and decapitated heads that denote their power.

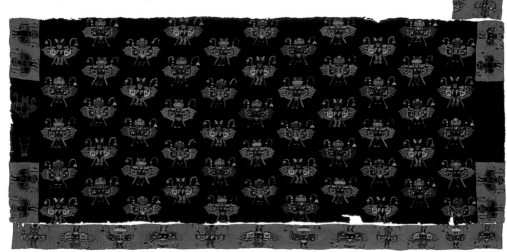

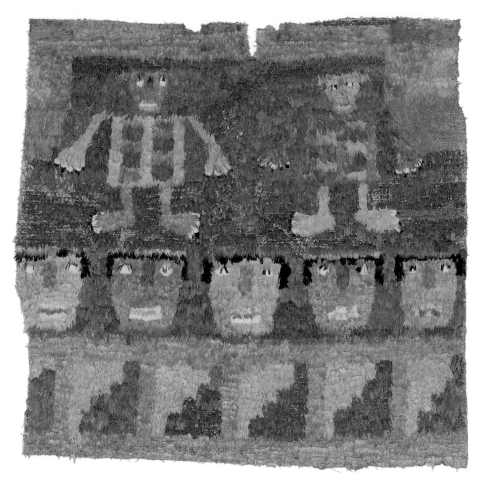

Tunic fragment
Wari-related culture, Peru,
Probably A.D. 500–800
Cotton and tropical bird feathers;
plain-weave ground cloth with
sewn rows of cut feathers
39 1/8 × 38 3/4 in. (99.5 × 98.5 cm)
J. H. and E. A. Payne Fund 60.253

The ancient Andean cultures of western South America (modern-day Peru and parts of Bolivia, Chile, and Ecuador) flourished in a harsh environment in which the world's second highest mountains—the Andes—are bounded on the west by coastal desert and on the east by Amazonian jungle. In these cultures, featherwork textiles were highly prized, and people of the highlands and coast were prepared to cross the Andes to trade with inhabitants of the jungle for the brilliant feathers of curassows, egrets, and various types of macaws. This textile, sewn with rows of cut feathers, shows standing figures wearing tapestry-woven tunics. The large faces below may represent the decapitated heads of defeated warriors.

This unusually large jar was created for use in the home, not for the collectors' market. In this period, women made the ceramic vessels necessary for ceremonial use and for the cooking, serving, and storage of food and water. Jars of this size, intended to hold grain, were highly valued and passed down from mother to daughter. The bold decorations evoke rain and water; they were painted with slip, a thin mixture of clay and water colored with mineral pigments.

Storage jar
New Mexico (Cochiti Pueblo), about 1875
Earthenware with slip paint
Height: 18 in. (45 cm)
Gift of Independence Investment Associates, Inc. 1997.175

Over many centuries, Plains Indians painted records of their battles, ceremonies, and tribal history on rock walls, hide robes, and tipi coverings. In the reservation period, some native artists continued this tradition using new materials—paper, pencils, crayons, and inks. Such works as this one are called "ledger drawings" because many were executed in ledger, or account, books. This lively image of a battle between Kiowa and Ute warriors is the work of Silver Horn, a member of a family known for its artists over several generations. The drawing is one of thirty-three in a sketchbook annotated by Horace Pope Jones, a civilian interpreter at Fort Sill, Oklahoma.

Silver Horn (Huangooah)
Kiowa Apache, 1861–1940
The once-famous Black Eagle (Ka-et-te-kone-ke) of the Kiowa in deadly conflict with Ute chief. Ute killed.
Oklahoma (Fort Sill), 1877–78
Graphite pencil and colored crayons on paper
10⅛ x 14 in. (25.7 x 35.6 cm)
Gift of the Grandchildren of Lucretia McIlvain Shoemaker and the M. and M. Karolik Fund
1994.429

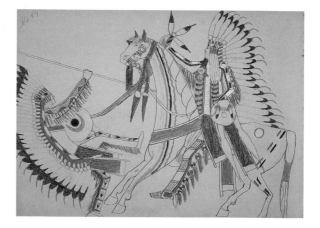

Tray
Southern California, (Mission culture, probably Cahuilla), about 1900
Attributed to **Guadelupe Arenas,** active about 1900–1920
Coiled grass stems, juncus grass, sumac
Diameter: 11½ in. (29.2 cm)
John Wheelock Elliot and John Morse Elliot Fund 1992.197

Basketry was the major art form of the Mission Indians (so named because they lived near the Spanish missions along the California coast). Coiled baskets and other objects were woven primarily of native sumac (often dyed) and juncus grass, whose stem changes naturally from deep brown to tan as it grows. Fine Mission baskets such as this were made for collectors from the 1890s into the 1930s, providing much-needed income for the weavers and their families. This tray may be the work of Guadelupe Arenas, who worked as a laundry woman in a Palm Springs tuberculosis sanitorium. The rattlesnake, a favorite motif on Mission baskets, was viewed as a symbol of power, an avenging spirit, and a protective deity that would bring good fortune to the weaver.

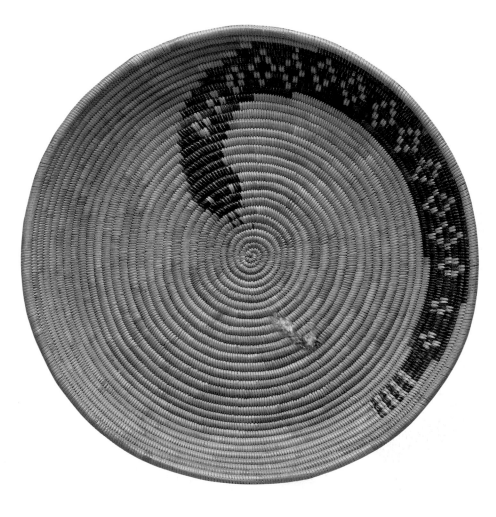

Bent-corner chief's chest
Probably Tsimshian culture
Canada (coastal British Columbia),
about 1860
Yellow cedar and red cedar with
black, red, and blue pigment
26 ¾ × 41 ⅜ × 24 ¼ in.
(67.7 × 105.1 × 61.8 cm)
Gift of a Friend of the
Department of American
Decorative Arts and Sculpture
1997.9

In traditional Tsimshian society, chests like this were used to store ritual objects such as masks and rattles, as well as the blankets and copper plaques that were indicators of wealth and status. The work of a highly skilled carpenter, the chest's four sides are made of a single piece of wood, which was steamed and bent into the shape of a box. Native people of the Northwest Coast believed in close and constant contact between the physical and spirit worlds, with humans and animals passing back and forth between the two realms, changing from one shape to another as they did so. Ravens, fish, and a mythical creature intermingle across the surface of this chest and defy any single interpretation.

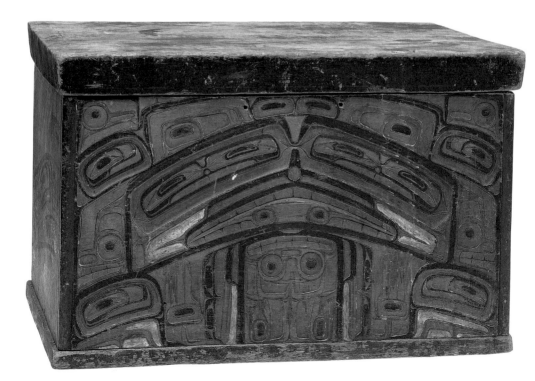

Rattle

Probably Tsimshian culture
Canada (coastal British Columbia),
about 1900
Probably alder and birch, paint and
pebbles
Height: 10½ in. (26.7 cm)
Gift of Elizabeth Wetherill McMeel
and the Seminarians 1996.28

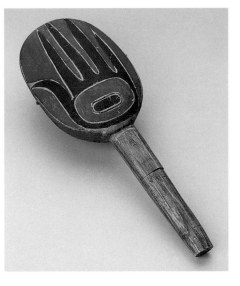

Among Northwest Coast cultures, rattles played important roles in rituals of power and healing. They were made in an immense variety of shapes and patterns. Because artistic motifs and actual works of art were shared among the groups of native people along the coast of British Columbia, it is often difficult to identify the origin of a particular object.

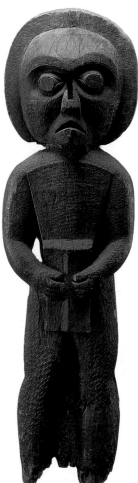

Potlatch figure

Canada (Northern Vancouver
Island), about 1840
Red cedar, paint (metal armature)
Height: 67¾ in. (168 cm)
Gift of a Friend of the
Department of American
Decorative Arts and Sculpture
1998.1

A center of social and ritual life among the peoples of the Northwest Coast, the potlatch was a feast in which the host showered his guests with food, drink, and gifts of blankets, masks, and valuable plaques of decorated copper. In this way the potlatch host demonstrated his wealth and ensured both the respect of his neighbors and his own future gain, since at a later time his guests would present him with even more lavish gifts at their ceremonies. This monumental figure would have been set up on the shore to welcome guests to the potlatch. The trapezoidal shape over his chest represents a copper plaque, symbol of the real goods that guests would receive during the festivities.

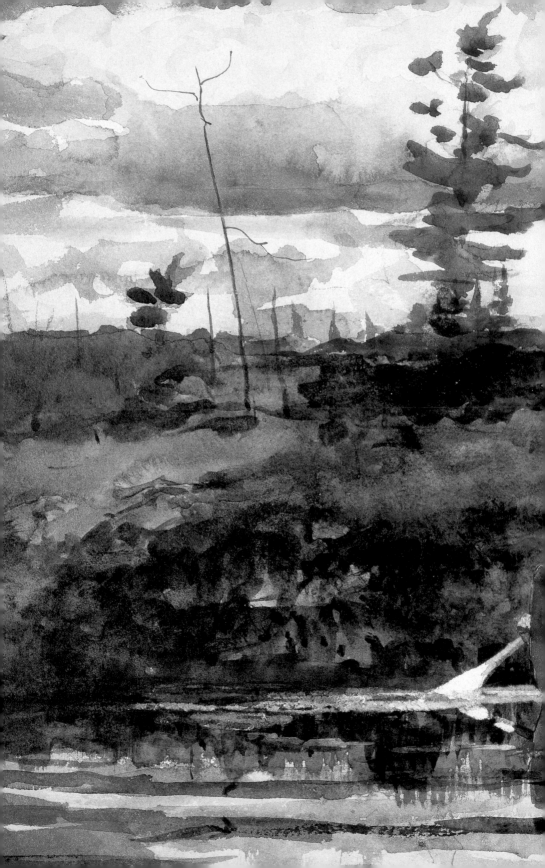

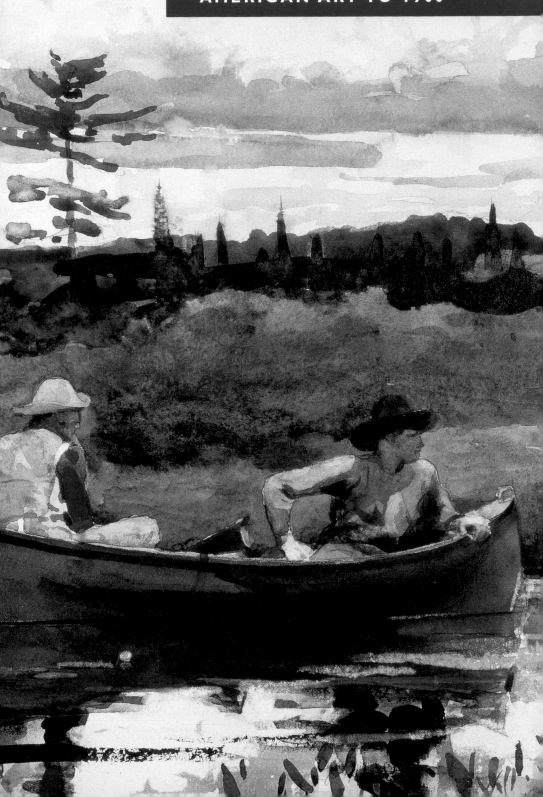

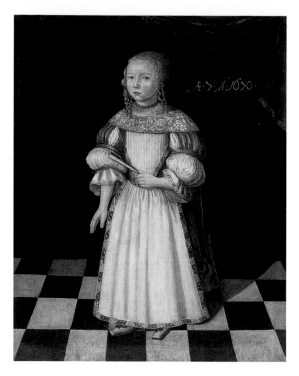

Robert Gibbs, the fourth son of a knight, left England to seek his fortune in the New World and became a prosperous Boston merchant. As a statement of his own social and economic success, Gibbs commissioned portraits of his children—Margaret, Robert (also in the Museum's collection), and Henry (Sunrise Museum, Charleston, West Virginia). Even the elaborate lace and needlework on Margaret's dress testify to her father's status, because Massachusetts law forbade the wearing of such finery unless the man of the house "possessed either a liberal education or an annual income of £200." This charming image of seven-year-old Margaret is one of very few surviving portraits from seventeenth-century New England; its emphasis on detail of costume and on line reflect a style—fashionable at the court of Queen Elizabeth—which was still current in parts of England in the 1660s.

Unidentified artist (called the
Freake-Gibbs painter)
Margaret Gibbs, 1670
Oil on canvas
40½ × 33⅛ in. (102.9 × 84.1 cm)
Bequest of Elsie Q. Giltinan
1995.800

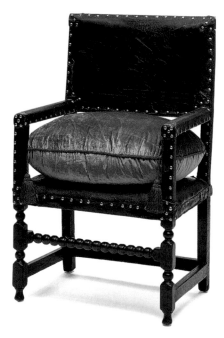

Great chair
Massachusetts (Boston), 1665–80
Oak and maple with original
upholstery foundation, leather
cover, and brass nails
38 × 23⅝ × 16⅜ in.
(96.5 × 60 × 41.6 cm)
Seth K. Sweetser Fund 1977.711

This oak chest is a highlight of the Museum's extensive collection of seventeenth-century New England furniture. The chest is believed to be from the shop of William Searle (1634–1667) or Thomas Dennis (1638–1706), furnituremakers (or joiners) trained in England. Chests of this kind, which could be used for seating as well as storage, were the most common furniture form in the small houses of the period. The vigorous carving—with its abundance of stylized leaves and flowers contained within geometric fields—and the indication of an original, brightly painted surface testify to the love of pattern and color in the Puritan society of early New England.

Joined chest
Massachusetts (Ipswich),
1670–1710
Attributed to the shop of
William Searle or
Thomas Dennis
Oak and white pine
30½ x 44⅜ x 19 in.
(77.5 x 112.7 x 48.3 cm)
Gift of J. Templeman Coolidge
29.1015

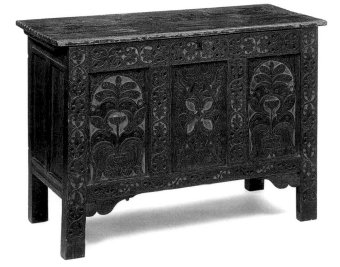

◄ With its leather coverings, marsh grass stuffing, and rows of brass nails, this is the only known upholstered great chair (armchair) to survive from seventeenth-century New England. Many families in this period did not even own a chair, and the great chair was a luxury item reserved for heads of families and honored guests. It became a possession of even more value and status when upholstered. This one belonged to Zerrubabel Endicott (1635–1683) of Salem, Massachusetts, a prominent surgeon and son of John Endicott, governor of the Massachusetts Bay Colony. The frame is virtually identical to those of London upholstered great chairs made at the same time, an indication of the determination and ability of colonial Americans to keep up with English fashions. The velvet cushion is a reproduction based on those depicted in prints and paintings of seventeenth-century interiors.

Sugar box
Massachusetts (Boston), 1680–85
Made by **John Coney,**
1655/56–1722
Silver
Height: 4⅞ in. (12.2 cm)
Gift of Mrs. Joseph Richmond
Churchill 13.421

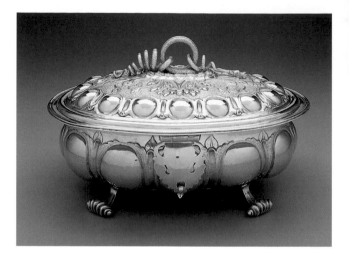

John Smibert
American (born Scotland),
1688–1751
Judge Samuel Sewall, 1729
Oil on canvas
30 × 25 in. (76.2 × 63.5 cm)
Bequest of William L. Barnard (by
exchange), and Emily L. Ainsley
Fund 58.358

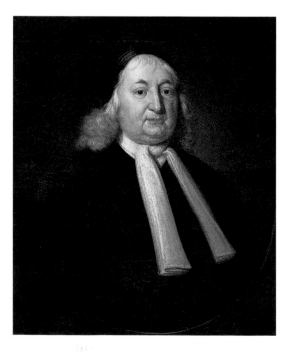

A judge at the 1692 Salem witch trials that convicted and executed nineteen people, Samuel Sewall (1625–1730) later publicly confessed his error. He was an eminent citizen of colonial Boston—a member of the Ancient and Honorable Artillery Company, manager of Boston's only licensed printing press, and chief justice of the Superior Court. His diaries provide a lively record of the social, political, and religious life of his time. This was among the first of almost 250 portraits that London-trained John Smibert made in Boston during his seventeen-year residence. His ability to capture character as well as appearance and his deft modeling of three-dimensional form caused a sensation in Boston, and his studio in Scollay Square became a mecca for aspiring artists.

John Coney was the most versatile and productive American silversmith of his generation. Like many silversmiths, he was an active citizen, engraving paper money for the colony of Massachusetts and serving as constable and tithingman. This sugar box, which weighs more than two pounds, testifies to the preciousness of sugar and demonstrates Coney's remarkable skill in embossing, engraving, and casting. Such boxes were often given as wedding presents, and the cast handle of this one takes the form of a coiled snake—a traditional emblem warning against interfering in quarrels between husband and wife. The box was made for Mary Mason Norton, wife of the Reverend John Norton of Hingham, Massachusetts.

Until the discovery of this chest-on-chest in the mid-1980s, little early eighteenth-century Boston furniture was known that was close to contemporary, high-style English furniture. Indeed, based on its stylistic features and construction, this chest was originally believed to be English. However, it is made of American woods and was owned in the eighteenth century by the Warland family of Cambridge, Massachusetts. In addition, microanalysis of dirt particles undisturbed by restoration or refinishing revealed not the expected English pollen but pollen from plants that grow in Massachusetts and Rhode Island—a strong indication of the chest's American origins. Thus, this chest-on-chest has provided exciting evidence that English furniture designs reached Boston very early, apparently brought by London-trained craftsmen attracted by Boston's thriving economy. A visitor, writing in 1725, commented: "A Gentleman from London would almost think himself at home at Boston when he observes the numbers of people, their Houses, their Furniture, their Tables, their Dress and Conversation, which perhaps is as splendid and showy as that of the most considerable Tradesman in London."

Chest-on-chest
Massachusetts (Boston), 1715–25
Black walnut, burl walnut veneer, and eastern white pine
70¾ × 42¼ × 21½ in.
(179.7 × 107.3 × 53.8 cm)
Gift of a Friend of the Department of American Decorative Arts and Sculpture and Otis Norcross Fund 1986.240

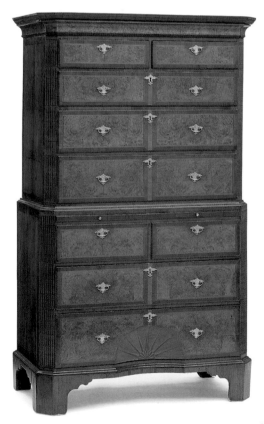

Colonial Silver

For the few colonial Americans who owned them, objects made of silver testified to wealth, social position, and discerning taste. They could also be (and often were) melted down and converted back to money in times of need. A Virginia gentleman wrote in 1688: "I esteem it as well politic as reputable, to furnish my self with an handsom Cupboard of plate which gives my self the present use & Credit, is a sure friend at a dead lift, without much loss, or is a certain portion for a Child after my decease."

Covered cup
Massachusetts (Boston), 1740–45
Made by **Jacob Hurd,**
1702/03–1758
Silver
Height: 13½ in. (34.3 cm)
Helen and Alice Colburn Fund
36.415

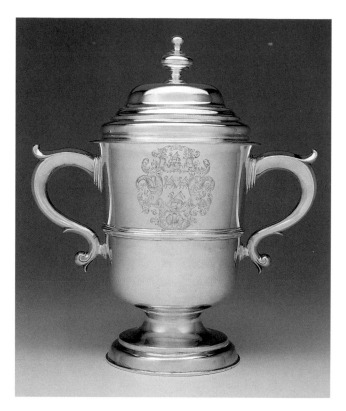

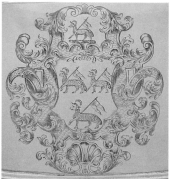

Jacob Hurd was among the most prolific of early American silversmiths, and this finely proportioned cup is evidence of his mastery of strong, sculptural form and elegant engraving. Such "grace cups" (traditionally passed around the table for a final toast after grace was said at the end of a meal) were favored in Boston as presentation pieces for ceremonial occasions. The cup bears the coat of arms of its first owner, John Rowe, a prosperous Boston merchant and shipowner.

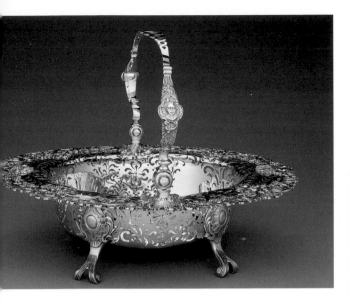

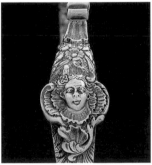

Bread basket
New York (New York),
about 1754–69
Made by **Daniel Christian Fueter,** 1720–1785
Silver
Height: 10 ¾ in. (27.1 cm)
Decorative Arts Special Fund
54.857

Elaborate pierced silver was a New York specialty, and this bread basket is the most sophisticated American example of its kind. The lacy openwork—lavish but perfectly controlled—is contained within a rim of cast scrolls, fruit, and flowers; unusual female masks decorate the handle. Daniel Christian Fueter, born and trained in Switzerland, fled into exile following his involvement in a plot to overthrow the local government; he worked in London before coming to New York.

Standing salt
Massachusetts (Boston),
1690–1700
Made by **Jeremiah Dummer,** 1645–1718
Silver
Height: 5 ½ in. (14 cm)
Bequest of Charles Hitchcock Tyler
32.371

In the Middle Ages, imposing standing salts were set on the head table in great halls, dividing the socially prominent from lesser guests who sat "below the salt." This salt, with four knops to support a cloth or plate, is a very rare example of a form soon to be replaced by individual trencher salts. Jeremiah Dummer, one of the first native-born American silversmiths, was also part-owner of a dozen ships. One of his sons became lieutenant governor of Massachusetts.

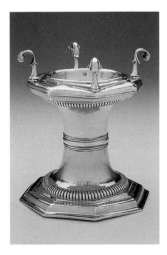

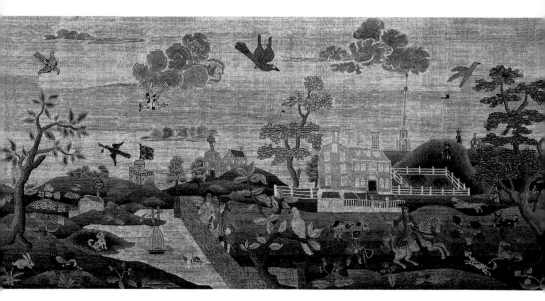

Embroidered picture
Massachusetts (Boston), about 1750
Made by **Hannah Otis,** 1732–1801
Silk, wool, metallic threads, and beads on linen canvas; predominantly tent stitch
24 1/4 × 52 3/4 in. (61.6 × 134 cm)
Gift of A Friend of the Department of American Decorative Arts and Sculpture and 15 other funds 1996.77

Like many well-to-do girls of her time, Hannah Otis learned fine needlework at school and embroidered a "chimneypiece" for display above the fireplace. Most schoolgirl embroidery reproduced standard compositions derived from European prints, but Otis's needlework picture is unique. She depicted a scene she knew—Boston Common, with the beacon on Beacon Hill and the fashionable stone mansion built in 1737 by wealthy merchant Thomas Hancock. The couple by the wall are believed to be Thomas and Lydia Henchman Hancock; the dashing figure on horseback may be their nephew and heir, John Hancock, later to be a governor of Massachusetts and signer of the Declaration of Independence.

Otis's brother James led radical colonial opposition to Britain, and her sister Mercy Otis Warren became the first historian of the American Revolution. Otis herself never married, but lived with her widowed father in Barnstable, Massachusetts, and later kept a shop and ran a boarding house in Boston.

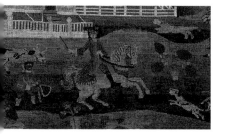

John Singleton Copley's portrait of Hannah Otis's sister Mercy Otis Warren is on page 304.

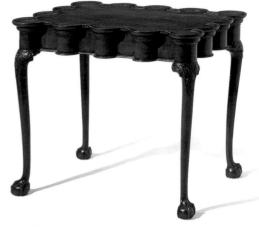

In 1740 an English visitor to Boston observed: "The ladies here visit, drink tea, and indulge every little piece of gentility to the height of the mode and neglect the affairs of their families with as good grace as the finest ladies in London." The social ritual of drinking tea, which became a passion on both sides of the Atlantic in the eighteenth century, spurred the creation of many new forms in furniture and silver. This table, made specifically for tea parties, has a scalloped-edge top with places for fourteen cups and saucers. This unusual type of table seems to have been a Boston specialty.

Tea table
Massachusetts (Boston),
about 1750
Mahogany
27 ¾ × 32 ⅜ × 23 ⅜ in.
(70.5 × 82.2 × 59.4 cm)
The M. and M. Karolik Collection
of Eighteenth-Century American
Arts 41.592

Trained in England, Joseph Blackburn came to New England from Bermuda in 1753. For the next ten years, he was a highly successful painter of portraits that reflected the decorative grace and silvery colors of current London style. He particularly delighted his female sitters by painting them with dainty heads on long, slender necks and by rendering their elegant dress and the textures of luxurious fabrics with skill and precision. In this ambitious group portrait, Blackburn posed the Winslows infor-

Joseph Blackburn
American (born England), active in
America 1753–1763
*Isaac Winslow and His
Family,* 1755
Oil on canvas
54 ½ ×79 ¼ in. (138.4 × 201.3 cm)
A. Shuman Collection 42.684

mally before an imaginary garden setting far grander than any existing in Boston. Isaac Winslow, who made his fortune in the shipping business, stands beside his wife Lucy; in her lap, baby Hannah holds a coral-and-bells teething toy. Daughter Lucy holds fruit, which may allude to the family's prosperity.

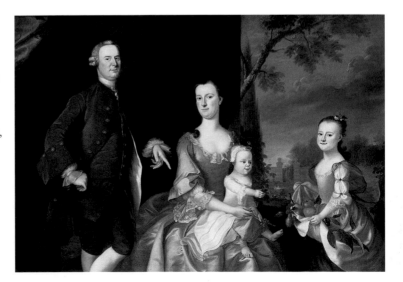

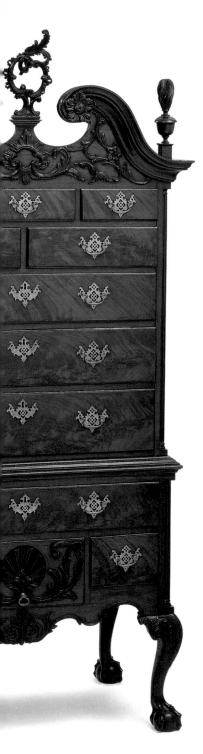

High chest of drawers
Pennsylvania (Philadelphia),
1755–95
Mahogany, yellow poplar, yellow pine
85¾ × 13 × 23 in.
(217.9 × 109.2 × 58.4 cm)
The M. and M. Karolik Collection of
Eighteenth-Century American Arts
39.545

Handsome, monumental high chests proclaimed their owners' wealth and taste while providing ample storage at a time when closets were still uncommon. In the last quarter of the eighteenth century, long after the high chest had lost favor in England, the form reached its artistic peak in Philadelphia—the fastest growing city in America. Fine Philadelphia high chests, like this one, are well-proportioned and richly ornamented. The wood is highly prized mahogany imported from the Spanish colonies of Cuba, Honduras, or Santo Domingo. On the drawer fronts, the warm color and lively patterns of mahogany crotch-grain veneer are enhanced by pierced brasses, placed to curve slightly inward, lightening the basic rectilinearity of the chest. The carved decoration, accentuated by the use of different-colored mahogany, reflects the fluid, graceful rococo style that dominated European art in the mid-eighteenth century. More than seven feet above the ground, the flourish of an asymmetrical cartouche provides the crowning touch.

The first porcelain factory in the colonies was established in Philadelphia in 1770 by Gousse Bonnin and George Anthony Morris, who imported English workers to produce domestic wares comparable to the soft-paste porcelain (a bone china) made in English factories. The Non-Importation Agreements of the late 1760s, which urged the boycott of imported British goods and encouraged colonial industry, made this seem a perfect moment for such a venture. However, expenses were much higher than expected, and many local merchants, ignoring the Non-Importation Agreements, continued to trade with England. Quantities of inexpensive English and Chinese wares were available in America, and after only two years, Bonnin's and Morris's factory closed. This open fretwork fruit basket is a very rare survivor of what was known, in its day, as "American China" (see page 130).

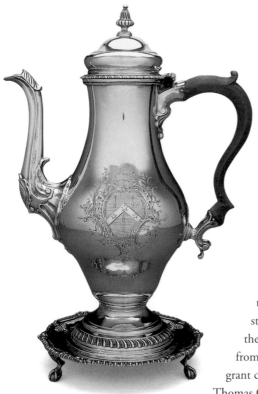

Coffeepot
Pennsylvania (Philadelphia),
1770–80
Made by **Richard Humphreys,**
1749–1832
Silver with wooden handle
Height: 13 5/8 in. (34.4 cm)
Gift in memory of Dr. George
Clymer by his wife, Mrs. Clymer
56.589

Philadelphia was the American center of the rococo style, with its animated ornament of entwined scrolls, shells, leaves, and other natural forms. The shape of this coffeepot, with its stepped foot and domed cover, expresses the rococo love of curving movement, as do the applied decoration and the delicate foliate engraving. The rococo style—also exemplified by the high chest on the preceding page—was introduced to America from England through imported objects, immigrant craftsmen, and such books of design as Thomas Chippendale's *The Gentleman and Cabinet-Maker's Director* (1754). Made by one of Philadelphia's foremost silversmiths, this coffeepot is unusual in that it retains its original stand.

Fruit basket
Pennsylvania (Philadelphia),
1771–72
Made by **American China Manufactory**
Soft-paste porcelain with underglaze blue decoration
Diameter: 6 7/8 in. (17.5 cm)
Frederick Brown Fund 1977.621

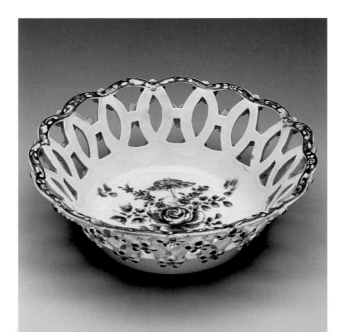

Looking at American Furniture

The Museum has one of the world's finest collections of colonial New England furniture. In the seventeenth and eighteenth centuries, such monumental chests as those illustrated here were the supreme expression of their makers' skill and their owners' affluence and status. Exploring the elegant proportions, handsome carving, rich surface ornamentation, and intricately worked brass handles of these solid and imposing pieces of furniture can offer the viewer visual delight.

A good example is the chest-on-chest on the facing page—among the greatest masterpieces of Salem furniture. The chest's form is of the eighteenth century, but its ornament reflects both the international taste for neoclassicism and the new American nation's search for cultural unity in symbols that

High chest of drawers
Massachusetts (Boston), 1725–40
Japanned butternut, maple, and
white pine
71 ¾ × 42 ⅞ × 24 ¾ in.
(182.2 × 108.9 × 62.9 cm)
Bequest of Charles Hitchcock Tyler
32.227

Cupboard
Massachusetts (Newbury area),
1670–1700
Attributed to the **Emery shops**
Oak, maple, poplar, pine
58 ¾ × 48 ½ × 19 ⅜ in.
(149.2 × 123.2 × 49.2 cm)
Gift of Maurice Geeraerts in
memory of Mr. and Mrs. William
R. Robeson 51.53

Desk and bookcase
Rhode Island (Newport),
about 1760–75
Mahogany, chestnut, pine, cherry
95 ¼ × 39 ⅞ × 23 ⅝ in.
(241.9 × 101.3 × 60 cm)
The M. and M. Karolik Collection
of Eighteenth-Century American
Arts 39.155

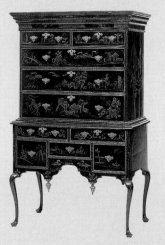
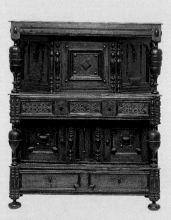
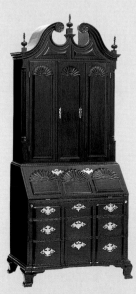

would be meaningful to all. The artistic vocabulary of ancient Greece and Rome seemed tailor-made for Americans who compared their infant democracy to the revered societies of the ancient world. Thus, on this chest, urns, garlands, and cornucopias overflowing with fruit speak optimistically of America's prosperity, and the crowning female figure bears attributes symbolic of the new nation's ideals—truth, virtue, and power. The chest was made for Elizabeth Derby West (see page 312), the daughter of Salem merchant Elias Hasket Derby whose success embodied the American dream. The chest was undoubtedly among its owner's proudest possessions, but when the collector Maxim Karolik (see page 322) rediscovered it in 1941, its drawers were being used for ripening pears.

Chest-on-chest
Massachusetts (Salem), 1796
Design and carving traditionally ascribed to **Samuel McIntire,** 1757–1811
Central figure probably carved by **Simeon Skillin, Jr.**, 1756–1806 or **John Skillin,** 1745–1800
Cabinetwork attributed to a **Mr. Lemon**
Mahogany and pine
102½ × 46¾ × 23 in.
(260.4 × 118.7 × 58.4 cm)
The M. and M. Karolik Collection of Eighteenth Century American Arts 41.580

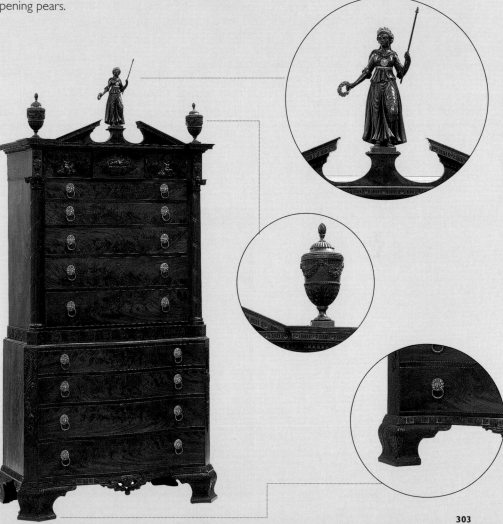

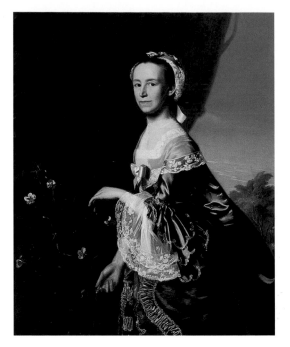

John Singleton Copley
American, 1738–1815
Mercy Otis Warren, about 1763
Oil on canvas
49 5/8 × 39 1/2 in. (126.1 × 100.3 cm)
Bequest of Winslow Warren
31.212

Virtually self-taught, Boston artist John Singleton Copley eclipsed all his rivals with his brilliant technique and his ability to portray wealthy and ambitious Americans as they wished to be seen. Copley looked to London for the latest styles, flattering his sitters with elegant costumes, grand settings, and confident poses often derived from mezzotint engravings that reproduced oil portraits of English aristocracy. Mercy Otis Warren (1728–1814), the wife of prosperous merchant and farmer James Warren, wears a sumptuous and expensive blue satin dress trimmed with silk, lace, and silver braid. She tends nasturtium vines, a metaphor for her nurturing role as mother and wife. Mercy Warren was also a formidable intellectual and a highly influential writer and activist for the patriot cause; her three-volume *Rise, Progress, and Termination of the American Revolution* was published in 1805.

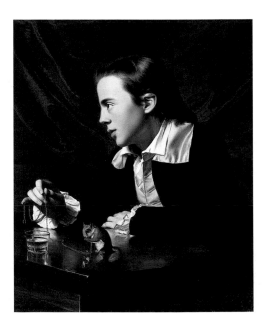

John Singleton Copley
American, 1738–1815
Henry Pelham (Boy with a Squirrel), 1765
Oil on canvas
30 3/8 × 25 1/8 in. (77.2 × 63.8 cm)
Gift of the artist's great-granddaughter 1978.297

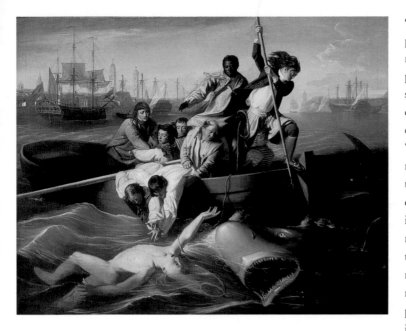

John Singleton Copley
American, 1738–1815
Watson and the Shark, 1778
Oil on canvas
72¼ x 90⅜ in. (183.5 x 229.6 cm)
Gift of Mrs. George von Lengerke
Meyer 89.481

"**W**as it not for preserving the resemblance of particular persons," Copley complained about colonial America, "painting would not be known in the place." He dreamed of working in England's more cosmopolitan artistic environment and of making "history paintings," those images of religious, mythological, or historical events that were traditionally considered the apex of artistic achievement. In 1774 Copley left America and began a forty-year career in London. *Watson and the Shark,* his first large-scale history painting, depicts the heroic rescue of English merchant Brook Watson (1735–1807) who, as a young cabin boy, lost a leg to a shark while swimming in the harbor of Havana, Cuba. *Watson and the Shark* is an astonishing achievement for an artist who had previously painted only portraits.

By 1765 Copley was eager to compare his work with that of the English portraitists he so much admired. This intimate image was not a commissioned portrait; rather, he painted it to be exhibited at the Society of Artists in London. In Boston, Copley was especially renowned for his ability to paint luxurious material objects—expensive textiles, furniture, and silver. He painted his half-brother Henry Pelham (1749–1806) to showcase his illusionistic skill in rendering animal fur, pink satin, metallic gold, polished wood, glass, and water. English portraitist Sir Joshua Reynolds praised the painting as "a very wonderful Performance" and urged Copley to come to England before his "Manner and Taste were corrupted or fixed by working in [his] little way at Boston."

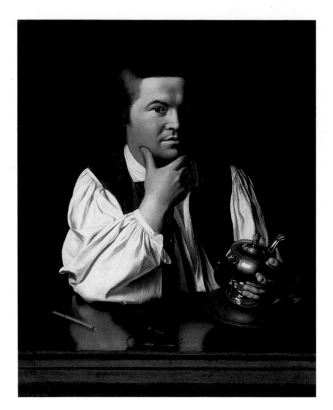

John Singleton Copley
American, 1738–1815
Paul Revere, 1768
Oil on canvas
35 ⅛ × 28 ½ in. (89.2 × 72.4 cm)
Gift of Joseph W. Revere, William
B. Revere, and Edward H. R. Revere
30.781

This image of a craftsman at work is unique in colonial portraiture and one of the most familiar and beloved icons of American art. Paul Revere (1735–1818) was a distinguished Bostonian, active in public affairs, an impassioned patriot, and a prominent silversmith. The circumstances surrounding the commissioning of this unusual portrait are unknown, but it was as a silversmith that Copley painted Revere—wigless and informally dressed in a white linen shirt and unbuttoned waistcoat. With his engraving tools spread before him, Revere seems to be contemplating the design he will engrave on a silver teapot. Teapots were among the most expensive items made by Revere; the inclusion of a teapot in his portrait may simply signify his craft, but the portrait was painted at the time of the much-resented Townshend Acts, which imposed heavy duties on imported tea. The teapot might thus be read as a provocative political statement.

This sugar bowl and creampot are highlights of the Museum's collection of almost 200 pieces of Paul Revere silver. The sheer variety of Revere's work is evident when we compare the intricate, curvilinear shapes and opulent decoration of these pieces with the simple elegance and rich, reflecting surface of the Sons of Liberty Bowl. The shape of the Liberty Bowl is influenced by imported Chinese porcelain bowls, while these objects are superb examples of the rococo style that dominated American and European decorative arts at the time.

The Liberty Bowl is a powerful and eloquent symbol of America's struggle for independence. It was commissioned by fifteen members of the Sons of Liberty, a secret, revolutionary organization to which Paul Revere belonged. The bowl was intended to honor ninety-two members of the Massachusetts House of Representatives who had refused to rescind the circular letter sent throughout the colonies to protest against the Townshend Acts (1767), which taxed tea, paper, glass, and other commodities imported from England. The legislators' defiant act of conscience directly embodied growing colonial resentment of high-handed British policies, and "the glorious Ninety-two" soon became a catchphrase expressing revolutionary sentiment. The Liberty Bowl, the Declaration of Independence, and the Constitution have been called the nation's three most cherished historical treasures. The bowl was purchased in 1949, with funds that included 700 donations by Boston public school children and the general public.

Sons of Liberty Bowl
Massachusetts (Boston), 1768
Made by **Paul Revere,** 1735–1818
Silver
Diameter: 11 in. (27.9 cm)
Gift by subscription and Francis Bartlett Fund 49.45

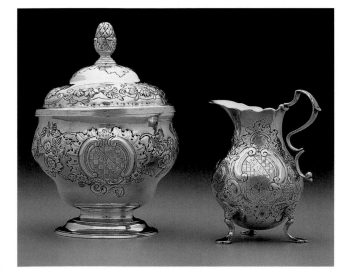

Sugar bowl and creampot
Massachusetts (Boston), 1761
Made by **Paul Revere,**
1735–1818
Silver
Sugar bowl height: 6½ in. (16.5 cm)
Creampot height: 4⅜ in. (11.1 cm)
Pauline Revere Thayer Collection
35.1781, 1782

Desk and bookcase
Massachusetts (Boston), 1770–85
Made by **George Bright,**
1726–1805
Mahogany and white pine
99½ x 43 x 24 in.
(252.7 x 109.2 x 61 cm)
Bequest of Miss Charlotte Hazen
56.1194

Admired as "the neatest workman in town," George Bright was among Boston's most successful cabinetmakers in the years just before and after the Revolution. The superb craftsmanship that made Bright famous is evident in this massive, handsomely proportioned desk and bookcase. The front and sides are bombé in form, from the French *bomber,* to bulge. In America, the bombé form was a specialty of Boston cabinetmakers, used on the most expensive and fashionable furniture. This desk and bookcase was made for wealthy merchant Samuel Barrett and is fitted with drawers, shelves, pigeonholes, and several secret compartments to hold the papers of a busy man. On the front of the doors are mirrors within curving gilded frames.

Covered goblet or pokal   >
Maryland (New Bremen),
about 1785–95
Probably made at the **New
Bremen Glass manufactory**
Glass
Height: 12⅜ in. (31.4 cm)
Gift of the Seminarians and Mr.
and Mrs. Daniel F. Morley 1994.82

Pewter chalice
New York (New York or Albany),
1775–95
Made by **Peter Young,** active
1775–1795
Height: 8½ in. (21.6 cm)
Pewter flagon
Connecticut (Hartford),
1795–1816
Made by **Samuel Danforth,**
1772–1827
Height: 11½ in. (29.2 cm)
Pewter teapot
Connecticut (Hartford),
about 1804–60
Made by **Thomas Danforth
Boardman,** 1784–1873
Height: 8¾ in. (22.2 cm)

Bequest of Mrs. Stephen S.
FitzGerald 64.1743, 64.1733,
64.1794

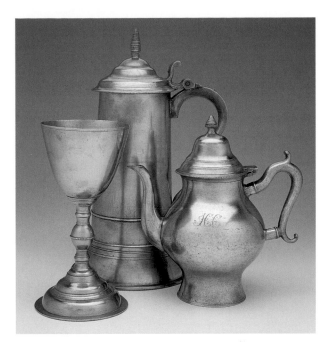

In early America, everyone who could afford to ate and drank from vessels made of pewter—an alloy consisting largely of tin, with small amounts of copper, antimony, bismuth, and lead. Pewter is shiny like silver (but ninety percent cheaper); it is longer-lasting than wood and less fragile than pottery. Some people insisted that a pewter mug gave a particularly tasty flavor to beer and ale. Pewter was cast in expensive brass or bronze molds that were passed down from generation to generation, so styles and forms persisted over long periods. Although most pewter was used in the home, the chalice here was made for use in church services.

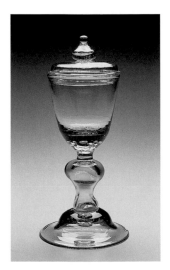

Although many glass factories were set up in the colonies, eighteenth-century American glass is very rare because few factories survived the competition from inexpensive, high-quality imported glass. In 1784 John Frederick Amelung (1741–1798) emigrated from Germany with sixty-eight skilled workers and established a factory at New Bremen, Maryland, that employed at its peak 500 people. This goblet bears no maker's mark, but its chemical composition matches that of objects known to be from Amelung's factory. Probably made for an Evangelical Lutheran church, the goblet's form seems appropriate for use in a church dedicated to "those who preach the Word [of God] in its simplicity and purity."

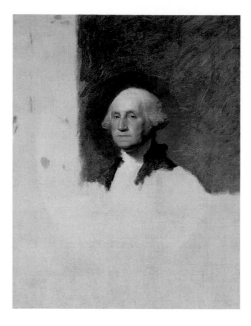 

This unfinished portrait of George Washington may well be the most famous of all American paintings—it even appears on the dollar bill. As Washington (1732–1799) neared the end of his second term as president, his wife Martha (1731–1802) commissioned paintings of them both from the celebrated portraitist Gilbert Stuart. Apparently Mrs. Washington was displeased with her husband's likeness, and the pair was never finished. Stuart kept them in his studio, using the head of the president as a model for more than sixty paintings of the heroic leader of the Revolution and the new republic. Stuart painted at least 114 portraits of Washington; this number testifies to America's hunger for visual symbols of the new nation's strength and pride. "Every American considers it his sacred duty," a French visitor observed, "to have a likeness of Washington in his home, just as we have images of God's saints."

Gilbert Stuart
American, 1755–1828
George Washington, 1796
Martha Washington, 1796
Oil on canvas
Each 47¾ × 37 in. (121.3 × 94 cm)
William Francis Warden Fund, John H. and Ernestine A. Payne Fund, Commonwealth Cultural Preservation Trust. Jointly owned by the Museum of Fine Arts, Boston, and the National Portrait Gallery, Washington, D. C. 1980.1 and 1980.2

Eagle >
Massachusetts (Salem), about 1786–99
Attributed to **Samuel McIntire,** 1757–1811
White pine and gilding
Height: 39 in. (99.1 cm)
Gift of a Friend of the Department of American Decorative Arts and Sculpture, the Estate of Gilbert L. Steward, Sr., Mrs. Ichabod F. Atwood and Mrs. Elaine Wilde, the French Foundation in Memory of Edward V. French, the Seminarians, and an Anonymous Donor 1991.535

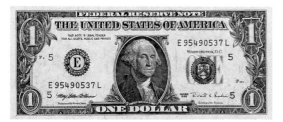

At the end of his career, the Philadelphia engineer Patrick Lyon (1779–1829) commissioned John Neagle to portray him as the lowly blacksmith he once was rather than as the successful businessman he had become. The portrait also includes, in the upper left, a view of Philadelphia's Walnut Street jail, where the young Lyon, falsely accused of theft, had been briefly imprisoned. In celebrating Lyon's humble origins and the dignity of skilled physical labor, the painting captures the optimistic spirit of America at a time when conviction was widespread that individuals could rise to greatness from poverty and adversity. Lyon is depicted on a heroic scale, his powerful forearms bared, his virile figure dramatically set off by the flames and smoke of his forge. Neagle's reputation rests almost entirely on this monumental work, which was acclaimed at exhibitions in Philadelphia, New York, and Boston.

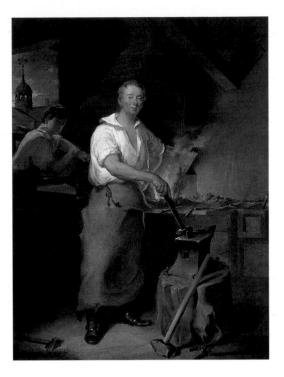

John Neagle
American, 1796–1865
Pat Lyon at the Forge, 1826–27
Oil on canvas
93¾ x 68 in. (238.1 x 172.7 cm)
Henry H. and Zoë Oliver Sherman Fund 1975.806

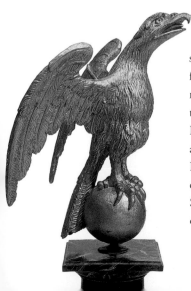

After the Revolution, Americans faced the challenge of how to unite thirteen disparate colonies into a single nation. One way was to create inspiring national symbols—such as images of George Washington—behind which people from all walks of life could rally. In 1782, by act of the Continental Congress, the eagle, an ancient symbol of power and victory, was chosen as the national emblem—in spite of Benjamin Franklin's sardonic disparagement ("a Bird of bad moral Character") and preference for the turkey ("a much more respectable Bird and withal a true original Native of America"). This spirited eagle is probably the work of versatile Salem architect Samuel McIntire (see pages 303 and 312), carved to crown the cupola of the home of merchant Elias Hasket Derby.

Parlor from Oak Hill

When the decorative arts wing opened in 1928, its most notable feature was three rooms reconstructed with woodwork from Oak Hill, a house built in 1800–01 in South Danvers, Massachusetts. Now meticulously restored and filled with furnishings that belonged to the Derby-West families, the Oak Hill rooms provide a vivid picture of the taste and lifestyle of prosperous New Englanders at the turn of the nineteenth century.

The house, probably designed by Samuel McIntire (see pages 303 and 311), was built for Captain Nathaniel West and his wife, Elizabeth, daughter of Salem millionaire-merchant Elias Hasket Derby. Elizabeth Derby West spared no expense in decorating her house with fashionable objects of the highest quality. The design and ornament of the magnificent commode below express the love of geometry and contrasting color fundamental to the neoclassical style. The commode survives with rare documentation: the bill from Thomas Seymour, which reads: "Large Mahogany Commode, $80.00. Paid Mr. Penniman's bill for painting Shels on Top of Do [ditto] $10.00."

In the parlor are carved mahogany side chairs and superb upholstered armchairs and sofas that testify unequivocally to Mrs. West's insistence on the best. Since the original fabrics did not survive, the Museum, following a description in the Oak Hill inventory, re-covered the furniture in an "orange" silk damask. Both the block-printed wallpaper and the woven Brussels carpet recreate costly items that Mrs. West probably imported from abroad. A selection of engravings and a gilded looking glass with a broadly reflecting convex surface complete the decoration of a room where visitors enjoyed conversation, tea parties, and games of cards.

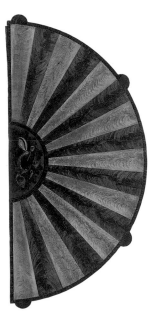

Commode
Massachusetts (Boston), 1809
Made by **Thomas Seymour,**
1771–1848
Painted by **John Ritto Penniman,**
1783–1837
Probably carved by **Thomas Whitman**
Mahogany and mahogany veneer; maple and satinwood veneer on pine, maple, and chestnut
41 ½ x 50 x 24½ in.
(105.4 x 127 x 62.4 cm)
The M. and M. Karolik Collection of Eighteenth-Century American Arts
23.19

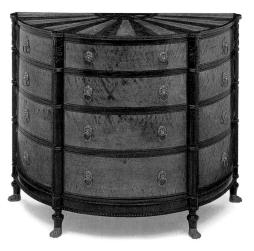

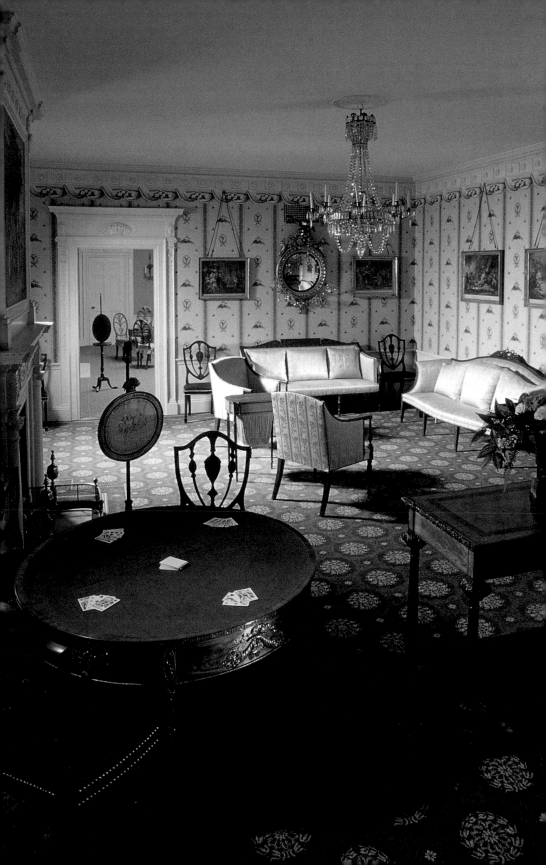

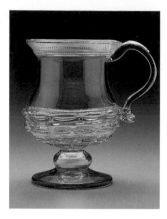

Mug
Massachusetts (Boston),
about 1825
Made by **Thomas Cains,**
1779–1865, of the **Phoenix
Glass Works**
Colorless free-blown glass with
applied decoration
Height: 9 3/8 in. (23.8 cm)
Gift of William, Nancy, and
Malcolm in Loving Memory of
their Father, William L. Johnston,
Great-Great-Grandson of Thomas
Cains 1995.765

Thomas Cains served his glassmaking apprenticeship in England before coming to the United States in 1812. His skills gave him an immediate advantage in the infant American glass industry, and by 1820 he was running his own firm, the Phoenix Glass Works in South Boston. A specialty was the "chain" decoration seen on this mug—strings of molten glass laid around the vessel and pinched together while still soft. Most early American glass is unmarked, but this mug can be approximately dated by the 1821 American quarter held in its hollow stem. While no one knows why it has always been called the "Bishop's Mug," its date and known history of descent in the Cains family make it a touchstone for identifying other objects from the Phoenix Glass Works.

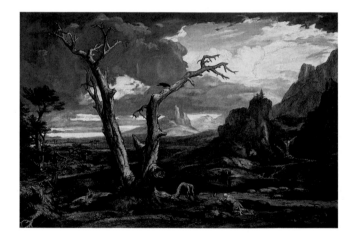

Washington Allston
American, 1779–1843
Elijah in the Desert, 1818
Oil on canvas
49 1/4 × 72 3/4 in. (125.1 × 184.8 cm)
Gift of Mrs. Samuel and Miss Alice
Hooper 70.1

According to the Bible's first Book of Kings, the Lord sent the prophet Elijah into the desert where "the ravens brought him bread and flesh in the morning and bread and flesh in the evening; and he drank of the brook." Allston conveyed the mood and meaning of this subject by the stark landscape, the turbulent clouds, and the dry texture of the paint. Elijah kneels in prayer, his figure echoed by the gnarled roots of a barren tree. Allston spent many years in Europe and viewed himself as a painter in the tradition of the old masters. His fellow Americans admired his learned biblical and literary subjects and romantic, imaginary landscapes. *Elijah in the Desert,* painted shortly before Allston returned to Boston from London, was the first work of art acquired by the Museum.

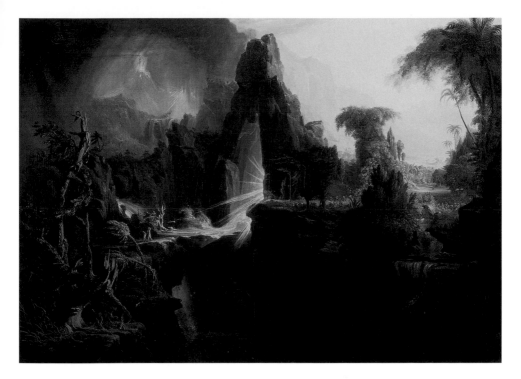

The pioneer of American landscape painting, Thomas Cole made his reputation with images of the wilderness of New York's Hudson River Valley. In this painting, which Cole called an attempt "at a higher type of landscape than I have hitherto tried," he combined landscape with the kind of religious theme accepted for centuries as the proper subject matter for "serious" artists. The story is that of Adam and Eve who, having angered God by eating the forbidden fruit that gave them knowledge of good and evil, were expelled from the Garden of Eden (see pages 186 and 240). Cole conveys their anguish, not through pose and expression (as was traditional) but through landscape—contrasting serene, light-filled Paradise with the harsh world outside. Dwarfed by the power of nature, the helpless figures seem propelled from the garden by a shaft of supernatural light.

Thomas Cole
American (born England),
1801–1848
Expulsion from the Garden of
Eden, 1828
Oil on canvas
39 3/4 x 54 1/2 in. (101 x 138.4 cm)
Gift of Martha C. Karolik for the
M. and M. Karolik Collection of
American Paintings, 1815–1865
47.1188

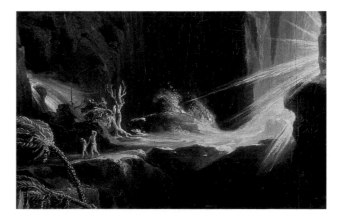

Henry Sargent
American, 1770–1845
The Dinner Party, about 1821
Oil on canvas
61 5/8 × 49 3/4 in. (156.5 × 126.4 cm)
Gift of Mrs. Horatio A. Lamb in
memory of Mr. and Mrs. Winthrop
Sargent 19.13

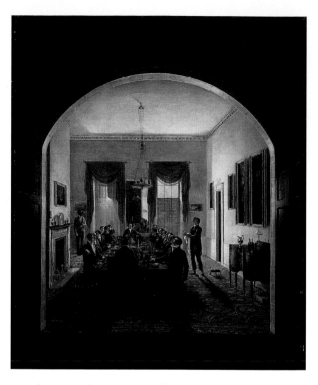

The meticulous detail of Henry Sargent's painting provides an invaluable document of upper-class life in early nineteenth-century Boston. It may depict a meeting of the Wednesday Evening Club, which gathered at the homes of its members to discuss the issues of the day. Mid-afternoon was the fashionable time for dining, and the gentlemen in Sargent's painting enjoy the final course of fruit, nuts, and wine, with a single candle to light their tobacco. The room is decorated in the latest neoclassical style, with swagged draperies above the shuttered windows and graceful carving on the mantelpiece and cornice. The sideboard was a new form in this period, as was the lead-lined cellarette, or wine cooler, at the end of the table. Beneath the table, a green baize "crumb cloth" protects the expensive carpet. Sargent, who studied with Benjamin West and John Singleton Copley in London, also served as a captain in the Boston Light Infantry and as a member of the Massachusetts State Legislature.

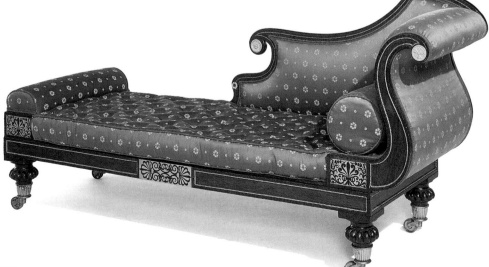

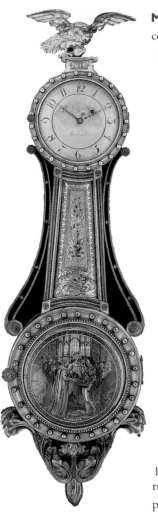

Made when clocks were still costly and prized possessions, the girandole is a design unique to America. It was patented by Lemuel Curtis in 1816 and took its name from the circular, convex looking glasses popular in the period. Such clocks, which were the work of many skilled craftsmen, are characterized by the convex glass of their dial faces and pendulum chambers, their gilded cases with eagle finials, and their reverse-painted glass panels—here, depicting a medieval wedding ceremony. Soon after this clock was made, Curtis's clockmaking business declined, undermined by the mass-production of thirty-hour shelf clocks. In 1832 he became a merchant and grocer, but was declared bankrupt ten years later and died in poverty.

Girandole wall clock
Massachusetts (Concord),
about 1816
Made by **Lemuel Curtis,**
1790–1857
Carved, painted, and gilded wood;
brass; reverse-glass painting
Height: 46 in. (116.8 cm)
Gift of Mrs. Charles C. Cabot in
memory of Dr. and Mrs. Charles J.
White 1991.241

Grecian couch
Massachusetts (Boston),
about 1818–30
Rosewood with rosewood
graining, brass, silk upholstery
34⅞ × 70¼ × 23¾ in.
(88.6 × 178.4 × 60.3 cm)
Gift of a Friend of the
Department of American
Decorative Arts and Sculpture, the
William N. Banks Foundation, the
Seminarians, Dr. and Mrs. J. Wallace
McMeel, and Anonymous
1977.726

< **T**he "Grecian" couch—with one high, bolstered end—was among the most stylish furnishings of early nineteenth-century parlors. This is one of four such couches that Boston merchant and banker Nathan Appleton ordered for his new house at 39 Beacon Street. The suave curves of the couch's silhouette are emphasized by lines of inlaid brass, and the imported rosewood is punctuated by finely crafted brass mounts. Unsurpassed among Boston furniture of the period for design and technical sophistication, the couch testifies to Appleton's discriminating taste, his awareness of the latest English and continental styles, and the considerable wealth he acquired trading arms and commodities during the War of 1812. The couch has been reupholstered in silk fabric of appropriate pattern, following the form of the original cushion, bolster, and back.

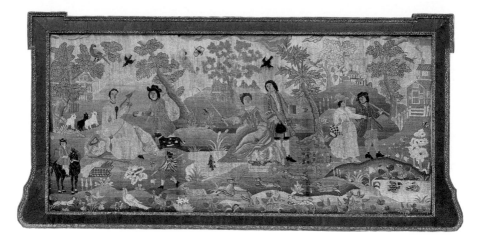

Embroidered picture
Massachusetts (Boston), about 1748
Attributed to **Eunice Bourne,** about 1732–1773/81
Wool, silk, metallic threads, and beads on linen; predominantly tent stitch
25 x 51 in. (63.5 x 129.5 cm)
Seth K. Sweetser Fund 21.2233

This is among the most skillfully worked and best preserved of the large, pictorial embroideries, usually derived from European prints, that were created by young women at Boston boarding schools. Like many of her peers, Eunice Bourne of Barnstable, Massachusetts, chose an idyllic, outdoor scene bustling with lively and detailed motifs—couples courting; ladies spinning and fishing; and an array of birds, animals, fish, and insects. Oversized strawberries provide bright notes of color. This overmantel or "chimney-piece" is one of very few still in its original frame; the projections at the bottom corners may have held candle sconces.

Mary S. Chapin
American, dates unknown
Solitude, 1815–20
Watercolor over graphite pencil on paper
15 ¼ x 13 ½ in. (38.7 x 34.4 cm)
M. and M. Karolik Collection of American Watercolors and Drawings 60.469

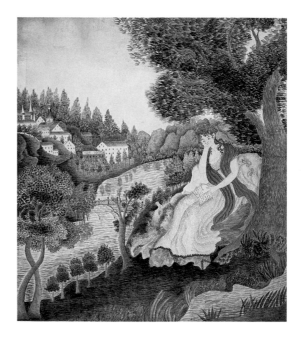

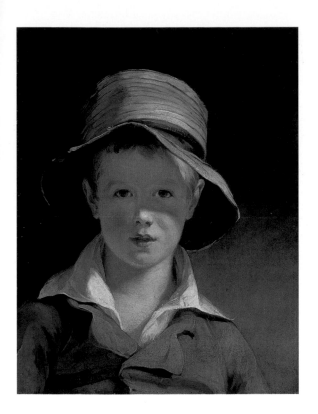

Thomas Sully
American (born England),
1783–1872
The Torn Hat, 1820
Oil on panel
19 1/8 x 14 5/8 in. (48.6 x 37.2 cm)
Gift of Miss Belle Greene and
Henry Copley Greene in memory
of their mother, Mary Abby
Greene (Mrs. J. S. Copley Greene)
16.104

In portraits of the seventeenth and eighteenth centuries, children were usually posed and dressed as miniature adults (see the portrait of Margaret Gibbs, page 292). But Philadelphia painter Thomas Sully discarded this convention in favor of more informal, naturalistic images, such as this one of his son Thomas. The curved brim of the boy's straw hat is torn, and this gives Sully the opportunity to display his skill at rendering the play of light and shadow on skin and fabric. The enthusiasm that greeted this unaffected image reflects the early nineteenth century's new appreciation of the appealing and distinctive nature of childhood.

Embroidery and watercolor painting, introduced to America from England in the seventeenth and eighteenth centuries, were considered requisite accomplishments of cultivated young ladies. Chapin's delightful watercolor shows a fashionably dressed young woman daydreaming in a bucolic setting. Although embroideries of such subjects were going out of fashion, Chapin rendered much of her picture with brushstrokes that imitate stitches. For example, the dots of white paint on the blue dress resemble French knots, and the foliage of the small trees in the background suggests featherstitch. But for the leaves of the large tree, the grass, and the roofs of the houses, the artist turned to the more fluid, "brushy" qualities of watercolor. Mary Chapin, most likely a student in her late teens, signed her name and wrote the picture's title on the back of the paper.

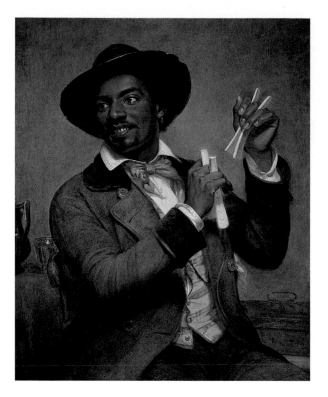

William Sidney Mount
American, 1807–1868
The Bone Player, 1856
Oil on canvas
36⅛ × 29⅛ in. (91.8 × 74 cm)
Bequest of Martha C. Karolik for
the M. and M. Karolik Collection of
American Paintings, 1815–1865
48.461

The musician depicted here plays "the bones," thin bars of ivory or bone that were clicked together to create complex and energetic rhythms. *The Bone Player* has the sensitivity and specificity of a portrait, but Mount created it to be reproduced as a color lithograph in Paris, where images of "exotic" figure types enjoyed widespread popularity.

Mount, who lived on rural Long Island, New York, was the first major American artist to devote his career to depictions of the work and play of ordinary people. He wrote in his diary: "Paint pictures that will take with the public. In other words, never paint for the few, but for the many. Some artists remain in the corner by not observing the above."

During the War of 1812, the infant American navy—to everyone's surprise—regularly defeated the supposedly invincible British fleet. Birch, who emigrated from England to Philadelphia in 1794, made his reputation with depictions of these naval battles, which were both as accurate as he could make them (details were often derived from interviews with members of the ships' crews) and romantically thrilling. In this picture, Birch documented, with fine patriotic passion, the defeat of the British warship *Guerrière* (on the right) by the USS *Constitution.* As the damaged *Guerrière* is driven up against the *Constitution,* the British standard sinks into the sea, and American flags wave triumphantly against a sky pink with clouds and smoke. The *Constitution,* nicknamed "Old Ironsides" for the virtually impenetrable oak planking of its hull, now is docked at the Charlestown Navy Yard in Boston.

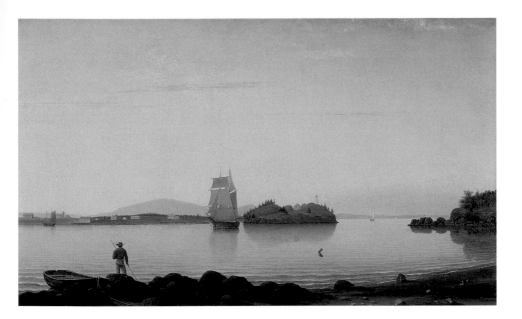

Fitz Hugh Lane
American, 1804–1865
Owl's Head, Penobscot Bay, Maine, 1862
Oil on canvas
15¾ × 26⅛ in. (40 × 66.4 cm)
Bequest of Martha C. Karolik for the M. and M. Karolik Collection of American Paintings, 1815–1865
48.448

The son of a sailmaker in Gloucester, Massachusetts, Lane spent his life painting the coast of New England. "The sea is his home," wrote a contemporary critic. "There he truly lives, and it is there, in that inexhaustible field, that his victories will be won." This is among the most spare and poetic of Lane's coastal views—small pictures whose horizontal shape emphasizes the line that separates land and sea from an expanse of clear, delicately tinted sky. Although Lane depicts a specific spot in Maine and a specific moment in time, this painting's true subject is light, and its evocative stillness renders it timeless.

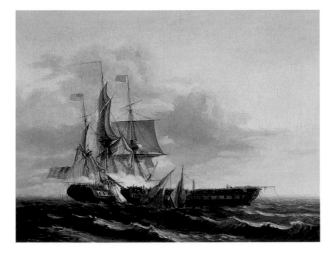

Thomas Birch
American (born England), 1779–1851
Engagement between the "Constitution" and the "Guerrière," 1813
Oil on canvas
28 × 36¼ in. (71.1 × 92.1 cm)
Ernest Wadsworth Longfellow Fund and Emily L. Ainsley Fund
1978.159

The Karoliks: Larger than Life

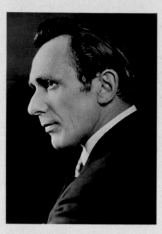

Maxim Karolik in 1941.

"Who ever accused me of being a gentleman? I am a tenor!" Trained as an opera singer in his native St. Petersburg, Russia, Maxim Karolik (1893–1963) came to the United States in the early 1920s and became a champion of American art and a great benefactor of the Museum. In 1927 he married Martha Codman (1858–1948), who was descended from several prominent New Englanders and was herself a distinguished collector of eighteenth-century American art. Together they assembled three huge collections for the Museum of Fine Arts that transformed the institution's holdings and rewrote the history of American art.

Martha Karolik was a more reserved figure than her husband—it would have been difficult not to be—but it was she who introduced him to the Museum and her money that allowed them to gather what Maxim called "the trilogy." The first collection was dedicated to eighteenth-century furniture and painting; the second to paintings of the half century between 1815 and 1865; and the last to drawings, watercolors, and folk art of the same period. It is for their taste in paintings that the Karoliks are best remembered, for before them it had been generally assumed that there was almost no art worthy of the name in mid-nineteenth-century America. The Karoliks were among the first to champion Fitz Hugh Lane and, above all, Martin Johnson Heade, whom Maxim called "the genius of our collection" (see pages 321 and 329). Presented to the Museum in 1949, the Karoliks' paintings spurred a nation-wide reassessment of nineteenth-century American art, and a number of the Karoliks' unknowns are today among the most sought-after American artists.

The Karoliks themselves were almost extravagantly modest, and Maxim refused to attend the

Chair
Pennsylvania (Philadelphia), about
1740
Walnut, white pine
Height: 42¾ in. (108.6 cm)
The M. and M. Karolik Collection
of Eighteenth-Century American
Arts 39.119

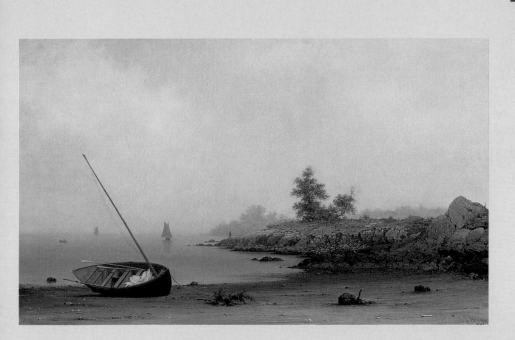

Martin Johnson Heade
American, 1819–1904
The Stranded Boat, 1863
Oil on canvas
22⅞ × 36⅞ in. (58.1 × 93.7 cm)
Gift of Maxim Karolik for the
M. and M. Karolik Collection of
American Paintings, 1815–1865
48.1026

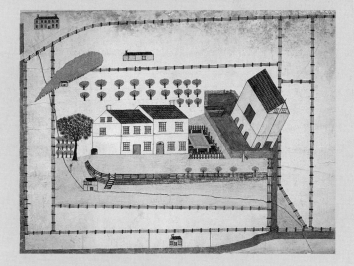

Unidentified artist
American, early 19th century
***Pennsylvania Farmstead with
Many Fences***
Pen and watercolor on paper
18 × 23⅞ in. (45.7 × 60.6 cm)
The M. and M. Karolik Collection
of American Watercolors and
Drawings 56.740

opening of the Museum's exhibition of the painting collection for fear his presence would distract from the art. Most movingly, he saw the trilogy as a celebration of his adopted country and the embodiment of its democratic spirit. In an open letter to the Museum's director, he concluded: "We are not 'Patrons of Art' or 'Public Benefactors.' We refuse to accept these banal labels. We accept with pleasure only one label: 'Useful Citizens.'"

Bostonian Horatio Greenough was the first of many American sculptors to train in Italy, drawn there by its famed marble quarries; the inspiring examples of ancient Greek, Roman, and Renaissance sculpture; and a thriving, international community of artists eager to recapture the glories of classical art. This sculpture, carved in subtly modulated low relief (see page 182) and influenced by Roman architectural friezes and sarcophagi, depicts the famous warriors Castor and Pollux. According to one legend, Zeus rewarded the love of these brothers, separated by death, by joining them eternally in the sky as the constellation of the twins, Gemini.

Horatio Greenough
American, 1805–1852
Castor and Pollux, about 1847
Marble
34 5/8 × 45 1/4 × 1 3/4 in.
(88 × 114.8 × 4.5 cm)
Bequest of Mrs. Horatio Greenough 92.2642

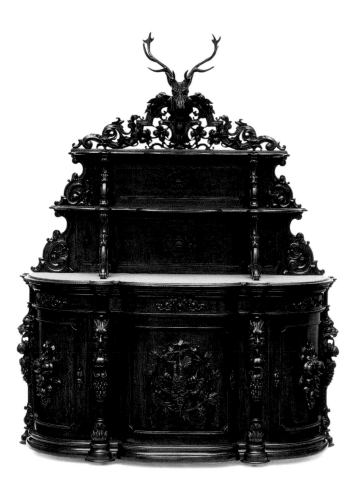

Sideboard
Pennsylvania (Philadelphia), 1850–60
Made by **Ignatius Lutz,** active 1844–1860
Oak and yellow-poplar, marble
94 × 74 × 25 in.
(238.8 × 188 × 63.5 cm)
Gift of the Estate of Richard Bruce E. Lacont 1990.1

Laura Eugenia, Sarah Isabella, and Augusta were the youngest of twelve children born to Otis and Sarah Lincoln of Newark Valley (near Binghamton), New York. Their father, who owned a hotel, commissioned this painting from Waters, a self-trained itinerant artist. For a period in the mid-1840s when her husband was ailing, Waters traveled from town to town painting portraits, presumably to supplement the family income.

This is the most ambitious of about thirty known portraits by Waters, and the rendering of pattern—in the children's dresses, the carpet or floorcloth, the leafy plants—is characteristic of the best folk art of the period. Note the intent little dog, whose neat, white feet echo the girls' pristine pantalettes. In the 1860s Waters turned from portraits to paintings of animals, which gained considerable acclaim. Her *Mallard Ducks and Pets of the Studio* was exhibited at the prestigious Philadelphia Centennial Exposition of 1876.

Susan Catherine Moore Waters
American, 1823–1900
The Lincoln Children, 1845
Oil on canvas
45 ¼ × 50 ¼ in. (114.9 × 127.6 cm)
Juliana Cheney Edwards Collection, by exchange 1981.438

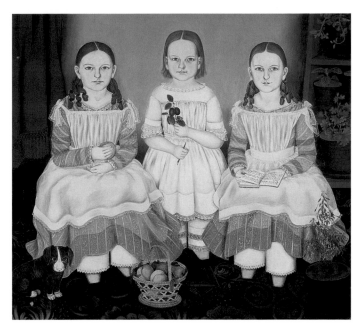

< **C**oncrete symbols of taste and social status change with changing times. In the mid-nineteenth century, massive sideboards—carved with fruit, vegetables, and animals and often laden with silver—adorned the dining rooms of the wealthy and style conscious. In a period when much furniture was at least partly made by machine, handcrafted objects began to assume new status. The rich and complex carving that gives this massive piece its exciting silhouette could not have been achieved by machine. The sideboard bears the label of French-trained cabinetmaker Ignatius Lutz, who came to Philadelphia in 1844. One of many French and German furnituremakers in American cities at this time, Lutz employed thirty craftsmen who mainly worked without power machinery in his successful shop.

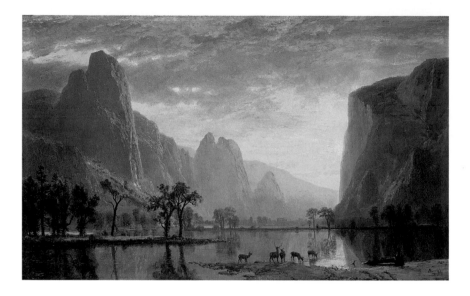

Albert Bierstadt
American (born Germany),
1830–1902
Valley of the Yosemite, 1864
Oil on paperboard
11 7/8 x 19 1/4 in. (30.2 x 48.9 cm)
Gift of Martha C. Karolik for the
M. and M. Karolik Collection of
American Paintings, 1815–1865
47.1236

The unspoiled grandeur of the West was an endless source of fascination for armchair travelers in the eastern United States. Bierstadt, a canny businessman as well as a gifted painter, made several trips to the West, and back in his New York studio, he used the oil sketches and photographs from these journeys to create hundreds of paintings that range from the tiny to the gargantuan. These images celebrate the West's natural splendors, many of which would soon be altered forever by railroads, settlers, and tourists. The emotional charge that Americans found in the Western landscape was conveyed by Bierstadt's companion on a trip to the recently discovered Yosemite Valley in 1864: "Far to the westward, widening more and more, it opens into the bosom of great mountain ranges,—into a field of perfect light, misty by its own excess,—into an unspeakable suffusion of glory created from the phoenix-pile of the dying sun."

During the 1850s, adherents of the Church of Jesus Christ of Latter Day Saints (the Mormons) migrated in great numbers from Europe and the eastern United States to the Utah territory. Mormons in Liverpool, England, hired English painter Piercy to document the trek in words and pictures and to produce a guidebook for future emigrants. In the course of a year-long journey, Piercy made a series of drawings and watercolors of the American plains that were reproduced as engravings in the book. This example, with its towering cottonwood trees, is typical of many nineteenth-century images of the West which contrast the diminutive fragility of human beings with the grand scale of the natural world.

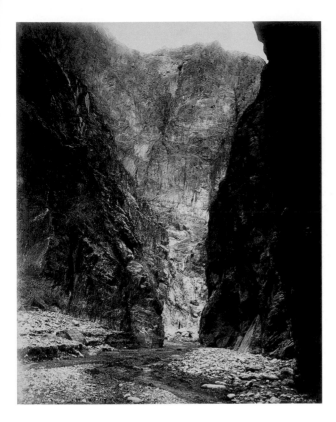

William Henry Jackson
American, 1843–1942
***Diamond River Canyon,
Colorado,*** after 1880
Photograph, albumen print
21 × 16½ in. (53.5 × 42 cm)
Abraham Shuman Fund 1979.44

After a fight with his fiancée, the young Jackson fled west and became a professional photographer, eventually settling in Denver. In the 1880s several railroad companies hired Jackson to document the mountains and deserts through which the trains snaked their way, hoping the photographs would lure tourists to visit the West. Jackson traveled with his own photographic lab on a special train. He photographed on glass plate negatives (measuring nearly two feet high and termed "mammoth") that required an enormous box camera and a heavy tripod to support it. However cumbersome the equipment, the extraordinary results convey the overwhelming scale of the landscape, the play of light, and the intricate textures of the canyon wall.

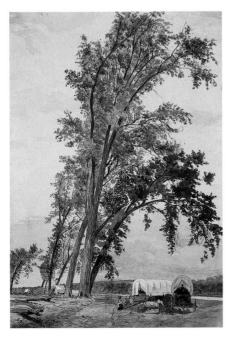

Frederick Piercy
English, 1830–1891
***Council Bluffs Ferry and Group
of Cottonwood Trees,*** 1853
Watercolor on paper
10¼ × 7 in. (26 × 17.8 cm)
M. and M. Karolik Collection of
American Watercolors and
Drawings 50.3870

Chalice and paten
New York (New York), about 1860
Made by **Francis W. Cooper**
and **Richard Fisher,** active
1858–1862
Silver, gilded silver, and enamel
Chalice height: 9 7/8 in. (25.1 cm)
Gift of the Seminarians, Curator's
Fund, and Ron Bourgeault
1996.271, 272

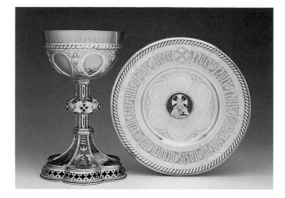

The chalice and the paten (a shallow dish) are used in the Christian church service of Communion, in which wine and bread are offered to the congregation as symbols of the blood and body of Christ. These are very rare examples of American silver in the Gothic Revival style, which emulated the perfection, grace, and exquisite workmanship of medieval liturgical vessels. Enriched with enamel and gilding, they reflect the "ecclesiological" movement in the mid-nineteenth-century Church of England and American Episcopal church, which called for a revival of the splendors of medieval Catholicism.

Parlor cabinet
New York (New York),
about 1870–90
Ebonized American cherry, raised
gilded gesso ornament, and brass
mounts
76 1/2 × 50 1/4 × 17 in.
(194.3 × 127.7 × 43.2 cm)
Helen and Alice Colburn Fund
1979.401

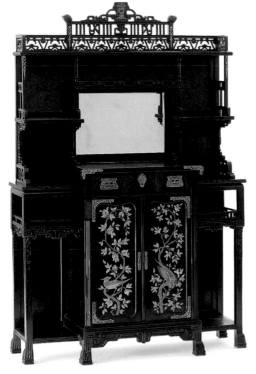

As the nineteenth century progressed, high-style furniture was increasingly characterized by eclectic design and abundant ornament, much of it made by machine. In response, some designers called for reform, advocating furniture with clean, straight lines and "honest" workmanship. Sir Charles Eastlake, spokesman for the reform movement in England, might have been writing about this cabinet when he stated: "The best and most picturesque furniture of all ages has been simple in general form. It may have been enriched by complex details of carved work or inlay, but its main outline was always chaste and sober in design, never running into extravagant contour or unnecessary curves." Made of ebonized cherry simulating lacquerwork, this cabinet also reflects the period's fascination with Asian art.

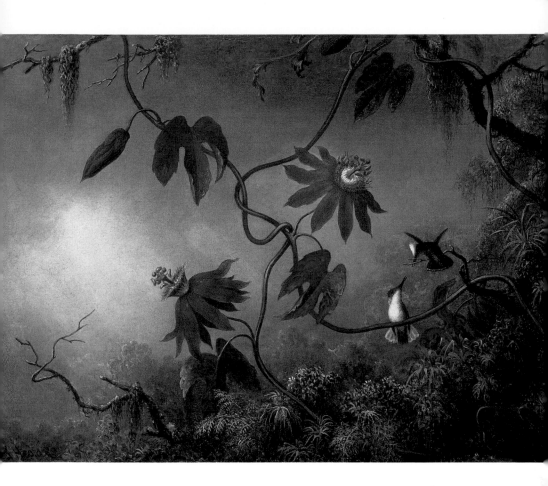

Martin Johnson Heade
American, 1819–1904
***Passion Flowers and
Hummingbirds,*** 1875–85
Oil on canvas
15 1/2 x 21 5/8 in. (39.4 x 54.9 cm)
Gift of Maxim Karolik for the
M. and M. Karolik Collection of
American Paintings, 1815–1865
47.1138

Heade traveled to Brazil in 1863 to paint illustrations for a
book about hummingbirds. Although the book never material-
ized, Heade continued to paint images of tiny hummingbirds
and exotic flowers—usually orchids—for more than forty years.
Reflecting mid-nineteenth-century beliefs in the unity of art
and science, Heade rendered his birds and blossoms with meticulous precision, but he was also clearly captivated by their sensuous beauty. Here, the brilliant flowers are silhouetted against
gray mist shot with light, and we look through sinuous, snaking
vines into a vast jungle landscape. Heade was the favorite
painter of eminent collector Maxim Karolik (see page 322).

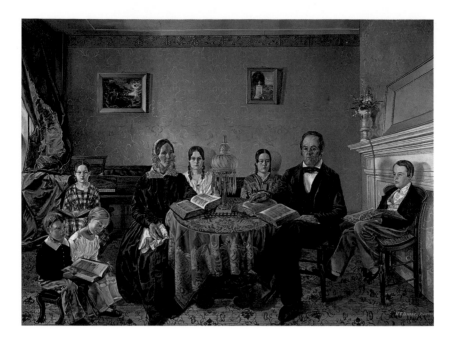

The advent of inexpensive and readily available photographic portraits threatened the livelihood of many portrait painters in the mid-nineteenth century. However, painted portraits had possibilities of color and scale that daguerreotypes did not. When only seventeen, Darby painted this group on a summer visit to Concord, New Hampshire. Reverend Atwood was a Baptist minister and chaplain of the state prison; five years later he became the Democratic Party's nominee for governor of New Hampshire. Darby depicted the Atwood family at their daily Bible study. On the back wall, a "mourning picture" includes a deceased son in the gathering. Family pride is underscored by the prominent placement of the elaborate lamp, a new invention burning oil pressed from lard, which was touted as "the greatest luminary in the world except the sun."

Henry F. Darby
American 1829–1897
The Reverend John Atwood and His Family, 1845
Oil on canvas
72⅛ × 96¼ in. (183.2 × 244.5 cm)
Gift of Maxim Karolik for the M. and M. Karolik Collection of American Paintings, 1815–1865
62.269

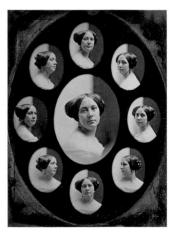

Unknown lady in nine views
Massachusetts (Boston), after 1855
Made by the firm of **Southworth and Hawes**
Framed daguerreotype
7⅞ × 6 in. (20 × 15.3 cm)
Gift of Edward Southworth Hawes, in memory of his father, Josiah Johnson Hawes 43.1405

Sargent was a young painter of fashionable portraits when he painted this unconventional image of the daughters of his artist friend Edward Darley Boit in the Boit's Paris apartment. The family traveled there each year from Boston, and the enormous Japanese vases in this picture survived sixteen trips across the Atlantic (they were given to the Museum in 1997). The painting's square format is unusual, as is the isolated placement of the children within a shadowy, cavernous space described by one critic as "four corners and a void." Each girl is individualized, expressing her age and personality by subtleties of pose and gaze. And "when," mused American writer Henry James, "was the pinafore ever painted with that power and made so poetic?"

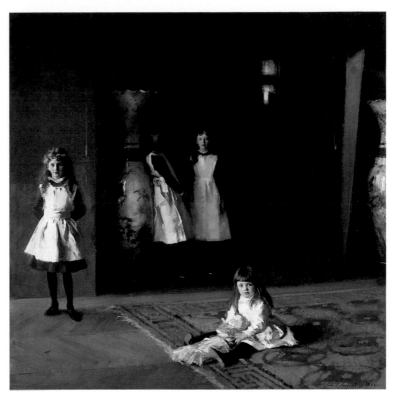

John Singer Sargent
American, 1856–1925
The Daughters of Edward Darley Boit, 1882
Oil on canvas
87 3/8 × 87 5/8 in. (221.9 × 222.6 cm)
Gift of Mary Louisa Boit, Julia Overing Boit, Jane Hubbard Boit and Florence D. Boit in memory of their father, Edward Darley Boit
19.124

< The daguerreotype, introduced in 1839, was one of the earliest photographic processes. The Boston firm established by Albert Sands Southworth (1811–1894) and Josiah Johnson Hawes (1808–1901) was renowned for its ability to capture personality and expression in daguerreotype portraits—no mean feat in a medium that required the sitter to remain absolutely motionless for up to thirty seconds. In 1855 Southworth patented a device for making multiple exposures on the same plate, explaining that they might be used to select "the best for a locket; or they may be different views of the same face taken upon the same plate for the purposes of preserving them together." This is the finest of only two known examples of this adventurous technique.

Childe Hassam
American, 1859–1935
Boston Common at Twilight,
1885–86
Oil on canvas
42 × 60 in. (106.7 × 152.4 cm)
Gift of Miss Maud E. Appleton
31.952

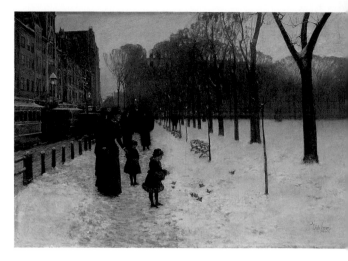

Along a snowy sidewalk, a fashionably dressed woman and her daughters, all wearing muffs against the cold, pause to feed some birds. Before them is the serene expanse of Boston Common; behind them, the gaslights are coming on and horse-drawn streetcars and cabs inch along crowded Tremont Street. This painting, one of the most evocative of images of life in nineteenth-century Boston, is also an early example of Hassam's lifelong interest in the varied effects of light and in subjects drawn from the modern city; he later became one of the first American Impressionists.

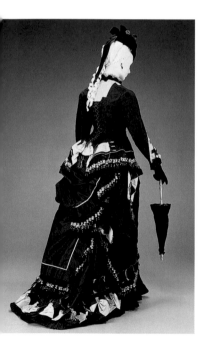

Walking dress
Massachusetts (Boston), 1874–75
Labeled: "**John J. Stevens**/282
Washington Street, Boston"
Silk, trimmed with knotted net
and tassels
Gift of Ruth Burke 56.818 a, b

Sarah Howe of Lowell, Massachusetts, purchased this dress at the popular Boston shop of John J. Stevens (1824–1902), a dressmaker who also advertised his firm as "importers and dealers of Paris modes." It is possible that Mrs. Howe's stylish dress, with its bustle and complex arrangement of sweeping folds, was made in Paris. Although designed as a "walking dress" for daytime strolls, it required the wearing of a corset and the cumbersome skirts would have been difficult to manage on the street. The dress reform movement, which had developed by the 1860s along with the women's suffrage movement, denounced such garments as restricting and unhealthy and scorned fashionable women as "upholstered bodies."

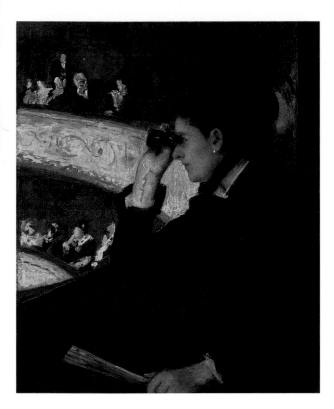

Mary Cassatt
American, 1844–1926
In the Loge, 1879
Oil on canvas
32 x 26 in. (81.3 x 66 cm)
The Hayden Collection 10.35

Born and raised in Pennsylvania, Cassatt settled in Paris in 1875 and became the only American to exhibit with the Impressionist group. Like her friend Edgar Degas (see page 260), she was a figure painter, attracted to detached and spontaneous views of modern life. Here, a woman in sober dress and hat uses her uptilted opera glasses to scan the occupants of other boxes. Self-contained and intent, she seems unaware of the man who leans out of another box, focusing his glasses on her. About the time this picture was painted, Cassatt began to carry a small sketchbook in which she swiftly recorded people and scenes that might later become subjects of paintings, as in the preparatory sketch for *In the Loge* (at right).

Mary Cassatt
American, 1844–1926
Study for the painting
In the Loge, about 1879
Graphite pencil on paper
4 x 6 in. (10.2 x 15.2 cm)
Gift of Dr. Hans Schaeffer 55.28

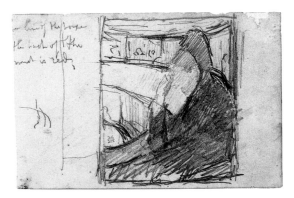

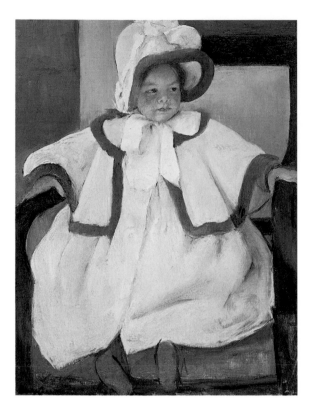

Cassatt was one of the first artists to explore the artistic possibilities of the sheltered domestic and social lives of upper-class women. This portrait of her niece Ellen Mary Cassatt (1894–1966) is unusual among the artist's many images of children for its directness and lack of sentimentality. Overdressed— indeed, almost overwhelmed—in a fashionable caped coat and bonnet, the baby sits waiting until the grownups are ready to go out. Her diminutive size is accentuated by the tiny hands and boots, but she fills the space of the picture entirely, touching every edge, and her firm personality dominates the portrait.

Mary Cassatt
American, 1844–1926
Ellen Mary in a White Coat,
about 1896
Oil on canvas
32 × 23¾ in. (81.3 × 60.3 cm)
Anonymous fractional gift in honor of Ellen Mary Cassatt 1982.630

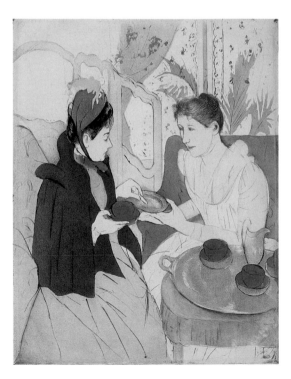

Mary Cassatt
American, 1844–1926
Afternoon Tea Party,
1890–1901
Drypoint and aquatint
13¾ × 10⅜ in. (34.8 × 26.3 cm)
Gift of William Emerson and Charles Henry Hayden Fund
41.811

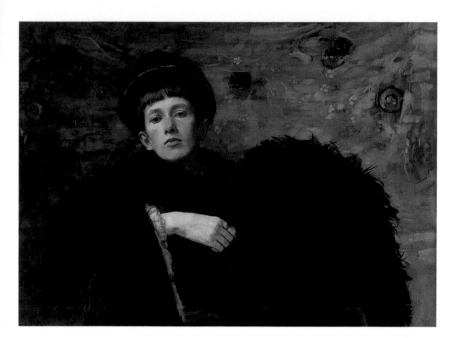

Hale studied in Boston, Philadelphia, and Paris and supported herself by teaching art in Boston, by selling her portraits and etchings, and by painting decorations in church interiors. This unconventional self-portrait was painted on Hale's return from Paris. Against a rather mysterious blue background decorated with swirling shapes and spots of bright color, her purposeful, unsmiling face and capable hand stand out from the surrounding soft blackness of dress, hat, and ostrich-feather fan. A critic writing in 1887 acknowledged the artist's originality and skill: "Miss Ellen Hale . . . displays a man's strength in the treatment and handling of her subjects—a massiveness and breadth of effect attained through sound training and native wit and courage."

Ellen Day Hale
American, 1855–1940
Self-Portrait, 1885
Oil on canvas
28½ x 39 in. (72.4 x 99.1 cm)
Gift of Nancy Hale Bowers
1986.645

After attending an 1890 Paris exhibition of more than 700 Japanese woodblock prints, Cassatt wrote: "You couldn't think of anything more beautiful. I dream of it." Like many of her contemporaries, Cassatt collected and admired Japanese prints for their modern-life subjects, emphasis on elegant line, unusual compositions, and barely modulated areas of color (see page 145). This is one of a set of ten images in which Cassatt focuses on daily domestic life—women bathing and dressing, tending their children, out for a dress-fitting or a social call. The several plates required to produce the variety of colors were each inked by hand, and every one of Cassatt's sophisticated etchings is a unique work of art.

Elihu Vedder
American, 1836–1923
The Questioner of the Sphinx,
1863
Oil on canvas
36 1/4x 42 1/4 in. (92.1 x 107.3 cm)
Bequest of Mrs. Martin Brimmer
06.2430

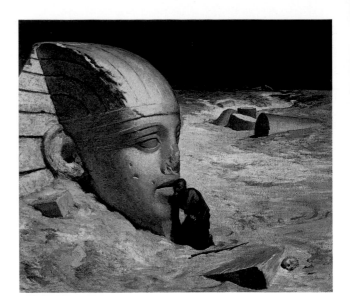

Raised in New York and Cuba, Vedder lived much of his life in
Europe, making frequent visits to America. This picture, painted
in his cramped and gloomy New York studio during the Civil
War, is typical of the subjects that Vedder found "wandering in
the little world of . . . [his] imagination." A Greek myth tells of
a sphinx who sat by the road to Thebes and devoured travelers
who could not solve her riddle. In Vedder's painting, it is not the
sphinx who asks questions, but a man. All around, the desolate
landscape is strewn with architectural ruins and a human skull.
"My idea of the sphinx," Vedder wrote, "was the hopelessness of
man before the immutable laws of nature."

William Rimmer
American (born England),
1816–1879
Flight and Pursuit, 1872
Oil on canvas
18 1/8 x 26 1/4 in.
(46.1 x 66.7 cm)
Bequest of Miss Edith Nichols
56.119

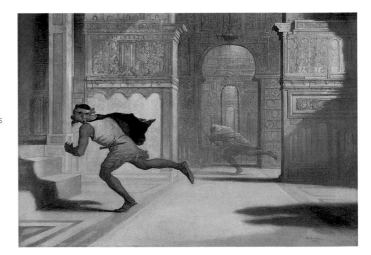

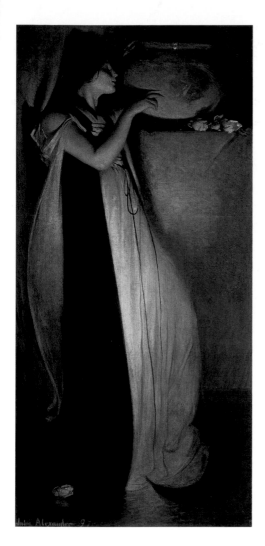

John White Alexander
American, 1856–1915
Isabella and the Pot of Basil,
1897
Oil on canvas
75 ⅝ × 36 ⅛ in. (192.1 × 91.8 cm)
Gift of Ernest Wadsworth
Longfellow 98.181

And she forgot the stars, the moon, and sun,
And she forgot the blue above the trees,
And she forgot the dells where waters run,
And she forgot the chilly autumn breeze;
She had no knowledge when the day was done,
And the new morn she saw not: but in peace
Hung over her sweet Basil evermore,
And moisten'd it with tears unto the core.

In John Keats's 1820 poem, "Isabella; or, The Pot of Basil," the ambitious brothers of wealthy Isabella, determined that she marry a nobleman, murder her humble suitor Lorenzo. Isabella discovers Lorenzo's body buried in the woods, cuts off the head, and hides it in a pot planted with sweet basil, a symbol of undying love. Painted in Paris at the very end of the nineteenth century, this picture's theatricality and macabre theme reflect the decadent tastes of the period known as the fin de siècle.

< What is the meaning of this nightmare vision of a man fleeing from a mysterious, shadowy figure? Suggested interpretations include man seeking to escape his conscience; the pursuit of John Surratt, suspected of scheming with John Wilkes Booth to assassinate Abraham Lincoln; and the biblical story of conspirators who raced to sanctuary after King David discovered their plot to usurp the throne. Whatever the intended subject of the painting may have been, Rimmer manipulated shadow and substance into a highly personal and disturbing vision.

The artist's own life was a troubled one, his childhood dominated by a father who believed he was the lost son of Louis XVI and Marie Antoinette. As an adult, Rimmer lived in many places on the periphery of Boston, working as a physician, sculptor, and teacher of drawing and anatomy; his paintings were little known during his lifetime.

William Michael Harnett
American (born Ireland),
1848–1892
Old Models, 1892
Oil on canvas
54 ⅜ × 28 ¼ in. (138.1 × 71.8 cm)
The Hayden Collection   39.761

"As a rule," Harnett said, "new things do not paint well."
Here, fastidiously arranged against a scuffed and cracked wooden door, are a dented bugle that has lost its shine, an old violin, volumes of Shakespeare and Homer frayed and stained from many readings, tattered scores of romantic songs, and a ceramic jar from Europe. These are the models that Harnett painted often—objects treasured both for their textures and shapes and for their evocation of past times. The American master of the time-honored trompe l'oeil ("deceive the eye") style, Harnett rendered his subjects with such minute precision that viewers are led to wonder: "Is this really only paint?" Scorned by the art establishment as virtuoso trickery, Harnett's pictures enchanted patrons in the hotels and saloons where they most often hung. *Old Models* was Harnett's last work, painted shortly before his death at the age of forty-four.

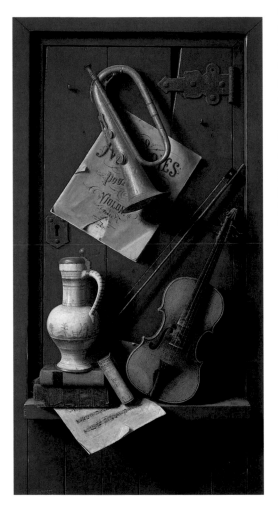

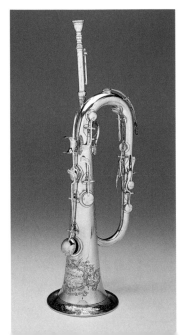

Keyed bugle in E-flat
Massachusetts (Boston),
about 1854
Made by **Elbridge G. Wright,**
1811–1871
Silver
Height: 17 ⅜ in. (44.2 cm)
Gift of the Seminarians and
Friends in Memory of Warren C.
Moffett 1990.85

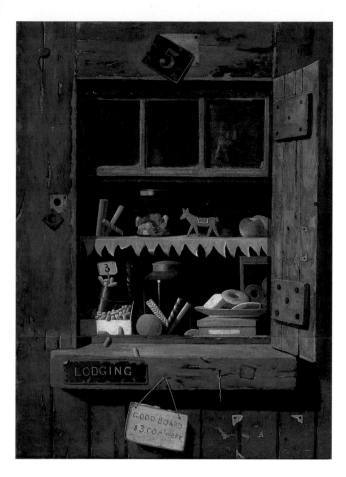

John Frederick Peto
American, 1854–1907
The Poor Man's Store, 1885
Oil on canvas and panel
35½ × 25⅝ in. (90.2 × 65.1 cm)
Gift of Maxim Karolik for the
M. and M. Karolik Collection of
American Paintings, 1815–1865
62.278

Peto had more success as a cornet player than as a painter and sold his pictures for a few dollars—or gave them away. Until about 1950, Peto's paintings were often attributed to his friend and fellow-Philadelphian William Harnett. This colorful image of a tiny street-front shop is Peto's masterpiece. He used a canvas for the central window area of the composition and set it into a wooden "frame" illusionistically painted to represent the wall, shelf, and door. Multiple meanings and visual jokes are characteristic of trompe l'oeil painting. Here, the sign "Good Board" below the window may refer to the availability of lodging, to the shelf from which the sign hangs, or to the actual wood of the painting's "frame."

< **B**y the time of the Civil War, virtually every American town had a brass band that performed at dances, election-day parades, and outdoor summer concerts. The keyed bugle pitched in E-flat was usually the solo instrument in such bands, and skilled bugle players could become celebrities. Most bugles were copper; this costly silver instrument, as indicated on the engraved bell, was a presentation piece, given in 1854 to Joseph J. Brenan, leader of the Marietta, Ohio, town band. By the 1860s, keyed bugles had passed out of favor and become—like the one in William Harnett's painting on the preceding page— sentimental reminders of days gone by.

American Folk Art

Although its extraordinary diversity resists generalization, much American folk art was made in rural areas and small towns by artists who lacked formal training in the fine arts. Some were professionals, some amateurs; many of their names are lost. Most of the objects they produced—like pottery and weathervanes—were primarily functional. Others were created for the pleasure of the artists and their friends, family, and community.

At its best, American folk art is far more than the unskilled imitation of work produced by trained practitioners in urban centers. Among its hallmarks is an originality of conception unhampered by the desire to be part of a recognized school or style. Although many folk artists were somewhat limited by their lack of training, they compensated for this with a directness of expression emphasizing pattern, contour, color, and simplified form in a way that is very pleasing to the twentieth-century eye.

The Museum's ever-increasing collection of American folk art was established by Maxim Karolik (see page 322), one of the first to recognize that folk art deserved serious, aesthetic consideration. In 1949 Karolik wrote: "One wonders whether from the artistic point of view the question of folk art vs. academic art has any meaning. The question I continue to ask is whether lack of technical proficiency limits the artist's ability to express his ideas. I do not believe that it does. . . . [Folk artists] sometimes lacked the ability to describe, but it certainly did not hinder their ability to express."

Peacock weathervane
American, 19th century
Copper, painted gold; iron rod
Height: 19 3/4 in. (50 cm),
including ball
Gift of Maxim Karolik 54.1089

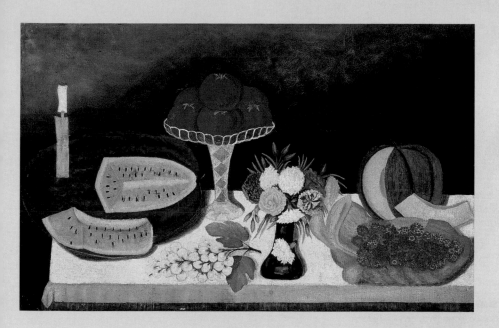

Unidentified artist
American, mid-19th century
Tomatoes, Fruit, and Flowers,
about 1860
Oil on canvas
20 x 31½ in. (50.8 x 80 cm)
Gift of Martha C. Karolik for the
M. and M. Karolik Collection of
American Paintings, 1815–1865
47.1265

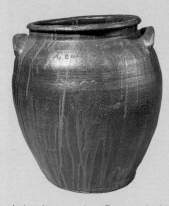

Dave the Potter
American, about 1783–about
1863
Storage jar
Made for the **Lewis J. Miles
Factory**, South Carolina
(Edgefield County), 1857
Stoneware with alkaline glaze
Height: 19 in. (48.3 cm)
Otis Norcross Fund and Harriet
Otis Cruft Fund 1997.10

A slave known only as Dave made this jar in the pottery of his owner.
Dave was literate and perhaps the only slave craftsman permitted to sign
his work. This jar is signed; dated August 22, 1857; and inscribed: "I made
this Jar for Cash/ Though its called lucre trash."

Mary Ann Willson
American, active about 1800–1825
***Young Woman Wearing a
Turban***
Watercolor on paper
7⅞ x 6½ in. (20 x 16.5 cm)
M. and M. Karolik Collection of
American Watercolors and
Drawings, 1800–1875 56.456

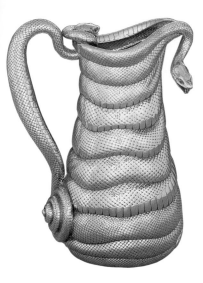

American mines were producing prodigious amounts of silver in the late nineteenth century, and a flourishing market for silver objects encouraged innovation in both form and technique. To keep pace with the demand, major silvermaking firms developed new production methods and hired skilled craftsmen and designers from Europe. This startling and seductive pitcher is a consummate expression of the period's love of novelty, surprise, and virtuoso craftsmanship. The work of the silversmith alone took fifty-five hours. The bodies of the two entwined snakes were embossed: pushed out or indented from the back. Another craftsman, the chaser, then articulated these basic snake forms from the front, defining the scales of backs and bellies in a process similar to engraving. The chasing required eighty-six hours to complete.

Snake pitcher
Rhode Island (Providence), 1885
Made by the **Gorham Manufacturing Company,**
1831–present
Silver
Height: 10 in. (25.4 cm)
Edwin E. Jack Fund 1983.331

John La Farge
American, 1835–1910
Vase of Flowers, 1864
Oil on gilded panel
18½ × 14 in. (47 × 35.6 cm)
Gift of Misses Louisa W. and
Marian R. Case 20.1873

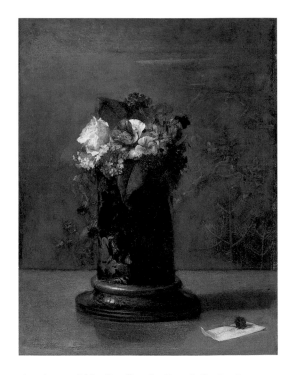

Best known for his murals and stained-glass windows, La Farge was also a gifted painter in watercolor and oil. His images of flowers are evocative rather than botanically accurate. Here, the spare composition and background (which may represent a Japanese screen, sketchily rendered on gold leaf) reflect La Farge's fascination with Asian art. The painting is given a distinctive, personal quality by the inclusion of a bent calling card (inscribed J. La Farge/1864) lying beneath a wilting bachelor's button.

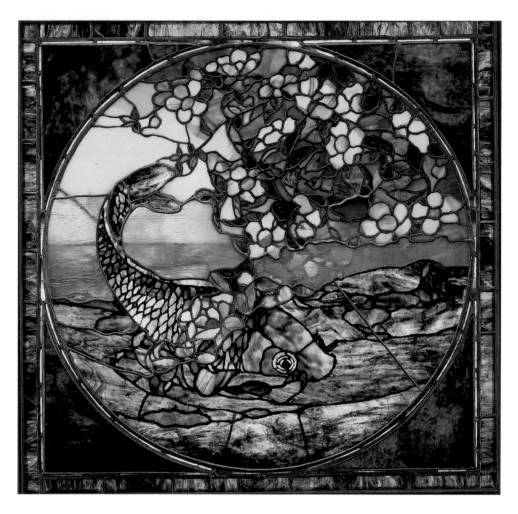

La Farge began his experiments with stained glass in the 1870s and soon gained an international reputation. Some three hundred La Farge windows survive, many made for churches, public buildings, and private houses designed by major architects of the day. In 1880 La Farge patented the use of opalescent glass, and here, he combined it with translucent and clear, colored glass to produce an exuberant pictorial illusionism. This window was made for the home of an ardent fisherman, Gordon Abbott of Manchester, Massachusetts.

The Fish
New York (New York), about 1890
Made by **John La Farge,**
1835–1910
Leaded stained glass
26½ in. × 26½ in (67.3 × 67.3 cm)
Anonymous gift and Edwin E. Jack Fund 69.1224

In 1879 a critic stated that Winslow Homer had gone "as far as anyone has ever done in   >
demonstrating the value of watercolors as a serious means of expressing dignified artistic
impressions." Spontaneous in effect, Homer's watercolors demonstrate an unequaled mastery of technique. He laid out his compositions with broad, overlapping washes of color
and then created a range of luminous coloristic and textural effects by both adding pigment
and "subtracting" it by blotting and scraping. "You will see," Homer said, "in the future I
will live by my watercolors." Although most watercolors fade over time, *The Blue Boat,*
painted on one of Homer's frequent trips to the Adirondacks in New York State, is in pristine condition. Homer acknowledged his satisfaction with this masterwork by noting on
the sheet: "This will do the business."

Winslow Homer
American, 1836–1910
Boys in a Pasture, 1874
Oil on canvas
15 7/8 × 22 7/8 in. (40.3 × 58.1 cm)
The Hayden Collection 53.2552

Born in Boston, Homer was trained as a commercial printmaker, and during the Civil War, he worked at the front for
the illustrated journal *Harper's Weekly.* In the 1870s, as
America began to recover from the war, Homer turned to
painting sunny, optimistic pictures of young women and
children enjoying themselves outdoors. The boys in this
painting—companionable, idle, at peace—may be seen as
emblems of America's nostalgia for a simpler, more innocent
time as well as of its hope for the future. Their faces are
shadowed and averted, a device Homer often used to make
his figures less individual and, therefore, more universal.

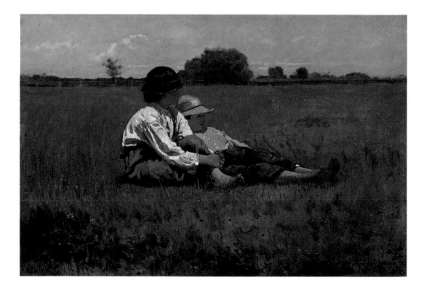

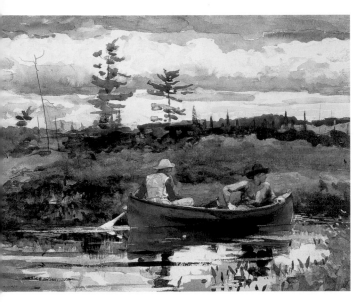

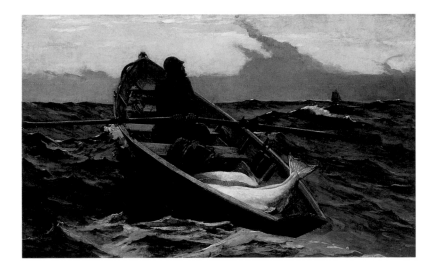

Homer moved to Prout's Neck, near Portland, on the rocky coast of Maine by 1883. There, for the rest of his life, he painted the sea and those who made their living from it. *The Fog Warning* was inspired by Homer's trip with a fishing fleet to the Grand Banks off Nova Scotia. Here, the lone fisherman, his dory weighed down by enormous halibut, tries to reach the mother ship before it becomes enveloped in the dark fog bank on the horizon. The painting explores man's constant struggle with the sea—the source of livelihood but also of danger. This was the first painting by Homer to enter a public collection.

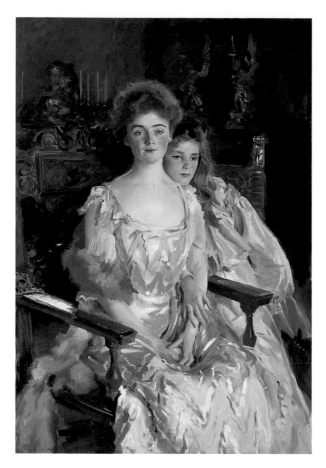

Born in Italy to American parents, Sargent became a highly successful portrait painter on both sides of the Atlantic. This portrait was painted in Boston at Fenway Court, which had just opened as the Isabella Stewart Gardner Museum and where the artist had a temporary studio. The portrait's imposing size, the Renaissance furniture, and Mrs. Warren's formal pose evoke aristocratic portraits of the past. At the same time, Sargent's style is very modern. He paints with freedom and confidence—notice the thick slash of white pigment that highlights the chair arm. Mrs. Warren, who wore at Sargent's insistence a borrowed pink dress, did not like the portrait, feeling that it focused on her social position and ignored her serious interest in poetry and the performing arts.

John Singer Sargent
American, 1856–1925
Mrs. Fiske Warren and Her Daughter Rachel, 1903
Oil on canvas
60 × 40⅜ in. (152.4 × 102.6 cm)
Gift of Mrs. Rachel Warren Barton
and the Emily L. Ainsley Fund 64.693

Sargent often produced more than twenty society portraits in a year; on holiday, he escaped to the freer, more personal, and more experimental medium of watercolor. He called his informal, anecdotal watercolors of friends and family "snapshots." Fluent and apparently spontaneous, they show a great mastery of complex techniques and are among Sargent's most admired works. Painted outdoors, they capture the colored shadows and the dappled effects of light; for this, watercolor—with its transparent washes of color over white paper—was the perfect medium. *The Tease* shows the artist's niece and a friend lounging on an outing at the Simplon Pass near the Italian-Swiss border.

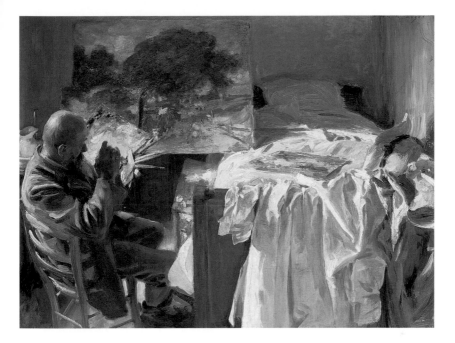

John Singer Sargent
American, 1856–1925
An Artist in His Studio, 1904
Oil on canvas
22 1/8 × 28 3/8 in. (56.2 × 72.1 cm)
The Hayden Collection 05.56

On a summer vacation in the Italian Alps, Sargent depicted his friend, the artist Ambrogio Raffele, painting a bucolic landscape. The setting is a cramped hotel bedroom. Surrounded by sketches presumably made outdoors, Raffele holds a palette that bears actual blobs of thick, bright paint. Half the composition is given over to rumpled sheets and a discarded smock—an extraordinary display of brilliant brushwork that gave Sargent the opportunity (which he loved) of painting white on white.

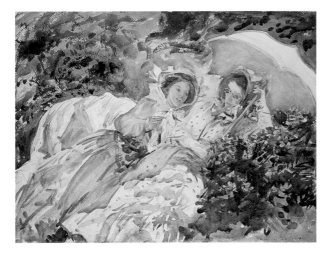

Sargent's portrait, *The Daughters of Edward Darley Boit* is on page 331.

John Singer Sargent
American, 1856–1925
Simplon Pass: The Tease, 1911
Transparent and opaque
watercolor over graphite pencil
15 3/4 × 20 5/8 in. (40.1 × 52.4 cm)
Hayden Collection. Charles Henry
Hayden Fund 12.216

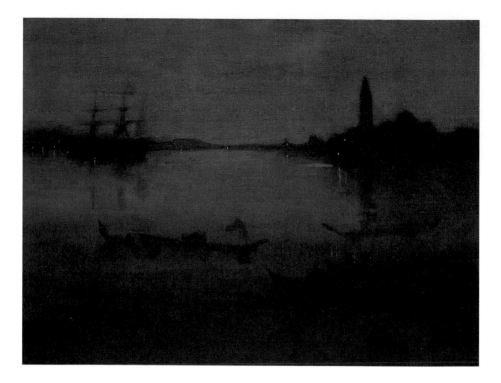

Whistler liked people to believe that he was born in Russia; in fact, although he made his career abroad, he was born in the mill town of Lowell, Massachusetts. Extraordinarily gifted and innovative, Whistler was determined to free his art from representation and narrative. "Art should be independent of all clap-trap," he asserted. "[It] should . . . appeal to the artistic sense of eye or ear, without confounding this with . . . devotion, pity, love, patriotism, and the like." In this night view of Venice, looking across still water to the church of San Giorgio Maggiore, Whistler painted the muted tones he loved. A friend who was with the artist when he created this image called it "possibly the most peace-bringing of Jimmy's pictures; certainly his finest night scene."

James Abbott McNeill Whistler
American, 1834–1903
Nocturne in Blue and Silver: The Lagoon, Venice, 1879–80
Oil on canvas
19 3/4 x 25 3/4 in. (50.2 x 65.4 cm)
Emily L. Ainsley Fund 42.302

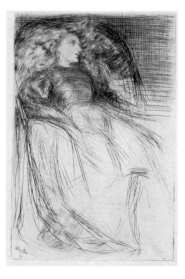

James Abbott McNeill Whistler
American, 1834–1903
Weary, 1863
Drypoint
7 3/4 x 5 1/8 in. (19.8 x 13 cm)
Lee M. Friedman Fund 69.1178

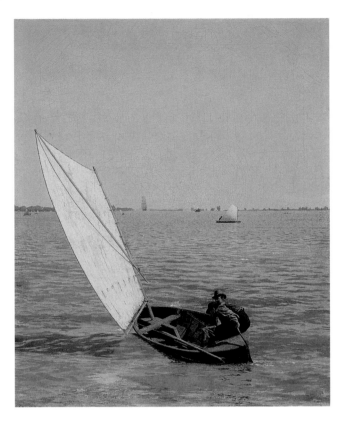

Thomas Eakins
American, 1844–1916
Starting Out After Rail, 1874
Oil on canvas mounted on
Masonite
24 1/4 × 19 7/8 in. (61.6 × 50.5 cm)
The Hayden Collection 35.1953

"A boat is the hardest thing I know to put in perspective," wrote Eakins. "It is so much like the human figure, there is something alive about it." This image of a boat skimming across water enlivened by the play of wind and light seems wonderfully immediate, but most of Eakins's paintings were the result of careful measurements, precise calculations, and many preparatory studies. He lived all his life in Philadelphia, and his family, friends, and the masculine world of sport were the subjects of his art. Here, he depicts two friends setting off to hunt for rail (a kind of bird) in the marshlands along the Delaware River, near Philadelphia.

< **W**histler was a prolific and influential printmaker, particularly interested in etching and drypoint, techniques very similar to drawing with pen on paper. *Weary* was printed on silky, tissue-like, Japanese paper to enhance the delicacy of fine and swiftly rendered drypoint lines. The model was Whistler's mistress, a red-haired Irish beauty named Joanna Hiffernan who also appears in a number of the artist's most celebrated paintings. Her pose in *Weary* was inspired by "Jenny," a poem by Whistler's friend Dante Gabriel Rossetti (see page 251) about a prostitute "fond of a kiss and fond of a guinea."

Pictorial quilt
Georgia (Athens), about 1895–98
Made by **Harriet Powers,**
1837–1911
Pieced and appliquéd printed
cotton, hand- and machine-
embroidered with cotton and
metallic yarns
69 × 105 in. (175 × 267 cm)
Bequest of Maxim Karolik 64.619

Described as "expressive in its every stitch of a most fiery
imagination," this quilt was created at the end of the nineteenth century by an African-American woman, born a slave,
who lived on a farm near Athens, Georgia. The fifteen squares
depict familiar biblical events—stories of Adam and Eve, Noah,
Job, Jonah, Moses, and Christ—and record local legends and
such fearful and marvelous natural phenomena as the Leonid
meteor shower of 1833. Although Powers probably could neither read nor write, she dictated a commentary on her work,
and those descriptions accompany the details illustrated here.
Narrative quilts are characteristically American, but Powers's
textile is strikingly similar in design and technique to the
appliquéd cotton cloths made by the Fon people of Abomey,
the ancient capital of Dahomey (now the Republic of Benin)
in West Africa.

Maurice Brazil Prendergast
American (born Newfoundland),
1858–1924
Umbrellas in the Rain, 1899
Watercolor over graphite pencil
14 × 20⅞ in. (35.4 × 53 cm)
Hayden Collection. Charles Henry
Hayden Fund 59.57

Prendergast was among the greatest American masters of watercolor. On a trip to Europe in 1898–99, he fell in love with
Venice, painting watercolors that are among his finest works.
Here, with the passing of a summer storm, a crowd of typically
anonymous figures moves among famous Venetian monuments—the somber facade of the prison at right; the delicate
arcades of the Doge's Palace; and the marble bridge, Ponte della
Paglia. The bright shapes of umbrellas lead the eye through a
composition that has the abstract, patterned quality of a mosaic. Although Prendergast
shared the Impressionists'
enthusiasm for outdoor subjects from modern life, his
exploratory style and his use
of watercolor rather than oil
as his primary medium place
him among American mod-
ernist artists of the early twentieth century.

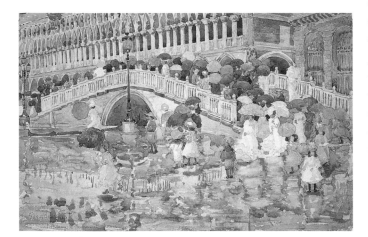

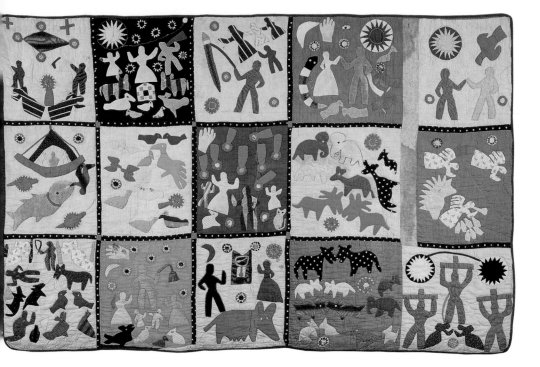

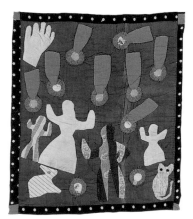

"The falling of the stars on Nov. 13, 1833. The people were frightened and thought that the end had come. God's hand staid the stars. The varmints rushed out of their beds." Accounts of the eight-hour meteor shower of 1833, passed down through the generations, were part of the oral tradition from which Powers drew for her imagery.

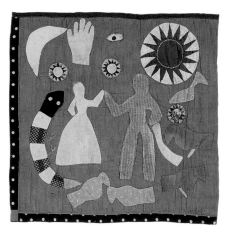

"Adam and Eve in the garden. Eve tempted by the serpent. Adam's rib by which Eve was made. The sun and moon. God's all-seeing eye and God's merciful hand."

Edmund Charles Tarbell
American, 1862–1938
Mother and Child in a Boat,
1892
Oil on canvas
30 ⅛ × 35 in. (76.5 × 88.9 cm)
Bequest of David P. Kimball in
memory of his wife, Clara Bertram
Kimball 23.532

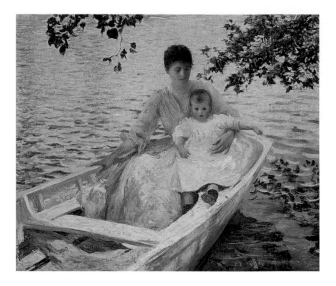

Boston artists played a major role in the recognition and practice of
Impressionism in America. Tarbell, who trained at the School of the
Museum of Fine Arts and later became one of its most influential
teachers, adopted a brilliantly colored Impressionist technique after
returning to Boston from studies in Paris. He was a founding member of The Ten, a group of painters working in Impressionist styles
whose exhibitions in New York, beginning in 1898, helped make
Impressionism the most popular "modern" style in America.

Child's bed
Massachusetts (Boston), about
1913
Designed by **Ralph Adams
Cram,** 1863–1942
Carved by **John Kirchmayer,**
1860–1930
Made by **William F. Ross and
Company,** active about
1904–1921
Walnut with polychrome and gilt
decoration
79 ½ × 37 × 76 in.
(201.9 × 94 × 193 cm)
Gift of David W. Scudder and
Judith S. Robinson in memory of
their grandfather, Ralph Adams
Cram 1997.210

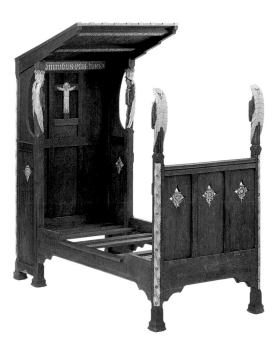

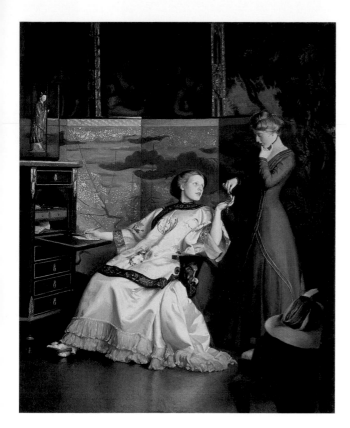

William McGregor Paxton
American, 1869–1941
The New Necklace, 1910
Oil on canvas
36 1/8 x 28 3/4 in. (91.8 x 73 cm)
Zoë Sherman Collection 22.644

At the turn of the twentieth century—a time of profound social, economic, and industrial change—Boston artists asserted a renewed ideal of beauty, extolling traditional values of fine drawing, rich color, and idealized compositions. Paxton believed that harmony and beauty were intrinsic to good art, and his paintings are carefully arranged and highly finished. Here, two elegantly dressed women appear to be discussing the implications of a recent gift from a suitor. Like the gold beads they hold, the women are exquisite ornaments in an opulent setting that includes a Japanese screen, a Chinese tunic and porcelain figurine, a Renaissance tapestry, and a copy of a painting by Titian. Paxton (who, like Tarbell, was a teacher at the School of the Museum of Fine Arts) was particularly inspired by the work of the seventeenth-century Dutch painter Jan Vermeer.

< **T**he leading architect of the Gothic-revival style in the early twentieth century, Cram designed this small bed for his new-born daughter Elizabeth. The design incorporates angels to protect the child and a biblical inscription in Latin from Psalm 91: "For he will entrust you to his angels to guard you in all your ways." The carving is the work of German immigrant John Kirchmayer, the leading ecclesiastical carver of the arts and crafts movement in New England, whom Cram considered "a true creative artist. . . possessed of the whole Mediaeval tradition. . . [yet] bent on working this out in vital contemporary forms." The bed reflects Boston's enthusiasm in this period for handcrafted objects, revered historical styles, and expensive, labor-intensive ornament.

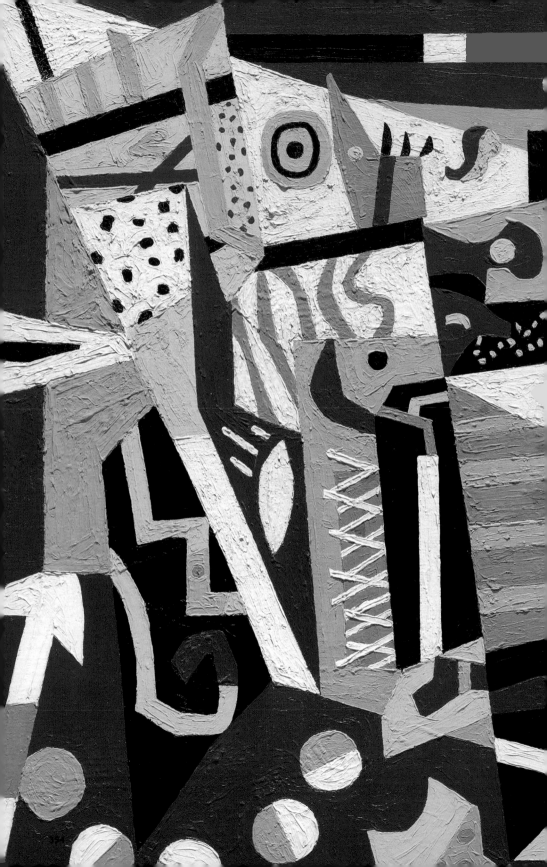

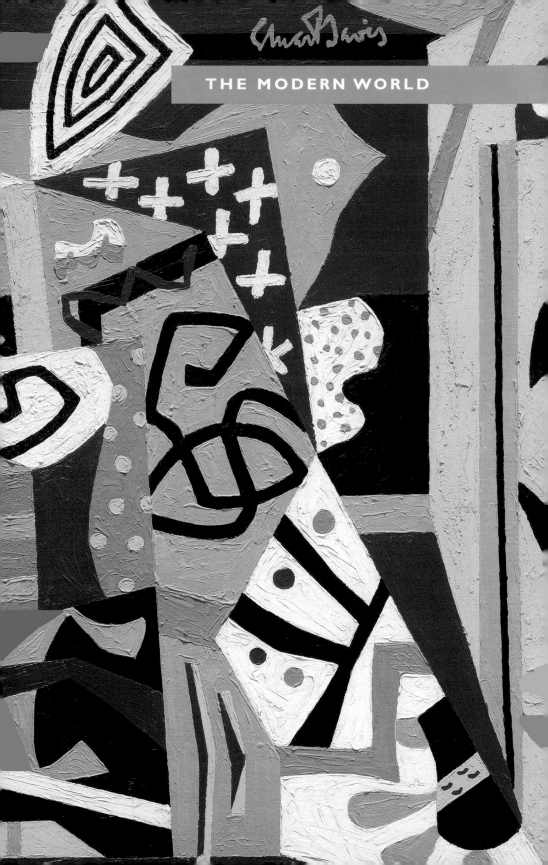

THE MODERN WORLD

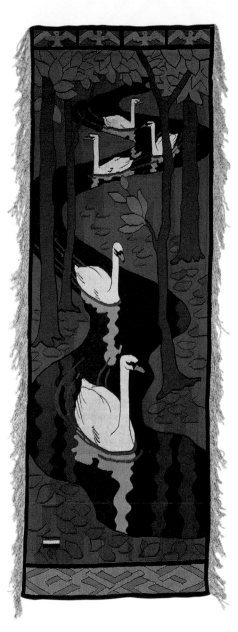

Wall hanging: *Five Swans*
Germany, 1897
Designed by **Otto Eckmann,**
1865–1902
Woven at the
Kunstgewerbeschule
Scherrebek, Schleswig-Holstein
Wool and cotton, tapestry weave
94 × 30 in. (240 × 76 cm)
Otis Norcross Fund, Curator's
Discretionary Fund, Charles Potter
Kling Fund, and Textile Purchase
Fund 1991.440

Five Swans is one of the masterpieces of
German Art Nouveau textile manufacture.
The idyllic composition of swans floating on a
meandering brook became a famous symbol of
the poetic naturalism characteristic of the style
known in Germany as Jugendstil. A leader of
the Jugendstil movement in Munich, Eckmann was known for his woodblock prints
and designs for stained glass, ceramics, book-
plates, furniture, metalwork, and interiors.
Five Swans was produced at the weaving
school at Scherrebek, which was inspired by
the tapestry workshop of Morris & Company
in England (see page 265).

In 1903 the Austrian architect Josef Hoffmann cofounded the Wiener Werkstätte (Viennese
Workshops) to "produce good and simple articles of everyday use." The Workshops made metalwork, jewelry, leatherwork, and furniture according to principles that emphasized function, pro-
portion, and the appropriate use of materials. Wishing to eliminate all historical references from
his work, Hoffmann created a new vocabulary of modular, geometric design to replace the lush,
curvilinear Art Nouveau style then current in Europe. Made from prefabricated, perforated metal
sheets, this imposing flower basket employs pure geometry with cylinders and rectangles formed
by repeated squares. Only thirteen of these baskets were manufactured by the Wiener Werkstätte
between 1906 and 1913.

Kandinsky, widely regarded as the originator of purely abstract art, abandoned a legal career in his native Russia at the age of thirty to study art in Munich, the center of modern German art, music, literature, and theater. This poster, in the Art Nouveau style, is imbued with graphic energy and charged with symbolic meaning. It was one of Kandinsky's first public graphic works and advertised the initial exhibition of the Phalanx society, an organization of avant-garde artists that he helped to found. The armor-clad warriors who form an interlocked battle line, or phalanx, allude to the members of this tightly knit and militant group.

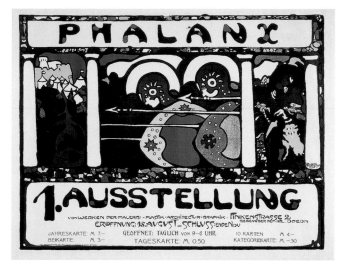

Wassily Kandinsky
Russian (worked in Germany), 1866–1944
Poster for the first Phalanx exhibition, 1901
Color lithograph
18 x 23¼ in. (45.7 x 59 cm)
Gift of Susan W. and Stephen D. Paine 1984.959

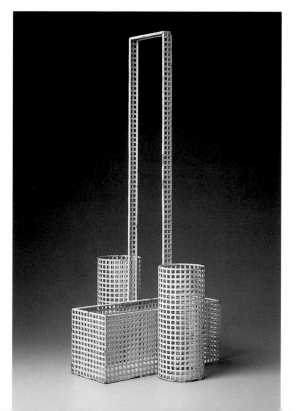

Flower basket
Austria (Vienna), 1906–13
Designed by **Josef Hoffmann,** 1870–1956
Manufactured by the **Wiener Werkstätte**
Painted metal
Height: 27½ in. (69.8 cm)
Bequest of the Estate of Mrs. Gertrude T. Taft, Gift of E. P. Warren, Gift of Alex Cochrane, Anonymous Gift, Gift of Charles Loring, and Estate of Mrs. William Dorr Boardman through Gift of Mrs. Bernard C. Weld, by exchange 1994.238

Determined to "revitalize German art," Kirchner joined with three other architectural students to found, in 1905, the idealistic artistic brotherhood called Die Brücke (The Bridge). The group

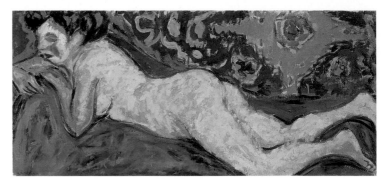

was active in Dresden and Berlin until 1913 and strove to form a bridge between art and life. Inspired by the psychological intensity and expressive form and color of van Gogh, Gauguin, Munch, and Matisse (although Kirchner vehemently denied the impact of these artists), Die Brücke developed the widely influential style known as German Expressionism. Here, Kirchner rendered a traditional studio nude in a forceful Expressionist style with rough brushwork, bold outlines, and strong acid colors that evoke feelings of tension and isolation.

Ernst Ludwig Kirchner
German, 1880–1938
Reclining Nude, 1909
Oil on canvas
29 1/8 x 59 5/8 in. (74 x 151.5 cm)
Tompkins Collection 57.2

Oskar Kokoschka
Austrian, 1886–1980
Two Nudes (Lovers),
about 1912–13
Oil on canvas
64 1/4 x 38 3/8 in. (163 x 97.5 cm)
Bequest of Mrs. Sarah Reed
Blodgett Platt 1973.196

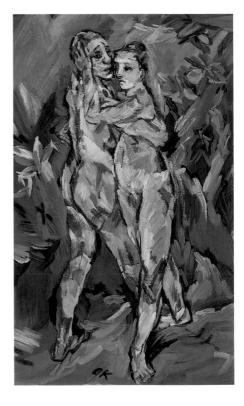

Painted in Vienna on the eve of World War I, Kokoschka's self-portrait with Alma Mahler— widow of the composer Gustav Mahler— is a monument to their intense and stormy love affair. Powerfully evoking the artist's tumultuous feelings, the painting is filled with restless, dynamic movement. Its brushwork is agitated and expressionistic, with light carefully manipulated to enliven the surface and create a sense of depth. There is, in addition, a tenderness to the image, evoked by the interlocked pose of the lovers, which suggests the formal intimacy of a dance.

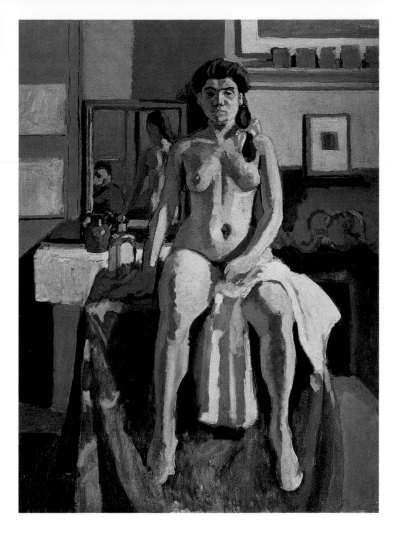

Henri Matisse
French, 1869–1954
Carmelina, 1903
Oil on canvas
32 × 23¼ in. (81.3 × 59 cm)
Tompkins Collection Res. 32.14

"What interests me most," Matisse wrote, "is neither still life nor landscape but the human figure. It is through it that I best succeed in expressing the nearly religious feeling that I have towards life." Here, in this rigorously balanced composition, the curves of the model's body are accentuated by the interlocking rectangles of the background, where the artist himself and the model's back are reflected in a mirror. Matisse declared that "the whole arrangement of my pictures is expressive. The place occupied by figures or objects, the empty spaces around them, the proportions, everything plays a part." In this early work, Matisse is already a master of color, playing off vibrating reds and blues against the blocks of warm earth tones representing furniture, walls, picture frames, and blank canvases.

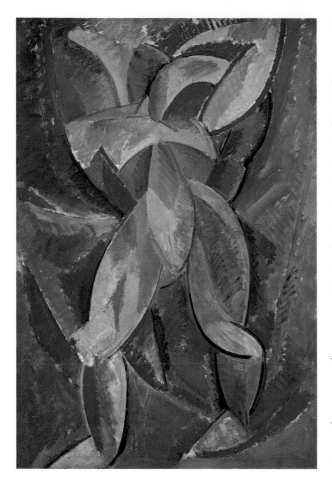

Pablo Picasso
Spanish (worked in France),
1881–1973
Standing Figure, 1908
Oil on canvas
59⅛ × 39½ in. (150.3 × 100.3 cm)
Juliana Cheney Edwards Collection
58.976

Picasso and Cubism

The three works on these pages are milestones in the early development of Cubism, possibly the most influential movement in twentieth-century art. The result of a unique collaboration between Pablo Picasso and Georges Braque, Cubism was an attempt to render three-dimensional forms on a two-dimensional surface in a radically new way—by breaking up the volumes into flat, angular facets or planes that imply multiple, simultaneous views of the object or figure.

In Standing Figure, *Picasso took a time-honored subject—the female nude—and divided the body into simplified components that interact so that the figure seems to turn on the surface of the canvas. Painted two years later,* Portrait of a Woman *is much more systematically fragmented, its forms open out into flat planes that dissolve into each other. Only a few details such as the hair at top left are identifiable; the background suggests a studio setting with canvases stacked*

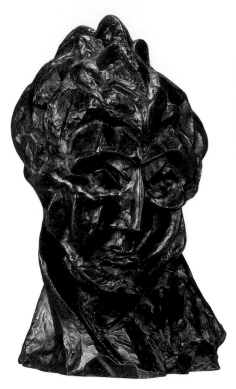

Pablo Picasso
Spanish (worked in France),
1881–1973
Head of a Woman, 1909
Bronze
Height: 16¼ in. (41.3 cm)
Gift of D. Gilbert Lehrman
1976.821

Pablo Picasso
Spanish (worked in France),
1881–1973
Portrait of a Woman, 1910
Oil on canvas
39⅝ × 32 in. (100.5 × 81.4 cm)
Charles H. Bayley Picture and
Painting Fund and Partial Gift of
Mrs. Gilbert W. Chapman 1977.15

against a wall. Picasso used a nearly monochromatic palette to distance this image from real-world associations and to focus more clearly on the painting's compositional structure.

In Head of a Woman, *Picasso translated the ideas he was exploring on canvas back into three dimensions, with the fragmented planes of the painting style reconfigured as convex and concave shapes. Cast in 1909 by Picasso's dealer Ambroise Vollard (only six examples are known), this is the most celebrated of all early Cubist sculptures.*

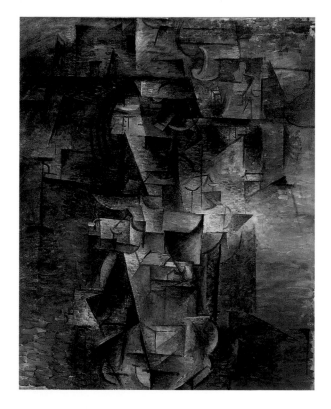

Marsden Hartley
American, 1877–1943
Painting No. 2, 1914
Oil on canvas
With frame: 42 ½ × 34 ¾ in.
(108 × 90.8 cm)
Gift of the William H. Lane
Foundation 1990.412

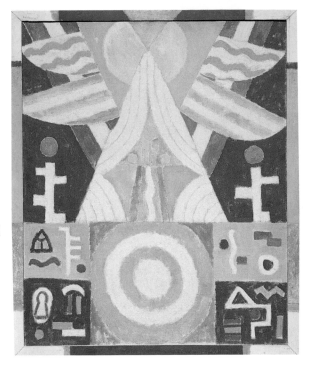

In 1912, Hartley went abroad for the first time, but unlike many American modernists who traveled to France, he spent most of his time in Germany. There, he came under the influence of the Blaue Reiter and other groups of young artists who were experimenting with new, basically abstract, forms of expression. He adopted their use of bright, flat color, emphasis on geometric patterns, and interest in folk culture. *Painting No. 2* is one of several that make up Hartley's *Amerika* series, and it uses forms derived from Native American cultures (see page 286), such as the triangular tipi and the geometric shapes evoking sand paintings. Hartley placed great emphasis on the presentation of his works, and he constructed and painted the frame of this picture to complement its design.

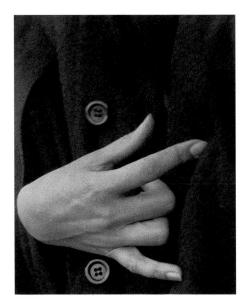

Alfred Stieglitz
American, 1864–1946
A Portrait: Georgia O'Keeffe,
1918
Photograph, platinum print
4 ⅞ × 4 in. (12.6 × 10 cm)
Gift of the Georgia O'Keeffe
Foundation, Jesse H. Wilkinson
Fund, and M. and M. Karolik Fund
1995.695

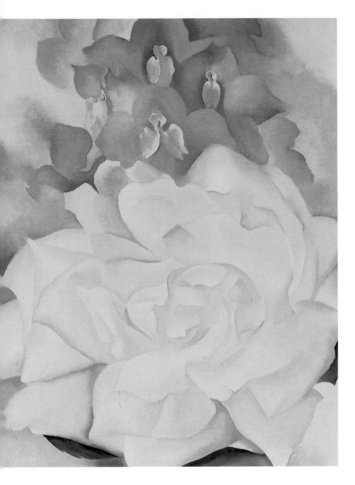

Georgia O'Keeffe
American, 1887–1986
***White Rose with Larkspur,
No. 2,*** 1927
Oil on canvas
40 × 30 in. (101.6 × 76.2 cm)
Henry H. and Zoë Oliver
Sherman Fund 1980.207

O'Keeffe often painted objects from nature whose formal qualities attracted her. She once wrote: "Nobody sees a flower—really—it is so small—we haven't time—and to see it takes time, like to have a friend takes time. . . . So I said to myself—I'll paint what I see—what the flower is to me—but I'll paint it big. . . . I will make even busy New Yorkers take time to see what I see of flowers." One of O'Keeffe's favorite paintings, *White Rose* hung in the bedroom of her Abiquiu, New Mexico, home until 1979, when she selected it for the Museum.

< One of the most significant photographers of the early twentieth century, Stieglitz said: "I was born in Hoboken. I am an American. Photography is my passion. The search for Truth my obsession." He also introduced modern European art to America through exhibitions in his New York galleries and supported the work of American modernist painters, including Georgia O'Keeffe, who became his wife. This image is part of Stieglitz's cumulative "portrait in time," several hundred photographs made of O'Keeffe between 1917 and 1933. He believed that a single image was not always sufficient to capture the complexity of a human personality and that, as long as it expressed some aspect of the sitter, any part of the body could be a portrait.

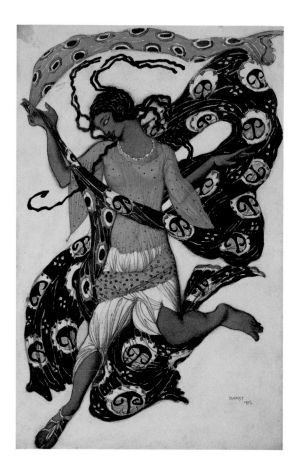

Léon Bakst
Russian, 1866–1924
The Butterfly, 1913
Costume design for Anna Pavlova
Graphite pencil and watercolor on
paper
17³/₄ × 11¹/₈ in. (45 × 28 cm)
Gift of Mrs. John Munro Longyear and
Mrs. Walter Scott Fitz 14.701

Emil Nolde
German, 1867–1956
Irises
Watercolor on white Asian paper
18½ × 13½ in. (47.2 × 34.2 cm)
Seth K. Sweetser Fund 57.667

Bakst dazzled early-twentieth-
century Europe with his opulent
designs for the ballet and theater.
His feeling for exotic styles,
voluptuous color, and sensuous
line profoundly influenced contemporary fashion, interior
design, and jewelry. Bakst created
many costumes for performances
by the great Russian ballerina
Anna Pavlova (1881–1931) at the
Imperial Ballet and the Ballets
Russes. After she started her own
troupe, the dramatic solo *The
Butterfly* was one of Pavlova's
most popular works.

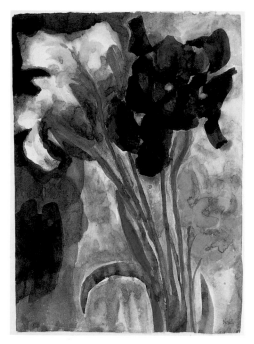

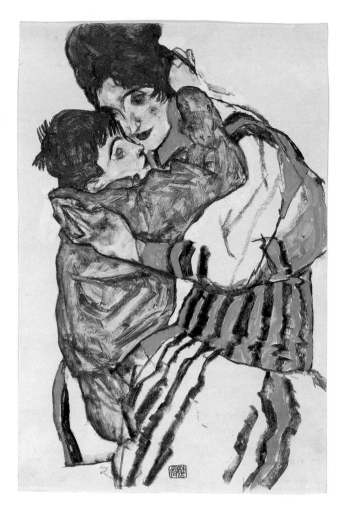

Egon Schiele
Austrian, 1890–1918
Schiele's Wife with Her Little Nephew, 1915
Charcoal and watercolor on paper
19 x 12½ in. (48.3 x 31.8 cm)
Edwin E. Jack Fund 65.1322

Schiele's distinctive style is characterized by an almost neurotic intensity of feeling, a love of pattern, and a magnificent energy of line. Here, he combines two media—broadly drawn charcoal and opaque watercolor. The woman's tight embrace and the yellow-and-black striping of her dress evoke a tigress fiercely protecting her cub. Since his early death in the influenza epidemic of 1918, Schiele has come to be regarded as one of the greatest Expressionist artists.

< Nolde was among the most original painters and printmakers of his time, and his inventive and rapidly executed watercolors are among his greatest works. He favored simple subjects and bold forms that fill the entire sheet, and he used damp, highly absorbent Japanese paper that gave extraordinary depth and luminosity to his colors.

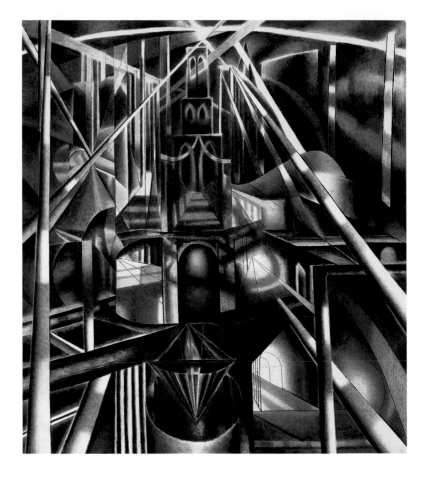

Joseph Stella
American (born Italy), 1877–1941
Old Brooklyn Bridge, about
1941
Oil on canvas
76¹/₄ × 68¹/₄ in. (193.7 × 173.4 cm)
Gift of Susan Morse Hilles in
memory of Paul Hellmuth
1980.197

New York's Brooklyn Bridge, completed in 1883 and hailed as an engineering marvel, spans the East River between Brooklyn and Manhattan. When Stella emigrated from Italy to Brooklyn in 1916, the borough's most famous landmark became a recurrent image in his work—a symbol of the dynamism and promise of the modern American city. Here, Stella shows the bridge at night: cables soar overhead, traffic signals and headlights flash through the darkness, and the bridge's Gothic arches rise in the background like those of a skyscraper or a church. The bridge, to Stella, was a "shrine containing all the efforts of the new civilization of AMERICA."

Margaret Bourke-White
American, 1904–1971
The George Washington
Bridge, 1933
Photograph, silver print
13 3/8 × 8 3/4 in. (33.8 × 22.3 cm)
Charles Amos Cummings Fund
1988.2

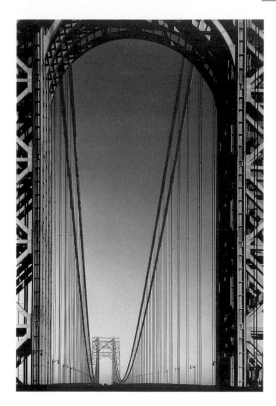

One of the original staff photographers at *Fortune, Life,* and *Time* magazines, Bourke-White is celebrated for her coverage of European battlefields and concentration camps during World War II as well as for her powerful images of the American South during the Depression, guerrilla warfare in Korea, and twentieth-century industry. This photograph—an icon of early, idealizing, machine-age art—was made when the monumental George Washington Bridge was still under construction, for a *Fortune* essay on the Port of New York.

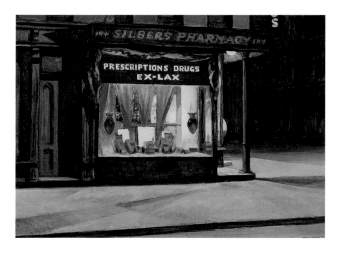

Edward Hopper
American, 1882–1967
Drug Store, 1927
Oil on canvas
29 × 40 1/8 in. (73.7 × 101.9 cm)
Bequest of John T. Spaulding 48.564

Among the first of Hopper's paintings to illustrate what became a favorite theme, *Drug Store* depicts nocturnal solitude in the city. Eerily illuminated by electric light, the drug store window (probably located near his studio in New York's Greenwich Village) is a bright spot in a picture otherwise made up of shadowy doorways and blank facades. The painting is full of subtle contradictions; for example, the patriotism expressed by the red, white, and blue bunting on the window display is undermined by the indelicacy of the product advertised above, and the acid colors and depopulated street discredit the window's ostensible welcome. Like much of Hopper's work, this painting is edgy and unsettling, creating a sense of melancholy and alienation.

Photography: Representation and Beyond

As anyone with a pocket camera knows, photography has evolved into a rapid, accessible medium in today's world, and the resulting images are as varied as the processes used to produce them. Yet contemporary photography often fulfills a much older and more traditional role than many other modern artforms: since the creation of the earliest cave drawings and the first crudely-shaped figures, artists have tried to describe the world in which they live, and the photographer is no different in this respect.

The earliest photographic processes, the calotype (see page 251) and the daguerreotype (see page 330), were both announced in 1839. While the two are aesthetically different in their results, they both originate in the fundamental premise upon which photography rests, namely, that certain chemicals change upon exposure to light. Calotype prints appear as shadowy, washlike images, settled deeply into the salted paper upon which they are printed, while the daguerreotype image, recorded on a polished, silver-coated copper plate, has a precise line and sharp detail. These were both followed by albumen prints, made on paper coated with sensitized egg white, leaving a glossy surface upon which the image appears to rest lightly (see page 327).

Albumen prints are made as contact prints, where the paper surface is the same size as the glass plates used to capture the image, and do not lose the sharpness that is often sacrificed with enlargements. This process was used extensively through the 1860–80s, eventually giving way to faster, more easily managed processes such as platinum prints (see page 362) and silver prints (see left). Platinum prints are characterized by a broad tonal range in browns and grays, a result of the color of the paper and the platinum com-

Charles Sheeler
American, 1883–1965
Wheels, 1939
Photograph, gelatin-silver print
6½ × 9½ in. (17 × 24 cm)
Gift of William H. and Saundra
B. Lane 1983.696

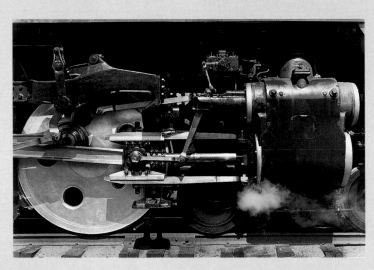

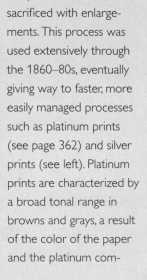

pound and iron salt with which the paper is treated; silver prints use silver salts to produce a crisper image with more reportorial qualities, favored by artists in the 1920s who renounced the painterly qualities of the earlier processes. More recent processes include color prints (introduced in the 1940s) such as the Cibachrome (below), popular for its bright, shiny surface and vivid, "bigger-than-life" colors, and state-of-the-art imaging methods such as digital photography.

Such artists as Robert Rauschenberg and Andy Warhol introduced photography into the printmaking process, using a variety of means to transfer photographic images from daily life and the mass media to the printing surface (see right and page 379). Works in the Museum's collections reflect the many methods and processes in which photographic images are produced and reproduced, from the portraits of the 1840s to modern works on paper, glass, plastic and other media.

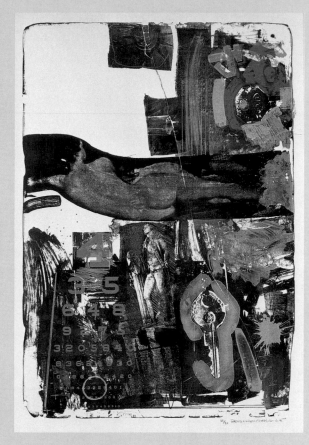

Robert Rauschenberg
American, born 1925
Breakthrough II, 1965
Lithograph
43½ x 29½ in. (110 x 75 cm)
Gift of Lewis P. Cabot 1970.515

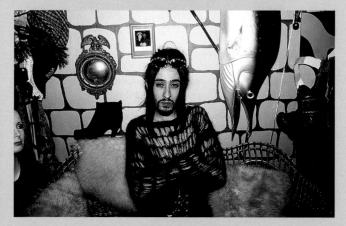

Nan Goldin
American, born 1953
Siobhan in the A House #1,
P-town, 1990
Cibachrome
20 x 24 in. (51 x 61 cm)
Curator's Grant Program of the
Peter Norton Family Foundation
1991.1098

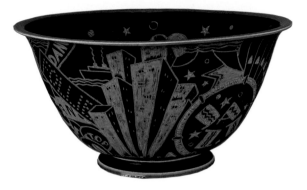

Punch bowl from the *Jazz Bowl* series
United States (Ohio, Rocky River), 1931
Designed and decorated by **Viktor Schreckengost,** born 1906
Thrown by **Reginald Guy Cowan** at the **Cowan Pottery Studio**
Glazed porcelain with sgrafitto decoration
Height: 9 in. (22.9 cm)
Gift of John P. Axelrod 1990.507

Between the world wars American ceramics underwent a transformation, with a new emphasis on modern, functional designs and streamlined, sometimes playful decoration. Viktor Schreckengost, who worked for the Cowan Pottery Studio near Cleveland, designed a series of twenty punch bowls commissioned by Eleanor Roosevelt for a party at the governor's mansion in Albany, New York. The bowls were decorated with motifs evoking contemporary New York—skyscrapers, ships, champagne glasses, moons, stars, and such words as follies, jazz, stop, and go. Later, Schreckengost refined the design, and Cowan produced a limited edition of fifty bowls, including this one.

Stuart Davis
American, 1892–1964
Hot Still-Scape for Six Colors—7th Avenue Style, 1940
Oil on canvas
36 x 44⅞ in. (91.4 x 114 cm)
Gift of the William H. Lane Foundation and the M. and M. Karolik Collection by exchange
1983.120

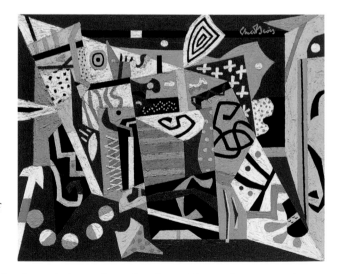

From the time Davis moved to the city in his late teens, New York was the principal subject of his art. With a title evoking jazz (a great love of Davis's), his "Still-Scape" combines still life and landscape, alluding both to the objects in his studio and to the world outside, on Seventh Avenue. Davis wrote: "The subject matter of this picture is well within the everyday experience of any modern city dweller. Fruit and flowers and kitchen utensils; fall skies; horizons; taxi cabs; radio; art exhibitions and reproductions; fast travel; Americana; movies; electric signs; dynamics of city sights and sounds." The artist's impressions of the city are captured with energy and flair by his jaunty line, vibrant palette (the "six colors" of the title), and the gritty texture of his paint.

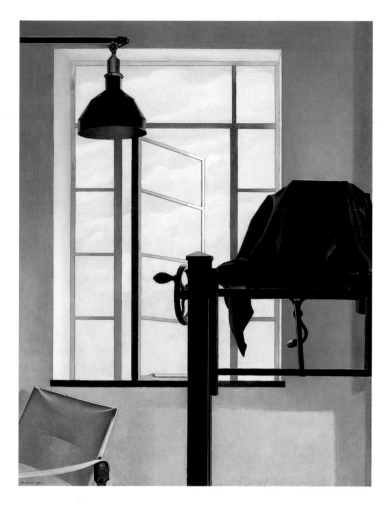

Charles Sheeler
American, 1883–1965
View of New York, 1931
Oil on canvas
48 × 36 ³⁄₈ in. (121.9 × 92.4 cm)
The Hayden Collection 35.69

Sheeler's ironically titled picture shows the interior of his own photography studio on an upper floor of a midtown New York apartment building and was painted at a pivotal time in his career. Through the 1920s he had enjoyed critical and financial success as a photographer while struggling to gain recognition as a painter. His difficult decision, made about 1931, to set aside photography and concentrate on painting is expressed through the studio's stillness and austerity—the camera is covered, the lamp turned off, and the chair vacant. Through the open window, we do not see the skyscrapers and bustling crowds normally associated with New York, but a cloudy sky. Sheeler thus gave universal meaning to his image of personal transition by contrasting the precisely defined, if barren, interior with an undefined external world full of uncertainties. He called *View of New York* "the most severe picture I ever painted."

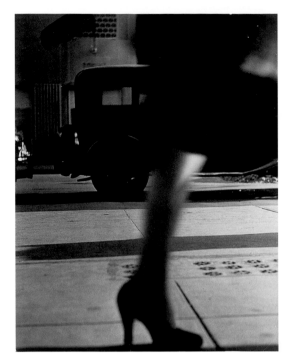

Lisette Model
American (born Austria),
1906–1983
***Running Legs, New York
(with Flag),*** 1940–41
Photograph, silver print
13 ⅜ × 10 ½ in. (34 × 26.7 cm)
Sophie M. Friedman Fund
1980.453

As a photographer and teacher, Model profoundly influenced the course of early twentieth-century American photography. Her *Running Legs* series, created soon after she settled in New York, overturned conventional ideas of perspective with its intriguing and radical viewpoints. A magazine review in 1941 called these photographs of New York pedestrians "an unusual and satisfying approach to a baffling subject, the legs, and specifically the feet, in motion. . . . Speed, stride, stamp, and strength—all are here."

Max Beckmann
German, 1884–1950
Still Life with Three Skulls,
1945
Oil on canvas
21 ¾ × 35 ¼ in. (55.2 × 89.5 cm)
Gift of Mrs. Culver Orswell
67.984

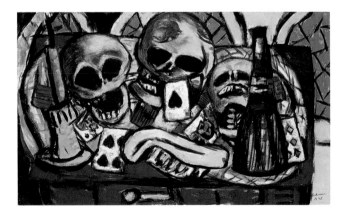

In this painting, Beckmann combined a modernist fondness for flattened space, schematic forms, and intense colors with traditional still-life subjects—skulls, an extinguished candle, playing cards—that signify the frailty and transience of human life. Identified by the Nazis as a "degenerate" artist, Beckmann had fled Germany in 1937 and sought refuge in Amsterdam, where this painting was made during the final stages of World War II. The artist described those years to a friend: "I have had a truly grotesque time, full to the brim with work, Nazi persecutions, bombs, hunger . . ." In the choice of objects, the predominance of black, and the thick, rough paint, this still life captures the grim feelings underlying these words.

Arthur G. Dove
American, 1880–1946
That Red One, 1944
Oil and wax on canvas
27 × 36 in. (68.6 × 91.4 cm)
Gift of the William H. Lane
Foundation 1990.408

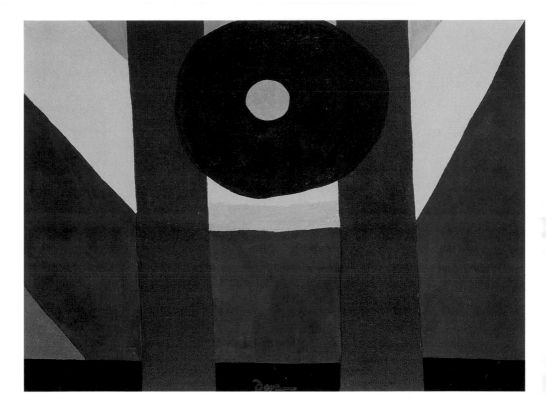

About 1910 Dove became the first American artist to experiment with pure abstraction. He painted abstractly throughout his career, but always with reference to the natural world. These adventurous paintings were admired by his fellow artists but rarely sold, and Dove's whole life was marked by financial struggle; *That Red One* was produced while the artist was living in an abandoned post office in Centerport, Long Island, New York. Despite Dove's personal difficulties, this painting is triumphant in mood, with the sunlike form in the center (a favorite Dove motif) dominating a design of broad shapes painted in clear, flat colors. Although the inspiration for the scene was commonplace—a view through trees across a pond at daybreak—the vision is monumental and heroic.

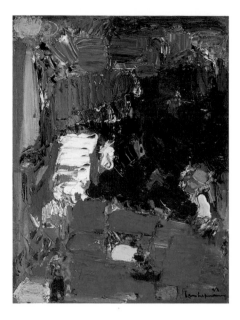

Hans Hofmann
American (born Germany),
1880–1966
Twilight, 1957
Oil on plywood
48 × 36 in. (122 × 91.4 cm)
Gift in name of Lois Ann Foster
1973.171

After studying art in Paris, Hofmann opened an
art school in New York City in the 1930s, bringing to his students not only knowledge of traditional European painting but also first-hand
experience of the work of such modernist artists as
Picasso, Braque, and Kandinsky. As a teacher,
Hofmann played a major role in the development
of American Abstract Expressionism. His own art,
however, did not attain the vigor and exuberance
of *Twilight* until the 1950s, when he was in his
seventies. Here, the paint is applied with brush and palette knife—layered, blended, and scraped
to produce a surface both physically rich and full of personal emotion. The painting's title suggests that it may have been inspired by the striking changes in color and light that occur at dusk.

At once the most controversial and the most influential artist of his generation, Pollock was the
leading figure of the Abstract Expressionist movement that made New York, for a time, the center
of the Western art world. The Abstract Expressionists painted freely, vigorously, and without calcu-
lation to capture their deepest feelings; the act of painting itself was the subject of their work.

This painting is characteristic of the mature style for which Pollock is best known. He placed
his canvases on the floor and moved around them, dripping and pouring paint with sweeping
movements of his arm. Line—freed of its traditional, shape-defining function—moves across the
surface with a nervous energy, producing overlapping skeins of paint. The smoothly pouring
industrial paint Pollock used (intended for automobiles, radiators, and pipes) was as revolutionary as his way of painting. Pollock himself described paintings like this one as "energy and
motion made visible—memories arrested in space."

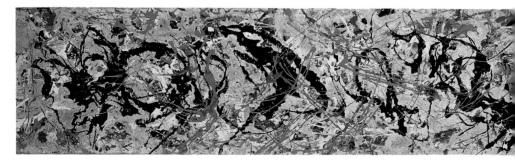

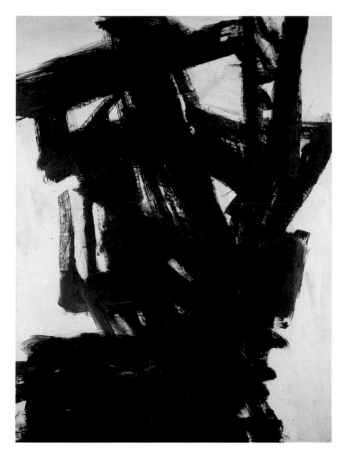

A major figure in the Abstract Expressionist movement, Kline's most characteristic and individual works are monumental, black-and-white paintings executed with very large brushes on a white ground. Although entirely nonrepresentational, this large painting suggests the massive girders and I-beams of buildings on the rise. Freely and expressively brushed, the broad lines also invoke a more lyrical tradition, the ancient Asian art of calligraphy. Named for an artist-friend in New York's Greenwich Village, *Probst I* is at once powerfully monochromatic and subtly colorful, enlivened with delicate touches of yellow, orange, and brown.

Franz Kline
American, 1910–1962
Probst I, 1960
Oil on canvas
107¼ × 79¾ in.
(272.4 × 202.6 cm)
Gift of Susan Morse Hilles
1973.636

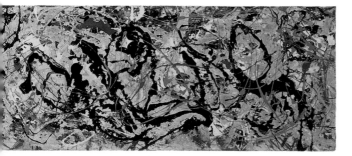

Jackson Pollock
American, 1912–1956
Number 10, 1949
Oil, enamel, and aluminum paint
on canvas mounted on panel
18⅛ × 107¼ in. (46.1 × 272.4 cm)
Tompkins Collection and Sophie
M. Friedman Fund 1971.638

Robert Rauschenberg
American, born 1925
Plain Salt (Cardboards), 1971
Cardboard and plywood
80½ × 37 in. (204.5 × 91 cm)
Gift of Martin Peretz 1992.396

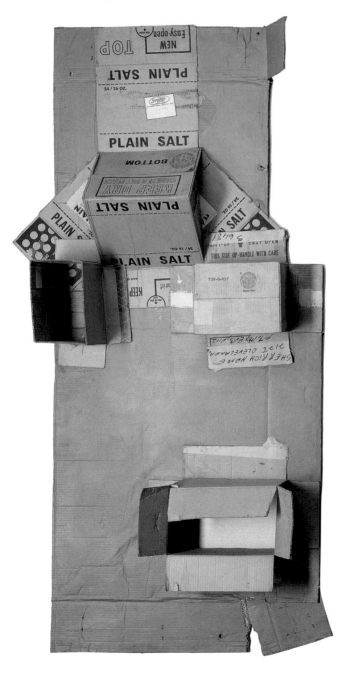

Painter, sculptor, printmaker, and photographer, Rauschenberg is one of the most innovative and individual of all twentieth-century American artists. Since the mid-1950s, he has incorporated such "found" materials as advertisements and street trash into loose, abstract compositions. This assemblage belongs to a group of constructions, first exhibited in 1971, that consist simply of opening out the sides of cardboard boxes and laying them flat against the wall, without the addition of painted marks of any kind. The artist's contribution was to visualize, compose, and construct. By focusing on cardboard, Rauschenberg invited comparison with the Cubist collages made by Braque and Picasso in the early twentieth century. At the same time, the exuberant way in which the boxes promote a product is in keeping with the "all-American" focus of much of Rauschenberg's work.

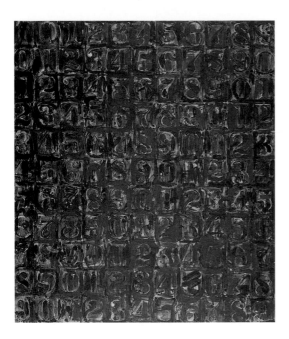

Jasper Johns
American, born 1930
Numbers, 1960
Graphite wash on pale cream
paper mounted on white paper
21 × 18 in. (53.3 × 45.7 cm)
Gift of Susan W. and Stephen D.
Paine 1996.362

Johns heralded the Pop Art movement in
New York in the 1950s with his transformation of everyday objects into art. This
drawing is one of a number of works in
several media in which Johns took simple
numbers and then pursued a game of art
and illusion, exploring spatial and formal
relationships through the layering of
transparent and opaque imagery. The
drawing is made even more subtle by the artist's use of a wash created from powdered graphite,
which produces an ambiguously shimmering surface.

A key figure in the movement called Color Field painting,
Louis poured streams of thinned, acrylic paint onto canvas left
raw and unsized so that the paint soaked into it. In this huge
piece, the simplicity of the format, with its empty and airy center, gives maximum impact to the visual power of the rippling,
brilliantly colored
stripes. The painting
takes its title from
the Greek alphabet,
reflecting Louis's life-
long preoccupation
with series and pro-
gressions. *Delta
Gamma* is one of the
major works in a
series Louis called
the *Unfurleds,* in ref-
erence to flags or
banners blowing in
the wind.

Morris Louis
American, 1912–1962
Delta Gamma, about 1960
Acrylic resin (Magna) on canvas
103¼ × 150 in. (259.7 × 382.9 cm)
Gift of Marcella Louis Brenner
1972.1074

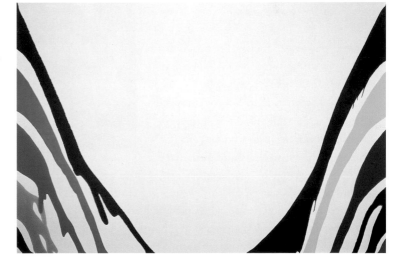

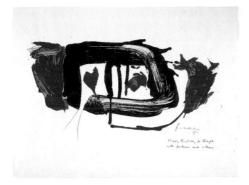

Helen Frankenthaler
American, born 1928
Untitled (study for *Postcard for James Schuyler*), 1962
Drawing in acrylic, oils, and crayon over a lithograph, on cream paper
19 7/8 × 25 3/4 in. (50.7 × 65.4 cm)
Gift of Mrs. George R. Rowland, Sr.
1994.118

While living in Italy in 1960 Frankenthaler began a postcard correspondence with the poet James Schuyler in New York. She would paint on postcards from Schuyler and send them back to him; he would add a poem and then return the cards to her. This process inspired Frankenthaler to make a lithograph, *Postcard for James Schuyler,* with which she experimented from 1962 until its eventual release in 1967. She elaborated this trial version of the lithograph with paint and crayon, essentially transforming it into a colored drawing on paper. The work is inscribed as a birthday gift to a young man named Padget who lived with Frankenthaler's family and helped with the children.

Pablo Picasso
Spanish (worked in France),
1881–1973
Rape of the Sabine Women,
1963
Oil on canvas
76 7/8 × 51 5/8 in. (195.4 × 131 cm)
Julia Cheney Edwards Collection, Tompkins Collection, and Fanny P. Mason Fund in Memory of Alice Thevin 64.709

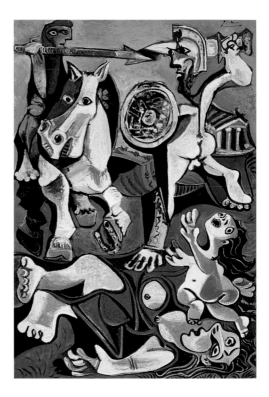

Painted when Picasso was eighty-two, this is his last major statement about the horrors of war, and is said to have been inspired by the Cuban missile crisis. In it, Picasso transforms a familiar subject from the art of the past— the story of early Romans who, suffering a shortage of marriageable women, invited the neighboring Sabines to Rome and then carried off all their young women. Against a sunny background of blue sky and green fields, the grotesquely distorted figures are compressed into the foreground space, the horses and soldiers trampling a woman and her child. Purchased by the Museum the year after it was painted, this powerful image of outrage and despair bears testimony to Picasso's productivity and energy in the last decade of his life.

Andy Warhol
American, 1928–1987
Red Disaster, 1963 and 1985
(one of two panels)
Silkscreen ink on synthetic
polymer paint on linen
Each panel: 93 × 80¼ in.
(236.2 × 203.8 cm)
Charles H. Bayley Picture and
Painting Fund 1986.161a

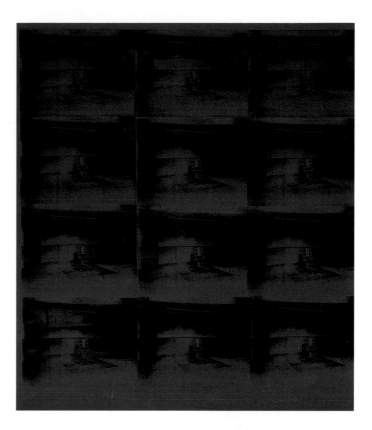

Beginning his career as a successful commercial artist, Warhol became, in the early 1960s, an underground filmmaker and a painter who sought to mechanize painting by including photographic images reproduced by the silkscreen process. His main subjects in 1962 were soup cans, soda bottles, Elvis Presley, and Marilyn Monroe. The following year—a time of enormous social and political change—he began to explore death in modern American society. The electric chair was the first subject in his series of "disasters" that also included car crashes and images of police brutality. *Red Disaster*, derived from a photograph of the death chamber at Sing Sing Prison, may be viewed as a grave and haunting plea against capital punishment; some, however, see its grim repetitiveness as an embodiment of callousness and inhumanity.

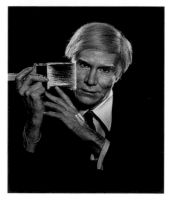

Yousuf Karsh
Canadian (born Armenia-in-
Turkey in 1908)
Andy Warhol, 1979
Photograph, silver print
23⅜ × 19½ in. (59.4 × 49.5 cm)
Gift of Yousuf and Estrellita Karsh
1996.182

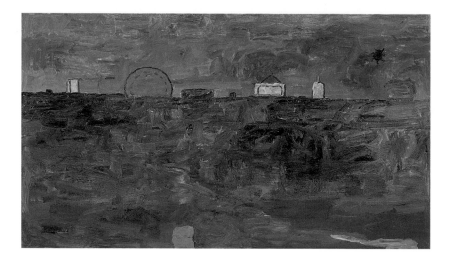

Philip Guston
American, 1913–1980
The Deluge, 1969
Oil on canvas
77 × 128 in. (195.6 × 325.2 cm)
Bequest of Musa Guston 1992.509

During the 1950s and early 1960s, Guston worked in a sensuous and luminous Abstract Expressionist style. In 1968, however, he began to introduce caricatural images into his freely painted abstract works, a movement from abstraction to representation that had a profound influence on many younger contemporaries. *The Deluge* is an early example of Guston's new direction. Both the image and the title suggest the aftermath of some cataclysmic event, with the objects on the horizon seeming about to be engulfed by the formless darkness below.

Robert Colescott
American, born 1925
Marching to a Different Drummer, 1989
Acrylic on canvas
84 × 72 in. (213.4 × 182.9 cm)
Ernest Wadsworth Longfellow
Fund 1990.494

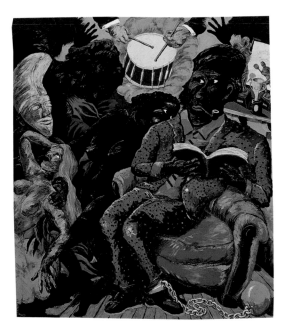

Although never formally trained as a sculptor, Smith became intrigued by Picasso's welded-steel sculptures while studying painting at the Art Students League in New York. Realizing that the skills he had acquired during summer jobs in a car factory could be used to make art, Smith created in 1933 the first constructed, welded-steel sculptures in American art. Made the year before Smith's death, *Cubi XVIII* is one of a series of structures in which cubes and cylinders of burnished and abraded steel are counterbalanced in relationships that dynamically expand into space while reflecting their surroundings.

David Smith
American, 1906–1965
Cubi XVIII, 1964
Polished stainless steel
Height: 115 3/4 in. (294 cm)
Gift of Susan W. and Stephen D. Paine 68.280

< Colescott's vivid and affecting paintings reflect on the complexity of racial perceptions in the United States today. With exaggerated forms, bold colors, and an exuberant and deliberately raw handling of paint, the artist uses humor and satire to explore difficult issues of identity and racial stereotypes. The trophies and diploma at the right suggest that the protagonist of *Marching to a Different Drummer* was educated on a sports scholarship. Above him is a drum played by white hands, and the ball chained to his foot suggests he is a prisoner. To what? The artist raises the question, and the viewer must decide.

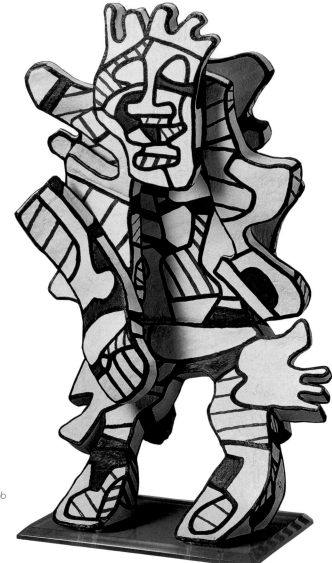

Jean Dubuffet
French, 1901–1985
The Inquisitor, 1973
Epoxy, polyurethane, paint
Height: 34 in. (86.4 cm)
Gift of Charlotte and Irving Rabb
1989.818

Throughout his career, Dubuffet's art deliberately challenged prevailing styles and traditional ideals of beauty. In 1962, reportedly inspired by doodling with a pen on scraps of paper, he began a series of sculptures and paintings in what he called his "Hourloupe" style. As here, the sculptures in this style are characterized by irregular, interlocking shapes that are colored blue, red, and white and heavily outlined in black. According to the artist, "Hourloupe" is a name "whose invention was based upon its sound. In French these sounds call to mind some wonderland or grotesque object or creature, while at the same time they evoke something rumbling and threatening with tragic overtones."

Dress
France (Paris), 1968
Designed by **André Courrèges,**
born 1923
Label: Courrèges/Paris
Cotton, gauze; appliquéd; silk lining
Gift of Elizabeth Lea   1991.681

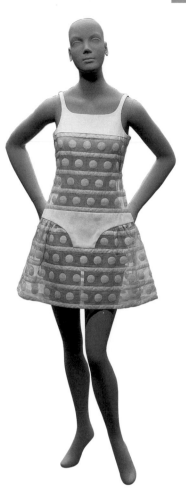

Courrèges, an engineer by training, has designed everything from watches to bathrooms and windsurfing equipment. During the second half of the 1960s, he became part of a revolution in fashion with his see-through styles, minidresses, and pantsuits intended for women to wear on all occasions. Simple, minimally decorated dresses like this one were designed to be more comfortable than clothes worn by men—celebrations of the modern woman's new, active lifestyle.

Animal Bowl
United States, 1990
Made by **Rob Butler,** born 1955
Silver, gilt
Height: 8½ in. (21.6 cm)
Anonymous gift 1990.604

Trained in London in the 1970s, Butler worked in Waltham, Massachusetts, before moving to New York's Hudson River Valley. This bowl is a virtuoso example of his silversmithing skills. The raised oval bowl is decorated with a band of cast zebras; the supports of the bowl are cast elephant heads, and intertwined, gilded giraffes form the handle of the top. At the base, Butler used a scroll saw to pierce the foot so that it resembles marsh grass with embossed crocodiles lurking in front.

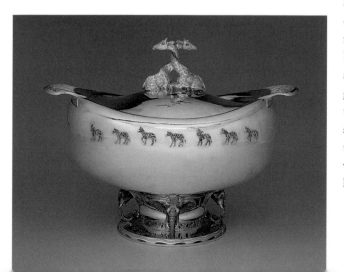

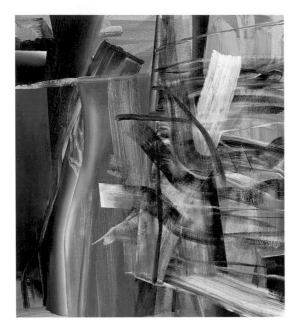

A key figure in the resurgence of German painting in the 1980s, Richter absorbed the disparate styles of Abstract Expressionism and Pop Art, refusing to paint in only one way. Some of his works are representational and figurative; others, such as *Vase,* explore color and form abstractly with wide, fluid brushwork that appears to be absolutely free and spontaneous but is, in fact, precisely calculated to achieve brilliant spatial effects.

Gerhard Richter
German, born 1932
Vase, 1984
Oil on canvas
88½ × 78¾ in. (224.8 × 200 cm)
Juliana Cheney Edwards Collection
1985.229

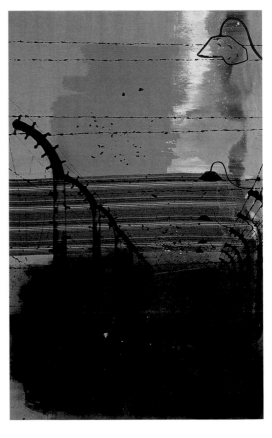

Sigmar Polke
German, born 1941
Lager, 1982
Acrylic and spattered pigment on pieced fabric support
158 × 98¾ in. (401.4 × 250.8 cm)
Gift of Charlene Engelhard
1993.961

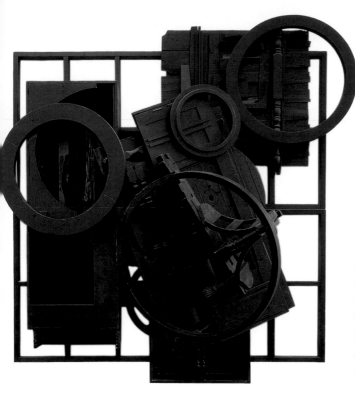

Louise Nevelson
American, 1899–1988
Mirror-Shadow VIII, 1985
Wood with paint
Height: 114 in. (289.6 cm)
Museum purchase with funds
provided by Charlotte and
Irving Rabb, Thomas H. Lee and
Ann Tenenbaum Lee, the Bruce
A. Beal, Enid L. Beal, and Robert
L. Beal Acquisition Fund, and
the Sophie M. Friedman Fund
1997.97

A leading innovator in twen-tieth-century American sculpture, Nevelson began making the powerful wooden constructions for which she is best known when she was in her fifties. These sculptures are typically made of stacked boxes filled with fragments of carved wood and such found objects as furniture pieces and bits of architectural orna-ment that she arranged into complex assemblages. She then painted these elements one color—usually black—to unify them and obscure their original identity. In this piece, an open, lattice-like support allows both for a dra-matic play of shadow and for the wall behind to interact with the relief's black sur-faces. Large rectangular areas are punctuated by four wood-en rings, the largest of which veers precipitously forward.

< Polke, who grew up in communist East Germany, escaped to West Germany in 1953. Working in collaboration with such artists as Gerhard Richter, Polke founded a German variation of Pop Art and often includes found objects in his work. His huge, multimedia *Lager,* which means "camp" in German, is one of a series of paintings in which the artist addressed the Holocaust. At the center is an image from a photograph of the electrified fence inside the concentration camp at Auschwitz, while the canvas is divided by an actual blanket that tangibly evokes the experience of the camp's prisoners. While *Lager* powerfully recalls the horrors of the Holocaust, the orange light of the sun in the background may symbolize the artist's hopes for an end to human atrocities.

Rocking chair
United States (Alta Loma,
California), 1975
Made by **Sam Maloof,**
born 1906
Walnut, ebony
Height: 45 in. (114.3 cm)
Purchased through funds provided
by the National Endowment for
the Arts and the Gillette
Corporation 1976.122

Maloof is preeminent among the first generation of studio furnituremakers who reacted against mass-produced furniture, asserting the values of high-quality workmanship, fine natural materials, and a more direct relationship between craftsman and client. Elegantly proportioned and comfortable, this rocking chair (an example of which is in the collection of the White House) reflects appreciation for the quality of the wood and for contrasts of soft, rounded edges and sharp, hard lines. This was one of the first examples of American furniture in the Museum's "Please Be Seated" program that provides works of art for seating in the galleries.

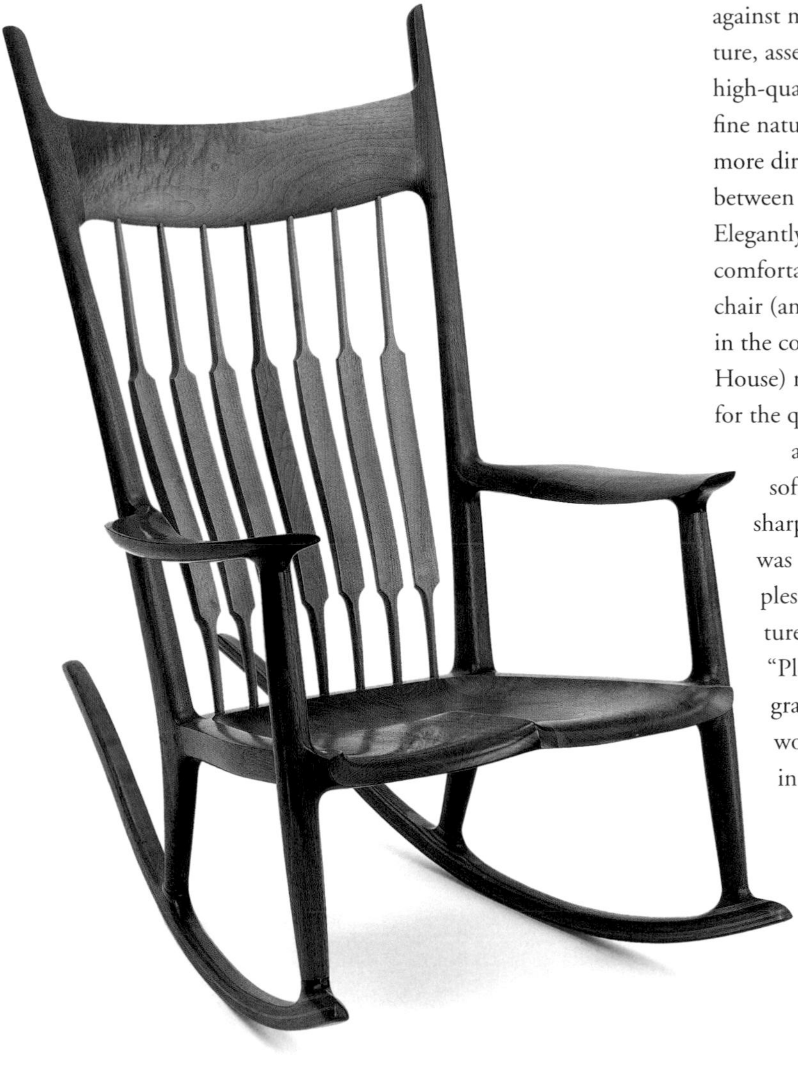

Kuramata's work is a unique blend of Japanese austerity, Western modernism, and his own sense of humor. Challenging traditional notions of look and materials, this chair is named for Blanche DuBois, the central figure in *A Streetcar Named Desire* by American playwright Tennessee Williams. Perhaps alluding to Blanche's romantic world of illusion, the suspended plastic roses are dramatically contrasted with the sharply angled slabs of clear acrylic resin. Kuramata is well known for the boutiques he created for fashion designer Issey Miyake (see page 391) in Tokyo, Paris, and New York.

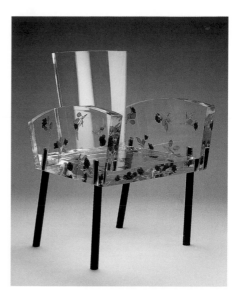

Miss Blanche
Japan (Tokyo), manufactured 1989
Designed in 1988 by
Shiro Kuramata, 1934–1991
Manufactured by **Kuramata Design Office**
Fabric and plastic flowers, acrylic resin, epoxy-coated aluminum
Height: 35½ in. (90.2 cm)
Maria Antoinette Evans Fund and Gift of Dr. John W. Elliott, by exchange, and EDA Curator's Fund
1996.32

Poltrona di Proust (Proust's Armchair)
Italy (Milan), manufactured 1991
by **Studio Alchimia**
Designed in 1978 by **Alessandro Mendini,** born 1931
Carved and painted wood, painted cotton upholstery
Height: 42½ in. (108 cm)
Gift of Mrs. S. M. B. Roby and Samuel P. Avery Fund, by exchange
1995.10

Studio Alchimia was established in 1976 as part of the "anti-design" movement that rejected mainstream modernist works and created furnishings in banal and outmoded styles to mock the pretensions of "tasteful design." Here, Mendini caricatures a Victorian armchair that French novelist Marcel Proust might have sat in. The frame and upholstery are hand-painted with a pointillist pattern of brushstrokes, a reference to the Neo-Impressionist painting (see page 269) that Proust admired.

Ellsworth Kelly
American, born 1923
Black Panel II, 1985
Oil on canvas
100½ × 125 in. (255.3 × 317.6 cm)
Ernest Wadsworth Longfellow
Fund 1987.119

Kelly began his training at
the School of the Museum
of Fine Arts in 1946, as a
student on the G.I. Bill.
He has worked with
abstraction through most of his
career, saying that "structure" is the con-
tent of his art. *Black Panel II* belongs to a group
of shaped, monochrome canvases that was the culmina-
tion of three decades of work. Although he is inspired by observation of things ranging from the
curve of a hill to the shape of a shadow, his rigorously spare forms are seemingly far removed
from their real-world associations. They are created to hang on expansive white walls where the
work itself functions as the depicted object and the wall behind as the background. Shape, size,
and blackness at first seem aggressive, but with prolonged looking, the viewer finds both subtlety
and ambiguity.

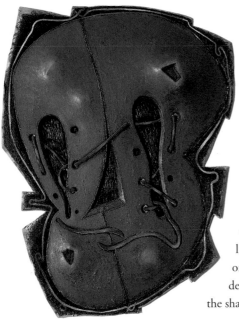

Elizabeth Murray
American, born 1940
Formerly Fleet, 1994–95
Oil on canvas on wood
Height: 99 in. (251.5 cm)
Museum purchase with funds provided by
Charlotte and Irving Rabb, Thomas H. Lee
and Ann Tenenbaum Lee, the Bruce A.
Beal, Enid L. Beal, and Robert L. Beal
Acquisition Fund, and the Sophie M.
Friedman Fund 1997.96

Murray's brightly colored, three-dimensional works
of the mid-1990s reveal the artist's interest in literally
constructing an illusion. They are carefully composed
of interlocking, irregularly shaped elements arranged
like puzzles in which the pieces do not quite fit. Relying
on the familiar for her subject matter, Murray here renders worn shoes in her signature, cartoon-like style, but
the shape, resembling a skull, may invite a darker reading.

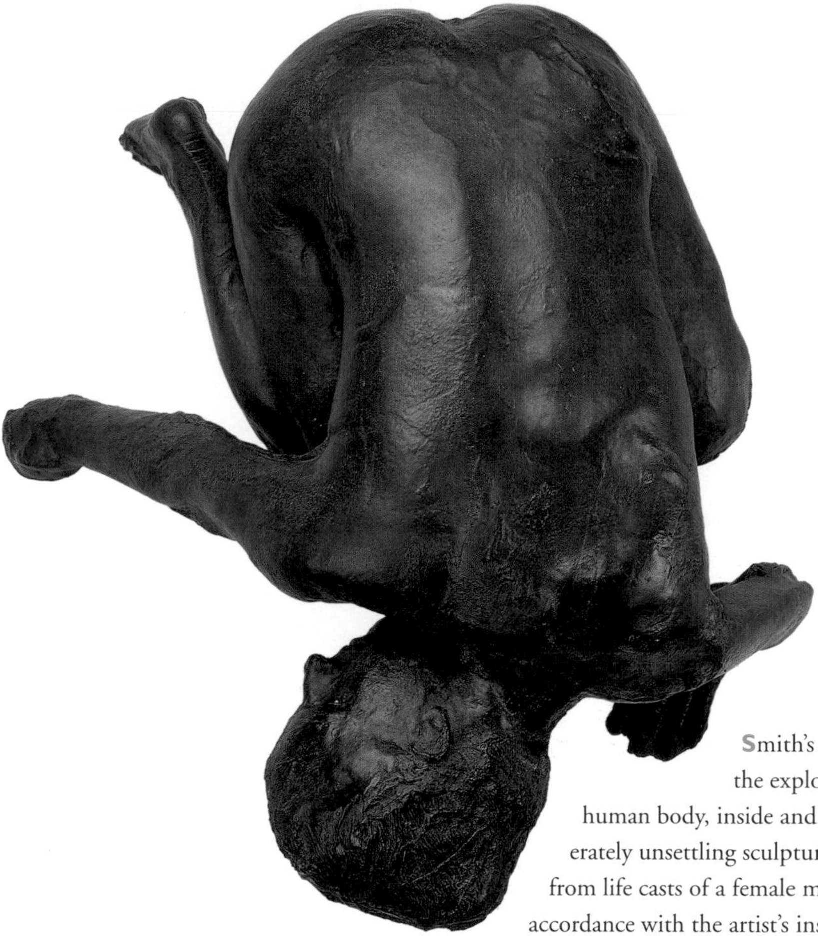

Kiki Smith
American, born 1954
Lilith, 1994
Edition 2 of 3
Silicon bronze and glass
Height: 33 in. (83.2 cm)
Contemporary Art Support
Group Fund, the Bruce A. Beal,
Enid L. Beal, and Robert L. Beal
Acquisition Fund, Barbara Fish Lee,
and the Lorna and Robert M.
Rosenberg Fund 1996.60

Smith's art is devoted to the exploration of the human body, inside and out. This deliberately unsettling sculpture was created from life casts of a female model, and in accordance with the artist's instructions, it is hung so that *Lilith* clings to the wall upside down, staring up at the viewer with glass eyes. The title refers to an ancient Sumerian demon, a creature of the air who, in post-biblical Hebrew legend is identified as Adam's intended first wife, who flew away when he refused to accept her as his equal. Long relegated to the realms of superstition and viewed as an evil spirit dangerous to men and children, Lilith has been reinterpreted in recent decades as an ideal of female strength and independence.

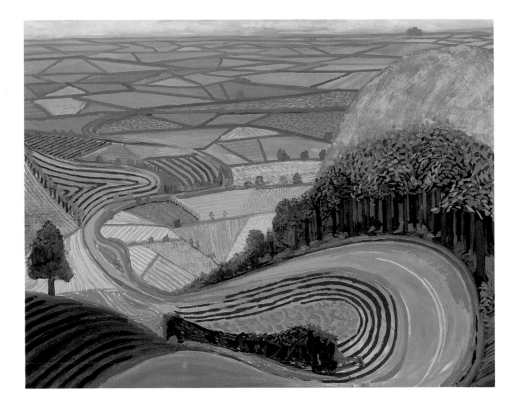

David Hockney
English, born 1937
Garrowby Hill, 1998
Oil on canvas
60 × 76 in. (152.4 × 193 cm)
Juliana Cheney Edwards
Collection, Seth K. Sweetser Fund,
and Tompkins Collection 1998.56

Coming to prominence as part of the British Pop Art movement in the early 1960s, Hockney is a painter and printmaker
who has also worked innovatively as a photographer and stage
designer. With the brilliant palette characteristic of many of his
works, *Garrowby Hill* is one of series of soaring, panoramic
landscapes of his native Yorkshire, in northern England, begun
in 1997. Hockney has long worked with painting and photography together, and this painting's multiple perspectives are the
result of photographs that the artist made while traveling in an
open car and later synthesized in his Los Angeles studio.

Lichtenstein made history in the 1960s with paintings, inspired by comic strips, that have
become classics of American Pop Art. Using bold primary colors, prominent black outlines, and
patterns derived from the screens of halftone dots used in newspaper printing, Lichtenstein has
drawn his subject matter from a wide range of sources—from advertising to the world of art and
art history. Beginning in 1996, the artist applied his trademark style to the tradition of ancient
Chinese landscape painting, subtly manipulating the size and density of the dots to capture the
atmospheric quality of these expansive views of water and sky.

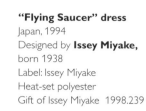

"Flying Saucer" dress
Japan, 1994
Designed by **Issey Miyake,**
born 1938
Label: Issey Miyake
Heat-set polyester
Gift of Issey Miyake 1998.239

Born in Hiroshima, Japan, Miyake studied graphic design and fashion in Tokyo and Paris and established Miyake Design Studios in 1970. Considered by many the most visionary designer of the late twentieth century, Miyake's fashions rely on a graceful collaboration of art and technology. This dress, which suggests traditional Japanese paper lanterns, is composed of permanently pleated and ingeniously seamed cylinders that hold the shape of the dress when it is worn and collapse flat when stored.

Roy Lichtenstein
American, 1923–1997
Seascape, 1996
Oil and Magna on canvas
49 × 102 in. (124.5 × 259.1 cm)
Gift of Dorothy Lichtenstein in memory of Roy Lichtenstein
1997.271

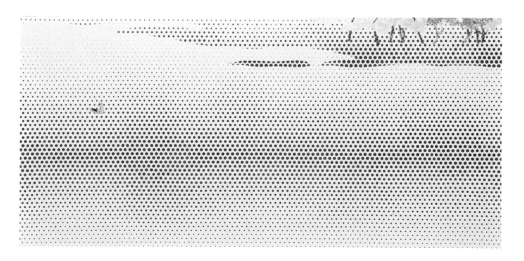

INDEX
OF ARTISTS
AND WORKS

Substantial assistance was provided by the following people:

Administrative
Brent Benjamin
Malcolm Rogers
Carl Zahn

Curatorial
Julia Bailey
Erin Bennett
Cheryl Brutvan
Elizabeth Ann Coleman
Joan Cummins
Sue D'Auria
Deanna Griffin
Timothy Kendall
Yvonne Markowitz
Anne Morse
Jeffrey Munger
Sue Welsh Reed
Pamela Russell
Carol Troyen
Wu Tung
Gerald Ward
Lauren Whitley

Photographic
Hilary Block
Greg Heins
Tom Lang
Gary Ruuska
Mary Sluskonis
John Woolf

Research
Nancy Eder
April Eisman
Randi Hopkins
Heather Horn
Guy Jordan
Ellen Roberts

Design
Joanna Bodenweber
Anne McLaughlin
Cynthia Rockwell Randall

Rights and Licensing
David Sturtevant

Consultation
Dorie Reents-Budet
Allen Wardwell

Photographs on cover, frontispiece, and pages 7, 9 18, 313
© Lou Jones 1999
